THE YEARBOOK OF CONSUMER LAW 2009

Markets and the Law

Series Editor:
Geraint Howells
Lancaster University, UK

Series Advisory Board:
Stefan Grundmann – Humboldt University of Berlin, Germany
Hans Micklitz – Bamberg Univeristy, Germany
James P. Nehf – Indiana University , USA
Iain Ramsay – University of Kent, UK
Charles Rickett – University of Queensland, Australia
Reiner Schulze – Münster University, Germany
Jules Stuyck – Katholieke Universiteit Leuven, Belgium
Stephen Weatherill –University of Oxford, UK
Thomas Wilhelmsson – University of Helsinki, Finland

Markets and the Law is concerned with the way the law interacts with the market through regulation, self-regulation and the impact of private law regimes. It looks at the impact of regional and international organizations (e.g. EC and WTO) and many of the works adopt a comparative approach and/or appeal to an international audience. Examples of subjects covered include trade laws, intellectual property, sales law, insurance, consumer law, banking, financial markets, labour law, environmental law and social regulation affecting the market as well as competition law. The series includes texts covering a broad area, monographs on focused issues, and collections of essays dealing with particular themes.

Other titles in the series

The Yearbook of Consumer Law 2009

Edited by
DEBORAH PARRY
Independent Consultant on Consumer Law, Hull

ANNETTE NORDHAUSEN
University of Manchester, UK

GERAINT HOWELLS
University of Lancaster, UK

CHRISTIAN TWIGG-FLESNER
University of Hull, UK

ASHGATE

Published by
Ashgate Publishing Limited
Wey Court East
Union Road
Farnham
Surrey GU9 7PT
England

Ashgate Publishing Company
Suite 420
101 Cherry Street
Burlington, VT 05401-4405
USA

www.ashgate.com

British Library Cataloguing in Publication Data
The yearbook of consumer law 2009. - (Markets and the law)
   1. Consumer protection - Law and legislation
   I. Parry, Deborah L.
   343'071

ISBN 978-0-7546-7574-7

Mixed Sources
Product group from well-managed
forests and other controlled sources
www.fsc.org Cert no. SGS-COC-2482
© 1996 Forest Stewardship Council
FSC

Printed and bound in Great Britain by
TJ International Ltd, Padstow, Cornwall

Contents

PART 2: CURRENT DEVELOPMENTS

Unfair Commercial Practices Directive:

Credit:

General:

Contributors

Richard M. Alderman Associate Dean for Academic Affairs, Dwight Olds Chair in Law and Director of the Centre for Consumer Law, University of Houston Law Centre, USA.

Alan Barron Lecturer in Commercial Law, University of Abertay, Dundee, Scotland.

Mary Donnelly Senior Lecturer, University College Cork, Ireland.

Nicola Howell Director, Centre for Credit and Consumer Law, Griffith University, Australia.

Jens Karsten EU Regulatory Affairs Adviser, Federation of European Direct Selling Association (FEDSA).

Souichirou Kozuka Professor, Sophia Law School, Tokyo, Japan.

Andrew Laidlaw Internal Market Policy Executive, Joint Brussels Office of the Law Societies, Belgium.

Paul Edgar Micallef Member of Malta Consumer Affairs Council.

Susana Navas Navarro Professor of Civil Law, Autonomous University of Barcelona, Spain.

Paul Nihoul Professor of Law, University of Louvain, Belgium, and University of Groningen, The Netherlands. Director, Centre de droit de la consummation.

Luke Nottage Associate Professor and Co-director, Australian Network for Japanese Law (ANJeL), University of Sydney, Australia.

Cristina Poncibò Researcher, Comparative Private Law, Faculty of Law, University of Turin, Italy.

Alexandre Regniault Avocat à la Cour, Simmons & Simmons, Paris, France.

Norbert Reich Visiting Professor (extraordinarius), University of Tartu, Estonia, Emeritus Professor, University of Bremen, and Senior Fellow, ZERP (Centre for European Legal Policy), Bremen, Germany.

James Ross Barrister, Gough Square Chambers, London.

Therese Wilson Senior Lecturer, Griffith Law School and Member, Socio-Legal Research Centre, Griffith University, Australia.

Preface

The *Yearbook of Consumer Law* is now an established series, this being the third volume to be published. It is edited under the auspices of the Consumer Law Academic Network (CLAN), a cooperation of consumer law scholars and practitioners led by Geraint Howells (Lancaster), Annette Nordhausen (Manchester), Deborah Parry and Christian Twigg-Flesner (Hull). It contains a stimulating range of peer-reviewed scholarly articles and a selection of shorter chapters exploring current developments in a variety of jurisdictions. As has been the case with the earlier volumes, there has been no difficulty in attracting submissions of a high calibre and prospective contributors are already in contact regarding the fourth volume. The managing editorship for the 2010 *Yearbook* will be assumed by Annette Nordhausen, who was co-editor of this volume, assisted by Geraint Howells as co-editor.

As might be expected, and following the pattern of contributions in the first two volumes of the *Yearbook of Consumer Law*, the influence of Europe is a central feature of many of the contributions to this volume. It commences with a far-ranging analysis of the intrinsic, extrinsic and global problems of the development of European Consumer Law by Norbert Reich. Paul Nihoul then provides a critical analysis of the position of European consumers of telecommunications services, postal services and energy for which the EU has passed liberalisation directives. The impact of the European Union on domestic law is the subject of Paul Micallef's chapter on Consumer Law in Malta.

The focus then moves to financial regulation and control. Nicola Howell and Therese Wilson, in their chapter on the position of consumer protection and fair trading in competitive markets, use the Australian consumer credit market as a case study to assess the effectiveness of competition as a regulatory tool. Mary Donnelly follows, with an analysis of the Irish Consumer Protection Code, an innovatory measure introduced by the Irish Financial Services Regulation Authority. The regulation of unsecured credit in Japan is the subject matter of the next chapter. Many European consumer lawyers are unfamiliar with consumer protection measures in Japan. Souichirou Kozuka and Luke Nottage seek to rectify this and to reduce the considerable gap in the literature available in English on Japanese Law.

Regional developments on the theme of methods of obtaining redress for consumers and their strengths and weaknesses are examined in the final two chapters. Cristina Poncibò looks at European developments encouraging collective redress for consumers, using the Italian system as an example of their practical application. Finally, Richard Alderman expresses concerns at the growth of arbitration as a means of dispute resolution in the United States.

It can be seen from these chapters that, whilst there may be local variations, in many different jurisdictions similar issues and concerns arise. Consumer lawyers can greatly benefit from studies conducted throughout the world and it is important that research and scholarship from a diverse variety of national perspectives is widely disseminated.

The section on current developments begins with two chapters on the implementation of the Unfair Commercial Practices Directive, which is already having a major impact on the laws of Member States of the European Union, and which has also been considered in some of the previous chapters. Alan Barron develops further some of his findings from his chapter on 'Reasonable Expectations, Good Faith and Self-Regulatory Codes' in the *Yearbook of Consumer Law 2007*, by looking at provisions in the Directive and their effects on codes of conduct in the United Kingdom. Paul Micallef then explains how the Directive has been implemented in Malta.

Recent developments in United Kingdom case law on the Consumer Credit Act 1974 are the focus of the chapter by James Ross. This is followed by Susanna Navarro, who comments on Spanish legislation affecting long term contracts. New legislation in France, aimed at developing competition for the benefit of consumers, is the subject matter of a chapter by Alexandre Regniault. Having examined passenger rights for sea and inland waterway transport in the *Yearbook of Consumer Law 2008*, Jens Karsten turns his attention to the regulation of rail passengers' rights in this volume. The final chapter, by Andrew Laidlaw, returns to the topic of methods of redress, raised in the full chapters, by discussing the scope for class actions in Europe.

The editors are grateful to everyone at Ashgate involved in producing the *Yearbook*.

Deborah Parry,
Hull

Editors

Deborah Parry, Independent Consultant on Consumer Law, Hull
Annette Nordhausen, University of Manchester
Geraint Howells, University of Lancaster
Christian Twigg-Flesner, University of Hull

Editorial Board

Claire Andrews, Gough Square Chambers

Richard Bragg, University of Manchester
Stephen Crampton, Independent EU and Consumer Affairs Consultant
Cowan Ervine, University of Dundee
Duncan Fairgrieve, British Institute of International and Comparative Law
Rod Freeman, Lovells
Suzanne Lace, OFCOM
Hans Micklitz, University of Bamburg
James Nehf, University of Indiana
Luke Nottage, University of Sydney
Iain Ramsay, University of Kent
Reiner Schulze, University of Münster
Thomas Wilhelmsson, University of Helsinki
Chris Willett, De Montfort University

Part 1 : Articles 2009

1   Crisis or Future of European Consumer Law?

Norbert Reich*

'Whither EU Consumer Law': A Legitimation Crisis?

1. 'Heute keine Ware' – a poster from 1973, in the old German Democratic Republic, saying 'WE HAVE GOT NOTHING TO SELL TODAY', was typical for the socialist 'economy of scarcity'. With the change in the political system, the 'economy of affluence/consumption' is now omnipresent. The 'economy of consumption' in Western Europe led to the development of a specific European 'consumer law'. For many authors[1] European consumer law has been, despite its technical weaknesses, its 'pointillistic character' and the pressure it puts on the coherence of national contract law[2] – a success story. It has put consumer protection on the agenda of the EU which cannot be abandoned. The EU has enacted a number of legal instruments – mostly directives – which have been

*   Visiting professor (extraordinarius), University of Tartu till 30.6.2008; Emeritus, University of Bremen; Senior Fellow, ZERP (Centre for European Legal Policy), Bremen. I thank my colleagues Hans Micklitz, Florence EUI, Annette Nordhausen, Manchester, Peer Zumbansen, Osgoode Hall/York University and Jacob Ziegel, Toronto University for valuable comments. Responsibility lies exclusively with the author.

1   N. Reich, 'Protection of Consumer's Economic Interests – Some Follow-Up Remarks', *Sydney Law Review* (2006): 37–62, at 37; H.-W. Micklitz, 'Der gemeinschaftsrechtliche Verbraucherschutz-Acquis – Rechtspolitischer Überblick und Perspektiven', in A. Wagner, V. Wedl (eds), *Bilanz und Perspektiven zum Europäischen Recht* (Wien, 2007), pp. 293–324, at p. 294; H. Rösler, 'Auslegungsgrundsätze des Europäischen Verbaucherprivatrechts in Theorie und Praxis', *RabelsZ* (2007): 495–526, at 495 concerning 'consumer friendly interpretation'; G. Howells, 'The Rise of European Consumer Law – Wither National Consumer Law?', *Sydney Law Review* (2006): 63–86, at 63; with some qualifications, S. Weatherill, *EU Consumer Law and Policy* (Cheltenham, 2006) at p. 245; J. Stuyck, 'European Consumer Law after the Treaty of Amsterdam: Consumer Policy in or beyond the Internal market?', *CMLRev.* (2000): 357–400, at 399 although insisting that 'EC consumer law has come of age'.

2   For a recent example see M. Loos, 'The Influence of European Consumer Law on General Contract Law and the Need for Spontaneous Harmonisation', *ERPrL* (2007): 515–31; for a different view see S. Grundmann, 'The Optional Code on the Basis of the *Acquis Communautaire* – Starting Points and Trends', *ELJ* (2004), 698–711.

implemented in Member States and which have contributed to the transformation of civil justice and trade practices law. These measures have led to a growing body of case-law at EU-level and even more so at national level, which has improved the position of the consumer in everyday transactions, against unfair advertising, against product risks, and in the enforcement of rights. Most of all, they have created a new subject of law, namely the consumer, who – similar to the EU citizen – is empowered with a number of rights laid down in Article 153(1) EC. The most important is the right to information, which must be surrounded by a protection of legitimate interests and effective enforcement mechanisms (judicial or Alternative Dispute Resolution (ADR)).[3]

From a socio-philosophical point of view, this emergence of the consumer has been criticised by Krämer as reducing the citizen to an economic subject, to a nearly parasitic 'middle-class' shopper who tries to get the best bargain at the lowest price, notwithstanding environmental concerns and gross inequalities of income distribution and mobility.[4] Hesselink[5] has recently put doubts on the one-sided market approach of consumer law disregarding the citizen and more fundamental values of justice which are the basis of contract law. But, in my opinion, this reduction of 'consumer law' to mere economic transactions and to 'middle-class values', is not a necessary consequence (see Part V below).

Other critics have insisted on the one-sidedness and the paternalistic approach of consumer law to contractual freedom: in imposing a set of mandatory rules on consumer transactions and communications, optimal decisions on markets for consumer goods may be made impossible, 'reliable' consumers may indirectly subsidise 'bad consumers', choice of consumers is limited and business may be burdened with compliance costs which will eventually be passed on to consumers.[6] For other authors, there is no general principle of consumer protection, and there

---

3   For an overview see H.-W. Micklitz and N. Reich, *The Basics of European Consumer Law* (Macao, 2007), pp. 21–36 same and P. Rott, *Understanding European Consumer Law* (Antwerp, 2008) 19, 1–19.

4   L. Krämer, 'The European Union, Consumption and Consumer Law', in L. Thévenoz and N. Reich (eds), *Droit de la consummation – Konsumentenrecht – Consumer Law, Liber amicorum Bernd Stauder* (Baden Baden, 2006), pp. 177–94 at p. 177.

5   M.W. Hesselink, 'Consumer Protection, Citizenship, or Justice?', *ERPrL* (2007): 323–48, at p. 329: 'consumer protection becomes market protection'.

6   G.Hadfield, R. Howse and M. Trebilcock, 'Information-Based Principles for Rethinking Consumer Protection Policy', *Journal of Consumer Policy (JCP)*, (1998): 131–69; B. Schäfer and C. Ott, *The Economic Analysis of Civil Law* (Cheltenham, 2004), at p. 9; for a differentiated view on 'paternalism' see W. Kerber and V. Vanbergh, 'Constitutional Aspects of Party Autonomy and its Limits – The Perspective of Constitutional Economics', in S. Grundmann, W. Kerber and S. Weatherill (eds), *Party Autonomy and the Role of Information in the Internal Market* (Berlin, 2001), at pp. 49, 75–9; for Poland see E. Letowska and A. Wiewirowska-Domagalska, 'The Common Frame of Reference – The Perspective of a New Member State', *European Review of Contract Law (ERCL)*, (2007): 277, at 283.

should not be one in EC law,[7] there are only selective measures of protection. A recent paper by Unberath and Johnston[8] has criticised the paradox of the ECJ in approaching consumer law questions in primary and in secondary law: while the first rests upon a liberalising philosophy, the second is based on an interventionist approach without considering Community policy 'in the light of proportionality and the possible applicability of theories of regulatory competition'.

Too much, too little or all wrong? The apparent success story of European consumer law is under review by a number of recent developments in the EU itself which deserve attention. We agree with Weatherill, that 'EC consumer policy is set to enjoy deservedly close attention as it enters its mid-life, if not its mid-life crisis'.[9]

If our observations are correct, the challenges facing EC consumer policy and law today should be discussed around three problem areas:

- An 'intrinsic', conceptual shortcoming despite achievements: the seeming reduction of consumer law to consumer information. This should, in our view, be widened both by an extension of the concept of the consumer – at least in some areas – to the user, and in the widening of certain 'minimum standards' beyond information, already done in some areas however inconsistently.
- An 'extrinsic', competence shortcoming: the unclear place of consumer law in the multi-level system of governance of the EU. This must be overcome by reconsidering the broad impact of Article 153 as the 'general consumer policy norm', which has to be read in conjunction with Article 3(t) EC as a 'measure which is essential to the accomplishment of the tasks entrusted to the Community and, in particular, to raising the standard of living and the quality of life in its territory'.[10]
- A 'global', jurisdictional shortcoming: reconsidering the territorial and personal limits of EU consumer law, eventually by referring to a 'transnational consumer law' beyond the state and the EU.

---

7   K. Riesenhuber, *Europäisches Vertragsrecht* (Berlin, 2003), at paras 895, 954, only specific protection against certain risks, no general principle; for an opposing view H. Rösler, *Europäisches Konsumentenvertragsrecht* (München, 2005).
8   H. Unberath and A. Johnston, 'The Double-Headed Approach of the ECJ Concerning Consumer Protection', *CMLRev.* (2007): 1237, at 1283–4.
9   Weatherill, at p. 250.
10   In this sense ECJ C-168/05 *Elisa Maria Mostaza Claro* v. *Centro Movil Milenium* [2006] ECR I-10421 at para. 37.

'Intrinsic', Conceptual Problems

The overall priority of consumer information

2. The importance of consumer information is laid down in Article 153(1) EC, which was introduced with the Amsterdam Treaty of 1999. Article 129a EEC did not contain such a right.[11] However, the Court of Justice, in its well known *GB Inno* case of 1990,[12] already derived a right of information from the principle of free movement.

This right of information contains four different aspects:[13]

- prohibition of misleading information;
- transparency of commercial statements and contract forms;
- certain information and disclosure obligations in secondary EC law;
- a right of cancellation (cooling-off period) in certain types of transactions, either depending on the marketing technique ('doorstep contracts' via Directive 85/577/EEC,[14] distance contracts via Directive 97/7/EC[15] and for financial services Directive 2002/65/EC[16]), or the subject matter of the contract (timeshare in Directive 94/47/EC,[17] life assurance by Directive 2002/83/EC,[18] in the future also consumer credit by the Consumer Credit Directive (CCD) 2008/48/EC.[19]

This is not the place to analyse the different aspects and extent of information obligations in detail. The prohibition of *misleading information* is a general principle of market law and was included into secondary Community law as early as

---

11   For details see Stuyck, 'European Consumer Law after the Treaty of Amsterdam: Consumer Policy in or beyond the Internal market?': 379–85.
12   ECJ case C-362/88 *GB Inno BM* v. *CCL* [1990] ECR I-667 at para. 19.
13   N. Reich, *Understanding EU Law*, 2nd edn (Antwerp, 2005), at pp. 294–302; R. Zimmermann, 'Consumer Contract Law and General Contract Terms: The German Experience', in *Current Legal Problems 2005* (Oxford, 2006), pp. 414–89, at pp. 473–9.
14   Council Directive 85/577/EEC of 20 December 1985 to protect the consumer in respect of contracts negotiated away from business premises [1985] OJ L 372/31.
15   Directive 97/7/EC of the European Parliament and of the Council of 20 May 1997 on the protection of consumers in respect of distance contracts [1997] OJ L 144/19.
16   Directive 2002/65/EC of the European Parliament and of the Council of 23 September 2002 concerning the distance marketing of consumer financial services and amending Council Directive 90/619/EEC and Directives 97/7/EC and 98/27/EC [2002] OJ L 271/16.
17   [1994] OJ L 280/83.
18   [2002] OJ L 345/1.
19   [2008] OJ L 133/66.

1984 when the misleading advertising Directive 84/450/EEC[20] was adopted. Many documents have repeated this principle and it can be said to be part of the general law of the EC, the *acquis communautaire*. It is, however, not confined to consumer markets, though it is most important here. It applies to any market communication, but the standards for measuring 'deception' will be a different one for business-to-business (B2B) and business–to–consumer (B2C) communications. With regard to the latter, the ECJ developed the so-called 'informed consumer standard', which can also take into account linguistic and cultural specificities.[21]

The principle of *'transparency'* relates mostly to consumer transactions and has found its explicit expression in Articles 4 and 5 of the Unfair Contract Terms Directive 93/13.[22] It has been repeated in other directives relating to pre-contractual information, for example on consumer guarantees (Article 6 of Directive 99/44)[23] or on financial services.[24] It must also be regarded as an element of effective competition.

3. *Disclosure obligations* have been included in most consumer directives, starting with the Doorstep Directive up to the recent Unfair Commercial Practices Directive 2005/29/EC (UPCD)[25] which has created the concept of 'misleading omissions'. This indirectly imposes information obligations onto the trader by making it an unfair practice not to disclose certain information.[26] An even more detailed approach is proposed in the CCD. The new Directive on Services in the Internal

---

20   Council Directive 84/450/EEC of 10 September 1984 relating to the approximation of the laws, regulations and administrative provisions of the Member States concerning misleading advertising [1984] OJ L 250/17.

21   For details see Reich, *Understanding EU Law*, at pp. 297–8; Micklitz and Reich, *The Basics of European Consumer Law*, pp. 121–8; G. Howells, H.-W. Micklitz and T. Wilhelmsson, *European Fair Trading Law – The Unfair Commercial Practices Directive* (Aldershot, 2006), at pp. 123–46; Weatherill at pp. 170–98; this has been developed by the case law of the ECJ, see C-210/96 *Gut Springenheide* [1998] ECR I-4657, para. 31; C-220/98 *Estée Lauder Cosmetics* v. *Lancaster Group* [2000] ECRI-117, para. 29; for a recent overview see Unberath and Johnston: 1250: 'preference for the provision of compulsory information over more severe marketing restrictions'.

22   Its importance for implementing the directive see ECJ case C-144/99 *Commission* v. *Netherlands* [2001] ECR I-3541, para. 21; scepticism has been voiced by Riesenhuber, at para. 930.

23   Directive 1999/44/EC of the European Parliament and of the Council of 25 May 1999 on certain aspects of the sale of consumer goods and associated guarantees [1999] OJ 171/12.

24   N. Reich and H.-W. Micklitz, *Europäisches Verbraucherrecht* (Baden-Baden, 2003) at p. 80.

25   Directive 2005/29/EC of the European Parliament and the Council of 11 May 2005 concerning unfair business to consumer commercial practices ('Unfair Commercial Practices Directive') [2005] OJ L 149/22.

26   For details see Wilhelmsson on misleading omissions at pp. 147–58.

Market 2006/123/EC[27] (DSIM) regulates, in Article 22, 'information on providers and their services' which are not limited to consumer transactions.

Finally, the *cancellation right*, which is granted in several directives, must also be regarded as an information-type instrument. The consumer must always be informed about this right (the consequences of non-information are discussed in para. 11). The effect of the contract depends on whether the consumer exercises his right of revocation or not. The cancellation right does not regulate the content but only the conclusion of the contract and aims to guarantee the consumer an informed choice after the conclusion of the contract, either because he has not been able to do so by the way he has been induced into the contract (doorstep situation or distance marketing system), or because of the complexity and the long-term financial consequences of the contract for him (timeshare, life assurance, consumer credit). The benchmark is the rational, informed consumer; at the same time the right of cancellation serves competition because it allows the consumer to switch to more advantageous conditions if he becomes aware of them within the time for revocation; Micklitz has derived from this a new paradigm of 'competitive contract law'.[28]

This analysis shall be completed by a reference to primary law where the Court, ever since its seminal *Cassis* case,[29] developed indirect information obligations under the free movement rules: where a Member State invokes non-discriminatory restrictions on cross-border transactions of goods (and later services) justified in the consumer interest, it should prefer information measures to more restrictive instruments like prohibitions, controls and other intrusive means of regulation. The principle of 'information first' is a sequel to the overall trust in consumer choice and autonomy as an adequate instrument of creating the Single Market. Consumer policy is part of this overall goal in respecting the proportionality principle.[30]

Missing links

No direct effect of Article 153 EC but possible use for interpretation purposes
4. This well developed 'information paradigm' however, has a number of drawbacks both from a legal and from a consumer policy point of view. One

---

27 Directive 2006/123/EC of the European Parliament and of the Council of 12 December 2006 on services in the internal market [2006] OJ L 36/12.

28 H.-W. Micklitz, 'The Concept of Competitive Contract Law', *PennState Int.L.Rev.* (2005): 549; for a critique against the concept of 'competitive contract law' see Riesenhuber at paras 943–5.

29 ECJ case 120/78 *Rewe-Zentral AG* v. *Bundesmonopolverwaltung für Branntwein* (*Cassis de Dijon*) [1979] ECR 649.

30 For an evaluation see Grundmann, Kerber, Weatherill, at pp. 18, 24; for a more sceptical view see T. Wilhelmsson, 'Cooperation and Competition Regarding Standard Terms in Consumer Contracts', *EBLR* (2006): 49–72, at 50–6 (need for mandatory standards).

reason may be the 'information overkill' which can be observed in areas where EC law has been active. Instead of concentrating on those parts of information which are really relevant for the consumer, the legislator seems to regulate a black box without asking what the 'normal consumer' can bear and what limits exist to information take-in. This is particularly true for information concerning adverse effects or certain risks inherent in a transaction or an action, as could be shown with cigarette warnings. Even dramatic forms of warning like 'smoking kills' do not seem to be able to overcome the cognitive dissonance of consumers.[31] In the end they may serve to exempt the trader from liability, but not to provide the consumer with relevant market information.

There are some other structural limits to the information paradigm in EC law. Most importantly, the 'right to information' in Article 153 EC has not been shaped into an autonomous right taking direct effect in favour of the individual consumer or the collective interest of consumers *vis-à-vis* Member States, the Community itself, or traders in consumer markets. The ECJ has denied any direct effect of Article 153 or the similar Article 95(3) (which requires a high level of consumer protection in proposals by the Commission) and refused to use it to close existing loopholes in information obligations, or to overcome shortcomings in existing Member State or EC regulations.[32] But Article 153, read in conjunction with Article 3(t) EC, may be used for interpretative purposes and allows a 'dynamic interpretation' to enhance existing consumer protection law.[33]

Selective character

5. Another critical point of the information paradigm in consumer law is its highly selective character. Since there is no general information obligation under primary law,[34] each act of secondary law has to prescribe special information obligations which are tailored to the specific field of application of the directive or regulation. This may lead, in some cases, to an accumulation of information requirements, in others to gaps or contradictions. A good example are regulations on distance marketing which are found in three directives starting from different premises, namely Distance Selling, Distance Marketing of Financial Services and E-

---

31   This is not discussed by Hadfield, Howse and Trebilcock: 159, in their preference for information based principles of consumer protection.

32   See cases C-91/92 *Paola Faccini Dori* v. *Recreb* [1994] ECR I-3325; C-192/94 *El Corte Inglés* v. *Cristina Blásquez Rivero* [1996] ECR I-1281; case C-350/03, *Schulte* [2005] ECR I-9215 para. 61 referring to the similar Article 95(3); critique Weatherill at p. 234.

33   Rösler, 'Auslegungsgrundsätze des Europäischen Verbaucherprivatrechts in Theorie und Praxis': 508; also the *Claro* case by the ECJ above at n. 10; N. Reich, 'More clarity after *Claro*?', *ERCL* (2007): 41–61, at 42; M. Loss, Case note on *Claro*, *ERCL* (2007): 439.

34   Riesenhuber, at para. 931.

commerce 2000/31/EC.[35] All three grant the consumer some specific information rights, for example, on the name and address of the trader, but only the first and the second contain a right of withdrawal of the consumer with many exceptions.[36,37] They also refer to the process of contracting as such, without defining when a contract is concluded or not. This hodge-podge of requirements can only be explained by the fact that different Directorates of the Commission initiated this legislation which then followed its path through the somewhat protracted legislative process in the EU.

Another well-known problem stems from different solutions for similar problems which cannot rationally be explained. It is concerned with different time-limits for rights of withdrawal which are granted in several directives, for example for doorstep contracts seven days, for distance contracts seven working days, for distance marketing of financial services 14 days, 30 days for insurance contracts. The intensity of disclosure about these rights of withdrawal, as well as the consequences of non-disclosure, again differ from directive to directive. There are some attempts to remedy this situation,[38] but so far no proposals have been presented to the EC legislature. Member States must remedy this situation, but this requires that they have discretion on how they want to implement a directive – a freedom more and more restricted by Court practice and the Commission's quest for 'full harmonisation' (see below para. 27).

The unsolved question of language 6. The EU is a multi-language Community, and all official languages are said to be on an equal footing. The citizenship concept may allow the citizen even to communicate in his native language in a different jurisdiction if this is allowed to nationals belonging to a protected minority.[39]

---

35   Directive 2000/31/EC of the European Parliament and of the Council of 8 June 2000 on certain legal aspects of information society services, in particular electronic commerce, in the Internal Market ('Directive on electronic commerce') [2000] OJ L 178/1.

36   Concerning 'transport services' exempted from Directive 97/7 see the surprisingly broad interpretation of the exception by ECJ 10.3.2005 case C-336/03 *Easy Car* v. *Office of Fair Trading* [2005] ECR I-1947 and the differing opinion of A.G. Stix-Hackl of 11.11.2004.

37   See N. Reich and A. Halfmeier, 'Consumer Protection in the Global Village: Recent Developments in German and European Law', *Dickinson L. Rev.* (2001): 111–38, at 128–34.

38   Report from the Commission – First Annual Progress Report on European Contract Law and the *Acquis* Review, COM (2005) 456 final (Sept. 23, 2005) [hereinafter First Annual Progress Report]; Green Paper of the Commission of 8 February 2007 concerning the review of the consumer *acquis*, COM (2006) 744 final. See also the recent proposals of the '*acquis*'-group, below, para. 19.

39   ECJ case C-274/96 *Criminal proceedings against H.O. Bickel und U. Franz* [1998] ECR I-7637; Micklitz and Reich, *The Basics of European Consumer Law*, pp. 28–31.

It is obvious that such a principle cannot be simply taken over to communications and transactions in the consumer market consisting of 27 different jurisdictions with 21 different languages. Primary EC law has been concerned with language questions, not so much whether they empower consumers, but whether they contain (open or hidden) restrictions of free movement in products or services.[40] Secondary law, in proclaiming this information paradigm, is usually silent on the language in which this information is to be provided. The transparency principle relies on 'clear and intelligible' language, but does not say what language may be used.[41] One could guess that this should be the language of the country of residence of the consumer. However, such a simple rule is nowhere stated, with the only exception of life insurance contracts. Other principles have to be consulted, for example on conflicts of law.[42] Some recent directives, for example Article 10(1)(d) of the E-Commerce Directive and Article 3(1) Nr. 3g of the Distance Marketing of Financial Services Directive, make it an obligation of the trader to at least propose a language in which transactions are to be performed, but this is an exception. Thus the Community withdraws from a central area of consumer protection and does not guarantee an effective right of information under Article 153 if it does not clearly impose a language rule.

Admittedly, this would almost certainly provoke costs for the trader doing cross-border business. But traders cannot expect to gain the benefits of the internal market without a price, and this includes respecting the cultural and linguistic diversity of its citizens.[43] A compromise would be to insist that the trader, who offers his goods or services cross-border, for example on the internet, proposes a language on his website in which the contract is to be governed. If a specific country is targeted, both the language of the place of origin of the trader and of the county of the consumer's residence should be offered – a practice already used

---

40   For a recent example see case C-490/04 *Commission* v. *Germany* [2007] ECR I-(18.7.2007) para. 71, concerning documents for posted workers from non-member countries to be translated into German; for an overview and its importance for consumer law see H.-W. Micklitz, 'Zum Recht des Verbrauchers uf die eigene Sprache (C.cas.)', *ZEuP* (2003): 653.

41   There are exceptions in the Timeshare Directive 94/47 and in Annex III of the Life Assurance Dir. 2002/83/EC, [2002] OJ L 345/1; see the somewhat protracted *Piageme*-controversies, case C-369/89 [1991] ECR I-2971 at para. 13 (*Piageme I*); C-85/94 [1995] ECR I-2955 paras 15, 29 concerning the imposition of a mandatory language requirement of the area in which the product is marketed beyond the 'easily understood language' which may be another language, maybe even English as *lingua franca* of the EU; see C. Twigg-Flesner, *The Europeanisation of Contract Law* (Ashgate, 2008) at p. 70.

42   P. Rott, 'Informationspflichten in Fernabsatzverträgen als Paradigma für die Sprachenproblematik im Vertragsrecht', *ZVglRWiss* (1999), 382–409, at 394 (applicability of the *lex causae – Vertragsstatut*).

43   For a plea in this direction see T. Wilhelmsson, E. Paunio and A. Pohjolainen (eds), *Private Law and the Many Cultures of Europe* (The Netherlands, 2007).

by many European traders, particularly with regard to financial services where language is a prerequisite of contracting. As a minimum, the trader should offer at least two languages in which the transaction can be performed. The consumer would thus have a choice in which language to do the transaction – or to abstain from it. Such an obligation does not put an unreasonable burden on the trader. He profits from a 'vast' internal market, and should therefore be aware of linguistic differences. An offer only in English directed at consumers outside of English speaking countries would not be enough. Since choice is one of the central elements of consumer protection, the consumer should be offered a genuine choice also in matters of language. If the consumer voluntarily reacts in the language proposed by the trader, then this should be the language of the transaction.

Consumer responsibilities arising out of information requirements? 7. EU consumer policy follows the information approach, but only creates obligations for providers. This may seem contradictory, but a well informed consumer should not only enjoy rights but also have obligations as a citizen under Article 17(2) EC or resident (see below para. 42). An example is transparency: if a clause is phrased in a transparent and understandable form (including language) should the consumer not be required to read it before contracting and, in case he does not do so, be prevented from opposing this clause (see para. 9)? If Article 5(4) of Directive 90/314/EEC[44] on package holidays requires the consumer to communicate expressly a defect to the organiser, should he not see his rights reduced if he has not done so? In product liability law, the presentation of a product maybe an indication of a product defect. Can the producer overcome this defect with an adequate warning, or at least invoke contributory negligence or causation under Article 8(2) of Directive 85/374? On the other hand, the Consumer Sales Directive makes it an option for Member States to require that the consumer inform the seller within a reasonable time (two months) about the non-conformity of the product according to Article 5(2). Could this be made into a general obligation of the consumer to minimise costs in order to increase efficiency of consumer transactions and therefore overall consumer welfare?

This other side of consumer information is rarely put forward in EC law, even though it would create an adequate symmetry of rights and obligations, not only of traders but also of consumers. Heiderhoff[45] has, ironically, called the EC-consumer model an imposed model measured only by the maximum satisfaction and cross-border market activity of the European consumer. 'In order to attain his maximal market activity, he is treated like in need of protection (*Unterlegener*), and therefore must be protected.' This is in stark contrast to the model of the

---

44   Council Directive 90/314/EEC of 13 June 1990 on package travel, package holidays and package tours [1990] OJ L 158/59.

45   B. Heiderhoff, *Grundstrukturen des nationalen und europäischen Verbrauchervertragsrechts* (Tübingen, 2004), at p. 278.

'responsible consumer' upon which a fairness obligation can be imposed and which we will advocate later (below para. 42).

Is information sufficient?

Vulnerable groups of consumers (that is, children, old people, foreigners) 8. It is a well known fact in consumer law that information may be useful for rational consumer decisions, but cannot reasonably be expected to be used by certain groups of consumers, like children, handicapped people, old persons, foreigners and migrants. Usually this problem is left to Member State law because they are closer to the specific needs of certain vulnerable consumer groups. All that is demanded from EC law is to allow Member States enough flexibility to impose special rules on the form and intensity of this targeted information to protect such consumers which cannot be reached by general information, even if this implies additional compliance costs on traders which seemingly contradicts the idea of an 'internal market' without impediments to the free movement of goods and services.[46] This problem has found limited attention in the UCPD in Article 5(3), in conjunction with Recital 19.[47]

Other directives are less concerned with vulnerable groups of consumers and users. In its attempt to completely cover market access and regulation, EC law becomes more and more critical to attempts of social protection by specific information requirements. A recent example is the DSIM: Article 22(5) allows Member States to impose information requirements beyond existing Community law, but only onto those providers which are established in their territory, not against providers coming from other EC countries.[48] This rule not only puts national providers at a disadvantage – which means that Member States will usually not make use of this possibility to avoid a 'reverse discrimination' of their home providers – but privileges providers from other countries with a general exemption from any group specific information requirements protecting vulnerable groups, at least in the area of application of the DSIM, thus creating unequal competition conditions against the very idea of the internal market!

Mandatory standards 9. It is well established in consumer theory, that information requirements may be a useful tool of protection, but may not be enough. In the above example of unfair terms the consumer is clearly informed and warned about them. It may still be necessary to protect him against his own seemingly rational decisions, especially in situations where he is in a situation of 'take it or leave it'. This is usually the case with pre-formulated standard terms presented to him in

---

46   See Wilhelmsson, 'The Average European Consumer: a Legal Fiction?' in: Wilhelmsson, Paunio and Pohjolainen, pp. 241–68.

47   For details see Howells, Micklitz andWilhelmsson, at pp. 111–16.

48   For a discussion see W.-H. Roth, 'FreierDienstleistungsverkehr und Verbraucherschutz', *VuR* (2007): 161–72, at 169.

written documents or on the internet; he either clicks the 'acceptance' button, or the transaction is closed (so called clickwrap- or browsewrap-clauses).[49] In these cases mandatory standards are imposed by consumer law, in particular Member State law, but also EC law.

A good example is the Consumer Sales Directive: Article 6 requires certain information about voluntary guarantees 'in plain intelligible language', but expressly wants to make sure that the consumer will not lose his legal right to receive a conforming product because of an exemption clause, Article 7(1), or because of the restrictive wording of the guarantee. A similar rule is contained in Article 22(3) CCD where even 'circumventing clauses' (for example lease or agency contracts) are prohibited. Some observers have criticised this approach as being 'paternalistic': the consumer is deprived of choosing two types of contract, one containing the mandatory provisions which are a sort of insurance cover for quality risks for which he has to pay a premium at a higher price, and another with the possibility to waive such protection in order to get a better price but take the risk of non-conformity himself. Mandatory rules on consumer protection may deprive the consumer of choice – this is the central point of critique of advocates of an economic analysis of consumer law like Grundmann and Kerber.[50]

To a certain extent these debates rest on a theoretical model and not on a realistic approach to consumer behaviour. Since the consumer is mostly concerned with price and quality, the bargain will usually not extend to negotiating contract clauses – and this may technically not be possible, as the existence of 'clickwrap-clauses' demonstrates. The normal consumer is not aware of the risk concerning the special content of contract clauses which later, in cases of non-performance, maybe used against him – and advertising does everything to avoid 'risk awareness'! This behaviour is even rational from a market efficiency point of view: the consumer is not an expert and should not be treated as one. Consumer law may therefore step into areas where no true choice of the consumer can be expected.[51]

Another problem posed by EC law has been the question whether the existence of information requirements prevents more intrusive regulatory mechanisms like a ban of a certain marketing practice. This was argued by the Commission in a case concerning an Austrian ban on doorstep sales for silverware; however the Court

---

49   For a critical comparative evaluation see D. Clapperton and S. Corones, 'Unfair terms in 'click-wrap' and other electronic contracts', *Australian Business Law Review* (2007): 152–80, at 156.
50   In Grundmann, Kerber and Weatherill, at p. 282.
51   This is recognised as efficient even by adherents of the economic analysis of law, Schäfer and Ott, at pp. 370–73. From the viewpoint of behavioural economics see F. Rischowsky and T. Döring, 'Consumer Policy in a Market Economy: Considerations from the Perspective of the Economics of Information as well as Behavioural Economics', *JCP* (2008): 281–314, at p. 294.

did not decide this issue but left it to the Member States' courts.[52] The debate makes clear the deregulatory spirit surrounding consumer law: information is not so much seen as a consumer remedy, but as a measure precluding Member States from introducing more restrictive measures for consumer protection. This is in line with the argument of Hadfield et al.[53] that 'there is a need to weigh the costs of regulation against the benefits to be derived from regulation'. But, who is determining the costs and benefits, and who is 'weighing them'?

This deregulatory tendency does not relieve consumer law from the challenge to develop an adequate regulatory mix, combining information requirements with mandatory standards. The main problem of EU consumer law is not the balancing of the mix in certain directives, but the absence of an overall approach which creates a bias towards consumer choice and information and a tendency to avoid the setting of mandatory standards. This preference for consumer information has been clearly spelled out in the recent EU Consumer Policy Strategy 2007–2013:[54] 'Consumer policy can equip consumers to make rational choices and to take on responsibility to promote their own interests'.

Is this all? Can one always and in every area of the consumer market rely on consumers promoting their own interests? Is this not simply a return to the '*caveat emptor*' – principle which consumer law from its very beginning wanted to overcome?[55] If this regulatory mix cannot be achieved at EU level, it must be attained by national law. This, however, is put into question under the new strategy of the EU towards full harmonisation (below, para. 27).

Special problems of long-term contracts 10. The information paradigm is usually confined to pre-contractual information in order to allow the consumer a rational choice before entering into a contract; sometimes it may go beyond. Practice has shown that long term contracts like credit, insurance, or services of general interest comprise much more serious problems to consumers than so called 'spot contracts' like sales or certain services which are usually limited to a one-time transaction, where the only problems are quality and safety questions arising after the transaction has been performed. Information rules cannot solve problems of access, adaptation, modification, frustration and so on, present in long-term or 'relational contracts'.[56] National contract law, supplemented by rules on unfair contract terms, has developed specific protective mechanisms which differ widely

---

52 Case C-441/04 *A Punkt Schmuckhandels-GmbH* v. *Claudia Schmidt* [2006] ECR I-2093; see Unberath and Johnston: 1247.

53 Hadfield, Howse and Trebilcock: 148.

54 Com [2007] 99 final of 13.3.2007, p. 4.

55 For an overview of the US-E(E)C discussion see T. Bourgoignie and D. Trubek, *Consumer Law, Common Market and Federalism* (Berlin, 1987); N. Reich, *Staatliche Regulierung zwischen Marktversagen und Politikversagen* (Heidelberg, 1984).

56 U. Reifner, 'Renting a Slave – European Contract Law in the Credit Society', in Wilhelmsson, Paunio and Pohjolainen, pp. 325–42.

among jurisdictions. The on-going process of an 'Europeanisation of contract law' may take up some of these problems to generalise them within the EU based on a broader concept of 'social justice'.[57]

The answer of EU consumer law beyond information has so far been rather modest. The Unfair Terms Directive contains a general clause on unfairness and transparency which is elaborated in the annex and is particularly important for long-term contracts. Some provisions of the annex cover long-term transactions, for example paragraph (g) on unilateral termination, (h) on automatic extension, (j) and (k) on modification, (l) on price increases, with special exceptions for financial services in part 2 of the Annex. Unfortunately, these clauses, which in the first drafts where conceived as a 'black-list', are now only indications of unfairness without any specific legal value, neither in implementing them in national legislation, nor in assessing the fairness of a contract term. In its *Freiburger Kommunalbauten* judgment,[58] the Court has effectively withdrawn from controlling unfairness of contract terms. Different approaches to unfairness exist in Member State law.[59] Community law thereby has missed the chance to develop some basic standards for long term contracts going beyond mere information requirements like transparency. This makes the role of national law for consumer protection ever more important.

It is true that the EC has been concerned with some specific long-term contracts, for example life-insurance where information is extended from the entering phase to the performance of the contract and most recently in consumer credit. The detailed regulation of services of general interest (telecommunication, energy) is however concerned mostly with competition and free choice of the provider in order to promote competition, not so much with the content of the contract (para. 13).[60]

Adequate remedies?   11. Another problem with information requirements is the frequent inadequacy of remedies if information is not provided at all, or if it is provided only in an 'unclear, unintelligible' way, against the transparency requirement written into many EC documents.[61] Given the character of EC law

---

57   See Study Group on Social Justice in European Private Law, A Manifesto, *ELJ* (2004): 653 at 664.

58   Case C-237/02 *Freiburger Kommunalbauten GmbH Baugesellschaft & Co.KG* v. *Ludger Hofstetter und Ulrike Hofstetter* [2004] ECR I-3403.

59   H.-W. Micklitz, *The Politics of Judicial Cooperation* (Cambridge, 2005), at pp. 401–40.

60   P. Rott, 'Consumers and Services of General Interest: Is EC Consumer Law the Future?', *Journal of Consumer Policy* (2007): 49–60, 54; Micklitz, 'The Concept of Competitive Contract Law': 574–7; C. Willet, 'General Clauses on Fairness and the Promotion of Values Important in Services of General Interest', in C. Twigg-Flesner *et al.* (eds), *The Yearbook of Consumer Law 2008* (Ashgate, 2007) pp. 67–106.

61   T. Wilhelmsson and C. Twigg-Flesner, 'Pre-contractual information duties in the *acquis communautaire*', *ERCL* (2006): 441–70, with legislative proposals; Green

as incomplete law, it refers to national law to provide for adequate remedies in case of information deficiencies. Rarely EC law itself contains certain remedies. Sometimes the ECJ may be asked to fill the gaps in existing EU legislation.[62]

The best known example is the so-called '*Heininger*'[63] saga. The questions submitted to the ECJ by the German Federal Court concerned mortgage credit agreements for financing a legally separated, but economically tied, real estate transaction, marketed by seemingly independent sales agents in the interest of banks and entered at the doorstep by a consumer without being informed of an eventual right of cancellation according to the Doorstep Directive. After the Court had confirmed the applicability of the Directive to this type of credit transaction – not to the purchase of the real estate as such – the question remained what should happen in case the consumer had not been informed of his right of withdrawal. The Court bluntly insisted that this right did not lapse because the bank could simply have prevented this consequence by informing the consumer!

On the other hand, this seeming 'victory' of consumer law over marketing practices by banks turned out to be a pyrrhic victory. Since the credit was tied to the separate sale of an immovable good or to the financing of a property fund which, as such, did not fall under the Directive, the consumer could cancel the credit agreement but had to repay the debt plus interest without being relieved of servicing the linked contract. As a follow up to the *Heininger* case, the Court held in *Schulte*[64] that *Article 4(3) of the Doorstep Directive requires Member States:*

> to ensure that their legislation protects consumers who have been unable to avoid exposure to such risks [loss of rental income and property value incurred because of not knowing of their right of cancellation under the Directive, NR], by adopting suitable measures to allow them to avoid bearing the consequences of the materialisation of those risks.

It left it to the Member State courts to ensure such protection without hinting how this could be achieved. This case shows that even a well meant information requirement like the right of withdrawal which does not lapse in case of non-information will not guarantee effective substantive protection of consumers

Paper of 8.2.2007, above, n. 38.

62   Reich, *Understanding EU Law*, at p. 300; P. Rott, Effektivität des Verbraucherrechtsschutzes? Rahmenfestlegungen des Gemeinschaftsrechts, Typescript (Bremen, 2006), at p. 19 insisting on the principle of effective protection even if the directive confers the availability of adequate remedies to Member State law; P. Rott, 'Effective Enforcement and Different Enforcement Cultures in Europe', in: Wilhelmsson, Paunio and Pohjolainen, pp. 305–22.

63   ECJ case C-481/99 *Heininger* v. *Bayr. Hypo und Vereinsbank* [2001] ECR I-9945.

64   Case C-350/03 [2005] *E & W. Schulte* v. *Badenia Bausparkasse* ECR I-9215 at para. 101; critique from a narrow reading of the information duty by Unberath and Johnston: 1260–61.

in cases of complex linked transactions, unless Member State courts develop adequate remedies, which was not the case in Germany.[65]

From consumer law to user protection

The role of the passive market citizen 12. EC consumer law uses a narrow definition of the consumer. With some slight variations, a consumer is a natural person who, in the type of transaction covered by a directive, is acting outside its business or profession. In the case law of the ECJ, this definition has been interpreted as not covering non-profit legal persons, commercial persons acting outside their normal business, and assignees of consumer contracts.[66] Mixed contracts depend on what element is most prominent – there is a presumption that the contract has been concluded for business or professional purposes which must be refuted by the consumer.[67] This case law creates a number of arbitrary delimitations and excludes persons who are also in need of protection. It should not be forgotten that this narrow definition has first been developed in matters of jurisdiction where, according to the Court, not only questions of consumer protection, but also of legal and procedural certainty concerning the place where a case is to be heard must be taken into account. Since the Brussels Convention[68] resp. Regulation (EC) 44/2001[69] take as a starting point the rule '*actor sequitur forum rei*', meaning that usually the domicile of the defendant is relevant to determine jurisdiction within the EC, any rule departing from this principle, like in the area of consumer cases, is an exception and must be interpreted narrowly in the interest of legal certainty.[70] This argument however is not true for consumer transactions where only the position of the 'non-professional market participant' outside the court room is at stake, like in all transactions which are pre-determined by the marketing strategies of business (including use of pre-formulated terms) where the receiving party (the consumer or user) is usually in a 'take it or leave it' situation.

It should also not be forgotten that such a narrow interpretation of the consumer concept as advocated by the ECJ is not in itself written into Article 153 EC, which leaves it to the discretion of the EU legislator or Member States to

---

65   An (incomplete) overview for the English speaking reader of the highly controversial case law of the *Bundesgerichtshof* (BGH-Federal Court) which in the end denied effective protection of consumers in *Heininger*-like situations is given by Unberath and Johnston: 1261–2.

66   Case C-541 + 542/99 *Idealservice* [2001] ECR I-9049; C-361/89 *di Pinto* [1991] ECR I-1189; C-89/91 *Shearson Lehmann Hutton* v. *TVB Treuhandgesellschaft* [1993] ECR I-139.

67   Case C-464/01 *Johann Gruber* v. *Bay Wa AG* [2005] ECR I-439.

68   [1998] OJ C 27/1 (consolidated version).

69   Council Regulation (EC) No 44/2001 of 22 December 2000 on jurisdiction and the recognition and enforcement of judgments in civil and commercial matters [2001] OJ L 12/1; comments Reich, *Understanding EU Law*, at p. 246.

70   C-269/95 *Benincasa* [1997] ECR I-3767 at paras 14–17.

define the concept of consumer. The Court, in cases involving marketing practices and consumer contracts, had no problems with allowing Member State law, being closer to real consumer problems than EC law, to extend the consumer concept to other persons acting without professional expertise.[71] Member State law has done so extensively[72] by allowing different rules on the personal application of a consumer protective measure, thereby, of course, creating distortions of competition in the internal market which are not 'popular' with EC institutions. This explains attempts at a 'full harmonisation' of the consumer concept which will be critically scrutinised later (below, para. 27).

It has been suggested that one should not to be concerned so much with the purpose of the transaction but rather with the position of the private person in the marketplace. Consumer in this sense is the 'passive market individual', the '*homo economicus passivus*' who is entering into transactions to satisfy his needs without producing the product or service himself.[73] EC law, in some areas, seems to recognise this broadening of the consumer concept by being concerned with user protection in general. The most obvious example is the new DSIM. Articles 19–22 contain detailed rules protecting the 'recipient of services' against non-discrimination, and for providing assistance and detailed information on services covered by the directive, not limited to the traditional consumer. Similar principles are emerging in the area of tourist and passenger protection (below, para. 15).

Similar rules can be found in directives on financial services like payment,[74] insurance, investment, or information society services. It is usually the non-professional user of services who comes into the sphere of application, whatever the sphere of use of this service, for example, for his profession, work, or household which may not be known to the trader nor important for qualifying the transaction as 'consumer' or 'non-consumer'. What is more important is the professional expertise of the provider versus the non-professional activity of the user to determine the scope of application of a protective measure. This widens the concept of consumer law, but makes sure at the same time that rules on information,

---

71   C-361/89 *di Pinto* above, at n. 66.

72   For France see J. Calais-Auloy, F. Steinmetz, *Droit de la consommation*, 6th edn (Paris, 2003), paras 12–15, ('*extensions possibles de la notion du consommateur*'); for the UK see G. Howells, S. Weatherill, *Consumer Protection Law*, 2nd edn (Aldershot, 2005), at p. 593 also including persons setting up a business; for Germany S. Grundmann and F. Ochmann, 'German Contract Law Five Years after the Fundamental Contract Law Reform', *ERCL* (2007): 450–67 at 452–6 (narrowing the consumer concept by following ECJ case law); for an overall discussion see E. Hondius, 'The Notion of Consumer: EU vs Member States', *Sydney Law Review* (2006): 89–98; M. Ebers, Concept of Consumer, in H. Schulte-Nölke *et al. Consumer Law Compendium* (Munich, 2007), pp. 670–99, insisting that Member States must be allowed to extend the concept of consumer beyond the directives, at p. 687.

73   Micklitz, Reich, *The Basics of European Consumer Law*, at p. 7.

74   *Ibid.*, at p. 80. Now Directive 2007/64/EC of 13 Nov. 2007 on payment services in the internal market [2007] OJ L 319/1.

mandatory standards and legal protection cannot depend on the rather haphazard intention to use a certain product or service 'within' or 'outside' a profession.

Services of general interest 13. Services of general interest like communication, energy, transport have only recently come into the scope of Community law, together with a trend of deregulation and privatisation of these services. While in the 'old days' these services were highly regulated by public law, the new regime which is more concerned with competition and choice had to develop standards of its own, in particular by transposing, somewhat hesitantly, the idea of *solidarity* also to a more economic and competitive understanding of public services, thus including questions of consumer, or rather user, access and quality.[75] The EC Commission has proposed to include these services in its work on consumer protection.[76]

The most important elements of this strategy have been, on the one hand, the internal market approach, and on the other the so-called 'universal service obligation' of providers.[77] The impact, therefore, is on free choice in the access to services and in non-discriminatory treatment, without distinguishing between consumers in the traditional sense and other users. Under the Universal Services Directive 2002/22/EC[78] and the revised Electricity Directive 2003/54/EC[79] 'household customers' should not be prevented from switching to another provider through direct or indirect impediments.[80]

The 'universal' or public service obligations concern access to services which should be open to anybody, details to be regulated by Member States. It cannot easily be terminated; freedom of contract is suspended by mandatory rules in favour of non-professional users. These provisions however are rather weak at EU-level according to which Member States must only ensure that there are 'adequate safeguards to protect vulnerable consumers, including appropriate measures to help them to avoid disconnection' under Article 3(5) of the Electricity Directive. Annex A gives consumers 'a right to a contract' with some basic information. They

---

75 M. Ross, 'Promoting Solidarity: From Public Service to a European Model of Competition?', *CMLRev.* (2007): 1057–1080, at 1070 insisting on the applicability of the general norm of Article 16 EC.

76 Consumer Policy strategy, COM (2002) para. 3.1.5; also COM (2007) 99 at 12: EU Consumer Policy Strategy 2007–2013.

77 Rott, 'Consumers and Services of General Interest: Is EC Consumer Law the Future?': 53.

78 Directive 2002/22/EC of the European Parliament and the Council of 2002 on universal service and user's rights relating to electronic communications, networks and services (Universal Services Directive) [2002] OJ L 108/51.

79 Directive 2003/54/EC of the European Parliament and the Council of 26 June 2003 concerning Common Rules for the Internal Market for Electricity [2003] OJ L 176, 32.

80 Rott, 'Consumers and Services of General Interest: Is EC Consumer Law the Future?': 56; Micklitz, 'The Concept of Competitive Contract Law': 576; Willet, pp. 95–100.

must be given notice 'of any increase of charges' and have a right to withdraw from contracts if they do not accept the new conditions, but there is no right to be informed about the calculation of the increase and a possible right to challenge it. The Unfair Terms Directive is a weak substitute in this field, even though it may be applied in principle, in particular the transparency principle of Article 4. The EU legislator seems to have confidence in competition which is, however, particularly distorted in the area of energy supply.[81]

Passengers, tourists and travellers 14. Another area where EC law has extended the traditional borders of consumer law is developments concerning passenger rights in transportation, in particular air transport. The role of the passenger does not depend on whether he undertakes a trip 'outside' or 'within' his business or profession; delays, cancellations and accidents concern him notwithstanding the purpose of his trip. Thereby Regulation (EC) 261/2004[82] provides for detailed remedies of the passenger in case of overbooking, delays and cancellations. This Regulation has not been based on the internal market or consumer competence of the EC, but on its competence in the area of transportation (Article 80).

A similar Regulation (EC) 1371/2007 of 23 October 2007[83] concerns rail passengers' rights. As Karsten[84] writes:

> The body of EC consumer law, as widely understood, is expanding into new areas. However, an enlargement of consumer law, narrowly understood, and a change of the narrow notion of "consumer" have not accompanied this growth. Rather, in passenger law, traditional EC consumer law has developed as an independent branch. Passenger law is thereby generally adding to the edifice of consumer law; though without touching its core domain of 'shopping law'.

---

81   Rott, 'Consumers and Services of General Interest: Is EC Consumer Law the Future?': 57.
82   Regulation (EC) No 261/2004 of the European Parliament and of the Council of 11 February 2004 establishing common rules on compensation and assistance to passengers in the event of denied boarding and of cancellation or long delay of flights, and repealing Regulation (EEC) No 295/91 [2004] OJ L 46, 1. See Case C-344/04 *IATA and ELFAA* v. *Department for Transport* [2006] ECR I-403; for a definition of 'extraordinary circumstances' excluding compensation see opinion of AG Sharpston, case C-396/06 *Eivid F. Kramme* v. *SAS Scandinavian Airlines Denmark A/.S.* A critical overview has been given by E. and M. Varney, 'Grounded? Air Passenger Rights in the EU', in Twigg-Flesner *et al.*, pp. 171–200.
83   [2007] OJ L 315, 14.
84   J. Karsten, 'Passengers, Consumers and Travellers: The Rise of Passenger Rights in EC Transport law and its Repercussion for Community Consumer Law and Policy', *Journal of Consumer Policy* (2007): 117–36, at 135; for further developments see same author, 'European Passenger Law of Sea and Inland Waterway Transport', in Twigg-Flesner *et al.*, pp. 201–32.

A certain precedent for this extension had already been set by the Package Holidays Directive. The definition of consumer, according to Article 2(1), has been extended to: the principal contractor, other beneficiaries and the transferee. The rules in the Directive concerning liability and compensation are mandatory and – with minor exceptions – cannot be waived by contract clauses, Article 5(4). These provisions are usually regarded as 'extensions' of the consumer concept which, being exceptions to the general rule, must be interpreted narrowly.[85] But the argument could be turned upside down, as we will demonstrate later (para. 40).

IP users?   15. Intellectual property matters have hardly been discussed under consumer protection aspects, even though the consumer – or rather user – will usually have to pay the 'price' for the use, copy or purchase of a product or service protected by an IP-right, or otherwise be excluded from its use. This price may be directly calculated as a licence fee, possibly imposed by a right-management institution, or may be part of the overall purchase itself. Consumers or potential users may simply be denied access at the discretion of the right-holder which is particularly relevant for 'information-goods' in the so-called 'information society'; EC law does not know a 'fair use' principle.[86] Protection is exclusively attributed to the right-holder, not to the user, as can be clearly seen from Directive 2004/48[87] which does not even mention user rights.

It was only the ECJ which, in its spectacular and controversial *Magill* case[88] gave user rights an adequate footing under the competition rules. The Court had to evaluate the practice of (market dominating) Irish radio and TV stations invoking their copyright to refuse the release of their programmes to independent consumer magazines. The Court followed the Commission and the Court of First Instance, against the opinion of AG Gulmann, in that this practice amounted to an abuse of a dominant position of the Irish TV stations in the regional market for programme magazines:

---

85   For the relevance of his argument see Reich, *Understanding EU Law*, at p. 30.
86   The leading US Supreme Court case concerning fair use is *Campell* v. *Acuff-Rose Music, Inc*. 510 U.S. 580, explaining the 'four factor test'. For its (reduced) relevance in US and TRIPS law, R. Okedij, 'Access to Copyrighted Digitalised Information Works', in K. Maskus and J. Reichmann (eds), *International Public Goods and the Transfer of Technology* (Cambridge, 2006), pp. 142–87, at p. 142, pleading for an 'international fair use doctrine' at p. 182, and insisting on an access rule for copyrighted digital works at p. 187.
87   Directive 2004/48/EC of the EP and the Council of 29 April on the enforcement of intellectual property rights [2004] OJ L 157/45.
88   Cases C-241 + 242/91P *Radio Telefis Eireann (RTE) and Independent TV Publications Ltd (ITP)* v. *Commission* [1995] ECR I-743.

The appellants' refusal to provide basic information by relying on national copyright provisions thus prevented the appearance of a new product, a comprehensive weekly guide to TV programmes which the appellants did not offer and for which there was potential consumer demand ... (para. 54).

The judgment aroused and still arouses protests among the IP community which does not seem to appreciate user rights and prefers a nearly unlimited protection of IP rights.[89] The Court in later cases had to clarify its case law by insisting it did not want to attack the very substance matter of IP rights.[90]

Similar controversies were provoked by the rules on exhaustion for intellectual property rights as developed by the case law of the ECJ. They have an indirect effect on consumer protection because they preclude the right-holder from invoking his IP right to control or to limit the distribution or repackaging of a protected product within the internal market, or to be able to cash-in twice for its licensing once the product has been placed on the market with his consent.[91] With regard to copyright, in *Laserdisken*, the ECJ[92] insisted that the exhaustion of the right of distribution guaranteed under Directive 2001/29/EC on copyright in the information society[93] is limited to the internal market; only the placing on the internal market (including the EEA), not on the world market is valid reason for exhaustion. This territorial limitation of exhaustion obviously limits the access of consumers to copyrighted products already put on non-EU/EEA markets.[94]

Also directly important for consumer protection – for example, the right to information and education under Article 153(1) EC – are those cases where questions of 'fair use' in the area of copyright are in conflict with the protection of the right-holder. This will concern cases of non-commercial use, for example the reproduction of copyrighted material already in circulation for personal purposes, the citation, caricature or parody of a work in later personal creations and the use of copyrighted material for educational purposes. Usually questions of 'fair use'

---

89 S.D. Anderman, *EC Competition Law and Intellectual Property Rights* (Oxford, 2000) at p. 178; H.K.S. Schmidt, 'Article 82's Exceptional Circumstances that restrict intellectual property rights', *ECLR* (2002): 210, at 215: lack of clarification of exceptional circumstances; for differentiated view insisting on the limits of antitrust see H. Ulrich, 'Intellectual Property, Access to Information, and Antitrust', in R.C. Dreyfus, D.L. Zimmermann and H. First (eds), *Expanding the Boundaries of IP* (The Hague, 2001), pp. 367–402, at pp. 381–98.

90 Case C-7/97 *Oscar Bronner GmbH & Co KG* v. *Mediaprint* [1998] ECR I-7791; later case C-418/01 *IMS Health* v. *NDC Health* [2004] ECR I-5939. See also case T-504/93, *Tierce Ladbroke* v. *Commission* [1997] ECR II-923.

91 Reich, *Understanding EU Law*, at pp. 170–73; for a recent example see case C-348/04 *Boehringer Ingelheim et al.* v. *Swingward et al.* [2007] ECR I-3391.

92 Case C-479/04 *Laserdisken* [2006] ECR I-8089.

93 [2001] OJ L 167/10.

94 This argument was used by the EFTA-Court in its *Maglite* opinion of 3.12.1997, cited by A.G. Jacobs in his opinion to *Silhouette* [1998] ECR I-4799 at 4813.

are not regarded as part of consumer law, but have been defined by Member States as exceptions to their general rules on copyright. In our opinion, this view is too narrow because the position of the consumer as the non-active market citizen is greatly influenced by the corresponding rights of the IP-holder. In many cases his right to receive information, which was recognised by the Court in *Laserdisken*, will be greatly influenced by the extent of copyright protection and by the possibility of invoking a 'fair use' exception for non-commercial, that is, personal purposes.

But Directive 2001/29 left the question of 'fair use' (a concept not mentioned in the Directive) to the Member States – in contrast to the idea of creating a 'single market' for copyright in the information society. Article 5(3) contains numerous exceptions to the reproduction and public communication right enshrined in copyright which must be invoked by the Member States, for example, for the sole purpose of illustration for teaching for scientific research duly quoting the source, quotations for review and criticism in accordance with 'fair practice' (lit. d), use for the purpose of caricature, parody or pastiche (lit. k), use in connection with the demonstration or repair of equipment (lit. l), use for educational and similar purposes. Under the so-called 'three step-test', these exceptions must not, however, conflict with 'normal exploitation' of the work and 'not unreasonably prejudice the legitimate interests of the right-holder' (para. 5 of Article 5). It is quite obvious that the EC legislator does not have trust in Member States which may possibly extend user rights to the detriment of right-holders.[95] Article 6(3) allows for 'technological measures' to prevent a circumvention of protected copyright, including *access control*. Paragraph 4, as an exception, requires Member States to 'take appropriate measures to ensure that right-holders make available to the beneficiary the above mentioned exceptions', but it is not clear how this can be implemented. At the moment, this seems to be a dead letter provision practically making free access as provided in the 'fair use' provisions nearly impossible.

From a broadly understood consumer law approach, the non-harmonisation of these exceptions must be regretted. It means that the non-professional user is subject to different national regimes which may not even be very effective in allowing access in areas expressly covered by the Directive, while the right-holder enjoys a broad protection with at least comparable standards. EC law does not even try to adequately balance these interests. The only possibility to avoid an 'overprotection' of right-holders and an 'under-protection' of consumers and users against their right to free access to information is to limit the threshold of copyright itself.[96] Article 2 refers to 'works' of authors, but does not define their originality or individuality as basis of protection. This must still be done by applicable Member

---

95   Critique of this 'three step' test by Okediji, at p. 170, pleading for a 'proportional approach to access' at p. 184.

96   Reich and Micklitz, *Europäisches Verbraucherrecht*, at p. 279 criticising that the right of the user concerning access to information has been regulated in a rather restrictive manner.

State law which uses different thresholds in this respect but which should not be 'levelled up' to the detriment of users.[97]

An important question involving a balancing between the protection of right-holders under the Directive on enforcement of intellectual property rights on the one hand, and the protection of users concerning their personal data relating to the use of the internet by means of connections provided by a telephone company, arose in *Promusicae*.[98] The question put before the ECJ concerned the obligation of Member States to allow right-holders, or their management societies, access in civil infringement proceedings to data of users held by internet providers. The Court did not give a straightforward answer, but required Member States and their courts, in answering such request, to balance the two opposing fundamental rights, namely of right-holders concerning an effective protection of their intellectual property and 'a further fundamental right, namely the right that guarantees protection of personal data and hence of private life'. Indirectly the Court recognised user rights at least insofar as their personal data are concerned. However this protection is not absolute and has to be balanced against the protection of right-holders. The Court did not say how this conflict is to be settled, but left this to Member States. It did not voice opposition to a provision in State law which allowed access to personal data only in criminal, not in civil proceedings.

Non-discrimination in consumer markets

Nationality 16. Community freedoms take two directions: they protect the active market citizen (producer, importer, trader, service provider, commercial agent and so on) against unjustified discriminations – whether direct or indirect – and restrictions of entry and marketing into the entire internal market. They also have a reverse side in protecting the recipient of services (and goods!) which has been labelled 'passive freedom of services'.[99] It does not matter whether the potential recipient is a consumer in the narrow sense or user in a broader context; both are protected against direct or indirect discriminations based on nationality limiting or making less attractive their right to receive services from other EC countries. The ECJ reads Article 49 in conjunction with Article 12 EC; this reading was extended also to the principle of Union citizenship under Article 18 meaning that every EU citizen cannot be discriminated against his freedom to receive services from providers established all over the EU and to enjoy the ancillary entitlements accompanying this freedom. These principles even take 'horizontal direct effect' if the restrictions or discriminations result from collective regulations in particular

---

97   D. Beldiman, *Functionality, Information Works, and Copyright*, PhD thesis (Bremen, 2008).

98   ECJ, 29.1.2008, C-275/06, *Productores de Musica de Espana (Promusicae)* v. *Telefonica de Espana* [2008] ECR I-nyr para. 63.

99   Reich, *Understanding EU Law*, at pp. 66–8.

in consumer markets.[100] An interesting situation arose in *Cowan*.[101] This case concerned freedom to provide services, but from the standpoint of the recipient – here, a consumer/user of (public) transportation services. As such, the consumer enjoys the right to free movement in order to receive these services.[102] If a Member State attaches certain rights to such a – primarily economic – position, then the tourist from another EC country should not be discriminated against in the exercise of these rights. That is, the tourist should be treated in the same way as nationals. The Court went on to say:

> When Community law guarantees a natural person the freedom to go to another Member State the protection of that person from harm in the Member States in question, on the same basis as that of nationals and persons residing there, is a corollary of that freedom of movement ... (para. 17).

Another case concerned discriminatory regulations for entry to (local) museums in Italy.[103] The Court rejected rules allowing free entry to state museums for EU citizens of pension age, but for local museums limiting this right only to Italian citizens or local residents of pension age. Such differentiation amounted either to direct discrimination based on nationality, or indirect discrimination based on residence. In both cases, this would affect foreign tourists more seriously than local ones. The discrimination could not be justified because it was based on purely economic reasons. This case law combines the economic right of free movement (here the freedom to provide and receive services) with other fundamental rights like non-discrimination. It is mostly directed against the state (in a broad sense) providing certain services, but may be extended to private law relations under the above mentioned qualification when originating from 'collective regulations'.

More recent cases concern the provision of health services to members of national health care or insurance systems who need to receive these services abroad. In a controversial and highly contested case law, the Court has extended the free movement rights of citizens by the corollary to receive health services under certain circumstances in other EU countries without needing prior authorisation.[104]

---

100 N. Reich, 'Horizontal liability in EC law: "Hybridisation" of remedies for compensation in case of breaches of EC rights', *CMLRev* (2007): 705–42, at 724–5; critique against this horizontal direct effect has been voiced by Riesenhuber, paras 100–104 referring to the state as being obliged to protect private relations.
101 Case 186/87 *Cowan* v. *Trésor public* [1989] ECR 195.
102 Case 286/82 + 26/83 *Luisi & Carbone* v. *Ministerio del Tesoro* [1984] 377.
103 Case C-388/01 *Commission* v. *Italy* [2003] ECR I-721.
104 Case C-158/96 *Raymond Kohll* v. *Union des Caisses de Maladie* [1998] ECR I-1931; with regard to hospital services see case C-372/04 *Yvonne Watts* v. *Bedford Primary Care Trust* [2006] ECR I-4325, allowing proportionate derogations under the public health proviso to 'attain a high level of health protection', paras 104–105.

Non-discrimination with regard to ethnic origin 17. The Race Directive 2000/43/ EC of 29.6.2000,[105] based on Article 13 EC, addresses discrimination based on racial or ethnic origin. It relates mostly to employment relations, but also covers social and consumer protection, including social security and healthcare; social advantages; and education. Most important has been the extension to the sphere of consumption because 'access to and supply of goods and services which are available to the public, including housing' are also covered, Article 3(1)(h). The meaning of this extension is somewhat unclear and will certainly be subject to further litigation and potential clarification by the Court. Some observers fear an overstepping of Community competences and a violation of the principle of freedom of contract, inherent in EC and Member State law.[106] There is however no *excès de pouvoir*, since the Community can legislate in the sphere of consumption, as Article 153 shows (below para. 22). This fear of an infringement of the fundamental freedoms is not justified, given the fact that in practice of financial services and tourist operations, open or hidden racial or ethnic discrimination seemed to be quite common and should not be allowed under the pretext of 'freedom of contract'.[107] The main criteria to be determined concern whether a good or a service is '*available to the public*'. The availability must be judged by eliminating potential discriminatory factors. Even if there is no duty to contract by any supplier of goods or services in the market under EC law (but may be introduced by Member State law), public advertising may make goods or services 'available' to the public, so that a refusal to sell or the imposition of discriminatory conditions may be caught by Article 3(1)(h). The Race Directive forbids direct as well as indirect discrimination.

Non-discrimination with regard to gender 18. On 5 November 2003, the Commission proposed a 'Council Directive implementing the principle of equal treatment between women and men in the access to and supply of goods and services'.[108] It would not allow different insurance tariffs for men and women, for example, in life, health or car insurance. The proposal has been severely criticised for invading into the freedom to contract and in making realistic calculations in insurance policies impossible which may lead to higher premiums in general.

---

105 Council Directive 2000/43/EC of 29 June 2000 implementing the principle of equal treatment between persons irrespective of racial or ethnic origin [2000] OJ L 180/22.
106 For a discussion see P. Eeckhout, 'The EU Charter of Fundamental Rights and the federal questions', *CMLRev.* (2002): 945, 986–8; from an economic point of view see A.-S. Vandenberghe, 'The Economics of the Non-Discrimination Principle in General Contract Law', *ERCL* (2007): 410–33.
107 D. Schiek, *Differenzierte Gerechtigkeit* (Baden-Baden, 2000) at p. 220 onwards; Reich and Micklitz, *Europäisches Verbraucherrecht*, at p. 426 concerning marketing activities; D. Schiek, L. Waddington and M. Bell, *Non-Discrimination Law* (Oxford, 2007), at p. 304.
108 Com (2003) 657 final.

In the meantime, Directive 2004/113/EC of the Council of 13 December 2004[109] has been adopted. It must be implemented by 21 December 2007. Article 3(2) and Recital 14 expressly guarantee freedom to choose a contractual partner, unless this is not based on that person's sex. The rules concerning insurance contracts have been somewhat modified to allow, to a limited and transparent extent, the use of actuarial factors for the different risks of men and women in insurance policies where measures may be delayed until 21 December 2009. The non-discrimination principle of the directive is limited, according to Article 3(1), to goods and services 'available to the public irrespective of the person' which depends on the marketing practice of the provider.[110] There are certain exceptions, for example, private and family life, education, the media. Differentiations may still be justified by objective reasons within the limits of the principle of proportionality, Article 4(5). According to Recital 16, this may include rules of private associations allowing access only to one sex – a somewhat problematic exception which may easily allow possibilities of circumvention.

Recent proposals by the 'acquis'-group

19. Within the process initiated by the European Commission of preparing a so-called 'Common Frame of Reference' for European Contract Law,[111] a group of researchers has been established to review and consolidate the 'consumer–*acquis*' and to make proposals for a legislative initiative at Community level. The so-called '*acquis*–group' has recently published a comprehensive draft on the '*acquis*' principles.[112] The principles take up some of the critique voiced in this paper against the existing EC consumer law directives, try to eliminate certain

---

109 [2004] OJ L 373/37.
110 N. Reich, 'Diskriminierungsverbote und Gemeinschaftsprivatrecht', in: A. Halfmeier *et al.* (eds), *Zugang und Ausschluss als Gegenstand des Privatrechts* (Stuttgart, 2005), pp. 1–32, at p. 18.
111 A critical overview has been given by N. Reich, 'A European Contract law – Ghost or Host for Integration?', *Wisc. Int. L. J.* (2006): 425–70. Critical questions have also been raised by R. Zimmermann, 'European Contract Law: General Report', *EuZW* (2007): 455–62, at 462. In the meantime, the 'Draft Common Frame of Reference' (2008) has been published.
112 For a detailed comment see Research Group on Existing EC Private Law (*Acquis Group) Principles of the Existing EC Contract Law (Acquis Principles)* (Berlin, 2007). A first evaluation has been given by R. Schulze, '"Acquis-Grundregeln" und Gemeinsamer Referenzrahmen', *ZEuP* (2007): 731–4, himself a member of the *acquis*–group. Some reservation has been voiced by R. Zimmermann, 'European Contract Law: General Report': 460–61; N. Jansen and R. Zimmermann, 'Grundregeln des bestehenden Gemeinschaftsprivatrechts?', *JZ*, 62 (2007), 1113–26 same, Restating the Acquis Communautaire,? A critical examination of the "Principles of Existing EC Contract Law, *Modern Law Review* (2008) 505-534; J. Basedow, 'Der Grundsatz der Nichtdiskriminierung im europäischen Privatrecht', *ZEup* (2009) 230-251 at 244

contradictions and to extend their sphere of application to create a 'general part of European consumer law' – a strategy certainly to be welcomed even though a political agreement and a legal structure still have to be debated and found.

Some remarkable innovations of the principles should be mentioned:

- According to Article 1:201 'consumer' means any natural person who is *mainly* (italics added) acting for purposes which are outside the person's business activity; this would extend the existing narrow definition mainly into the area of 'mixed contracts' (above, para. 12).
- Article 2:201 contains a general pre-contractual information duty of business towards consumers which is specified in detail in later provisions (see para. 5); there is a special rule in Article 2:203 concerning information towards disadvantaged consumers (above, para. 8).
- Article 2:206 contains a duty to provide and express information in clear and intelligible language; this seems to refer also to the language issue (above, para. 6).
- Article 2:207 contains remedies for breach of information duties, including prolongation of the right of withdrawal up to one year in case of missing information and a right to receive 'reliance damages' (above para. 11).
- Chapter 3 contains general rules on non-discrimination (above paras 16–18), without however mentioning EU-nationality discrimination.
- Article 5:103 consolidates withdrawal periods to 14 days, thus eliminating the existing contradictions in the different directives (para. 5).
- Article 5:106 contains a definition of so-called 'linked contracts', a problem that had not been adequately resolved by the so-called *Heininger* saga (above para. 11).
- Chapter 6 consolidates the law of 'non-negotiated terms', without, however, transforming the indicative list into a blacklist (see para. 10) or taking up Member State law with goes beyond the Directive under the principle of 'minimum harmonisation'.

It is too early to discuss the further destiny of the 'principles'. They certainly deserve close attention – a closer one than can be given in this context. These *acquis* principles have been included in the recently published draft common frame of reference (DCFR).[113] The legal status of this document is not yet known and it will therefore not be considered further here.

---

because of their going beyond the *acquis* by developing some general principles of contract law. See also Wilhelmsson and Twigg-Flesner: 441.

113 For an overall discussion see the contributions in R. Schulze (ed.), *Common Frame of Reference and Existing Contract Law* (Munich, 2008).

'Extrinsic', Competence Problems

The competence dilemma

The 'market' bias of EC consumer law   20. Consumer protection has been on the E(E)C agenda ever since its first 1975 consumer programme,[114] where it proclaimed five consumer rights:

1. The right to protection of health and safety.
2. The right to protection of economic interests.
3. The right of redress.
4. The right of information and education.
5. The right to representation (right to be heard).

There are two fundamental problems with this generous, but limited and, to some extent dated, grant of 'consumer rights' in the EU:

* Important consumer 'rights', or perhaps somewhat more modestly 'consumer interests' are not included which we mentioned above (paras 13–15), in particular *non-discriminatory access* of (potential) users to services of general interest (public services) and to information networks – a problem which seemingly did not exist at that time!
* These 'rights' are not legally enforceable, or, in EC terminology, do not take 'direct effect'. They must be implemented by secondary law and paralleled by effective enforcement mechanisms, which is a question of competence in a 'quasi-federal'-system of divided jurisdiction between the Union (the EC) and Members States to which we will turn now.

The competence basis for consumer protection measures in the then Treaty of the European Economic Community (EEC), which was renamed the European Community (EC) in 1993 by the Maastricht Treaty, has always been rather weak and contested. The original version of Article 100 EEC allowed measures for the approximation of laws having a direct effect on the establishment and functioning of the common market by directives, based on a unanimous decision of the Council as main legislator of the Community; the European Parliament had only a consultation right. This formula was used to enact the first consumer protection directives, but the rather vague substantive criteria on competence were compensated by the requirement of *unanimity* of the Member States in the Council. Therefore, little discussion on competence existed when – after protracted compromise formulations which usually considerably 'watered down' original proposals of the Commission – the directives on misleading advertising,

---

114   [1975] OJ C 92; Micklitz, Reich, *The Basics of European Consumer Law*, at p. 13.

on doorstep selling, product liability and consumer credit 87/102/EEC[115] were enacted. These directives are still in force today, even though with a very different scope of application and content following later case law and amendments. The consumer credit directive is soon to be replaced by a new one, the CCD. The Doorstep Selling Directive is – together with other seven consumer directives – subject to review.[116] Their common characteristic besides *minimal harmonisation* – which will be treated in the next section (para. 26 with the notable exception of product liability, see para. 29) – was an attempt to reconcile the requirements of the common market with the creation of consumer rights, for example to information, to legal protection and to compensation. Consumer law started from a 'productivist concept', as has been said elsewhere.[117]

In the 1980s the EEC was increasingly concerned with the issue of opening the markets and the concept of a 'Single European Market' or 'Internal Market' emerged. This had been applied beforehand in judicial decisions. Specific protective consumer policies were only of relevance for the Community to the extent to which they increased the freedom of choice of individual consumers; the approach is a liberal one related to free trade rather than a social state protective approach. Initially, the Single European Act of 1987 pursued this concept in Article 14 EC (formerly Article 8a EEC) establishing firmly the objective of achieving the Single European Market by 31 December 1992 in terms of free movement of goods, persons, services and capital. Consumer protection was only indirectly recognised as an objective of the EEC.[118]

21. An explicit recognition only occurred by Article 129a E(E)C as amended by the Maastricht Treaty of 1993 via the so-called 'co-decision procedure', giving the European Parliament a genuine legislative power jointly with the Council in the areas covered by the internal market competence. This allowed a two way road to consumer protection, namely:

- by measures adopted pursuant to Article 100a in the context of the completion of the internal market
- by specific action which supports and supplements the policy pursued by the Member States to protect the health, safety and economic interests of consumers and to provide adequate information to consumers.

---

115 [1987] OJ L 42/48.
116 Discussion paper on the Review of the Consumer *Acquis*, COM (2006) 744 final of 8.2.2007 published by the Commission.
117 Micklitz, Reich, *The Basics of European Consumer Law*, at p. 11.
118 See Stuyck, 'European Consumer Law after the Treaty of Amsterdam: Consumer Policy in or beyond the Internal market?': 378.

Article 153 EC in the version of the Amsterdam Treaty again reformulated the provision on consumer policy by spelling out the consumer right to information and education in para. (1), by introducing a 'horizontal clause' in para. (2) whereby 'consumer protection requirements shall be taken into account in defining and implementing other Community policies', and by replacing the phrase 'specific action' by '*measures*', thus in the Community jargon meaning to include legislative action.[119] This is still the legal basis of consumer policy today.

Another important change has been the addition of a separate chapter on creating an area of 'Freedom, Justice and Home affairs', allowing certain measures regarding judicial protection of citizens in civil matters, including consumers, but granting an opt-out to Denmark and containing opt-in provisions for the UK and Ireland.

How has this new competence been used in later action? We will briefly take a look at the relevant competence entitlements and the debate surrounding them, without going into details of the proposed or enacted measures.

Article 153 and its limits 22. For an independent observer, it might seem that Article 153 would become the main motor for consumer protection in the EC. This however was not the case. The main reason was the ambivalent, double faced nature of Article 153 itself in its para. 3, either referring in lit. (a) to measures concerning the internal market itself, or in lit. (b) to 'supporting and supplementing measures' linked to consumer policies pursued by the Member States. Since the Commission is the main player in proposing legislative measures, it has the freedom to choose the optimal legislative basis for measures, depending on its priorities, and these were clearly in the direction of establishing the 'internal market' and making it work by eliminating still existing limits to free movement and distortions of competition, and not in an effort of pursuing an independent, autonomous consumer policy. In effect, only one directive[120] is based on Article 153(2)(b). But this remained the only exemption and the directive is now under reconsideration which may well lead to a change in its legislative basis.[121]

The limits of Article 153(3)(b) have never been tested, but there seems to be an overwhelming agreement that the scope left for Community legislation is rather small and will, in particular limit, 'innovative legislation' to create new rights and obligations of consumers and business in areas not yet covered by Member

---

119 For an analysis see *ibid.*, 379–84; Weatherill at pp. 18, 70; Micklitz, Reich, *The Basics of European Consumer Law*, at pp. 41–3; N. Reich, 'A European Contract Law, or an EU Contract Law Regulation for Consumers?', *JCP* (2005): 383–407, at 398–401.

120 Directive 98/6/EC of the European Parliament and of the Council of 16 February 1998 on consumer protection in the indication of the prices of products offered to consumers [1998] OJ L 80/27; insofar Unberath and Johnston: 1243 are not correct in alleging that 'not a single legislative measure' has been based on Article 153(3)(b) EC.

121 COM [2006] 744 Annex II on the review of the consumer *acquis*.

States.[122] It has been argued that lit. (b) could at least be used to codify and amend existing EC consumer marketing practices and contract law.[123] All Member States now have – either on their own or implementing EU directives – their national consumer law, including general principles of an overall EU approach to consumer protection based on information and fairness before entering into and within transactions, and specific rules on 'cooling-off' periods in direct and distance marketing, on unfair terms, and on legitimate quality expectations. These quite well developed areas of EU consumer contract law could easily be elaborated and codified in a comprehensive consumer code. The above mentioned *'acquis principles'* (para. 19) could be enacted on the basis of Article 153(3)(b) as a 'European Consumer Contract Law Regulation' (ECCLR).[124]

Article 95 and the 'tobacco follow-up' 23. Article 95 EC became the main basis for adopting consumer policy measures, thus following the former approach on the basis of (the nearly void) Articles 100 and of 100a EEC (now Article 94/95 EC). There was little debate on whether the mentioning of Article 95 in Article 153(3)(a) gave consumer policy a particular and autonomous status, or whether it remained a mere technical reference not changing the substantive requirement of internal market legislation, namely to contribute to the establishment or functioning of the internal market. This is, of course, particularly relevant with regard to measures which do not make free movement of goods and services easier by eliminating Member State restrictions, but by 'positive measures' whose main purpose is to improve the health, safety, or economic wellbeing of the consumer. These may even create additional (indirect) obstacles to free movement, for example mandatory rules on consumer contracts, restrictions on advertising, or regulations on product safety.[125]

Since the ECJ is the final arbiter on disputes of Community competence, it is not surprising that such questions finally had to be decided in Luxembourg. These competences are not unlimited despite the wide interpretation given in earlier Court decisions, as can be seen in the judgment of 5 October 2000 on advertising and sponsorship of tobacco products.[126] This dealt with the complaint of the Federal

---

122 Weatherill at p. 74; for a more extensive reading see Stuyck, 'European Consumer Law after the Treaty of Amsterdam: Consumer Policy in or beyond the Internal market?': 387; it is sufficient that a policy (not a law) of Member States already exists.

123 Reich, 'A European Contract Law, or an EU Contract Law Regulation for Consumers?': 401; similar Rösler, 'Auslegungsgrundsätze des Europäischen Verbaucherprivatrechts in Theorie und Praxis': 502.

124 Reich, 'A European Contract Law, or an EU Contract Law Regulation for Consumers?': 405.

125 This had been already litigated by case C-359/92 *Germany* v. *Council* [1994] ECR I-3681 paras 34–7.

126 ECJ, C-376/98, *Germany* v. *European Parliament and Council* [2000] ECR I-8149; compare Weatherill at pp. 73–9.

Republic of Germany against the tobacco advertising directive 98/43/EC[127] which almost entirely prohibited advertising and sponsoring of tobacco products, but had allowed the Member States to enact still stricter provisions. Article 152 EC had been ruled out as a legal basis as the Community's competence to protect health did not embrace the enactment of harmonisation measures. In the end, only the general clause regarding internal market policies in connection with the free movement of services remained to justify competence. The ECJ insisted that Article 95 may not simply be invoked because of differences in Member State legislation; otherwise the powers of the Community would be without limitations, and contrary to the principle of enumerated powers contained in Article 5(1) EC. The ECJ then criticised that the directive did not actually abolish existing obstacles to the free movement of goods and services. Furthermore, it found that there was no evidence proving that the different existing advertising rules in the Member States resulted in an 'appreciable'[128] distortion of competition. However, in certain areas the ECJ allowed Community bans on advertising, such as in the area of print advertising and the sponsoring of sporting events. Nonetheless the ECJ was incapable of distinguishing admissible and inadmissible provisions of the directive, since this concerned a legislative issue. Thus the Tobacco Advertising Directive was declared void in its entirety.

The significance of the tobacco decision for consumer policy in the Community on the basis of internal market competence is still subject to controversy. Roth[129] alleges that the Directives on (consumer) contract law will be of short duration considering the latest court decisions of the ECJ as they do not provably contribute to free movement or elimination of distortion of competition; they 'merely' concern legal protection. The coordination of the different legal systems in the Community is realised by international private law, not by harmonisation of laws. Other authors, such as Grundmann and Kerber,[130] primarily refer the Community competence to information regulations; otherwise the principle of *pacta sunt servanda* applies. Weatherill reads the tobacco-judgment as insisting that the 'EC measure must work harder in the service of market integration. This raises questions about the

---

127 Directive 98/43/EC of 6.7.1998 relating to the approximation of laws, regulations and administrative provisions of Member States relating to the advertising and sponsorship of tobacco products [1998] OJ, L 213, 9.
128 This criterion was not repeated in the later *BAT* judgment of 13.12.2002, C-491/01 [2002] ECR I-11453, para. 60.
129 W.-H. Roth, 'Die Schuldrechtsmodernisierung im Kontext des Europarechts', in W. Ernst and R. Zimmermann (eds), *Zivilrechtswissenschaft und Schuldrechtsreform* (Tübingen, 2001), pp. 225, 231–5; W.-H. Roth, 'Europäischer Verbraucherschutz und BGB', *JZ* (2001): 475–80, at 477; similar Unberath and Johnston: 1255.
130 S. Grundmann and W. Kerber, in Grundmann, Kerber and Weatherill, pp. 264, 281–3 considering financial services.

legal validity of some already adopted directives that affect contract law but assert their contribution to market making in a laconic fashion ...'.[131]

This view is not supported by the latest practice of the ECJ.[132] In its decision on the validity of Directive 98/44/EG on the legal protection of biotechnological inventions[133] the ECJ stated: 'The purpose of harmonisation is to reduce the obstacles, whatever their origin, to the operation of the internal market which differences between the situations in the Member States represent.'

In the area of consumer protection the obstacles result from the different levels of protection which undermine the trust of the consumer in the functioning of the markets, increase misallocations based on false or incomplete information and limit the consumer's freedom of choice. Later judgments concerned, in particular, health and safety aspects of internal market legislation which may even justify complete bans on products or severe restrictions on advertising. There is thus no real conflict between free movement on one hand and a high level of protection in the areas named in Article 153(1) on the other hand. In its subsequent judgment concerning the complaint of Germany against the revised tobacco advertising directive 2003/33/EC the Court[134] upheld the somewhat 'softened' prohibition of tobacco advertising even if it restricted free movement, and it allowed human health and consumer protection objectives to be included in the legislative discretion on the extent of harmonisation.

The case was mostly concerned with free movement, not so much with distortions of competition which may also affect the functioning of the internal market. Consumer protection rules in contract and tort law usually do not impede free movement as such, or make it more difficult or costly,[135] but may distort competition by imposing different regulatory standards on traders and different intensities of consumer protection. Harmonisation may therefore be necessary; it need not result in a 'levelling down', but may also serve to improve and intensify protection, which the Court has clearly recognised in health related issues.[136] This case law can be transferred to improving consumer protection standards in economic matters like marketing practices or contract standards. It is true that Community law aims at liberalising trade, but not at any price, as can be seen by the horizontal clauses of Articles 3(t), 95(3) and 153(2) EC (above, para. 4).[137] Of

---

131 Weatherill, at p. 157; see also S. Weatherill, 'The Constitutional Competence of the EU to Deliver Social Justice', *ERCL* (2006), 136–58, at 141.
132 N. Reich, 'Die Vorlagepfllicht in harmonisierten Bereichen', *RabelsZ* (2002): 531.
133 ECJ, case C-377/98, *Netherlands* v. *European Parliament and Council* [2001] ECR I-7079.
134 ECJ, case C-380/03 *Germany* v. *European Parliament and Council* [2006] ECR I-11573 paras 37–40.
135 Schäfer and Ott, at p. 294.
136 Joined cases C-453/03 and others, *ABNA and others* v. *Secretary of State for Health* [2005] ECR I-10423, para. 108.
137 See the recent opinion of 15.11.2007 of A.G. Trstenjak in case C-404/06 *Quelle* v. *BVVZ*, para. 51 concerning the interpretation of the Consumer Sales Directive.

course, there must always be some relationship of the measure to the establishment and functioning of the internal market, either by limiting restrictions on free movement by divergent rules on advertising of the Member States, or by avoiding distortions of competition by different rules on consumer contracts or torts. The debate nowadays is not concerned with the basis of competence for consumer matters as such, but rather its extent under the conflicting principles of 'minimal versus full harmonisation' which will be discussed later (below, para. 27).

Article 65 on judicial cooperation in civil matters 24. The new chapter on freedom, justice and home affairs in the Amsterdam Treaty also extended competence in the area of civil justice which is important for judicial consumer protection in civil matters. This has been recognised in Article 65 with regard to 'measures ... having cross-border implications ... in so far as necessary for the proper functioning of the internal market ...', by 'promoting the compatibility of the rules applicable in the Member States concerning the conflict of laws and of jurisdiction'. In Community practice, this article is only concerned with cross-border protection of citizens (including consumers) in general by rules on applicable law and on jurisdiction. It has been used on several occasions, the most notable outcome is the above (para. 12) mentioned Regulation (EC) 44/2001 on jurisdiction and enforcement of judgments in civil and commercial matters, and later Regulation (EC) 1896/2006 on a European payment order procedure.[138] Lately, Regulation 861/2007[139] establishing a European small claims procedure has been adopted, to be applied from 1 January 2009. The main intention of these instruments is to ensure that the consumer, who has been actively approached by the trader to enter into a contract, is not deprived of the jurisdiction of his home country and cannot be subjected to the country of the trader or another country under a choice of jurisdiction clause. In this area, the EC, as well as preceding international agreements like the Brussels Convention of 1968 (as amended) had no problems recognising the need for special protection of the consumer against opting out of his home jurisdiction. The exact extent of this privilege is subject to debate, but has been extended during recent amendments.

Today the main problem concerns the possible use (or, in my opinion, misuse) of pre-litigation arbitration clauses forcing the consumer to take his claim to arbitration in the name of 'freedom of contract' (below para. 40), and thereby making the protection granted by the existing Community and national instruments ineffective – a practice well familiar to the US consumer law thus *de facto* eliminating consumer protection legislation.[140] The questions have not yet

---

138 Regulation (EC) No 1896/2006 of the European Parliament and of the Council of 12 Dec. 2006 on creating a European order for payment procedure [2006] OJ L 399, 1.

139 Regulation (EC) No. 861/2007 of the European Parliament and the Council of 11 July 2007 establishing a European Small Claims Procedure [2007] OJ L 199/1.

140 Reich, 'More clarity through *Claro*?': 49–52; R. Alderman, 'Consumer Arbitration: The Destruction of the Common Law', *Journal of American Arbitration* (2003): 1–

been finally decided in EC law, but the ECJ had to decide whether the national court, in an action for annulment of an arbitration award against a consumer, can, on its own motion, determine the unfairness of the arbitration clause.[141] The Court answered positively, insisting that consumer protection:

> as measure which is essential to the accomplishment of the tasks entrusted to the Community and, in particular, to raising the standard of living and the quality of life in its territory…, (require the court) to assess of its own motion whether a contractual term is unfair, compensating in this way for the imbalance which exists between the consumer and the seller or supplier (para. 37).

The Court did not answer the question of unfairness of such clauses but left this to Member State law. It should however be mentioned, that with regard to cross-border litigation in the EU regarding consumer contracts, not only jurisdiction but also arbitration clauses which have the same effect, namely forcing the consumer to a jurisdiction outside his place of residence, should be severely restricted under the applicable rules of Regulation 44/2001 even though its Article 17 is only concerned with limiting jurisdiction clauses in consumer contracts entered into before litigation.[142]

Minimal changes in the 'competence sensitivity'[143] by the Lisbon Reform Treaty
25. The existing state of competence of the ECJ in consumer matters is highly unsatisfactory. It leads to a fragmentation of legislative actions which must respect the different requirements and limitations following from Article 95 and, to a more specific and selective extent, also Article 153(3)(b) and Article 65 EC. It supports the 'internal market bias' of consumer law which is more or less seen as an instrument to support cross-border shopping, not to empower the consumer in his position as the non-professional market citizen. Also the federal element of EC jurisdiction should be remembered. Since it is limited in scope and intensity, the power of national states is even more important and must always be respected. Consumer policy becomes a truly federal matter, ruled by the subsidiarity principle of Article 5(3).

Attempts at rewriting or amending the Treaty to give the Community greater, or at least clearer, competence in the area of consumer policy have been rather

---

17; The future of Consumer Law in the US, U of Houston Law Center No. 2008-A-09, with further references to the US-American situation, fearing a 'Destruction of the Common Law'.

141 Case C-168/05 *Elisa Maria Mostaza Claro* v. *Centro Movil Milenium* [2006] ECR I-10421; critique has been voiced by P. Landolt, 'Limits on Court Review of International Arbitration Awards Assessed in light of States' Interests and in particular in light of EU Law Requirements', *Arbitration Int.* (2007): 63–91, at 77–82.

142 Reich, 'More clarity after *Claro*?': 53–5.

143 Weatherill, p. 70.

scant. The Lisbon Reform Treaty of 13 December 2007 will not change the existing competence arrangements. The EC Treaty will be replaced by a Treaty 'on the Functioning of the European Union (TFEU)'. The numbering of the articles will be amended; Article 153 EC will become Article 169 TFEU. Article 4(2)(f) lists 'Consumer Protection' under the heading of 'shared competences' between the Union and Member States, parallel with the 'Internal Market'. A new Article 12 takes over the wording of Article 153(2), namely that 'consumer protection requirements shall be taken into account when defining and implementing other Community policies and activities'. Article 65 on 'judicial cooperation in civil matters' will become Article 81, also to include measures 'ensuring an effective access to justice'. It mentions in particular the 'development of alternative methods of dispute settlement'.[144]

Minimum versus complete harmonisation

The original approach and its problems 26. The first consumer directives – with the exception of product liability to which we will turn later (below para. 29) – had been adopted as so-called minimum directives. This was due to the necessity of unanimity in the Council under the old procedure of Article 100 EEC, which forced compromise solutions on the Community legislator. Member States did not want to lose control over the further development of their own consumer law. Even after the Single Act allowed majority voting under the new Article 100a EEC, now Article 95 EC, minimum harmonisation was still the main road to consumer protection both in the area of trade practices and consumer contract law.

The last example for this is the Consumer Sales Directive[145] which justified this approach in Recital (5) with the following words: 'Whereas the creation of a common set of minimum rules of consumer law, valid no matter where the goods are purchased within the Community, will strengthen consumer confidence and enable consumers to make the most of the internal market'.

The minimum clause was described in Article 8(2) in a wording similar to other directives: 'Member States may adopt or maintain in force more stringent provisions, compatible with the Treaty in the field covered by this directive, to ensure a higher level of consumer protection.'

In a number of judgments, the ECJ ruled in favour of this minimum protection clause,[146] thereby allowing an extension of consumer protection rules to non-

---

144　For proposals in this direction see already H.-W. Micklitz, N. Reich, S. Weatherill, 'EU Treaty Revision and Consumer Protection', *JCP* (2004): 367–399, at 384.

145　For a discussion see P. Rott, 'Minimum harmonisation for the completion of the internal market?', *CMLRev* (2003):1107–30, at 1107, justifying minimum harmonisation with different expectations and hence vulnerability of consumers in the EC, at 1131.

146　ECJ, cases 382/87 *Buet et al.* v. *Min. Public* [1989] ECR 1235; C-361/89 *Criminal proceedings against Di Pinto* [1991] ECR I-1189; C-183/00 *Gonzales Sanchez* v. *Medicina Asturiana* [2002] ECR I-3901 para. 27; C-71/02, *Karner* v. *Troostwijk*

consumers in the narrow sense of EC law, to more intrusive remedies and to a widening of the scope of application. The only limit to this extension was set by general Treaty provisions, such as on discrimination or artificial segregation of the market. However, no national consumer protection law was ever successfully challenged for its negative effect on the internal market, even though the minimum protection clause allowed considerable variations of consumer law in the Member States.

The minimum harmonisation principle was taken over in Article 153(5) EC at least for those measures where the Community acts in support of Member States under para. (3)(b) (above, para. 22). Other areas of social protection had similar rules, for example in environmental law, social standards and non-discrimination. Even measures on intellectual property based on the internal market competence were governed by the minimum clause.[147]

In areas which related directly to the free movement of goods and services, the Community however opted for a stronger harmonisation, either by full harmonisation or, as we will discuss later, by the so-called mutual recognition or by the country of origin–approach; in cases of free circulation of goods causing harm to consumers a strict safeguard procedure was foreseen.[148] These differentiations can be explained by the different impact on free movement caused by rules on consumer protection on the one hand, and by standards of goods or services on the other. While the first only have an indirect, sometimes rather hypothetical, effect on the internal market by forcing the trader to respect different rules of trade practices or contract law,[149] the second are a direct impediment to free movement by restricting market access of goods and services as such. Thereby it seemed justified to allow different thresholds for Member States to 'opt out' from Community standards.

[2004] ECR I-3025 para. 33 a different view has been developed by AG Trstenjak in her opinion of 17.7.2008 in case C-205/07 *Criminal proceedings against Lodwijk Gysbrechts und Sangturel Inter BVBA*; critical comment by Reich/Michlitz, *Vur* (2008): 349–351.

147 With an important exception concerning the EU wide exhaustion, see case C-355/96 *Silhouette International Schmied GmbH & Co KG* v. *Hartlauer Handelsgesellschaft GmbH* [1998] ECR I-4799.

148 Case C-470/03 *A.G.M.-COS.MET* [2007] ECR I-2749; critical comment N. Reich, 'A.G.M.COS.MET, Or Who is protected by EC Safety Regulation?', *ELRev* (2008) forthcoming.

149 O. Remien, *Zwingendes Vertragrecht und Grundfreiheiten des EG-Vertrages* (Tübingen, 2004), pp. 193 onwards; N. Reich, 'Der Common Frame of Reference und Sonderprivatrechte im Europäischen Vertragsrecht', *Zeitschrift für Europäisches Privatrecht* (2007): 161–79, 172.

The new approach: how 'complete' is 'complete' harmonisation? 27. The new Consumer policy strategy of the Commission since 2002[150] however changed the existing method of harmonisation, at least as far as Commission proposals were concerned, by opting for full harmonisation in order to reach its first midterm objective, namely 'an equally high common level of protection':

> We must go further to enable consumers and business to realise the benefits of the internal market. Central to this is the establishment of common protection rules and practices across Europe. This means moving away from the present situation of different sets of rules in the Member States towards a more consistent environment for consumer protection across Europe ...

This is an important policy change couched in the terminology of the internal market and consumer confidence which was critically 'welcomed' in the literature.[151] The Commission only incidentally, not yet empirically, proved its point that 'common' and 'uniform' standards are necessary for cross-border shopping, or that minimum harmonisation was an impediment to consumers shopping abroad and to traders going cross-borders. More important for consumer confidence in the internal market, as Wilhelmsson convincingly stated, are effective complaint systems, taking into account language problems, to which the consumer can turn in case of difficulties.

From an EU-constitutional point of view[152] full harmonisation has a positive and a negative effect: the positive effect is to require the Member States to enact the protective provisions of a directive fully, thus in compliance with general principles of EC law. The negative consequence, however, is concerned with the *pre-emptive* effect of EC law: Member States are prevented from 'upgrading' their

---

150 COM [2002] 208 at 12.
151 Micklitz, Reich and Weatherill: 385; T. Wilhelmsson, 'The Abuse of the "Confident Consumer" as Justification for EC Consumer Law', *JCP* (2004): 317–37; scepticism is also voiced by Weatherill, 'The Constitutional Competence of the EU to Deliver Social Justice': 156: need for '*diverse* patterns of consumer protection, underpinned by a *unified* minimum standard' (italics W.); B. Lurger, 'The Common Frame of Reference/Optional Code and the Various Understandings of Social Justice in Europe', in Wilhelmsson, Paunio and Pohjolainen, pp. 177–200, at pp. 180–86, particularly concerning competence transfer to the EU and thus undermining Member State policy; a more positive view has been taken by E.-M. Kieninger, *Wettbewerb der Rechtsordnungen im Europäischen Binnenmarkt* (Baden-Baden, 2002) at p. 380; see also R. Michaels and N. Jansen, 'Private Law Beyond the State: Europeanisation, Globalisation, Privatisation', *American Journal of Comparative Law* (2006): 843–90, at 863–4 referring to tensions between the different concepts of European private law.
152 These questions are rarely discussed in EU law, see remarks by J. Lindholm, 'State Procedure and Unions Rights', *Umäa Justus Förlag* (2007): 249 concerning similar problems in the area of enforcement of Community rights through national courts.

consumer law to allow higher standards of protection. Legislative power to amend and modify consumer law is thus transferred to the EU, a consequence not in conformity with the principle of limited jurisdiction of the EC as laid down in Article 5(1) and the principle of subsidiarity in Article 5(3) EC. It is also not clear whether and how far courts are bound by the full harmonisation principle: can they extend protection to non-consumers, or may they devise remedies under their national law if EC law proves to be inefficient for consumer protection?

28. The most important example of full harmonisation has been the Unfair Commercial Practices Directive. Even though Article 4 follows the principle of full harmonisation, there are a number of exceptions which provoke uncertainties both for traders and for consumers, as Wilhelmsson[153] points out. Following, he argues for a justified differentiation between the 'positive' and the 'negative' scope of application of the Directive. While health related claims may be covered by the prohibitions of the Directive, this should not necessarily pre-empt stricter Member State standards justified for (proportionate) health reasons. It is however not sure that such a differentiation will be followed by the ECJ.

A similar full harmonisation approach has been adopted by Parliament and Council in the Consumer Credit Directive 2008/48/CC (CCD). Article 22(1) reads explicitly: 'Insofar as this Directive contains harmonised provisions, Member States may not maintain or introduce provisions other than those said laid down in this Directive.'

The main point of debate will refer to the scope of harmonisation by the Directive itself as set out in Article 2(2). Consumer information has been completely harmonised under the EC information paradigm by introducing '*standard European consumer credit information*' and a right of withdrawal. However, it seems clear that questions of 'social protection' of the consumer–debtor, for example against usurious credit agreements, against unfair and harsh collection clauses, or about protection in cases of inability to repay and in situations of insolvency, are not, and cannot be, harmonised. This will of course limit the cross-border effects of the directive despite its pro-consumer rhetoric in Recital (9): 'Full harmonisation is necessary in order to ensure that all consumers in the Community a high and equivalent level of protection of their interests and in order to create a genuine internal market.'

The example of product liability 29. Product liability was harmonised by the early Directive 85/374. As can be seen from the preamble, the objective of the Directive is two-fold; ease the free movement of goods and improve consumer protection. This was used to justify a 'no fault' liability scheme of the producer in the consumer interest. The protective purpose of the directive is repeated several times throughout the Directive although the Directive allows the producer the

153 In Howells, Micklitz and Wilhelmsson, at p. 58.

so-called 'state of the art defence' with regard to the controversial 'development risk',[154] which the Member States may waive.

The supplier was liable only under limited conditions according to Article 3(3).The directive contains neither a minimum nor a maximum protection clause, but its Article 13 reads somewhat ambiguously: 'This Directive shall not affect any rights which an injured person may have according to the rules of the law of contractual or non-contractual liability or a special liability system existing at the moment when this Directive is notified.'

The ECJ[155] had to decide the question how far Member States could go beyond the Directive in order to improve the position of the victim, especially by introducing strict liability for the supplier beyond the limits of Article 3(3), with the possibility of taking recourse against the producer or EC-importer. Such a remedy might be necessary in cases of false statements of the supplier concerning the producer, or the latter's insolvency. In *Skov* the Court[156] ruled that the Directive created full harmonisation and therefore rejected any strict liability of suppliers to be introduced by Member States; a fault-based system would however be in conformity with the Directive.

The main argument is a purely formal one; the Court does not even consider the position of the victim (the consumer) which the Directive aimed to improve in achieving 'effective protection' without total harmonisation.[157] It argues about the conceptual difference between 'no-fault' and 'fault' liability without mentioning the safety obligation which is inherent in the Directive. In any case, the supplier is 'closer' to the producer than the consumer and should bear the risk of not being able to enforce his claim against the producer (or EU-importer); he can take out insurance, or draft his contracts in such a way that the producer will be finally liable.

The Council adopted a resolution on 19 December 2002 on the amendment of liability for defective products[158] proposing to allow national law to extend liability to suppliers. This, however, was not followed up by any action or initiative by

---

154 See C-300/95 *Commission* v. *UK* [1997] ECR I-2649 para. 24 and in particular the interesting opinion of A.G. Tesauro at para. 19.

155 Cases C-52/00 *Commission* v. *France* [2002] ECR I-3827; critique Howells, 'The Rise of European Consumer Law – Wither National Consumer Law?': 75–7; M. Sengayen, 'Recent Judgments of the ECJ and the Elusive Goal of Harmonisation of Product Liability Law in Europe, in: Twigg-Flesner *et al.*, pp. 447–64; N. Reich, 'Horizontal Liability in Secondary EC Law', in: *Liber amicorum Guido Alpa* (London, 2007), pp. 846–68, at pp. 850–53.

156 Case C-402/03 *Skov* v. *Bilka Lavprisvarehus* and *Bilka Lavprisvarehus* v. *Jette Mikkelsen et al.* [2006] ECR I-199, critical comment by S. Whittaker, Commentary, *ZEuP* (2007): 865; as a follow up case C-177/04 *Commission* v. *France* [2006] ECR I-2461 and my critique Kommentar, *VuR* (2006): 241.

157 Recitals 12, 13, 18; Micklitz, Reich, *The Basics of European Consumer Law*, at p. 266.

158 [2003] OJ C 26/2.

the Commission.[159] Following the ECJ ruling, the Danish Product Liability Act was amended. Suppliers are now liable for fault, including vicarious liability for negligence of the producer; in the latter case he can take recourse against the producer.[160] This is an elegant way to circumvent the strict ruling of the Court by using 'fault' liability to make it conform with 'no-fault' principles. This example shows that the objective of the Commission to stop Member States from devising remedies in favour of their citizens going beyond EC law cannot and should not be halted. Obviously this will lead to a partitioning of the internal market from a legal point of view, but this is a consequence of a quasi-federal system[161] of 'multi-level governance' (below, para. 41) well known to other, more federal, entities like the US and Australia. This implies that regulation for the internal market may be necessary on two levels, one concerned with market access on federal level, the other concerned with different social and consumer protection standards on a Member State level. But there will always be a dilemma balancing the two levels.

A seemingly elegant, some say radical, way out of this dilemma seems to be the country of origin (or mutual recognition) principle to which we will turn now.

Country of origin versus country of activity

Mutual recognition and/or country of origin 30. In areas without full harmonisation, under general rules of the conflict of laws usually the law of the country of a marketing activity directed at consumers, and not the law of the supplier established in another EU country, would apply. This rule is, however, subject to critique from a free movement point of view, and therefore the Court, in its seminal *Cassis de Dijon* judgment of 1979, has developed the principle of mutual recognition for product standards. This has later been extended to services and the freedom of establishment. It has a close link to the 'country of origin principle' but these principles are not identical.

The ECJ has a long standing practice[162] of scrutinising regulations of the country of destination or activity for their potential effect on cross-border trade.

---

159 Third Commission Report, COM (2006) 495 final of 14.9.2006, at 5, 11.

160 W. Wurmnest and W. Doralt, 'Die Entwicklung des Gemeinschaftsprivatrechts 2004–2006 – Obligationenrecht', *GPR (Gemeinschaftsprivatrecht)* (2007): 118–130, at 120; Whittaker: 868 pointing to the rather formal difference between (forbidden) strict liability of the supplier and (allowed) vicarious liability of the supplier for product defects caused by the producer.

161 Bourgoignie and Trubek, at pp. 2–10; Lindholm, at p. 251, referring to the lack of remedies in EC law which therefore must be left to the Member States, and at p. 276 insisting on the limits of pre-emption requiring, as in US practice, a 'clear and manifest intention' of the legislator.

162 The literature can hardly be overlooked any more, seen for the modern case on free movement of goods P. Oliver and S. Enchelmaier, 'Free movement of goods – Recent developments in the case law', *CMLRev.* (2007): 649–704, on services V. Hatzopoulos,

The starting point is a set of different, rather broad, tests to define the concepts of 'indirect discrimination' or 'restriction'. Once this is established, the Member State may justify its regulations under a public interest test allowing, *inter alia*, considerations of consumer, environmental and social protection to be taken into account. Any regulation must meet the principle of 'proportionality' which is subject to close Court scrutiny depending on the invoked public interest test; mere economic and financial considerations of Member States will usually not suffice to justify a measure restricting free movement. As mentioned before, the Court will usually give preference to information requirements over mandatory standards or pre-marketing controls. Services may be subject to a broader range of justifications, especially in sensitive areas such as health and legal services, but they cannot avoid scrutiny under EU law principles either.

This mechanism had led to a *mutual recognition* or *respect* principle meaning that, unless otherwise proven, regulatory requirements, controls, tests, certifications, exams or similar requirements complied within the country of origin of the product or service should be recognised as sufficient in the country of destination. At least the Member State of activity should establish a procedure whereby this equivalence can be objectively and transparently tested. This principle is based on Member States' owing each other mutual trust and confidence under the cooperation rule of Article 10 EC until the contrary is proven. But the country of activity can always verify whether there is equivalence, and whether some special and proportionate public policy considerations still justify its (stricter) regulatory standards.

This mutual recognition principle is similar to the 'country of origin-principle' since both operate in the area of non-harmonised EU-standards, but they are not identical. The mutual recognition principle does not affect jurisdiction with regard to verification and justification of restrictions; the country of activity remains responsible for this process of evaluation, always of course respecting the relevant EC law principles. This may, in practice, come close to the 'country of origin principle', but avoids an automatic shift of jurisdiction and competence. Mutual recognition, therefore, seems to be more in line with the subsidiarity principle of Article 5(3) EC, even though it requires a protracted case-by-case evaluation of still existing restrictions to free movement, or secondary legislation which establishes EC wide standards.

The Commission however does not seem to be satisfied with this state of affairs, and ever since its 1984 paper on 'Television without Frontiers'[163] has not only promoted, but also put forward in legislative proposals, the more radical country of origin principle. To understand its importance and the controversies surrounding it, we will look at some important initiatives in this respect. With regard to consumer policy, its main danger lies in a feared 'race to the bottom':[164]

T.U. Do, 'The Case law of the ECJ concerning free provision of services', *CMLRev.* (2006): 923.

163   See Reich, Micklitz, *Europäisches Verbraucherrecht*, at pp. 117–21.

164   This is doubted by Kieninger, at p. 329 because of missing incentives for suppliers.

businesses may establish themselves in the country with the 'lowest regulatory standards' in environmental, consumer or social protection issues (which seems easy in a Union of 27 Member States all competing for business investments under a liberalised regime!), and the mechanism of 'country of origin' will allow these standards also to govern environmental, consumer or social relations in the country of activity, thereby setting aside its 'established and traditional standards which eventually must be downgraded to avoid regulatory competition harming the economy of the receiving state'.[165] Whether this fear is true or not, is at the moment more subject to speculation than empirical verification.

The example of E-commerce Directive 31. The country of origin principle was and is used by the Commission to promote the development of new technologies under the Lisbon strategy, in an attempt to make the Union's internal market the most dynamic and competitive economy in the world. A predecessor (in this regard) to the E-commerce Directive was the Directive 89/552/EEC on 'Television without frontiers'[166] which allowed broadcasters established within the EU to transmit their programs into all Member States, subject only to home–country control which, however, had to respect certain common standards on advertising and consumer protection. Receiving countries lost jurisdiction of control, subject to some very narrowly defined safeguard clauses to protect children. This principle was upheld but also restricted by the Court in its *de Agostini* case to its genuine scope of application,[167] thus pre-empting special TV regulations of the receiving country, but still allowing the application of its general marketing practices legislation to combat unfair and misleading advertising.

This approach was later followed in the much more important and more widely applied E-commerce Directive which became the starting point for later similar proposals of the Commission; it is therefore important to briefly evaluate its impact. The country of origin principle is laid down under the heading of 'Internal market', similar to the TV-Directive. The most important provision is Article 3 para. (1/2). This rule is supposed to liberalise e-commerce within the EU. It is supplemented by Article 4 expressly excluding prior authorisation procedures. Its legal content and importance is subject to controversies. These can be summarised as follows:

---

165 This has become a popular paradigm in EC law, see N. Reich, 'Competition between Legal Orders', *CMLRev.* (1992): 845; Kieninger, throughout.

166 Council Directive 89/552/EEC of 3 October 1989 on the coordination of certain provisions laid down by Law, Regulation or Administrative Action in Member States concerning the pursuit of television broadcasting activities [1989] OJ L 298/23, amended by Directive 97/36/EC of the European Parliament and of the Council of 30 June 1997 [1997] OJ L 202/60.

167 C-34-36/95 *Konsumentenombudsmannen (KO)* v. *De Agostini (Svenska) Forlag AB and TV Shop Sverge AG* [1997] ECR I-3843.

- It is not clear whether the country of origin principle should be understood as a conflict-of-law rule determining the applicable law in cross-border conflicts as the law of the 'information society service provider', as some authors suggest.[168] This seems to contradict Article 1(4), according to which the Directive does not establish 'additional rules on private international law nor does it deal with the jurisdiction of courts'.

- The country of origin principle depends on the 'coordinated field' as broadly defined in Article 1(h) of the E-Commerce Directive. However, it specifically exempts requirements applying to goods as such, to the delivery of goods, and to services not provided by electronic means. These distinctions are not always easy to apply in practice, since they may lead to the applicability of different laws depending on what aspect of the supply of goods or provision of services is involved.[169]

- The Directive does not apply to certain services, per Article 1(5), such as gambling, representation before the courts, and taxation. As a general rule of Community law, these exceptions have to be construed narrowly, thereby allowing lawyers to offer their out-of-court services cross-border without being subjected to restrictive rules of the receiving country which may not, for instance, forbid advertising on websites of lawyers for reasons of 'professional ethics' as in Germany. The excluded services will however come under the general EC rules, in particular gambling.[170]

- The Annex contains express derogations from Article 3, in particular copyright and other industrial property rights, 'contractual obligations concerning consumer contracts', the permissibility of forbidding unsolicited commercial communications by electronic mail, and others.

- Article 1(3) of the E-Commerce Directive is without prejudice to existing Community law protecting 'in particular public health and consumer interests, as established by Community acts and national legislation implementing them in so far as this does not restrict the freedom to provide information society services'. The latter qualification is again subject to doubt, since rules on health and consumer protection can only operate to restrict the freedom to provide services, but are usually justified by the general interest.[171]

- A special safeguard procedure is provided in Article 3(4)–(6) to combat crime, for example, pornography on the internet.

---

168 In this sense S. Leible, 'Die neue EG-Verordnung über das auf außervertragliche Schuldverhältnisse anzuwendende Recht (Rom, II)', *Recht der Internationalen Wirtschaft* (1997): 721–35, at 729.

169 Reich, Halfmeier, 'Consumer Protection in the Global Village: Recent Developments in German and European Law': 132; for a recent example see case C-244/06 *Dynamik Medien* v. *Avides* [2008] ECR I-(14.2.2008) concerning a restriction to sell image store media to young persons.

170 See most recently joined case C-338, 359 + 360/04 *Massimiliano Placanica* [2007] ECR I-1891.

171 C-322/01 *Deutscher Apothekerverband* v. *Doc Morris NV and Jacques Waterval* [2003] ECR I-14887.

- The country of origin principle only applies to information society service providers established in the EU. Service providers established in third countries (including association countries) have to follow the general rules on jurisdiction and conflict of laws.

- According to Recital 22 competent authorities of the country of origin are obliged to protect not only citizens of their own country but *all* Community citizens. Although an extension of the principle of territoriality of control, this is not reflected in the provisions of the directive itself, for example on information exchange between competent authorities.[172] To some extent this 'home country control' rule is without meaning because most internet service providers can simply avoid this control by being established outside the EU; control by the country of activity will usually not be possible due to factual impediments. The internet is to some extent creating a legal vacuum which some authors want to fill by 'transnational consumer law' (below, para. 35).

The importance of the E-Commerce Directive is most substantially felt in the area of advertising and commercial communication. Here, the liberalising effect of the country of origin principle may encourage traders to shop for the 'best' (that is, the most liberal and least restrictive) regulatory environment. In this way, the Directive undermines higher standards in the receiving country. In the somewhat futile attempt to avoid such a 'race to the bottom', the Directive also contains minimum requirements on information, transparency and contracting, but no substantive standards, thus following the 'information paradigm' of EC law which we criticized already (above, paras 4–7). At the same time it has *de facto* abolished Member State restrictions on advertising and sales promotion methods. It is therefore questionable whether the country of origin principle has achieved what was its intention, as expressed in Recital (7): 'In order to ensure legal certainty and consumer confidence, this Directive must lay down a clear and general framework to cover certain legal aspects of electronic commerce in the internal market.'

More recent proposals for the country of origin-approach and their failure
32. The example of the E-commerce Directive became the model for later proposals of the Commission concerning directives on 'unfair commercial

---

172 The constitutional and economic problems involved in this extension of the principle of home country control are discussed by S. Weatherill, 'Pre-emption, Harmonisation and the Distribution of Competence to Regulate the Internal Market', in C. Barnard and J. Scott (eds), *The Law of the Single European Market* (Oxford, 2002), pp. 41–74, at pp. 66–9; H. Muir Watt, 'Integration and Diversity', in F. Cafaggi (ed.), *The Institutional Framework of European Private Law* (Oxford, 2005), pp. 107–148, at p. 107 criticising that costs of deregulation are transferred to the country of activity at the detriment of local consumer, environmental and social standards, a consequence against the principle of 'economic due process'.

practices',[173] earlier proposals of 2004 on 'services in the internal market'[174] and the modified proposal on consumer credit.[175] In addition to the 'full harmonisation' rule excluding the minimum protection principle in the areas covered by the proposed directives (above, para. 27), they contained an 'internal market clause' for areas not explicitly regulated by the Directive. The general rule was in all proposals that the goods or services covered by the Directive could circulate within the EU only if complying with the harmonised EU standards and the rules of the country of establishment, not of the country of destination. Control should lie with the supervisory authorities of the country of origin which had to be assisted by rules on administrative cooperation with the remaining (26!) Member States, coordinated by the Commission, which emerged as a kind of 'regulatory superpower'.

The most controversial document was the 2004 services proposal which suggested the introduction of the country of origin principle to many services not particularly regulated and offered in the internal market. The proposed Article 16(1) stated:

> Member States shall ensure that providers are subject only to the national provisions of their Member State or origin which fall within the coordinated field.

> Para. 1 shall cover national provisions relating to access to and the exercise of a service activity, in particular those requirements governing the behaviour of the provider, the quality or content of the service, advertising, contracts and the provider's liability.

Even though there were certain exceptions to this country of origin principle, it would have meant that service providers had only been subject to the rules and supervision of their home country, including contract law and civil liability (with the express exceptions of consumer contracts and liability of the provider for personal injury). If such a principle had been enacted, it would have turned upside-down well established rules on jurisdiction and conflict of laws. These allow at least a residual competence of the country of activity, even though subject to monitoring by EC law.[176] It would have set a precedent for other areas of economic activities not (yet) covered by EC law. It would not have completely derogated from consumer protection since the proposal itself and other applicable EC law instruments contained rules on information to be provided to service recipients

---

173 COM (2003) 356.
174 Com [2004] 2 final.
175 Com [2005] 483 final of 7.10.2005.
176 C. Calliess, *Die Dienstleistungsrichtlinie*, Zentrum für Europ, Wirtschaftsrecht Bonn (2007), at pp. 17–27; G. Davies, 'The Services Directive: Extending the country of origin-principle and reforming public administration', *ELRev* (2007): 232.

(including consumers). Important questions like rules on civil liability of service providers were not even touched in the proposal.[177]

After strong opposition, the Commission had to reduce its original proposal considerably. The final wording of Article 16 of the Service Directive 2006/123 is a compromise negotiated between the European Parliament, the Commission and the Council. The exact meaning of this will almost certainly be tested before the ECJ. It reads: 'Member States shall respect the right of providers to provide services in a Member State other than that in which they are established. The Member State in which the service is provided shall ensure free access to and free exercise of a service activity within its territory ...'. It recalls the main principles for restrictions as developed in the case law of the ECJ (the so-called *Gebhard* test),[178] namely the principles of:

- Non-discrimination,
- Necessity, and
- Proportionality.

Article 16(2) contains a 'black-list' of prohibited requirements which was already proposed in the draft Article 16(3) and has a special new escape clause.

The term '*respect*' in Article 16(1) takes a lower threshold than the principle of mutual recognition. It seems to exclude direct effect of the right to provide services – a consequence which would be in clear contradiction to the existing case law of the ECJ. This is 'corrected' by the next sentence which contains a precise and unconditional obligation of the Member State where the service is provided to ensure free access to and exercise of the service. Interestingly, it is only concerned with 'vertical', not with 'horizontal' direct effect of this freedom. Regarding these uncertainties, the directive must be interpreted by referring to the existing case law of the ECJ.

Article 16(3) is important insofar as it repeats the public policy provision in Article 46 EC. It has been widened as it includes the protection of the environment, while consumer protection beyond health matters is not mentioned, even though it figures high in the case law of the ECJ regarding restrictions in the public interest.[179] This should be criticised from an EU constitutional point of view because the Directive considerably narrows the Member State's competence in the area of (economic) consumer protection as established by the case law of the

---

177 U. Magnus and H.-W. Micklitz, *Liability for the Safety of Services* (Baden-Baden, 2006), at pp. 113–27 with an overview of (missing!) general EC law on liability for defective services.

178 C-55/94 *Gebhard* v. *Consiglio dell'Ordine degli Advocati e procuratori di Milano* [1995] ECR I-4165 para. 37.

179 Case C-384/93 *Alpine Investments BV* v. *Minister van Financien* [1995] ECR I-1141; Roth, 'Freier Dienstleistungsverkehr und Verbraucherschutz': 171; Calliess, *Die Dienstleistungsrichtlinie*, at p. 34.

ECJ, without giving any reason for this encroachment on state prerogatives.[180] In referring to national labour law on employment conditions the directive wants to prevent a 'race to the bottom' by service providers from other Member States with lower standards.

One may argue that Article 16(1) does not modify the existing case law of the ECJ. The black-list in Article 16(2) is, however, not subject to any justification. The elimination of consumer protection from a justified restriction is contrary to the case law of the ECJ and is a problematic deviation from existing principles of Community law. It implies a downgrading of consumer protection, despite the Commission assuring the opposite.[181]

All other proposals which contained – alongside the principle of 'full harmonisation' – 'internal market clauses', such as on unfair commercial communications and on 'consumer credit' had to abandon them during the legislative process. The consumer credit proposal relates to a particularly sensitive area of consumer protection. Recital 10 of the modified 2005 proposal suggested, with surprising clarity, the mutual recognition principle in areas not harmonised in 'order to avoid additional burdens on creditors', not even considering consumer interests. The Commission refers to 'mutual recognition', but actually means the country of origin principle. Consumer protection is set aside in favour of creditor 'protection'. As Micklitz[182] remarked, the Commission promotes a harmonisation which is a leap into the unknown (*ins Blaue hinein*) – without even mentioning the constitutional problem of undermining Member States' competence in sensitive areas like consumer protection. Finally, this proposed Article 21 – which was rejected in the final reading – is contrary to EC rules and proposals on jurisdiction and conflict law rules on consumer protection to which we will turn now.

Consumer protection in conflict situations of private law 33. Consumer protection beyond harmonisation of rules on private transactions can be achieved in different ways, in particular:

- rules on jurisdiction, or/and
- rules on applicable law

The main thrust of consumer law is to allow the consumer access to the (more familiar and usually less costly) courts and ADR-mechanisms of his home country. In addition, the standards of his domicile apply and proceedings have to be in the national languages. Legal representation and legal aid also follow the rules of the consumer's domicile. This is in clear contrast to the country of origin principle which unilaterally favours the trader. There are however exceptions to

---

180 Roth, 'Freier Dienstleistungsverkehr und Verbraucherschutz': 171.
181 See the last *Consumer Policy Strategy 2007–2013*, COM [2007] 99.
182 H.-W. Micklitz, N. Reich, 'Europäisches Verbraucherrecht – quo vadis?', *VuR* (2007): 121–30, at 129.

this 'consumer country of domicile' principle, for example when the consumer himself went to a foreign market for a transaction, or where he misinformed the trader about his place of domicile, especially in case of electronic contracting.

It is therefore no surprise that the relevant EC rules on jurisdiction and conflict of laws start exactly from these premises. Both the Brussels Convention of 1968 (as amended) on jurisdiction in civil and commercial matters, and the Rome Convention of 1980[183] on applicable law for obligations arising out of contracts contained special rules on consumer litigation and consumer contracts whereby the so-called 'passive consumer' – the consumer doing the relevant transaction in his country of domicile where he was approached by the trader – has the privilege of access to his home country courts and the application of the mandatory consumer protective provisions of his home legislation.

The Brussels Convention is now largely transposed into Regulation (EC) 44/2001 under the new competence of Article 65 EC (above, para. 24). One of the key changes in the Regulation compared to the Convention is the new approach towards marketing activities in B2C relations. According to Article 13(1)(c) of the Convention, the right of the consumer to sue the supplier in the consumer's country of domicile was originally subject to the existence of advertising or a specific invitation addressed to the consumer and limited to certain transactions, excluding consumer credit. Moreover, the consumer should have taken the necessary steps to conclude the contract in that state.

Article 15(1)(c) of Regulation 44/2001 replaced these two conditions with one: the consumer may sue the company in the country of his domicile if the company '... by any means, directs such activities to that Member State or several States including that Member State'. It applies to all consumer transactions (excluding transportation contracts, but including package holidays). This provision has sparked debate with regard to e-commerce, as it can be interpreted that the mere accessibility of the website of a company situated in one Member State by a consumer domiciled in another Member State may give such consumer the right to sue the company in the consumer's domicile. As a result marketing in e-commerce could be subject to now 27 different and diverging jurisdictions. Traders may also be provoked to avoid contracting and thereby discriminating against consumers in some jurisdictions. On the other hand, the E-commerce Directive did not solve this dilemma because it expressly excluded rules on jurisdiction from its scope of application and therefore did not impose the county of origin in jurisdiction matters. It does not transfer competence to hear consumer cases to the country of the trader instead of the consumer. This may pose some practical problems which will not be discussed here.[184]

---

183 Text in Micklitz, Reich, *The Basics of European Consumer Law*, at pp. 505–18.
184 Different solutions have been proposed by P. Mankowski, 'Entwicklung und Stand des Europäischen Verbraucherschutzrechts', in A. Wagner and V. Wedl (eds), *Bilanz und Perspektiven zum Europäischen Recht* (Wien, 2007), pp. 325–58 at p. 325.

This consumer-friendly jurisdiction rule has also been adopted in the recent Regulation (EC) No 1896/2006 of 12 December 2006 creating a European order for payment procedure. The competence for the procedure is determined by reference to the rules of Regulation 44/2001. This means that usually the court of the domicile of the defendant is competent. According to Article 6(2), an order against the consumer can only be sought in the court where the consumer is domiciled.

34. Another area of consumer protection in cross-border situations is the Rome Convention of 1980, now enacted in all 'old' Member States.[185] It should, following the model of the Brussels Convention of 1968, be transformed into a Regulation. This would undoubtedly allow a further integration of Europe even if the different laws are very much alike already. The Commission published a Green book preparing such a proposal in 2002.[186] On 15 December 2005, the Commission published its proposal for a 'Regulation ... on the law applicable to contractual obligations (Rome I)'.[187] It is based on the Rome Convention, but includes some innovations which are of importance for consumer contracts. Its legal basis is Article 65/61 EC which means that Denmark will not participate, while the UK and Ireland may opt in (which they have refused so far).

Most important for our argument is the proposed conflict rule on consumer contracts. A new Article 5 will substantially modify the rules on consumer protection by taking up some of the critique voiced against the Rome Convention. The basic rule will be that the consumer contract will be governed by 'the law of the Member State in which the consumer has his habitual residence'. Such a rule should be welcomed as a clarification and simplification of the existing law,[188] despite the criticism by e-business representatives as well as academics.[189] Article 5(2) defines the concept of consumer contract which is identical with the narrow one already used by secondary EU law; however, it is not limited to the supply of goods and services, but also includes credit contracts, without special reference to instalment transactions. The basic criteria for applying the law of residence of the consumer is the fact that the:

> contract has been concluded with a person who pursues a trade or profession in the Member State in which the consumer has his habitual residence or, by any means, directs such activities to that Member State or to several Member States including that Member State, and the contract falls within the scope of such activities, unless

---

185 D. Martiny, 'Europäisches Internationales Vertragsrecht', *ZeuP* (2008): 79–108.
186 COM (2002) 654.
187 COM (2005) 650 final; MPI comments, available at: www.mpipriv-hh.mpg.de/ deutsch/main/Pressemitteilungen/Comments_RomeI/Comments_RomI_proposal.
188 Mankowski, at p. 343.
189 G.-P. Calliess, 'Kollisionsrecht, Richtlinienrecht, oder Einheitsrecht', *ZEuP* (2006): 742, at 748 with a critique Reich, 'Der Common Frame of Reference und Sonderprivatrechte im Europäischen Vertragsrecht': 179.

the professional did not know where the consumer had his habitual residence and this ignorance was not attributable to his negligence.

This abandons the former approach of merely protecting the 'passive consumer'. The terminology follows closely Article 15 of the Brussels Regulation 44/2001, with one important exception: the professional who did not know or could not have known the residence of the consumer is not subjected to Article 5; the applicable law will then be determined either by a choice of law-clause or by the principle of closest connection, which will usually be the law of the home country of the professional. This new rule is meant to 'protect' the seller in distance contracts or e-commerce who has been misled about the consumer's residence; it is not clear whether it also includes the question whether the contracting party is a consumer. It contradicts, to some extent, the mandatory character of these rules, but seems to follow the problematic judgment of the Court in *Gruber*,[190] which concerned jurisdiction, not the applicable law.

The proposal has been before the EU Parliament and the Council. The newly drafted Article 5 has met strong opposition both from stake holders and from governments. The 'consumer country' principle in Article 5 is criticised. It is suggested that the phrasing of the Rome Convention is retained, which now has been taken up by the amendments of the European Parliament. This has been taken up in Article 6 of Regulation (EC) 593/2008 (Rome I). [191]

1. a contract concluded by a natural person for a purpose which can be regarded as being outside his trade or profession (the consumer), with another person acting in the exercise of his trade of professioin (the professional) shall be governed by the law of the country where the consumer has his or her habitual residence provided that the professional:
    a. pursues his commercial or professional activities in the country where the consumer has his habitual residence, or
    b. by any means, directs such activities to that country or to several countries including that country, and the contract falls within the scope of such activities.
2. Notwithstanding this, the parties may choose the law applicable to a contract which this Article applies, in accordance with Article 3. Such a choice may not, however, have the result of depriving the consumer of the protection afforded to him by provisions that cannot be derogated from by

---

190 ECJ, C-464/01, *Johannes Gruber* v. *BayWa*, ECR 2005, I-439 paras 51–52 ; critique Reich, comment, *EuZW* (2005): 244; Reich, *Understanding EU Law*, at p. 351.

191 In document A6-0450/2007. [2008] OJ L 177/6. For a discussion see F. Garcimartin Alférez, 'The Rome I Regulation: Much ado about nothing?', The European Legal Forum (2008) pp.I-61-79 at I-71-73; Micklitz/Reich/Rott, *Understanding European Consumer law*, 2008, paras 7.16-7.19.

contract by virture of the law which, in the absence of choice, would have
been applicable on the basis of para 1.

The new conflict regulations adopted in the consumer interest may not solve
the problems posed by 'globalisation' to trade, especially by the widespread use
of the internet for commercial and consumer transactions. Not only Member
State law, but also EU law comes to the limits of its effectiveness because of
territorial restrictions of jurisdiction. Completely different instruments bypassing
the traditional state, supra- or international law regulations may be necessary. We
will now turn to these problems, which are still relatively new and unresolved by
EC law.

'Global', Jurisdictional Problems

Beyond space and time: Cyber law

35. The traditional mechanisms of consumer protection via law are usually limited
to national law, to some extent to the law of supranational organisations like the
EU. There may be trends to extend the sphere of application, or to make sure that
EU nationals can always refer to the protection of their home country, but this will
be difficult to implement in a globalised market with transactions easily crossing
borders, especially by the use of the internet. This is particular obvious in cases
of software transactions: there is not a national, only a virtual, market place, not
determined by space and time. The partners may not know each others residence
but only their IP number; the payment and the download is done via the internet,
without any personal contact of the parties being a necessary or usual prerequisite
of the transaction. It seems impossible or at least very complicated under existing
conflict rules to determine jurisdiction and applicable law.[192]

International uniform law like the CSIG as an International Convention for the
sale of goods ratified by most States (with the exception of the UK, Portugal and
Ireland) exclude consumer transactions 'unless the seller … neither knew or ought
to have known that the goods were bought for (personal, family or household)
use' in Article 2(a) and are not mandatory in their legal application according
to Article 6.[193] They are, therefore, not appropriate for (cross-border) consumer

---

192 There is abundant literature of this phenomenon, see Micklitz, Reich, *The Basics of
     European Consumer Law*, pp. 300–311 concerning the practical application of the
     Rome Convention and of specific EC directives to cross-border transactions.

193 J. Ramberg, *International commercial transactions*, 3rd edn (Dordrecht, 2004), at p. 25;
     U. Magnus, in A. Staudinger, *CISG in BGB-Kommentar*, 13th edn (Berlin, 2005), Article
     2 paras 10–31.

transactions. Other soft-law initiatives like the UNIDROIT principles[194] are limited to commercial transactions, while the Principles of European Contract Law contain some rather weak consumer protection provisions,[195] but are applicable (if at all) only to transactions within the EU. Both are without prejudice to mandatory consumer protection law. The globalisation of trade in consumer markets, in particular via the internet, has not been followed up by a globalisation of law. 'Cyber law' is still a catchword not being met by reality which forces transactions via e-commerce into the national legal frame which is not adequate any more for these transactions.

The World Trade Organisation (WTO) has not yet emerged as an actor in transnational private law, in particular consumer law, with the exception of intellectual property via the TRIPS agreement.[196] This is in particular due to its mostly 'negative' impact on national (and supranational) law: it is concerned with impediments to international trade mostly by product – to a lesser extent service – related regulations which cannot be justified by mandatory and proportionate public interests like health or safety.[197] Therefore, the WTO does not have jurisdiction for setting mandatory standards for international commercial and consumer transactions, including conflict resolution.

Consumer law as an impediment to e-commerce?

36. Some authors go even further in their critique. Consumer law in the narrow sense as used by the EU, or in a broader sense as advocated here, is always based on mandatory standards, such as on information, quality, fairness in pre-formulated contract terms, adequate remedies, non-discrimination rules and access to justice. This entire complex of protection is vested upon a functioning state legal order which makes the judge the final arbiter in consumer disputes. Law is state oriented and guaranteed. In the EU, this follows the fundamental right to judicial protection under Article 6 ECHR, confirmed on many occasions

---

194 M.J. Bonell, 'The UNIDROIT Principles and Transnational Law', in: K.P. Berger (ed.), *The Practice of Transnational Law* (The Hague, 2001), pp. 23–41, at p. 23; M.J. Bonell and R. Peleggi, 'UNIDROIT Principles of International Commercial Contracts and Principles of European Contract Law: A Synoptical Table', *Uniform L Rev.* (2004): 315–396, comparing the Unidroit principles with the Principles of European Contract Law (Lando–Principles).

195 H.-W. Micklitz, 'The Principles of European Contract Law and the Protection of the Weaker Party', *JCP*, (2004): 339–56.

196 Michaels and Jansen: 867.

197 For details see H.-W. Micklitz, *Internationales Produktsicherheitsrecht* (Baden-Baden, 1995), at p. 257, arguing it should be transformed into a 'human right of safety'; a detailed commentary on the clause concerning actions 'necessary to protect human, animal or plant life or health' of Article XX (b) GATT and related agreements has been published by R. Wolfrum, *et al.* (eds): *WTO – Technical Barriers and SPS Measures* (Leiden, 2007), at pp. 96–120.

by the ECJ[198] and to be included in Article 6 of the Lisbon Treaty on European Union integrating the Charter of Fundamental Rights in the EU and in particular Article 47 on judicial protection into EU law. In its numerous cases concerning the obligations of Member States to implement and enforce Community consumer law, the Court has insisted on this *obligation de résultat* of states also under Article 10 EC; a violation may even make the state directly liable towards consumers under the *Francovich* doctrine.[199]

This concept of consumer protection is challenged as a consequence of a globalised trade and consumer market. This challenge comes in a seemingly contradictory direction:

* Consumer law is criticised because it becomes an impediment to trade by imposing mandatory standards on business which differ from country to country or region to region. As a result, search costs for finding out applicable law to consumer transactions become unreasonably high.
* As a seemingly contradictory consequence, consumer law cannot be fully be implemented in a globalised world. State borders are still legal borders, especially in the enforcement of consumer rights.

Consumer law in the traditional, state based concept runs the risk of becoming an ideology: instead of protection, it compartmentalises the (global) market, and at the same time it promises a protective standard which it cannot possibly achieve. For some authors there seems to be only one way out of this dilemma: if mandatory consumer protection standards prove to be dysfunctional to trade, the easiest way therefore to overcome this dilemma would be a system of liberalised world trade based on self-regulation while guaranteeing freedom of contract for business and freedom of choice for consumers.

Lex mercatoria electronica as emerging 'transnational law'?

37. International commercial law had to face the challenges of globalisation already for many years because trade is from its very nature directed across borders, and the emerging *lex mercatoria* seemingly has been an answer to these challenges. The concept of *lex mercatoria* is quite controversial and cannot be discussed here in detail.[200] It relates to a set of norms, practices, and standards in international

---

198 T. Tridimas, *The General Principles of Community Law*, 2nd edn (Oxford, 2006) at p. 418; Reich, *Understanding EU Law*, at p. 239.

199 Case C-178/94 *Dillenkofer et al.* v. *Germany* [1996] ECR I-4845.

200 See K.P. Berger, *The Creeping Codification of the Lex Mercatoria* (The Hague/London/Boston, 1999); contribution in Berger (ed.), *The Practice of Transnational Law*; C. Joerges, I.-J. Sand and G. Teubner, *Transnational Governance and Constitutionalism* (Oxford, 2004); Michaels and Jansen: 870, also referring to the 'private law created within the internet community'.

trade and conflict resolution mechanisms, mostly through arbitration, which have evolved through commercial usage and customs, and have to some extent been 'codified' by private international organisations like the International Chamber of Commerce (ICC), International Standardising Organisations like ISO, international law harmonising institutions like UNIDROIT, and specialised organisations for special business areas or for specific ways of communication, in particular the internet like ICANN.[201] The basis of applicability in commercial contracts is not state law or an international treaty, but usually agreement of the parties which need not be express and formalised, but can be implied. This practice may result in *general principles* which are accepted by the relevant business community as guidelines for their commercial transactions. They will usually be enforced in arbitration; arbitrators will use them in contract interpretation and decision making unless the arbitration agreement provides otherwise. Therefore, some authors argue for a 'private ordering', meaning a law created by the economic agents themselves which results in a 'global governance' of self-regulation.[202] Other authors refer to a 'global civil society' which emerges as a 'law creating instance' via a 'creeping codification of transnational law'.[203]

These concepts seem however to be somewhat exaggerated and misleading because in the end the basis of their applicability to international commercial transactions is the free will of the parties. The parties can always opt-out of these 'standards', or 'principles', even though there may be no incentives to do so, or transaction cost economics will force the parties to subscribe to these standards. It may also be imputed that, if the parties did not come to an agreement on applicable law or if there are doubts on interpretation, the *lex mercatoria* like the UNIDROIT principles will be applicable as 'general principles', commercial practice or custom, in particular in commercial arbitration.[204] But arbitration is subject to second level control in enforcement proceedings by Member State or EU '*ordre public*', as the ECJ has said in its seminal *ECO-Swiss*[205] and *Claro* judgments.[206]

38. Can these concepts of 'lex mercatoria', of 'private ordering of markets', of 'global governance via self-regulation' be transferred to consumer law? This is indeed the thesis G.-P. Calliess proposes as an alternative to the erosion of

---

201   See G. Teubner, 'Societal Constitutionalism: Alternatives to State Centred Constitutional Theory?', in Joerges, Sand and Teubner, at p. 18; somewhat more critical v. Bernstorff, 'The Structural Limitations of Network Governance: ICANN as a Case in Point', *ibid.*, at p. 257. This is not the place to discuss these concepts.

202   See P.-G. Calliess, *Grenzüberschreitende Verbraucherverträge* (Tübingen, 2006), p. 196.

203   K.P. Berger, in Berger (ed.) *The Practice of Transnational Law*, at pp. 12–19.

204   For the UNIDROIT principles see Bonell, 'The UNIDROIT Principles and Transnational Law', at pp. 28–36.

205   ECJ case C-126/97 *Eco Swiss China Time* v. *Benetton Int.* [1999] ECR I-3055 concerning the competition *ordre public*.

206   Above n. 141.

national (and EU) consumer law in a globalised context. He discusses a number of initiatives and mechanisms which seem to confirm his theory:

> By establishing a global civil constitution for a transnational consumer contract law, reflexive institutions must be created which organise the phenomena of self-regulation and of private ordering in such a way, that on one hand they promote effective legal protection via alternative consumer protection mechanisms, and on the other guarantee fairness and justice of such procedures *vis-à-vis* the consumer.[207]

This radical separation of (transnational) consumer law from the state (or the EU) – and as a consequence from the existing state controlled mechanisms of consumer protection – provokes critique. Such a concept has a number of weaknesses. No representative consumer association exists world wide which could promote or at least monitor and support these standards in some sort of collective consumer interest. It cannot be implied that this would be taken care of by business institutions themselves. Neither state power nor collective action by social partners can guarantee the promises which Calliess sets out himself.[208] There is no consumer consensus to accept unilaterally imposed standards by the international 'business' or 'e-commerce' community. A 'global civil society' may exist on the business side using the internet (even though this seems quite doubtful due to conflicting interests as v. Bernstorff has shown with regard to ICANN[209]); it certainly is not true with regard to highly fragmented consumer markets.

In his search for an alternative to the traditional state oriented consumer law, Calliess is satisfied if the soft-law mechanisms of 'transnational consumer law' at least attain what he calls '*rough justice*'[210] – probably meaning lower standards of protection than already guaranteed within existing consumer law. This must be achieved through different ADR mechanisms, including possibly consumer arbitration. What are the standards by which these mechanisms are supposed to function? What about third-party effects of these 'private orderings' *vis-à-vis* consumers as individuals or as a group which must be legitimised either by democratic processes or by agreement of those concerned? Is there an international consensus on certain minimal standards for consumer protection? How far is the principle of freedom of contract – which indeed is a basic rule of international commercial transactions – extended to consumer transactions which are, as we have seen, excluded both from the 'hard law' of the CISG and the 'soft law' of the UNIDROIT-principles?

---

207 Calliess, *Grenzüberschreitende Verbraucherverträge,* at p. 340; translation NR.
208 See D. Schiek, 'Private rulemaking and European governance – issues of legitimacy', *ELRev.* (2007): 443 concerning the need for (collective) autonomy to justify private rulemaking in the EU context; this also applies to international law.
209 Bernstorff at pp. 274–81.
210 Calliess, *Grenzüberschreitende Verbraucherverträge*, p. 351.

'Rough justice' as advocated by Calliess means indeed *'rough justice'* – only a vague guarantee of certain consumer expectations which can hardly be called 'rights' and which usually can be 'enforced' only via private arbitration not subject to any public control or transparency, and without clear rules on applicable law. The concept of 'transnational law' remains unclear and illusionary; it hits the death stroke to the consumer *acquis* either on an EU or a national basis. It is already doubtful whether it can really be called 'law' at all. This either requires some state monitoring, or a minimum consensus between the parties – two elements well set out in Article 1134 of the French Code Civil whereby *'les conventions légalement formées tiennent lieu de loi à ceux qui les ont faites'* ('contracts legally entered into take force of law for those who have made them').

Calliess defends his concept with the following words:

> Transnational law describes a third category of autonomous legal systems beyond the traditional categories of national or international law. Transnational law is created and developed by the global civil society through acts creating law (*Rechtsschöpfungskräfte*). (1) It is based (a) on general principles of law and (b) on practice and custom in the civil society, which leads to their confirmation and further development. (2) Its application, interpretation and development is regularly *conferred* (italics added) to private providers of dispute resolution mechanisms. (3) Its mandatory character is based on legally (*rechtsförmig*) organised orders and enactment of social-economic sanctions. (4) A codification of transnational law – if at all – occurs in the form of general catalogues of principles and rules, standardised contract forms and codes of conduct which are established by private standard setting institutions (*Normierungsinstitutionen*).[211]

This definition may be true for the classical *lex mercatoria* but always requires some express or implied agreement between the parties to be applicable in their relations if there has been no constitutionally delegated power behind its enactment. It cannot be used against third parties like consumers who have not participated in the elaboration of this 'transnational law', neither personally nor via their representatives. We do not argue that law always requires state enactment – but if this is not the case there must at least be some other mechanisms substituting the decision of the legislator which can only be party autonomy of those concerned, whether individual or collective. Even the argument of Calliess set out above requires some sort of 'conferral' of power to (binding?) dispute resolution mechanisms, but does not explain who has validly effected this transferral to the detriment of state or other legitimate mechanisms; the idea of an 'international civil society' is too vague and too abstract to have this power of conferral. Therefore, the concept of 'transnational law' cannot be transferred to consumer transactions even in a globalised setting without the state, because of the lack of equality of parties and the limited freedom of choice for consumers.

---

211 *Ibid.*, at p. 371; own translation, NR.

It is interesting to see that the so-called institutions of an international 'civil society' upon which Calliess relies for his concept of 'transnational law' refer themselves to mandatory standards which are set by state (or international[212] respectively supranational) law. It seems that the international 'civil society' (which is, in my opinion, a fiction anyway) cannot live without the state as will be shown in the following section.

The evolution of soft-law standards – an alternative to 'hard' law?

39. It can be useful to look at some of the soft-law standards which have been developed by internet service providers. Most of these are American, being the main players on the global market for e-commerce. The surprising point in all these systems seems to be that they offer the consumer certain mechanisms to guarantee satisfaction and to resolve disputes, but they do not completely replace the traditional, state bound consumer law and protection. The following examples are documented by Calliess:

- The Better Business Bureau *OnLine* 'Code of Online Business Practice'[213] contains 5 principles, including consumer satisfaction. It recommends informal dispute settlement mechanisms, including non-binding or conditionally binding arbitration (under which the decision is binding on the company if the consumer elects to accept the decision, thereby making it binding on the consumer as well), without pre-empting further governmental actions in this field; the critical point for arbitration is obviously the 'election by the consumer' – can it be done in general contract terms communicated electronically to the consumer? – Calliess does not answer this question.
- Agreement between Consumers International and the Global Business Dialogue on Electronic Commerce – Alternative Dispute Resolution Guidelines.[214] ADR mechanisms are greatly encouraged; dispute resolution may be based on equity or codes of conduct. Binding arbitration before the dispute is to be avoided 'where such commitment would have the effect of depriving the consumer of the right to bring an action before the courts.' Development of ADR is left to governments. The guidelines contain a plea for deregulation of formal requirements for ADR and for a clarification of rules on jurisdiction and applicable law to be dealt with in 'a manner that encourages both business investment and consumer trust in electronic commerce'.
- American Bar Association (Task force) Recommendation on Best Practices for

---

212 The need for mandatory international standards has been emphasised by the International Council of Human Rights, *Beyond voluntarism. Human rights and the developing international obligations of companies* (2002); see also M. Micheletti and A. Follesdal, 'Shopping for Human Rights', *JCP* (2007): 167–75, at 167.
213 Calliess, *Grenzüberschreitende Verbraucherverträge*, at p. 422.
214 *Ibid.*, at p. 439.

Online Dispute Resolution Service (ODR) Providers:[215] It clearly states that ODR Providers 'should disclose the jurisdiction where complaints against the ODR provider can be brought, and any relevant jurisdictional limitations.'

* ICC 'Resolving disputes online' – Best practices for ODR in B2C and C2C transactions:[216] They insist that 'companies should not obligate consumers to agree to use binding dispute resolution processes prior to the materialisation of a dispute. However, where permissible under local law, pre-dispute commitments to binding dispute resolution are acceptable if they are clearly disclosed before the initial transaction is completed. This will allow consumers to take the dispute resolution provision into consideration and make an informed choice about doing business with the company.' Again, the main point is 'clear disclosure' which must be determined by the applicable law to the contract. US-American and Canadian law is much more generous in allowing electronically agreed arbitration clauses through so-called 'click-wrap' agreements than the law of the Member States or EU law itself.[217]

The examples show that a concept of 'transnational consumer law' based on self- or co-regulation by 'civil society' cannot work in practice. Therefore, the main argument against such '*lex mercatoria electronica*' is still the binding force of state consumer law and consumer protection mechanisms which are part of the constitutional heritage of Member States and the Union under Articles 6(2) EU, 6 ECHR. Traders may, of course, enhance consumer satisfaction and make dispute resolution easier by encouraging ADR mechanisms, a policy explicitly supported by EC initiatives.[218] Consumers should be given easy access to ADR mechanisms provided they are fair and transparent as proposed in EU recommendations 98/257/EC and 2001/310/EC.[219] But the final arbiter in a consumer dispute – even under transnational conditions – which cannot be resolved by ADR should always be a court of law. This may create obstacles and difficulties to e-commerce in a globalised 'virtual' market place; it may also be difficult and eventually impossible to enforce. But this is not an argument against national or EU consumer law; it is the price to be paid for globalisation allowing greater access for traders to world markets which does not automatically overcome legal barriers.

---

215 *Ibid.*, at p. 448.
216 *Ibid.*, at p. 458.
217 *Comb* v. *PayPal Inc* 218 F Supp 1165 (2002) at 1176; Canadian Supreme Court, *Dell Computer Corp.* v. *Union des Consommateurs*, 2007 SCC 34 (13.7.2007); for an overall critique Reich, 'More clarity after *Claro*?': 46.
218 Micklitz, Reich, *The Basics of European Consumer Law*, at pp. 359–64.
219 [1998] OJ L 115/31; [2001] OJ L 109/56.

What is Needed: Responsible EU Consumer Law Serving the Citizen

Consumer as citizen: User rights instead of consumer rights?

40. This article has argued for an expansion of consumer law into user's rights, insofar taking up a more citizen oriented approach to legal protection which is already inherent in EC law.[220] This expansion of consumer law into 'user relations' is, however, not without problems. It may indicate a paradigm change which has not yet been fully reflected in the law-making and law-application process in the EU. It is also not clear how some of the well established instruments of consumer law like information can be used in this concept, even though information rules are also present in the areas of user protection mentioned above. The most delicate problem will be how to define the circle of persons who come into the ambit of protection. Can a new definition of 'user' help, and how can conformity with the narrower definition of consumer contained in some earlier and more traditional instruments like the 'horizontal' Unfair Terms Directive, jurisdiction and conflict rules normally giving preference to the law of the domicile of the consumer and limiting choice-of-law and jurisdiction clauses, or the special rules on competence in EC procedural law be achieved?

The suggestion advocated here refers to the consumer as '*passive market individual/citizen*', contrasting the trader (and his agent) as active supplier of goods or – even more important – services. The trader devising marketing and contract strategies to win customers is also responsible to ensure that these practices meet certain standards. Protection is not an exclusive concern in favour of individuals acting outside their business or profession, but should be extended to all market participants who do not actively market a product or a service. This standard setting task must either be left to EC law, or to the Member States and should not be abandoned by referring to 'complete harmonisation'. Otherwise the balance of consumer interests and trader interests in the EU cannot be upheld. We therefore propose a '*flexible system of consumer protection in the EU*' which conforms with the principles set out in Article 153 EC. This must be done by a *wide* and not, as is practice now, by a narrow definition of the consumer, either provided by EC or by national law.

Some principles of this flexible system have already been set in an earlier publication where it had been suggested:[221]

- Consumers are generally only natural persons.
- The activities of the consumer are functionally to be distinguished from those of undertakings, self-employed persons and employees as described by the 'active side' of the fundamental freedoms of Community law.

---

220 N. Reich, 'The Consumer as Citizen, the Citizen as Consumer', in *Liber amicorum Jean Calais-Auloy* (Paris, 2004), p. 943.
221 Micklitz, Reich, *The Basics of European Consumer Law*, at pp. 80–81.

- The applicability of consumer provisions to *'mixed purposes'* will depend on the predominance of one or the other purpose; there is against the case law of the ECJ a presumption that the consumer as private person acts for private purposes.[222]
- The role of the consumer is not restricted to personal activities but may also serve the consumption of others provided this is done outside his trade, profession or business.
- In the field of the non-economic protection of legal interests, for example against accidents caused by defective products or services, the term 'consumer' is independent of any activity and may be employed to any natural person.

It should be added, as we have tried to show, that the main argument for consumer or, broader, user protection is the non-professional, 'passive' position of the private person in a consumer market, confronted with one sided marketing activities and pre-formulated contract terms which put him in a 'take-it-or-leave-it' situation. This broadening of the consumer concept – either in EU or in national law – opens a wider and more citizen-like perspective of consumer law[223] because it is not only concerned with 'optimal shopping', but is extended to other important areas of consumer interest as 'fair access' to services of general interest, in particular utilities, to concerns of non-discrimination in consumer markets, to user rights against IP right-holders, to victim compensation in case of defective products and services, and to effective access to justice in particular in cross-border transactions.

Freedom of contract and marketing, and its constitutional limits

41. The extension of consumer law as advocated here does not mean an abrogation of the basic rules on freedom of contract and marketing which are indeed guaranteed by primary EC law.[224] Quite to the contrary these are seen as effective instruments for enhancing consumer choice and welfare. But they must respect fundamental principles and rules which are set out in the different areas of consumer law. Competition and choice may help to create such principles, but should not be 'let alone' without democratic monitoring. Consumer law is not the opposition, but the realisation of these freedoms. Under the impact of globalisation, it may be difficult to enforce them across borders. But this should not result in abandoning them, but lead to rethinking their impact on conflict of laws, jurisdiction and, even more importantly, ADR.

Ongoing discussions in the Member States recognise the constitutional aspects and limits of freedom of contract and marketing.[225] Article 6(2) EU sets out that

---

222 See now the proposals of the *acquis*-group, above para. 19.
223 Hesselink: p. 332–43.
224 Reich, *Understanding EU Law*, at p. 268.
225 O. Cherenednychenko, 'EU Fundamental Rights, EC Fundamental Freedoms, and Private Law', *European Review of Private Law* (2006): 23–61, at 56; for an example

the Union respects fundamental rights as they are common to the constitutional traditions of Member States, and will therefore have to consider them also in the area of consumer law. Any rule which gives preference to an abstract interest in the 'internal market', by initiatives towards full harmonisation and the country of origin principle, deliberately cuts off this constitutional dialogue and becomes an agent of a one-sided preference towards the imposed law of the trader to the detriment of the consumer/non-professional user whose freedom to contract is thereby curtailed.

A 'market' versus a 'social approach' to consumer protection?

42. The question of competence in the EU has become one of the critical issues of the legitimacy of EC law making, resulting in the new tendency for total harmonisation, supplemented by the controversial country of origin principle. This paper has argued for continue usage of minimum harmonisation as Article 153(5) seems to intend this to be the regular instrument of consumer law. This does not exclude 'full harmonisation' for rules on technical aspects where needed, for example time limits for cancellation rights which should not differ within the EU.[226]

Whenever no clear priority of internal market measures is evident, as the free movement of goods or services, Article 153 EC should be the basis for consumer protection legislation. Article 153(3)(b) needs to be tested to find out the extent and limits of consumer protection measures in trade practices and contract law. The outstanding review of the consumer *acquis* by the EC Commission should be seen under these premises and allow the adoption of an 'EU consumer contract law regulation' (ECCLR, para. note 22) aiming to codify the existing, somewhat heterogeneous, consumer contract directives in a systematic way.[227] It should be based on a flexible concept of the consumer as developed above. Matters of cross-border jurisdiction will, as before, have to be based on Article 65, matters on non-discrimination on Article 13 EC.

The insistence on minimum protection advocated here should allow a well balanced constitutional approach to consumer law, as far as a division of EU and Member State competences are concerned. It is probably too simple to allocate to the EU the 'market building function' of consumer law, as recently suggested by Unberath and Johnston,[228] and to leave to the Member States the 'social aspects'.

---

see the studies in: A. Colombi Ciacchi (ed.), *Protection of Non-Professional Sureties in Europe: Formal and Substantive Disparity* (Baden-Baden, 2007).

226 See Schulte-Nölke, Ebers, *Consumer Law Compendium*, p. 753.

227 Reich, 'A European Contract Law, or an EU Contract Law Regulation for Consumers?': 398. For details of the proposed review see Micklitz and Reich, 'Europäisches Verbraucherrecht – quo vadis?': 121.

228 Unberath and Johnston: 1281 who criticise a 'double-headed approach towards consumer protection' in the case law of the ECJ, trade-oriented and liberal with regard

But the justification behind this division is the 'constitutional responsibility' of the EU to establish and enhance the functioning of the internal market, while the economic, ecological, social and cultural well being of their citizens is still a main challenge to Member States; the EU also has a 'social purpose'[229] and Member States should support market building – both arising out of the basic constitutional obligation of the EU and Member States to mutual support and trust. In all these areas the principle of 'minimum harmonisation' should be the rule, not the exception. There is no reason why this should be any different in consumer law in the wide sense as it is understood here.

The responsible consumer as citizen: 'good faith' as a two-sided rule

43. The consumer concept of EC law is based on rights and interests, as the wording of Article 153(1) shows, but it seems to exclude corresponding duties. It should be remembered that the concept of Union citizenship in Article 17 EC refers not only to rights but also to duties.[230] Shaw[231] remarks in this context: 'The tendency of any discourse of citizenship duties is to construct the figure of the citizen in the light of some conception – however vague – of moral virtue.'

This 'moral virtue' for the consumer seems to be 'good faith' or 'fairness' with regard to legally relevant behaviour in consumer markets. National law, when referring to these principles, defines them as being two-sided, imposed on both partners of a transaction whether B2B, B2C or C2C. EU law has not yet developed this concept in any detail; The Unfair Terms Directive uses it only in a unilateral way for controlling pre-formulated contract terms. The '*acquis*' principles (above, para. 19) very clearly formulate in Article 2:101: 'In pre-contractual dealings, parties must act in accordance with good faith.' This is repeated in Article 7: 101–104 for performance, including to some (lesser) extent the corresponding duties of the consumer.

As mentioned above, there are, however vague and sketchy, already some corresponding obligations of consumers in certain areas, for example the duty to notify complaints in package holiday contracts, or the possibility of Member States to impose a similar rule in sales contracts (above, para. 7). Product liability law

---

to negative harmonisation, 'interventionist' for secondary law, suggesting at 1284 a paradigm change also in secondary law with regard to 'proportionality' and 'the possible applicability of theories of regulatory competition'.

229 Case C-437/05 *ITF & FSU* v. *Viking et al.* [2007] ECR I-(11.12.2007) at para. 79 with regard to worker protection and social action; for an analysis see N. Reich, 'Free Movement v. Social Rights in an Enlarged Union', *German Law Journal*, 9 (2008): 125–60, 156.
230 Reich, *Understanding EU Law*, at p. 347.
231 J. Shaw, *Collected Courses of the European Academy VI-1* (The Hague, 1998) at p. 344.

may put (partial) liability on the victim when he contributed to the damage. In state liability cases the ECJ has allowed the defence of contributory negligence.[232]

Another area where some co-responsibility exists is advertising law. As the Court in the *Gut Springenheide* judgment[233] ruled: 'in order to determine whether ... the statement in question was liable to mislead the purchaser, the Court took into account the presumed expectations of an average consumer who is reasonable well-informed and *reasonably observant*' (italics added). This judgment has led to different interpretations concerning the consumer 'model' which is the starting point of EC (trade practices) law. It has been referred to in Article 6(1) of the Unfair Commercial Practices Directive as the 'average consumer' test. What is usually missed in discussions of this concept is reference to the consumer who is 'reasonably observant' or, as it was said in the *Mars* case,[234] 'reasonably circumspect'. This is an indirect acknowledgement of a corresponding duty (*'Obliegenheit'* in German) of the consumer to take a 'close look' at any advertising before being able to attack it as 'misleading'. Obviously, this test refers to a group of consumers, not to individual consumers, but makes clear that, in addition to rights, there are at least some (rather minor) responsibilities of consumers. AG Poiares Maduro uses this concept in limiting the consumer right to cancel a doorstep contract in the case of false information, even if this was not expressly stated in the Doorstep Selling Directive.[235]

It is still an open question whether a similar reasoning can be applied to unfair contract terms, at least as far as 'abstract control' is concerned. This is linked to the question of transparency of terms which, according to Micklitz, also contains a competitive function: 'the consumer needs to be in a situation to decide whether or not to enter into a more advantageous position.'[236] Conversely, if this relation to the decision making process of the consumer cannot be shown, the transparency argument cannot be invoked, and the clause cannot be held to be unfair.

On the other hand, the obligations of consumers should not be exaggerated. They should not serve as a pretext for denying protection where needed, but to allow a more efficient and 'fair' distribution of risks and responsibilities. This is

---

232 C-46 and C-48/93 *Brasserie du Pêcheur* v. *Germany* and *R.* v. *Secretary of State for Transport ex parte Factortame Ltd.* [1996] ECR I-1029 para. 85, referring to general principles of the law of Member States; for details Rott, *Effektivität des Verbraucherrechtsschutzes*, at p. 75.

233 Case C-210/96 *Gut Springenheide* v. *Oberkreisdirektor Steinfurt* [1998] ECR I-4657 at para. 31.

234 Case C-470/93 *Verein gegen Unwesen in Handel und Gewerbe Köln* v. *Mars GmbH.* [1995] ECR I-1923 para. 24.

235 Opinion of 21 November 2007 in case C-412/06 *Annelore Hamilton* v. *Volksbank Filder nyr* similarly the ECJ judgment of 10.4.2008 justifying a time-limit for cancellation of one month after performance in full of the contract by the parties.

236 Micklitz, Reich, *The Basics of European Consumer Law*, at p. 181, referring to; ECJ case C-386/00, *Axa Royale Belge* v. *Georges Ochoa et al.* [2002] ECR I-2209 para. 28.

typically done by Member State law, not by EC law. It remains to be seen how these functions will in future be fulfilled under the modified 'full harmonisation principle'.

Conclusion

44. This article discussed intrinsic (conceptual), extrinsic (competence) and global (jurisdictional) problems of EC consumer law as it developed over time and now being in a process of review. The reductionist approach by the EC Commission, being mostly concerned with information of the consumer–'shopper', and with complete harmonisation to promote a rather fictitious concept of the internal market, was critically appraised and confronted by a broader theory of the consumer also as user of services in the public interest and of networks of information, as well as a citizen asking for effective protection of his rights, which includes corresponding duties. In a globalised setting, the answer to difficulties in cross-border enforcement of consumer rights cannot be found in business self-regulation, but in a balance of voluntary and mandatory standards, which, finally, must always allow access to independent courts of law. This follows from the constitutional traditions common to the Member States of the EU. The article also makes reference to recent proposals of the '*acquis*'-group to codify and consolidate existing principles of EU consumer law. which should be based on the special consumer provisions of Article 153(3)(b) EC, to be taken over by the Lisbon Reform Treaty as Article 169 (2)(b) of the Treaty on the Functioning of the EU.

2 The Status of Consumers in EC Liberalisation Directives

*Paul Nihoul**

Introduction

The EC has gone through a wave of liberalisation in the last two decades. Measures were first adopted in the telecommunications sector, which has since become the sector of electronic communications. They were subsequently extended, in their substance, to other economic activities with similar characteristics (the so called 'public utilities').[1]

An important issue in consumer policy is whether these measures have done any good for consumers. The latter are often mentioned in the preamble to these instruments. Somehow, they form part of the 'justification tool kit' put forward by the European Commission to advance the liberalisation agenda. But what is concretely their situation in the liberalisation era?

One way to address the issue is to analyse the terms and conditions under which goods and services are presented to consumers in liberalised sectors. Are these terms and conditions better, effectively, than those available beforehand, or those which would have existed otherwise? For instance, have tariffs been lowered? Has quality improved? Has output expanded? These questions are examined by economists and statisticians. Some answers have already been provided. They do not always support the same conclusion. Often, they appear as confirmation

---

* Professor of Law, University of Louvain, Belgium and University of Groningen, The Netherlands. Director, Centre de droit de la consommation.
1 For a general presentation of liberalisation in the European context, see, among recent publications: J.L. Buendia Sierra, *Exclusive Rights and State Monopolies under EC Law* (Oxford, 2000); G. Haibach (ed.), *Services of general interest in the EU: Reconciling Competition and Social Responsibility* (Maastricht, 1999); P. Cameron, *Legal Aspects of EU Energy Regulation* (Oxford, 2005); P. Cameron, *Competition in Energy Markets – Law and Regulation in the European Union* (Oxford, 2007); P. Nihoul and P. Rodford, *EU Electronic Communications Law – Competition and Regulation in the European Telecommunications Markets* (Oxford, 2004); C. Henry, M. Matheu and A. Jeunemaître (eds), *Regulation of Network Utilities* (Oxford, 2001); OCDE, *Non-Commercial Service Obligations and Liberalization* (Paris, 2004).

of the position that the author of the document held before examining the data available.[2]

In this chapter, I propose a different approach. That approach is to analyse liberalisation from a consumer law perspective. The question to be examined in that context is whether the *legal* situation of consumers has advanced as a result of liberalisation in the sectors concerned – if so, how, and to what extent. Sub questions are: do liberalisation directives contain rules dealing specifically with consumers? If so, what objectives are pursued through these rules? Are these objectives different from those aimed at in other pieces of EC legislation dealing with consumers?

The material used for this analysis is primarily the body of rules adopted in the sector of electronic communications. The situation in other liberalised sectors is also addressed, but to a lesser extent. Why the emphasis on electronic communications? As that sector was the first to be liberalised the rules adopted in other sectors followed those set up for electronic communications. In substance, these rules replicate some deployed beforehand in the telecom sector – or are at least strongly inspired by them. Another reason for the emphasis on electronic communications is that the rules applicable in that sector are particularly complete. They have created a comprehensive framework where the position of all stakeholders in the sector – or almost all of them – is regulated. By contrast, the rules adopted in other sectors appear more partial, and fragmented. As a result, they form a less solid basis for an analysis on the status of consumers in EC liberalisation directives.

---

2   For instance, the Commission considers that the strategy of liberalisation has been a factor of economic growth and has stimulated the creation of jobs. In other words, it claims that the policy carried out by its own services has a (very) positive effect on the general economic and social situation, on the European continent. See the recent Commission Report – Report on Competition Policy 2006 (SEC(2007)0860), Brussels 25 June 2007 COM(2007)358 final. Not surprisingly, the former national monopolies sometimes defend a different version. They are assisted, in that respect, by trade unions, which fear, probably, a negative evolution in the working conditions of their members. Consumer associations generally welcome liberalisation as a mechanism giving consumers choices. At the same time, they criticise what they see as shortcomings or potential dangers: a decrease in the safety of users, a deficit in the quality of the services provided, access to services not necessarily open to all users. For an example of critical comment on the liberalisation programme carried out by the European Commission, see S. Thomas, *The 2006 Review on Gas and Electricity Markets*, Public Services International Research Unit, University of Greenwich, available at: http://www.psiru.org/reports/2007-03-E-EUEnergymarkets.doc.

Principles

Whatever the sector where they were adopted, the directives enacted by EC institutions in the context of liberalisation are based on a few principles which are analysed below.

Introduction of competition

One principle – the first probably in importance – is the introduction of competition on previously reserved markets. That principle has had vast consequences for consumers, particularly for those who were not satisfied with the goods and services provided by their supplier. Before liberalisation, these consumers had no alternative. If they wanted the good or service concerned, they had to remain in a business relationship with their supplier, independent of their level of satisfaction – and of their desire to continue that relation. With the advent of competition, they are granted the possibility to shift to other suppliers.

Authorisations

A corollary of competition is that a limitation was imposed on the power of the Member States to adopt measures affecting activities in liberalised markets. The idea, in that regard, was that Member States should not be permitted to adopt measures making it more difficult for firms to enter liberalised markets or to carry out activities in these markets. Such obstacles could, indeed, limit the incentive for new firms to enter the markets concerned and/or remain there in activity. To avoid these obstacles, the Parliament, the Council and the Commission[3] determined, in directives, what obligations and what conditions could be imposed on undertakings in the markets concerned.[4]

---

3   The accurate contribution of each of these institutions to the enactment and the implementation of the liberalisation programme is described below.

4   Among other rules, a limitation was imposed on the possibility for Member States to impose specific authorisations prior to firms being allowed to carry out their activities. Beforehand, States used to submit the activity to the fulfilment of conditions requiring an assessment and an approval by the national competent authority. In the terminology used in European regulation, these procedures are called 'specific authorisations' because they entail authorisations which may be given specifically to the firms concerned. They are different from general authorisations which, under the European regulatory framework, are designed in more general terms, and contain conditions which apply to all firms placed in the same situation.

Regulation of market power

Another corollary is that a control should be carried out on activities performed by powerful firms. In the philosophy underlying the reform, markets perform adequately where economic actors are free – where they enjoy sufficient freedom to exploit their talents and realize their projects. Yet, economic freedom and, thus, efficiency, are threatened where one or several firms acquire power in a market. Under the rules adopted by EC institutions, such a situation warrants control on the part of the authorities and even, in some instances, an intervention.[5]

Protection of users

Then comes the principle examined with more attention in this chapter. The introduction of competition, the limitation of the legislative competence of the Member States and the regulation of economic power do not necessarily create a context where users are adequately treated by undertakings. This is apparently the conclusion that the Parliament, the Council and the Commission have drawn from their observation of the markets concerned. That conclusion can be inferred from the fact that these institutions have introduced, in the liberalisation directives, provisions which, beyond the introduction of competition and the organisation of relations between firms, are aimed specifically at the protection of users.

In that context, three directions have retained their attention. First, the EC institutions decided that some categories of the population deserved special protection. These categories are, particularly, persons with social difficulties, or those suffering from a handicap (social dimension). Second, they identified services which, according to their analysis, should be provided on reasonable conditions to all members of society. Where these services are not provided spontaneously by the markets, initiatives should be taken by national authorities to ensure their provision (universal service). Third, the EC institutions defined general rights that users should have on liberalised markets in their relations with business interlocutors (rights of users).

Administrative framework

A last set of EC measures organises the administrative framework necessary to apply the principles mentioned above, as well as the rules implementing them. That application takes place at national level, with the creation of National Regulatory Authorities (NRAs).The objectives to be achieved by these authorities are set in

---

5   That authority is normally a National Regulatory Authority (NRA). It can also be, in some cases, a National Competition Authority (NCA). Whatever the authority, the object of the intervention is to ensure that the actors do not make use of the power they have acquired in a way which alters the terms and conditions under which goods and services are available to final or intermediate consumers (price, output, and so on).

the EC regulation, together with the type of measures which they can take to that effect.

Introduction of Competition

Before studying the rights granted to users, I propose to analyse further the first principle mentioned above. For this discussion, we do not need to refer to provisions concerning a specific sector. All sectors affected by liberalisation are thus concerned with the following remarks. Often, consumer lawyers tend to underestimate the change brought by the introduction of competition. The reason being that attitude may be that the measures introducing competition are rarely associated with rules granting rights to consumers or increasing the protection afforded to them. Most of the time, the two categories of rules are studied by different people. The rules of competition are often used by business lawyers or market-oriented academics, who are concerned with proper relations between business actors. By contrast, consumer protection concerns the relation between businesses and final users. In the practice of the law and in academic circles, it is traditionally associated with private law or even, in some instances, social law.

The virtues of competition

These differences should not cast a shadow on the importance of competition for consumers. Through the introduction of competition, the position of the consumer *vis-à-vis* business has changed dramatically – and positively.[6]

First, the possibility of shifting to another supplier may bring a solution to consumers who are not satisfied with the current provision of services. That aspect has been explained above. There is no need to develop it further. Only may it be useful to stress the comfort felt by consumers where they realize that they are not compelled to deal any longer with a supplier from which they have received bad service or disappointing products.

Second, the introduction of competition has strengthened, in general, the position of consumers, and particularly their bargaining position, *vis-à-vis* their business interlocutors. 'Treat me well – or else I go away' is the message that consumers may now address to firms. That message often has a certain efficacy. As they seek revenues,[7] the possibility of a departure by clients rarely leaves firms indifferent.

---

6   On that point, see P. Nihoul, *La concurrence et le droit – La position occupée par les entreprises, les consommateurs et les autorités* (Paris, 2001).

7   Clients represent a direct source of revenues for firms. They are also important, indirectly, for relations between the firms and their shareholders. The latter often consider the degree of satisfaction of clients as an indication of how good the firm performs. Furthermore, the number of clients, expressed in the form of the market

Third, competition places upon firms a pressure always to do better. Firms located in a competitive environment face a threat that other suppliers or providers may do better – and may be selected, as a result, by clients, in preference to them. As they are confronted with that threat, firms ideally examine, constantly, and systematically, their organisation, their performance, and their relations. The purpose is always: to improve, in all respects, and to propose, to partners, terms and conditions better than those put forward by competitors.

A fourth change, which may appear more abstract, but is nonetheless important, is the contribution brought by competition to the construction of a more active, conscious society. Law does influence behaviour. Beyond, it also has an impact on identities. So it is for competition and the measures associated with it. Beforehand, consumers were, somehow, passive. How could they be otherwise? Where they were not satisfied, they could hardly react.[8] With competition, consumers are invited and, even, in some instances, are compelled to become more active. A selection must be made amongst offers. To that effect, information must be collected. Offers must be analysed.[9]

'Problems of the past'

Is all this enough? Consumer lawyers are keen on maximising the protection of consumers and the promotion of the interests of the latter. It is legitimate, on their part, to wonder whether the introduction of competition has done enough for consumers. In that regard, they can relax: their presence remains necessary; their role will not end with the advent of competition, more can and – indeed – needs to be done.

One reason is that, despite all virtues mentioned above, competition mainly improves the situation of consumers as regards the future, but does not necessarily solve the problems that have occurred in the past. As an illustration, take a consumer of electronic communications services. Suppose that that consumer is not satisfied with the current supplier. In the last bill, there has been a significant

---

share retained by the firm, is an important element for shareholders. The market share indeed provides an indication as to, according to clients, how firms perform relative to one another. The analysis of market shares supplies information on the relative strengths and weaknesses of firms present.

8   They could not shift to other suppliers or providers as the market was reserved to one undertaking. The law provided for remedies against bad behaviour adopted by the monopolist. But these remedies were often limited and hardly accessible. Most of the time, national authorities limited the access to justice by users when it came to remedies against their own behaviour or against behaviour adopted by entities placed under their control.

9   Above all, consumers are invited, in a competitive environment, to analyse better, and identify their needs and desires. In our consumption society, choice requests, and makes possible, a better knowledge of oneself, even if the answers given to these enquiries and the ways to carry out that investigation differ with individuals.

error in the amount charged. The supplier does not agree to rectify the mistake. In a liberalised environment, that consumer has a possibility to shift to another supplier. Chances are that that consumer will be more satisfied, in the future, in a new business relationship.

But has the original problem been solved? If nothing is done, that consumer remains with an erroneous bill to be paid. To that problem, competition does not bring, *per se*, any direct solution. If the consumer wants the error committed by the supplier to be rectified, he or she has to use traditional consumer protection mechanisms. Among them are: the obligation, on the part of suppliers, to justify the amount charged to clients; the possibility, for consumers, to use alternative dispute mechanisms, in order to obtain a quick and equitable remedy; in the absence of such mechanism, the possibility to bring a case to court;[10] possibly, a right to demand compensation for the costs associated with that case in the countries allowing that sort of claim.

'Problems in the future'

Nor does competition solve all problems in the future. In the illustration provided above, we have wished the consumer a better relation with a new supplier. That wish does not always come true. The reason is that, in a competitive world, firms only survive if they attract revenues and, thus, clients. In theory, that 'law of attraction' normally imposes on firms a pressure to behave properly with clients. If they want to attract new clients, or at least not lose current ones, firms must provide good treatment. A difficulty, however, is that that theoretical prediction does not always come true. One reason may be that the law of attraction is tempered by a second rule important to firms – the 'law of revenues'. Firms need revenues. To collect them, they may resort to practices damaging for their reputation with clients in the long term but allowing them quickly to collect sometimes badly needed revenues.[11]

This is related, among others, to the degree of competition existing on markets. In an article published some time ago, I argued that in a competitive environment, the proportion of illegal behaviour increases with the degree of competition.[12]

---

10   Or, probably better, a refusal to pay the bill as the amount charged is excessive and, if an action is brought to court against the consumer, the presentation of these arguments to the judge.

11   Another reason may be that consumers tend to look at the main clauses of the contracts proposed to them without necessarily analysing the latter in their entirety. For instance, consumers often care about prices. They do not necessarily have the same attention for other aspects of the transactions – aspects which may in effect prove even more important at some point (for example, the length of the guarantee proposed by the producer). To compete against one another, firms may then concentrate their efforts on these central issues.

12   P. Nihoul, 'Concurrence et respect du droit – Pour une nouvelle articulation entre l'analyse juridique, le calcul rationnel et l'intérêt individuel', *Ethique publique*, 2

In that regard, markets are not different from sport races. Consider the following example. More than 200 cyclists participate, each summer, in the Tour de France. In substance, that race decides who will get a contract to participate in the following year(s). If, through his performance, a cyclist can attract attention, he will get a contract. Otherwise, he might have to stop his career. To attract attention, riders must win the Tour, or part of it. The number of possible victories is, however, limited. Thus, a very low proportion of individuals, compared with the total number of participating cyclists, will achieve victory. Examine now the situation of a cyclist who, for physical or psychological reasons, is not capable of winning. The incentive for such a rider to use illegal products is substantial – very substantial indeed. If he does not take any drug, that cyclist will be eliminated. If he wins, he gets it all – fame, money, contract ...[13]

The same analysis applies to firms in markets – and to men and women working in such firms. If firms get the feeling that they might be eliminated, the incentive to adopt illegal behaviour increases dramatically. The more competition there is in a market, the more it is difficult for firms to attract partners, the more they happen to see their situation as being threatened, the higher the incentive they have for cheating.

Coming back to liberalisation, one can contend, on the basis of that analysis, that firms are not unlikely to adopt illegal practices in liberalised markets. This is so, particularly, in the years following the introduction of competition. In these years, actors are still numerous, as no consolidation has yet taken place. As there are many actors, a lot will be eliminated and only a few will succeed. The probability of illegal behaviour is then not insignificant.

A typical behaviour used by firms after liberalisation is the announcement of performances that cannot be achieved realistically. Firms promise wonderful services, terms and conditions to clients. In doing so, they hope to attract consumers away from the incumbent or other major companies. However, they lack the capacity and skills to match their promises. Consumers are lured away – but the disappointment comes quickly.[14]

That scenario is important for our discussion. It demonstrates that shifting to another supplier does not necessarily translate into an improvement in the situation

---

(1999): 91–105.

13   The use of drugs may be detected. In that case, the rider would be eliminated. But he would get eliminated anyway given his poor performances.

14   Surveys show that consumers rarely change supplier where competition is introduced – or at least do not necessarily shift readily to another business interlocutor. That result is sometimes followed by a critique addressed to consumers. 'They do not play by the rules of competition', it is said, 'they do not study the offers made to them', 'they do not choose the best offer'. In light of the likelihood that illegal behaviour may be adopted by firms in liberalised markets, the attitude adopted by consumers appears, on the contrary, reasonable. Consumers have understood that, in a competitive environment, firms have to catch their attention and are sometimes ready, to that effect, to make promises they cannot comply with.

of the consumer. Thus, competition does not always solve the problems in the future. It may, on the contrary, create new problems, as consumers are sometimes even less happy with the new supplier. Then, new 'problems of the past' emerge, requiring a solution that competition does not provide.[15]

Categories of consumers

In an additional comment, nuances must be brought to a statement made above that firms constantly seek clients and improve their offers to attract/retain them. This corresponds to what is seen as a virtue of the competitive process. That statement, however, supposes that all clients are always welcome. Yet, in a competitive environment, as is the case on liberalised markets, clients do not have equal importance. Plainly, they are treated differently depending on what – and how much – they can bring to businesses. Do they spend much? Do they pay on time? Are there risks that they may not pay? Are they faithful to the firm? Are they likely to refer other clients to the firm? And so on. Firms like clients for which the answer to these questions is positive – less so where answers are negative.

This analysis shows that, for some clients, the virtues of competition, which normally induces firms to take care of their relations with consumers, may not materialize. Some consumers may not see their situation improve with liberalisation, quite the contrary. Beforehand, they faced one company compelled by authorities to serve them. In the liberalisation era, they may be left aside as they provide little financial perspective to business interlocutors. The fate of these consumers is rarely explored by competition lawyers. But they may not be forgotten by consumer lawyers, as they are central in that legal discipline. By nature, consumer law is not essential for those who have the – intellectual, social, financial – resources to defend themselves.

Consumer Protection in Electronic Communications

We now turn to provisions dealing with rights granted to users. We start with the situation existing in the sector of electronic communications. The situation in other liberalised sectors is examined later in this chapter.

---

15 This clearly appears from reports published by consumer associations about the situation in liberalised markets. These reports generally contain a first part where the association welcomes the introduction of competition as a mechanism granting consumers a choice – and thus increasing the degree of liberty that these stakeholders have in the market. Then often follows a second part where the association points out difficulties in the relation between consumers and business actors. See for instance BEUC (Bureau européen des unions de consommateurs), 2006 *Review of the electronic communications regulatory framework – comments by BEUC*, BEUC/X/064/2006, 27 October 2006, available at http://www.beuc.eu.

Electronic communications

The regulatory framework now in force in electronic communications is made of five directives.[16] Among these directives, four were based on Article 95 EC which provides that national legislation may be approximated where their disparity would otherwise affect the internal market. These directives were adopted by the Parliament and the Council in the co-decision procedure. The procedure started with a proposal submitted by the European Commission. These directives deal, respectively, with:

- the authorisations that Member States may still require from undertakings before the latter are allowed to start their activities: European Parliament and Council Directive (EC) 2002/20 on the authorisation of electronic communications networks and services (Authorisations Directive),[17]
- the access of alternative service provides to fix infrastructure: European Parliament and Council Directive (EC) 2002/19 on access to, and interconnection of, electronic communications networks and associated facilities (Access Directive),[18]
- the provision of a universal service throughout the European territory: European Parliament and Council Directive (EC) 2002/22 on universal service and user's rights relating to electronic communications networks and services (Universal Service Directive),[19]
- the establishment of a administrative framework for the implementation of the rules and principles laid down in the above mentioned instruments: European Parliament and Council Directive (EC) 2002/21 on a common regulatory framework for electronic communications networks and services (Framework Directive).[20]

A last instrument – the so called 'competition directive' – was issued by the European Commission at the same time as the above mentioned directives: Commission Directive (EC) 2002/77 on competition in the markets for electronic communications networks and services.[21] That instrument repealed Directive

---

16   For a general presentation of the reform carried out in the sector of telecommunications, see Nihoul, Rodford, 1.96–1.129. A. Bavasso, *Communications in EU Antitrust Law: Antitrust, Market Power, and Public Interest* (Oxford, 2003); R. Bell and N. Ray, *EU Electronic Communications Law* (London, 2004); L.Garzaniti, *Telecommunications, Broadcasting and the Internet* (London, 2003); P. Larouche, *Competition Law and Regulation in European Telecommunications* (Oxford, 2000).
17   [2002] OJ L 108/21.
18   [2002] OJ L 108/7.
19   [2002] OJ L108/51.
20   [2002] OJ L 108/33.
21   [2002] OJ L 249/21.

90/388, several times amended.[22] The Competition Directive in substance reiterates a principle already enshrined in the previous instruments it repealed. That principle is that Member States are prohibited from granting a special or exclusive right to undertakings for the provision of an electronic communications service, whatever the nature of that service.

Three directions

Earlier I emphasised that three directions were followed, as regards users, in these various instruments, by the Parliament, the Council and the Commission. First, social provisions were adopted. Second, a universal service was defined. Third, rights were granted to users. In the following paragraphs, I examine these directions and attempt to determine to what extent they contribute to the protection of consumers.

Social provisions

Under the Universal Service Directive, Member States may take measures ensuring that users with low incomes or special social needs are not prevented from accessing or using the publicly available telephone services (Article 9(2)). These measures may take the form of tariff options or packages departing from those

---

22   Commission Directive (EEC) 90/388 on competition in the markets for telecommunications services, [1990] OJ L 192/10. Through that original instrument, competition was introduced, for the first time, by the European Commission, in the markets for telecommunications services. The Directive was amended in 1992, 1994 and 1996. Commission Directive (EEC) 94/46 amending Directive 88/301 and Directive 90/388 in particular with regard to satellite communications [1994] OJ L 268/15; Commission Directive (EC) 95/51 amending Directive 90/388 with regard to the abolition of the restrictions on the use of cable television networks for the provision of already liberalised telecommunications services [1995] OJ L 256/49; Commission Directive (EC) 96/2 amending Directive 90/388 with regard to personal and mobile communications [1996] OJ L 20/59; Commission Directive (EC) 96/19 amending Directive 90/388/EEC with regard to the implementation of full competition in telecommunications markets [1996] OJ L 74/24. The purpose of these amendments was to expand the realm of competition in the so far spared telecommunications markets, with a final aim to achieve full competition by 1998. In 1999, the Commission adopted a last instrument to amend Directive 90/388: Commission Directive (EC) 1999/64 amending Directive 90/388 in order to ensure that telecommunications networks and cable TV networks owned by a single operator are separate legal entities [1999] OJ L 1175/39. That latter directive addressed situations where telecommunications and cable TV networks were owned by a single company. Under the Directive, these infrastructures had to be placed in separate legal structures. The purpose was to ensure that the two networks would be managed separately – in competition against each other.

provided under normal commercial conditions (*idem*). Beyond these measures, 'support'[23] may be granted by authorities to these users (Article 9(3)).

Suppose a situation where measures are adopted by a Member State on the basis of these empowering provisions. Would these measures contribute to the protection of consumers? In some respects, probably, as consumer law often seeks to restore equilibriums and improve the lot of less privileged categories of the population. With measures adopted in the sense provided by the directive, the users pertaining to these categories would have access to services otherwise remaining out of their reach, and/or would access these services at more favourable conditions.

It remains that these social actions and measures are to be financed. Under the Universal Service Directive, three methods may be used to that effect. One is for the firm(s) concerned to finance the cost relating to social provisions through its own resources. Another one is the payment of subsidies by authorities to compensate the extra cost deriving from the provision of the universal service. Under the Directive, this can only occur where the burden imposed on the firm(s) concerned may be regarded as 'unfair'. The subsidy paid in that situation can only cover the net cost of providing the service concerned, and/or of complying with the obligations affected.[24] A third method also involves the payment of a subsidy. This time, however, the subsidy is not paid out of resources belonging to a public authority. It rather comes from a fund established by Member States and collecting dues among service providers active on the national territory concerned. The conditions seen above as regards the use of that method also apply in that third scenario.[25]

Among these three methods, the second is hardly used. Nowadays, it is difficult for authorities to find resources to invest in the provision of the universal service. This is so, particularly, in a time when States are selling their participation in the capital of former public undertakings, thereby renouncing the prospect of receiving substantial dividends each year. The period is also difficult for States as they are invited to reduce the level of taxation on businesses, and hence accept a diminution in the resources they can collect from the markets, in an attempt to attract foreign investors.

The methods thus commonly used in electronic communications for the financing of the universal service are the first and the third ones, described above.

Yet, these methods are not consumer neutral. In the first case (self financing), the firm must find, by itself, the resources needed to compensate the cost caused by

---

23   Thereby, it is probably meant that subsidies can be granted to these categories of users in order to facilitate their access to such services. It is not clear whether that possibility is limited to access or the use of telephone services or whether it concerns all sorts of electronic communications services.

24   See the Universal Service Directive, Articles 12 and 13.

25   Intervention only if the burden is unfair, payment limited to what is strictly necessary to ensure the realisation of the universal service. See the Universal Service Directive, same provisions.

the 'social provisions'. These resources can hardly be found from shareholders. In a context of worldwide capital mobility, investors do not easily accept a lower return on their financial contributions. The resources must thus be found elsewhere. In most cases, they are financed through increases in productivity. The stakeholders, then, financing the social measures proposed by the States are the workers. The second type of stakeholder from which resources can be obtained are consumers. Not those who enjoy these special social measures as, by definition, the consumers covered by the scheme are entitled to more favourable conditions. But those who are not envisaged in that scheme, that is those who do not have a right to these special social conditions.

The same can be stated regarding the subsidies paid out of a fund alimented by service providers active on the national territory. The contributions made by these providers must be financed. Again, the financing cannot come, in most cases, from investors. The effort must be borne, thus, by the workforce and, also, by consumers. This, again, is important to note; the subsidies possibly paid to firms in compensation for the extra costs relating to the provision of the universal service come partly, and probably, to a significant extent, from the consumers themselves. These measures are thus financed through a transfer of resources among consumers – to those who benefit the measures from those who do not.

Is this a contribution to the protection of consumers? Yes, to the extent certain consumers have access to services, or conditions, which would not have been available to them otherwise. No, because these measures are financed by the consumers themselves. In my view, consumer protection concerns relations between businesses and consumers. In these relations, the latter need a certain protection as they rarely enjoy a position equal to that maintained by the former. The social provisions enshrined in the universal service should better be compared with social security allowances – with the difference that, in the universal service, social provisions make it possible, for the persons concerned, to access particular services, whereas social security allowances are generally provided, at least on the continent, in the form of cash to be used by the beneficiaries at their discretion.

Universal service

Beyond these social provisions, the EC institutions have identified, in the Universal Service Directive, various services which, in their view, should be made available to all citizens under reasonable conditions whatever the geographic location where the service is to be provided – and thus whatever the cost of providing the service to the individual users concerned. As a rule, the items belonging to the universal service must be provided by market forces acting in a competitive environment. In various circumstances, however, these objectives of general availability and reasonable conditions may not be attained by the mere action of market forces. To address these situations, the Directive provides that, should one or both objective(s) not be attained, Member States have a right to intervene. As was the case for the social provisions examined above, the intervention by national authorities generally involves the designation of one or several undertakings which are entrusted with the provision of the service(s), or part(s) of the service(s) concerned. Compensation may be provided to the designated undertaking(s) if, and to the extent, that the performance of that task constitutes, for the firm(s) in question, an 'unfair burden'.[26]

Here again, we are confronted with the question: does such a mechanism contribute to the protection of consumers? The answer provided to that question may not be different from the one given regarding the social provisions examined above. It must be emphasised that the designation of fundamental services to be provided to all members of the community under reasonable conditions indeed ensures a certain protection for consumers. Those who would not have had access otherwise to these services, or to the same conditions, receive certain assistance. The problem, however, is that these measures must be financed and that, in most instances, the financing takes the form of a transfer of resources among consumers.

The three methods described in connexion with the social provisions examined above may also be used for the financing of the extra cost relating to the provision of items covered by the universal service: self financing by the firms, payment of a subsidy by a public authority, payment out of a subsidy alimented by service providers active on the national territory. As already observed, the second method (public subsidy) is not really used in the Member States, which prefer the first and third ways, in which they do not have to disburse any fund. The difficulty, however, is that these methods both involve a transfer of resources among consumers.

To illustrate this, let us consider the example of a user established on the top of a mountain. Suppose that there is no other user in the surroundings. The cost for providing a connexion to the public telephone network at that location is substantial as a specific line has to be provided for that user, this has to be done in a difficult environment and the cost of that work cannot be shared among numerous users. For such a consumer, the universal service constitutes a 'plus'. In the absence of that mechanism, the service would have been more expensive – if provided at all. For others, the universal service may create disadvantages. The provision of services under reasonable conditions indeed implies that a sort of 'averaging' has to be carried out by service providers. The high cost of providing services at certain locations will be borne, partly in that system, by consumers who, had markets been free, would have received the service under better conditions. In the scenario examined here, this would have been the situation of people living in cities, where the cost for providing access to the public telephone network is, in principle, much lower per user, as it can be shared among many. Under the universal

---

26   Universal Service Directive, Articles 3–9, and Articles 11–13. Nihoul, Rodford, pp. 491–629.

service mechanism, urban consumers would end up subsidising a portion of the cost incurred by the provider in supplying the service to mountainous users.

Rights of users

The last category of measures introduced by the Universal Service Directive relates to rights granted to users. In substance, these measures contain six rules which are described, then analysed, below.[27]

Rule 1. Liberalisation does not affect the application of EC consumer law. Traditional consumer law provisions remain applicable. As a result, the relations between consumers and businesses are subject, in the electronic communications sector, to two sets of rules: traditional consumer law and sector specific regulation.[28]

Rule 2. A contract must be signed with consumers seeking connexion and/or access to public telephone networks. That contract must detail the terms and conditions under which connection and/or access are provided.[29] Where contracts are concluded for other services, the same terms and conditions must be integrated in the covenants.[30]

---

27 The rules in question primarily come from the Universal Service Directive. Some were, however, extracted from other directives. The provision organising each of the rights examined will be mentioned in footnotes.

28 That rule is formulated in Article 20(1) of the Universal Service Directive. 'Paragraphs 2, 3 and 4 [of this provision] apply without prejudice to Community rules on consumer protection, in particular Directives 97/7/EC and 93/13/EC, and national rules in conformity with Community law' (see Directive 97/7/EC of the European Parliament and of the Council of 20 May 1997 on the protection of consumers in respect of distance contracts [1997] OJ L 144, pp. 19–27; Directive 93/13/EEC of 5 April 1993 on unfair terms in consumer contracts [1993] OJ L 95 pp. 29–34).

29 Article 20(2) of the Universal Service Directive:
[2]. Member States shall ensure that, where subscribing to services providing connection and/or access to the public telephone network, consumers have a right to a contract with an undertaking or undertakings providing such services. The contract shall specify at least: (a) the identity and address of the supplier; (b) services provided, the service quality levels offered, as well as the time for the initial connection; (c) the types of maintenance service offered; (d) particulars of prices and tariffs and the means by which up-to-date information on all applicable tariffs and maintenance charges may be obtained; (e) the duration of the contract, the conditions for renewal and termination of services and of the contract; (f) any compensation and the refund arrangements which apply if contracted service quality levels are not met; and (g) the method of initiating procedures for settlement of disputes … Member States may extend these obligations to cover other end-users.

30 *Ibid.*, Article 20(3): 'Where contracts are concluded between consumers and electronic communications services providers other than those providing connection and/or access to the public telephone network, the information in paragraph 2 shall also be

Rule 3. Consumers have a right to receive notice from the operator or the service provider when a modification is made to the terms and conditions inserted in the contracts mentioned above. The minimum delay is one month's notice. If they are not satisfied with the new terms and conditions, consumers have a right to withdraw without penalty. In the notice, they must be informed of that right.[31]

Rule 4. Member States must organise alternative mechanisms for the resolution of disputes involving consumers. These mechanisms must be transparent, simple, equitable, rapid and inexpensive.[32]

Rule 5. Network operators must organise the possibility, for consumers, to select, or pre select, the supplier from which they want to receive services.[33]

---

included in such contracts. Member States may extend this obligation to cover other end-users.'

31   *Ibid.*, Article 20(4):
Subscribers shall have a right to withdraw from their contracts without penalty upon notice of proposed modifications in the contractual conditions. Subscribers shall be given adequate notice, not shorter than one month, ahead of any such modifications and shall be informed at the same time of their right to withdraw, without penalty, from such contracts, if they do not accept the new conditions.

32   Alternative dispute resolution mechanisms, ADR. Articles 34(1) and (2) of the Universal Service Directive:
[1] Member States shall ensure that transparent, simple and inexpensive out-of-court procedures are available for dealing with unresolved disputes, involving consumers, relating to issues covered by this Directive. Member States shall adopt measures to ensure that such procedures enable disputes to be settled fairly and promptly and may, where warranted, adopt a system of reimbursement and/or compensation. Member States may extend these obligations to cover disputes involving other end-users. [2] Member States shall ensure that their legislation does not hamper the establishment of complaints offices and the provision of on-line services at the appropriate territorial level to facilitate access to dispute resolution by consumers and end-users.

33   Carrier selection and carrier pre-selection. That facility is limited to situations where operators have been notified as having significant market power for the provision of connection to and use of the public telephone network. Article 19(1) of the Universal Service Directive:
National regulatory authorities shall require undertakings notified as having significant market power for the provision of connection to and use of the public telephone network at a fixed location in accordance with Article 16(3) to enable their subscribers to access the services of any interconnected provider of publicly available telephone services: (a) on a call-by-call basis by dialling a carrier selection code; and (b) by means of pre-selection, with a facility to override any pre-selected choice on a call-by-call basis by dialling a carrier selection code.

Rule 6. Service suppliers must allow consumers to take their telephone number away with them where they shift to another supplier.[34]

Sector specific issues

Among these rules, two (Rules 5 and 6) relate to issues specific to the electronic communications sector. EC and national authorities have sought to introduce competition in the market for infrastructure. This implied that two networks at least should be made available for consumers. As establishing and/or maintaining a network is costly, the number of networks however remained limited to one in most Member States.

A better result was reached on markets for services. Introducing competition on these markets required the possibility, for providers, to use concurrently existing infrastructure for the delivery of their services, in competition against each other. To make this possible, the Parliament, the Council and the Commission organised, in the Universal Service Directive, a system where, among these providers, consumers have a right to make a 'selection'.[35] The 'selection' organised by the Directive comes down to an indication notified to the operator and identifying the provider from which consumers want to receive their service(s). The selection can be made per use of the network. It can also be made for a longer period, until the notification of a new choice to the operator ('pre selection')[36] (Rule 5).

---

34   Number portability. Article 30(1) and (2) of the Universal Service Directive:
     [1] Member States shall ensure that all subscribers of publicly available telephone services, including mobile services, who so request can retain their number(s) independently of the undertaking providing the service: (a) in the case of geographic numbers, at a specific location; and (b) in the case of non-geographic numbers, at any location. This paragraph does not apply to the porting of numbers between networks providing services at a fixed location and mobile networks. [2] National regulatory authorities shall ensure that pricing for interconnection related to the provision of number portability is cost oriented and that direct charges to subscribers, if any, do not act as a disincentive for the use of these facilities.

35   Among others, this makes it possible, for consumers, to choose a service provider other than the network operator. A danger, in effect, in electronic communications, was that the network operator could and would take advantage of its dominance on the network market to maintain, acquire or reinforce a power on the various existing markets for services.

36   It should be noted that, under the Universal Service Directive, carrier selection and pre-selection are limited to situations where consumers deal with operators notified as having a significant market power (a dominant position). In markets where operators do not have market power, no obligation of that sort is imposed. In these latter markets, operators have no obligation to 'share' the access to their network with service providers. As a result, a consumer dealing with such an operator would have to change network if he/she prefers dealing with another service provider.

Number portability is a second mechanism imagined in the Universal Service Directive to develop competition among service providers. Telephone numbers are divided by national regulatory authorities among service providers. They are then assigned by these providers to their clients – among which are the consumers.[37] Competition implies that consumers and, more generally, users, must have the possibility to shift to other suppliers, where they are not satisfied with the current provision. The existence of effective competition among providers depends upon these changes being relatively easy, and cheap. Yet, observation shows that, realistically, changes are unlikely where consumers must renounce their numbers.[38] Under the Universal Service Directive, that difficulty is solved through number portability[39] (Rule 6).

Do these rules regarding the (pre) selection of providers and number portability contribute to the protection of consumers? In some ways yes, as they provide consumers with a mechanism allowing them to choose their business relation. Are consumers satisfied with their current provider? They can select it using the first mechanism. Are they not satisfied? They have the possibility, and the right, to choose another one (first mechanism still) and take their number away with them to the new provider (second mechanism).

---

37 That number corresponds to the identity of consumers on the public telephone network. If the number changes, the possibility for correspondents to still be able to reach the number holder is remote. Of course, correspondents may be informed about the new number. But not all of them can be informed. Furthermore, the energy, and the expense necessary to inform them is not insignificant.

38 The 'cost' of shifting would then be too high for consumers. Consumers should notify all correspondents of the change. This costs time, money and effort. Furthermore, not all correspondents can be warned. Their details may have been lost by the consumer, or the notification may not reach its destination, and so on.

39 We have seen that carrier selection and pre-selection are limited to situations where consumers or users deal with operators notified to the national regulatory authority as having significant market power. This is due to the fact that the selection, or pre-selection, of the provider designated by the client, must be made to the operator. Yet, as stated above, the main issue, in electronic communications, as in other public utility markets, is to prevent operators using the power they have in the infrastructure market as a way to impose their own services on clients to the detriment of other providers. The situation is different with number portability. That measure makes it possible for consumers to shift to another supplier. Operators may be involved. That is the case where consumers receive their services from the operator itself. The obligation provided by the EC legislation applies in such a situation, as the operator would then have an obligation to let the consumer leave with the number associated with him/her on the network. But operators are not involved in all situations where consumers shift to other suppliers. The shift may take place from one service provider different from the operator, to another provider. The obligation thus had to be formulated in broader terms. This is the reason why its scope has not been restricted to markets where operators hold a significant market power.

But are these advantages specifically meant to improve the legal condition of consumers? In many respects, the two measures contained in the Universal Service Directive and described above appear as devices meant to ensure that competition functions effectively on the market. These measures thus help consumers, or affect positively their positions – but not to a greater extent than competition rules generally do. In other words, the measures at stake contribute to the general well being of consumers in markets. Thanks to them, consumers are not forced any longer to remain in business relations with a provider with which they are not satisfied. As a result of these measures, they can also expect, in principle, a general improvement in the offers made to them by firms, by virtue of the pressure placed by competition on these firms. Beyond these general positive effects, which come from the introduction of competition itself, no specific contribution can be found in those measures, as regards the legal position of consumers.

Information

The other rules are included in the electronic communications directives and dealing with users' rights address issues more traditional in consumer law and policy. Under the Universal Service Directive, a contract must be signed with consumers.[40] That obligation is mentioned explicitly in the Directive as regards the relation between consumers and operators for the connection and/or the access to the public telephone network.[41] It is also provided that, for other services, where a contract was concluded, the same elements should be included.[42]

Information to be provided   Under the Universal Service Directive, the pieces of information to be provided in relevant situations are the essential elements of the contract: description of the services concerned, determination of the prices to be charged, duration and termination of the contract (Rule 2 formulated above). Beyond these classical elements, information must be provided about the compensation to be given by the firms concerned if they fail to provide, or to provide adequately, the services concerned. Also, information must be supplied about how possible disputes may be solved using alternative resolution mechanisms (see later in this chapter).[43]

---

40   Universal Service Directive, Article 20.
41   *Ibid.*, Article 20 (2).
42   *Ibid.*, Article 20 (3).
43   The obligation to provide information on these aspects is rather classical in general contract law. It may be compared to a similar obligation to provide like information in the following EC consumer protection legislation: Council Directive 90/314/EEC of 13 June 1990 on package travel, package holidays and package tours, [1990] OJ L 158, pp. 59–64; European Parliament and Council Directive 94/47/EC of the European Parliament and the Council of 26 October 1994 on the protection of purchasers in

Relations with network operators   The first part of that rule concerns the relations between consumers and network operators. The connection and/or access to the public telephone network are granted by the operator exploiting that network. In these relations, the Universal Service Directive imposes, as I have stated, an obligation to conclude a contract, as well as the inclusion, in that contract, of specific information, to the benefit of consumers.

I have already emphasised that the number of public telephone networks is limited to one in most EC countries. There are not various operators among which consumers would have a choice. As a result, the obligation to provide information cannot be viewed as a desire, on the part of EC institutions, to assist consumers in making more enlightened choices in markets. Why, then, is that obligation imposed? One possibility could be the sort of 'mistrust' that the Parliament, the Council and the Commission still apparently feel *vis-à-vis* former national telecommunications monopolies. As there is only one such network in most Member States, consumers are under the dependency of the operators controlling these networks as regards connection and/or access. That dependency, it was probably feared, may induce operators not to treat consumers correctly – hence these obligations.[44]

Relations with service providers   The situation is analysed as being different regarding the relations between consumers and service providers. Under the Universal Service Directive, specific information must be included, regarding these relations, in contracts, 'where contracts are concluded'. Why is a difference made between the two contexts? The reason probably lies in the existence of competition. As competition exists in the markets for services, consumers have a choice. They can choose their provider; they can shift to others if they are not satisfied. In the philosophy underlying the reform, that possibility of shifting towards a competitor creates a strong incentive, for current providers, to treat consumers correctly.

From the words used in the provision, it may be inferred that, in the eyes of those who drafted the EC legislation, a contract does not need to be concluded in all circumstances involving consumers and service providers. This somehow comes as a surprise. In principle, service providers have an interest in concluding contracts with their clients. Conversely, it is also in the interest of clients to have

---

respect of certain aspects of contracts relating to the purchase of the right to use immovable properties on a timeshare basis, [1994] OJ L 280, 83–7; Directive 97/7/ EC of the European Parliament and of the Council of 20 May 1997 on the protection of consumers in respect of distance contracts – Statement by the Council and the Parliament re Article 6 (1), [1997] OJ L 144, 19–27.

44   The hope of this construction is that, through information provided in the contracts proposed to them, consumers will not engage in non favourable transactions – and will prefer dealing with other providers. Facing that reaction, network operators would be constrained to adapt their terms and conditions. They would not have the possibility any longer to behave as monopolists, which do not fear reactions by consumers as the latter may not shift away to competitors.

such a contract. In contracts, parties indeed define their rights and obligations. A context is thereby created where disputes are not likely to emerge – or at least are less likely.

The concept of a 'contract' is not defined in the relevant legislation. How then should that term be understood? The most classical approach, at least on the continent, is to consider that a contract is formed whenever parties agree on a transaction. The form – written, oral – of the agreement does not matter. The essence of the contract lies in the meeting of minds which take place between the parties.

That – ordinary – definition casts a doubt on the possibility, for service providers, to escape the obligation to provide the specific information that operators must supply where they deal with consumers. Is it possible for a service provider to avoid the conclusion of a contract with a client? This does not even appear to constitute a theoretical possibility. Under general private law, a contract must be deemed to exist as soon as the provider agrees with a consumer that a certain service will be provided under given conditions. In the practice, it thus seems that, as operators, service providers have to conclude written contracts with consumers, and must include, in these contracts, the specific pieces of information mentioned above.[45]

Differences in situations   Beyond these technical, but important, considerations, the difference in the words applicable to the two situations under the Universal Service Directive remains striking. In one scenario, a firm has a monopoly. That situation is submitted to a provision under which a written agreement must be concluded and specific information must be included in that instrument. To explain

---

45   The interest for providers not to conclude contracts came to light when the author was approached by a provider proposing interesting tariffs for fix telephony. The offer was made by telephone, through a call centre. In view of the tariffs proposed, I requested a document, which the correspondent refused to hand over. I then started to think about the reasons which may have led a firm to renounce a new client for the mere reason that that client had requested a written document. What could induce an undertaking to behave in such a manner? One reason could be haste. Exchanging documents takes time, and money. For the firm, that time, and that money were, possibly, not worth spending to attract a client. That reason, however, was not convincing. The correspondent had spent more than a quarter of an hour with me on the telephone. Sending a document would have added a little extra cost – but would have brought a new client to the firm. I then realized that the conversation had been taped by the provider. That record was only available to the latter. The provider thus had evidence that an agreement had been exchanged. On my part, I did not have any evidence whatsoever about the – interesting – tariffs that had been proposed. Suppose that I had signed on and, soon afterwards, a change occurred in the tariffs charged by the provider – making these tariffs less attractive. The provider could establish that I had signed on. For the rest, they could refer to their general terms and conditions where, for instance, no notice was provided in case of changes in tariffs …

the link existing between that scenario and the obligation, one must infer that, in the eyes of those who drafted the Universal Service Directive, monopolistic situations involve risks for consumers – hence the need for a legal protection. In the second scenario, the monopoly has ceased to exist and has been replaced by competition. The terms associated with that situation in the relevant provision do not involve the immediate conclusion of a written agreement. Only if a contract is concluded should specific information be included. The absence of an automatic obligation appears to imply that, in a competitive environment, consumers do not need legal protection or, at least, that the protection should not be as automatic, and comprehensive.

These two scenarios, and the obligations which are attached to them under the Universal Service Directive, demonstrate that, surely, the EC institutions aware of the evils associated with monopolies – but do not appear to consider that competition may also create legal issues for consumers ...

Dispute resolution

Another traditional key element in EC consumer policy is the resolution, outside the traditional judicial system, of disputes involving consumers. In the eyes of the EC institutions, the rights granted to consumers are meaningless and, in fact, nonexistent, if they cannot be enforced. Yet, traditional judicial enforcement is often regarded as inadequate for consumer claims. It takes too long, is too expensive and often depends on the quality of pleaders (this giving an advantage to firms which can often afford better lawyers than consumers).

For that reason, the European Commission has repeatedly stressed the importance of alternative dispute resolution. Two recommendations were adopted to that effect.[46] They established criteria that national schemes should offer to their users. In addition, the Commission issued a proposal for a European Directive on Mediation in Civil and Commercial Matters.[47] That draft Directive aims to build a relationship between the mediation process and judicial proceedings at national level. A number of key aspects of civil procedure are tentatively regulated. Finally, ADR[48] provisions were inserted in specific EC consumer law directives. These provisions compel Member States to introduce ADRs in the areas, or the fields, covered by the instruments containing them. That strategy has been followed in the

---

46   Commission Recommendation of 30 March 1998 on the principles applicable to the bodies responsible for out-of-court settlement of consumer disputes [1998] OJ L 115, 31–64; Commission Recommendation of 4 April 2001 on the principles for out-of-court bodies involved in the consensual resolution of consumer disputes [2001] OJ L 109, 56–61.

47   Proposal for a Directive of the European Parliament and of the Council on certain aspects of mediation in civil and commercial matters {SEC(2004) 1314}, COM/2004/0718 final – COD 2004/0251.

48   Alternative Dispute Resolutions.

sector of electronic communications where, under the Universal Service Directive, Member States must establish ADRs to solve disputes involving consumers (see Rule 4 formulated above).

An advantage of that latter strategy is that, in the fields concerned, ADRs are not only recommended, but are also made compulsory for the resolution of disputes. There is, however, a disadvantage attached to that technique. The measures contained in such a provision are, indeed, limited strictly to the fields concerned. They lack a general scope. No general obligation is thus imposed, as of today, on Member States, to reform their judicial system, with the aim of reinforcing and facilitating the protection meant for consumers.

Other Economic Sectors

In the previous section, I analysed the status of consumers in the sector of electronic communications. The next step is to check whether that analysis can be confirmed with an examination carried out in other European liberalised sectors. Three sectors, or groups of activities, are generally considered when it comes to liberalisation: postal services, the distribution of gas and electricity (energy), transportation (air, road and train). Among these sectors, transportation has a peculiar status. For that reason, it is not treated in this publication.[49, 50]

Postal services

I start with the sector where the provisions regarding the consumer protection are the most limited – postal services. In that sector, a liberalisation has taken place, and

---

49   One reason is the legal basis on which measures are adopted. The EC Treaty contains provisions dealing with transportation specifically (Articles 70–80). These provisions served as legal basis for the adoption of liberalisation measures in that sector. This is different from other liberalised sectors, where measures were based on general provisions (Articles 86 and 95 EC). Another difference is that, in the field of transportation, EC institutions are entrusted with the power to design and carry out a common policy. They thus have the power to determine what policy they want to carry out in that field. Such a power does not exist in other liberalised sectors.

50   The measures adopted by the EC institutions in the field of transportation, including those relating to consumer protection, are analysed in other publications. For a recent account, see J. Faull, A. Nikpay, *The EC Law of Competition* (Oxford, 2007), 14.01–14.257. For other presentations, see J. Goh, *European Transport Law and Competition* (New York, 1997); L. Ortiz Blanco and B. van Houtte, *EC Competition Law in the Transport Sector* (Oxford, 1996); B van Houtte, 'Community Competition Law in the Air Transport Sector(I)', *Air and Space Law* (1993): 61–70; B van Houtte, 'Community Competition Law in the Air Transport Sector(II)', *Air and Space Law* (1993): 275–7.

is still unfolding.[51] The main instrument in force is currently Directive 97/67/EC of the European Parliament and of the Council of 15 December 1997 on common rules for the development of the internal market of Community postal services and the improvement of quality of service, as amended, hereinafter 'Postal Directive'.[52]

The liberalisation in the postal sector was based on four pillars among those mentioned above: introduction of competition, limitation of interventions by Member States, establishment of an administrative framework, regulation of the provision of services to users.[53]

As regards this latter point, the Postal Directive did not go far. No social provisions were inserted. The Member States were not granted any power to introduce special tariffs for peculiar categories of the population. This is a major difference with the sectors of energy and electronic communications.

A universal service was created. Under the Postal Directive, users have a right to a service of good quality under reasonable terms and conditions. That universal service is meant for 'users' (Article 3). 'Users' are natural or legal persons covered by the universal service as senders or addressees (Article 2(17)).

Only one provision deals with the protection of users in their relations with providers. That provision organises an obligation, for the Member States, to establish transparent, simple and inexpensive procedures for the solution of disputes (Article 19). The disputes concerned are those opposing 'users' to businesses. Implicitly, the Postal Directive suggests that the scope of the provision is limited to beneficiaries of the universal service. But the possibility is provided for the Member States to broaden that scope to situations, and users, beyond that scheme (Article19).

The Postal Directive does not introduce any obligation, for service providers, to conclude contracts with users, and provide, in these contracts, specific information.[54]

---

51   For a general presentation of liberalisation in the postal sector, see D. Géradin (ed.), The Liberalization of Postal Services in the European Union (The Hague, 2002); L. Flynn and C. Rizza, 'Postal Services and Competition Law', World Competition, 24 (2004): 475–511.

52   [1997] OJ L 15, p. 14.

53   Pillar 3, concerning the regulation of access, was not taken over. The reason is that, in that sector, the existing infrastructure cannot be used by firms in competition. This is due to the nature of that infrastructure. Contrary to networks used for the distribution of energy, or the transmission of electronic communications, the infrastructure used for postal services is human in nature. It is made of personnel. The activity carried out by these men and women constitutes, at the same time, the infrastructure, and the service. In that sector, it is not possible to divide the two aspects, and organise, thus, competition among firms using the same infrastructure.

54   The reason may be the nature of the service rather than the lack of a desire to promote the interests of consumers. Postal service providers cannot be compelled to sign contracts with users for each and every letter sent. The administrative costs would largely outweigh the advantages in terms of protection. Similarly, the absence of

Energy

Gas and electricity are closer to electronic communications. Both sectors require a physical infrastructure for the conveyance, to clients, of energy products or services.[55] As we noted above, establishing and maintaining such infrastructure is costly – hence the earlier organisation of these markets in the form of public monopolies. At the end of the twentieth century, policy makers started to consider, as in electronic communications, that energy markets would be more efficient if the infrastructure were used by several firms operating in competition.

Measures were adopted to implement that new form of market organisation. These measures are, in essence, the same for gas and electricity markets. In the electricity sector, the relevant instrument is Directive 2003/54/EC of the European Parliament and of the Council of 26 June 2003 concerning common rules for the internal market in electricity and repealing Directive 96/92/EC, hereinafter 'Electricity Directive'.[56] For gas, the instrument is Directive 2003/55/EC of the European Parliament and of the Council of 26 June 2003 concerning common rules for the internal market in natural gas and repealing Directive 98/30/EC, hereinafter 'Gas Directive'.[57] These two instruments are, in substance, identical. In the discussion, I refer to provisions relating to electricity. The corresponding provisions dealing with gas are mentioned.

The liberalisation which took place in these two sectors were based on the five pillars delineated at the outset of this article: introduction of competition, organisation of access to networks, limitation of national interventions, establishment of an administrative framework and regulation of services provided to users.

In this chapter I am mainly concerned with the last principle: regulation of services to users. As regards that principle, the EC institutions worked in the directions delineated above: social provisions, universal service and regulation of relations with users.

---

reference to ordinary consumer law does not imply that that law does not apply. There is no reason for that part of the law not to apply, in the absence of counter-indication. The main impression remains, however, that the reform was not grasped to improve the status of consumers in that sector.

55 In this chapter, we do not consider other sources of energy (solar energy, and so on). For a general presentation of the legal regime applicable to energy in the European Union, see recently Cameron, *Competition in Energy Markets*; Faull and Nickpay, *The EC Law of Competition*, 12.01–12.467.

56 [2003] OJ L 176, p. 37.

57 *Ibid.*, p. 57.

Social provisions The Member States are empowered to take special measures for vulnerable consumers.[58] There is a lack of indication, however, in the Directives concerned, about the concrete implications for the Member States, for providers and for users.

Universal Service Under the relevant Directives, Member States may organise a system whereby residential consumers and small undertakings have access to electricity under reasonable terms and conditions whatever their localisation.[59]

Relations between consumers and businesses The EC legislator has opted for the same protection as used in electronic communications.

In Table 2.1 below, I identify the provisions dealing with user protection in the various sectors concerned. A comparison shows that that protection is extensive in the energy sector – more even than in electronic communications. The differences are minor. One is that, for energy, the service provider must communicate in advance, to consumers, the specific information to be included in the contract.[60] That obligation is not limited to situations where a contract is contemplated with a specific client. More generally, service providers must publish information about tariffs and terms/conditions applicable in their relations with clients.[61] These terms

---

58   'Member States shall take appropriate measures to protect final customers, and shall in particular ensure that there are adequate safeguards to protect vulnerable customers, including measures to help them avoid disconnection', Electricity Directive, Article 3(5). For similar, although shorter, terms, see the Gas Directive, Article 3(3).

59   'Member States shall ensure that all household customers, and, where Member States deem it appropriate, small enterprises; ... enjoy universal service, that is the right to be supplied with electricity of a specified quality within their territory at reasonable, easily and clearly comparable and transparent prices', Electricity Directive, Article 3. Surprisingly, there is no mention of a universal service in the Gas Directive. That instrument provides that Member States 'may take appropriate measures to protect customers in remote areas which are connected to the gas system', Article 3(3). In the same line, the Directive states that 'customers ... connected to the gas system are informed about their rights to be supplied, under the national legislation applicable, with natural gas of a specified quality at reasonable prices', Annex A(g). These two provisions show that no universal service, as such, is organised at European level in that economic Sector, but that Member States may organise a scheme having the features of it. In that case, customers must be informed about the features of the schemes.

60   'Conditions shall be fair and well known in advance. In any case, this information should be provided prior to the conclusion or confirmation of the contract. Where contracts are concluded through intermediaries, the above information shall also be provided prior to the conclusion of the contract', Electricity Directive, Annex A(a), second sentence; Gas Directive, same provision.

61   '...[T]he measures referred to in Article 3 are to ensure that customers: ... (c) receive transparent information on applicable prices and tariffs and on standard terms and

and conditions must be clear and comprehensible.[62] Customers must be warned about their rights regarding the provision of the universal service.[63]

The Gas and Electricity Directives do not organise explicitly a procedure for the selection or pre selection of service providers. This does not take away the fact that such a mechanism must be organised by the operator. Competition requires clients to have a choice among possible suppliers. The existence of that choice implies that clients must be given an opportunity to identify the provider from which they want to receive energy through the infrastructure dominated by the operator (see Rule 5 formulated above).

By contrast, no equivalent obligation exists for number portability (see Rule 6 formulated above). Portability was necessary in electronic communications because, otherwise, clients would not shift to other suppliers. In the absence of portability, they would fear losing contact with their correspondents. In the field of energy, no correspondent needs to be informed about a possible change in supplier. Information to that effect only needs to be given to the provider selected by the client and, in case of change, the original supplier. In that regard, the Electricity and Gas Directives indicate that, in case of shift, no payment may be requested from clients.[64]

Another specific obligation introduced in the sectors of gas and electricity is that clients must be granted a choice among several payment modalities. Providers are not allowed to impose a specific form of payment, for instance automatic bank payments. The extra cost possibly related to a specific payment means may be charged to the client.[65]

Beneficiaries Who benefits from these protective provisions? As was the case for electronic communications, the categories mentioned in the Energy Directives are diverse. In general, the term used in the Electricity Directive to designate the beneficiaries is 'customer'.

---

conditions, in respect of access to and use of electricity services', Electricity Directive, Annex A(c); Gas Directive, same provision.

62   'General terms and conditions shall be fair and transparent. They shall be given in clear and comprehensible language', Electricity Directive, Annex A(d); Gas Directive, same provision.

63   '…[T]he measures … are to ensure that customers: … (g) when having access to universal service under the provisions adopted by Member States … are informed about their rights regarding universal service', Electricity Directive, Annex A.

64   '…[T]he measures referred to in Article 3 are to ensure that customers: … (e) shall not be charged for changing supplier', Electricity Directive, Annex A; Gas Directive, same provision.

65   '… [T]he measures referred to in Article 3 are to ensure that customers: … (d) are offered a wide choice of payment methods. Any difference in terms and conditions shall reflect the costs to the supplier of the different payment systems', Electricity Directive, Annex A; Gas Directive, same provision.

a. The social provisions are meant for 'final customers'.[66] These are customers purchasing electricity for their own use.[67] They can be natural or legal persons. Thus, these social provisions are available for companies purchasing electricity without a view to resale. In other words, the protection provided in these social provisions is not limited to natural persons acting in a private capacity.[68]

b. The universal service is meant for 'household' customers.[69] This excludes, in principle, legal entities. By way of exception, the benefit of the universal service may be extended, by the Member States, to small enterprises. These are enterprises with fewer than fifty occupied persons and an annual turnover or balance sheet not exceeding EUR 10 million.[70]

c. The protection of users is not reserved to specific beneficiaries. It is available to all customers.[71] This is in contrast with electronic communication, where the benefit was limited to consumers but could be extended to all final users.

---

66   Electricity Directive, Article 3(5). Particularly where those customers are 'vulnerable': *ibid.*; Gas Directive, Article 3(3).

67   As opposed to for resale, Electricity Directive, Article 2(9). Customers purchasing energy for resale are called 'wholesale customers', Electricity Directive, Article 2(8); Gas Directive, Article 2(29).

68   These users are called 'household customers'. The term designates customers purchasing electricity for their own consumption, excluding commercial or professional activities. These customers can only be natural persons, as legal persons could not purchase electricity or gas independent of any commercial or professional activities, Electricity Directive, Article 2(10); Gas Directive, Article 2(25).

69   Electricity Directive, Article 3(3); Gas Directive, Article 2(25).

70   *Ibid.* An extension to small enterprises is not foreseen in the Gas Directive.

71   Electricity Directive, Article 3 and Annex A; Gas Directive, same provision.

Table 2.1   **Correspondence between provisions organising the relations with clients in the electronic communications and energy directives**

	Electronic Communications Universal Service Directive	Electricity Directive	Gas Directive	Postal Directive
Rule 1. – Application of traditional EC consumer law directives	Article 20(1)	Annex A(a)	Annex A(a)	–
Rule 2. – necessity to conclude a contract and provide information	Article 20(2)	Annex A(a)	Annex A(a)	–
Rule 3. – notice in case of change	Article 20(4)	Annex A(b)	Annex A(b)	–
Rule 4. – access to ADRs	Article 34	Annex A(f)	Annex A(f)	Article 19
Rule 5. – selection or pre selection	Article 19	–	–	–
Rule 6. – number portability	Article 30	–	–	–

What Consumers?

Traditional question

The provisions dealing with legal consumer protection in EC electronic communications directives have been examined. It is now time to wonder: who benefits from that protection? This is a traditional question in debates about EC consumer policy.[72] Among EC consumer lawyers, there is a suspicion that, through their so-called consumer policy, the Parliament, the Council and the Commission may strive to ensure the realisation of the internal market. That is to say: measures presented as protective for consumers may, in effect, be EC

---

72   See, for example, G. Howells and S. Weatherill, *Consumer Protection Law* (Hampshire, 2006), pp. 1–98; M. Raideiheh, *Fair Trading in EC Law – Information and Consumer Choice in the Internal Market* (Groningen, 2005), pp. 56–9; S. Weatherill, *EC Consumer Law and Policy*, 2nd edn (Harlow, 1997), pp. 1–36.

measures meant to approximate national legislation in order to make it easier for businesses to sell their goods and services outside their national territory.[73]

That attitude may be due, partly, from a so-called tendency, on the part of EC institutions, to emphasise economic growth, in the declarations made by their officials. By contrast, the statements urging businesses to better treat consumers appear less stringent. The attitude may also come, for another part, to the traditional perspective adopted by consumer lawyers, who see their legal discipline as part of social law or at least as being influenced by a social perspective. For them, the function of the law is to protect the poor, the feeble, those who could otherwise be exploited. In their minds, consumer law must make up the misbalance existing between, on the one hand, individuals contracting in their private capacity and, on the other hand, undertakings, which have the financial resources, the intellectual ability and the legal expertise to actively and decisively advance their own interests.[74]

As I have stated, specific measures have been inserted in EC directives applicable to electronic communications. These measures have been called 'social', in that they provide that, by derogation to normal market conditions, special tariffs or conditions could be proposed to categories of consumers with special needs. Other measures, relating to the universal service *stricto sensu*, have also been examined. The consumers concerned by these two categories of situations are those which, otherwise, would not have had access to the services concerned, or to the normal conditions under which these services would have been made available in a competitive environment.

In this section, we concentrate on the measures included in these directives, which are similar to classical consumer law provisions, particularly the organisation of ADRs and the obligation on firms to supply information to consumers. Whom do these provisions benefit?

Difficulties

Answering the question is not easy, because the concept of consumer is not defined in the directives examined. This lack of definition should not come as a surprise. Sometimes, that concept is not even defined in EC legislation dealing with consumer protection.[75]

---

73 Where national legislation diverges, companies may find it difficult to sell their goods or services outside their national borders. When the disparity threatens the realisation of the internal market, national legislation may be approximated, Article 95 EC.

74 Among others, undertakings have a command on the pieces of information which they hand over to consumers as regards their goods and services. They have inside data to determine the worth of their items whereas consumers must refer to the presentations made by these undertakings to make up their minds.

75 For instance, and without being exhaustive, the concept of is not defined in the following instruments although the latter deal specifically with consumer protection.

In the absence of specific indication, how should the concept be interpreted? A certainty or, at least, a quasi certainty, is that the definition should be pan–European. It should not be based on national legislation. Otherwise, an EC concept would receive an application varying with national territories.

To define the concept, one possibility could be to use definitions provided in other, similar, EC legislation. The difficulty, however, is to choose the legislation from which to extract a definition. The concept is not defined in the same manner in all directives. In some, 'consumer' refers to individuals[76] contracting in a private capacity.[77, 78] In others, it designates users – natural or legal persons acting in private or professional context.[79]

Returning to electronic communications, another difficulty is that, in the directives under investigation, it is sometimes difficult, beyond issues of definition, to identify the beneficiaries of the protective measures. This is due to the variation in the terms used in the directives to determine the scope of the measures introduced. In most instances, the protection goes, as it is stated in these directives, to 'consumers' but, under some provisions, that protection can be extended to other 'final users'.[80] In such a case, the protection can no longer be deemed to be

---

Council Directive 84/450/EEC of 10 September 1984 relating to the approximation of the laws, regulations and administrative provisions of the Member States concerning misleading advertising [1984] OJ L 250, 17–20; Council Directive of 25 July 1985 on the approximation of the laws, regulations and administrative provisions of the Member States concerning liability for defective products (85/374/EEC) [1985] OJ L 210, 29–33; the Timeshare Directive 94/47/EC; Directive 2001/95/EC of the European Parliament and of the Council of 3 December 2001 on general product safety [2001] OJ L 11, 4–17.

76　As opposed to legal persons (undertakings and so on).

77　As opposed to in the context of their professional activities.

78　That definition appears in the following directives: Council Directive 85/577/EEC of 20 December 1985 to protect the consumer in respect of contracts negotiated away from business premises [1985] OJ L 372, 31–3, Article 2; Distance Contracts Directive 97/7/EC, Article 2(2); Directive 1999/44/EC of the European Parliament and of the Council of 25 May 1999 on certain aspects of the sale of consumer goods and associated guarantees, OJ L 171, 12–16, Article 2(a); Directive 2005/29/EC of the European Parliament and of the Council of 11 May 2005 concerning unfair business–to–consumer commercial practices in the internal market and amending Council Directive 84/450/EEC, Directives 97/7/EC, 98/27/EC and 2002/65/EC of the European Parliament and of the Council and Regulation (EC) No 2006/2004 of the European Parliament and of the Council ('Unfair Commercial Practices Directive') [2005] OJ L 149, 22–39, Article 2(a).

79　For that second definition, see Package Travel Directive 90/314/EEC, Article 2(4). In a last set of instruments, the notion of consumer is associated with legal or natural persons acting outside their profession: the Timeshare Directive 94/47/EC, Article 2. The term used in that directive is 'purchaser'.

80　That possibility exists for the obligation to conclude a contract, and include specific information in that contract, as regards connexion and/or access to a public telephone

meant for consumers. It has a more general scope of application and goes beyond the measures that can be taken in the context of a consumer policy.

An additional difficulty is that the EC legislator sometimes uses different terms in connection with a same provision as if, although different, these terms were synonymous. For example, number portability is presented as being important for 'consumers' in the Preamble to the Universal Service Directive. But in the same paragraph, the EC legislator explains that, as portability is important, 'final users' should be able to carry their number away with them.[81] Are 'final users', thus, the same as 'consumers'? Another instance: the universal service is described in Universal Service Directive as a set of services that should be available to 'final users' under reasonable conditions.[82] But the term used in the annex to that same instrument in order to describe the revision procedure[83] is 'consumers'.[84]

Consumers, final users

To generalise the discussion, it appears, from a careful analysis of the provisions contained in that directive, that the EC legislator often refers to 'final users' and to 'consumers'. How do these concepts relate to one another? Both assuredly designate persons at the final stage of the economic chain. But nuances appear to differentiate them.

    a. 'Consumers' is generally interpreted as designating natural persons exclusively. Undertakings, for instance, are rarely called 'consumers'. The concept of 'final users' seems broader. It can encompass both types of users. For instance, an undertaking can be considered a final user to the extent the good or service is integrated in its activities without being commercialised to other clients.

    b. Another nuance is that consumers are often defined as people considered in their private activities. By contrast, the notion of final users may include persons (be they natural or legal) using the good or service in a professional capacity.

---

network, Universal Service Directive, Article 20(2) last sentence. It also exists for the possible extension of these obligations to services contracted with providers, *ibid.*, Article 20(3). These provisions have been cited above. The extension of obligations to relations with end-users can be decided by Member States. This does not imply that the EC level plays no role. The possibility of an extension is indeed organised by the Universal Service Directive, thus by an EC instrument.

81   Preamble para. 40.
82   Preamble para. 7 and Article 1 (2).
83   A procedure is organised in the directive in order to revise the scope of the universal service. This makes it possible to include new items where it appears that, as a result of an evolution in technology or needs, the universal service must be extended.
84   Annex V.

Table 2.2   Comparison between 'consumer' and 'final user'

Consumer	Final user
- User - Located at the last stage of the economic chain - Using the good or service in a private capacity - Thus a natural person as opposed to a legal person	- User - Located at the last stage of the economic chain - Using the good or service in a private capacity - But also in a professional activity - And thus being possibly a firm or an individual

Beyond the issue of definition, the use of a dual terminology ('final users', 'consumers') indicate that two categories of persons benefit from the measures adopted: one the one hand, the consumers *stricto sensu*, that is, the natural persons acting in a private capacity; but on the other hand, and more generally, all those who use the services concerned, be they natural or legal persons, independent of the private or professional character of their activity.

This dual definition of the beneficiaries is prone to reactivate the suspicion, earlier described in this article, about the real intentions animating the Parliament, the Council and the Commission in adopting measures organising a protection or giving rights to particular parties.

Consumers and Liberalisation

So far, we have examined, in the directives applicable in the so-called liberalised sector, the provisions having a special interest for consumers. But are all these instruments to be associated with liberalisation? Are the provisions examined above in connexion with consumer protection attached, *per se*, to liberalisation? As a mechanism, does liberalisation entail a better protection, in law, of consumers?

The concept of liberalisation

To examine that issue, we start with an attempt to define the concept of liberalisation. In general, liberalisation refers to the introduction of competition on markets. As a result of competition being introduced, markets are 'liberated'. They are more free; freer than they used to be.

The process of liberalisation is often associated with deregulation. This is because these processes sometimes take place simultaneously, and are often demanded by the same persons. Where markets are liberalised and deregulated, activities are 'liberated': more freedom is introduced on markets. There are, however, differences between the two concepts. Deregulation refers to rules: greater liberty is introduced in markets as a result of a diminution in the number of rules applicable to a sector. That mechanism, thus, concerns the general level of regulation existing in an economic field. As a result of deregulation, that level is brought downwards. Undertakings have fewer rules with which to comply. They can concentrate on producing and selling, without having to devote substantial resources to studying the law and ensuring that, in all circumstances, it is abided by.

Liberalisation is also a form of deregulation: as the latter, it consists of eliminating rules. The process, however, is more specific. The rules eliminated are determined: they are those which prohibit, market entry or make it more difficult. The concept of liberalisation is narrowly associated with public monopolies. The latter are undertakings to which exclusive rights were granted by public authorities: rights to be the only undertaking allowed to carry out given activities. As a result of liberalisation, these rights, considered as privileges, are eliminated, and firms can enter the markets concerned.

Liberalisation instruments

Are all the instruments examined earlier in this article associated with liberalisation? Yes, to the extent they regulate sectors which are considered as liberalised. Not necessarily, if we consider the object of these instruments and the provisions they contain. This position is further explained in the paragraphs below. For this discussion, I refer, again, primarily, for reasons mentioned above, to the sector of electronic communications; the perspective being afterwards broadened to other sectors.

In electronic communications, two categories of instruments may be distinguished. A first category is made of directives based on (now) Article 95 EC. These instruments were originally adopted by the Council, later by the Parliament and the Council (co-decision). In electronic communications, these instruments form the greater part of the applicable regulatory framework: four out of the five directives currently composing that framework.[85]

---

85   The directives on authorisations, access to networks, universal service and the administrative framework. These currently applicable directives follow other instruments also adopted originally by the Council, later by the Parliament and the Council. See Council Directive (EEC) 90/387 on the establishment of the internal market for telecommunications services through the implementation of open network provision [1990] OJ L 192/1, as amended several times; Council Directive (EEC) 92/44 on the application of open network provision to leased lines [1992] OJ L 165/27, amended several times; European Parliament and Council Directive (EC) 97/33 on interconnection in telecommunications with regard to ensuring universal service and interoperability through application of the principles of Open Network Provision (ONP) [1997] OJ L 199/32; European Parliament and Council Directive (EC) 98/10 on the application of open network provision (ONP) to voice telephony

A second category contains directives based on Article 86(3) EC. These instruments were unilaterally enacted by the European Commission. Their content was not negotiated with the Parliament or/nor the Council.[86] In the current regulatory framework, one directive pertains to that category: the Competition Directive, mentioned earlier.[87]

May the instruments pertaining to these two categories be considered 'liberalisation directives'? In the sector of telecom, the introduction of competition clearly came from the Commission. The Parliament and the Council played, on that subject matter, a secondary role. They intervened *ex post facto* and, rather than meaning to introduce competition, their intervention was aimed at managing, or regulating, the new markets.

If liberalisation is equivalent to the introduction of competition, an examination of the status of consumers under EC liberalisation directives would require the analysis to be limited to directives adopted by the Commission. Thus, can we consider that consumers are better protected, in law, through these directives? The answer must probably be negative. In substance, these directives only concern the first of the five principles[88] delineated above as being the pillars on which the reform was based. These directives left almost untouched the other principles, which were addressed at a later stage by the Council, or the Parliament and the Council.

Yet, liberalisation *stricto sensu*, that is, the introduction of competition, comes down to an authorisation, given to new firms, to enter markets. Such a process is beneficial, primarily, for new entrants: firms which are interested in carrying out activities in the markets concerned, without being allowed in them as a result of the exclusive rights granted by public authorities to specific undertakings. Consumers are also interested in competition. In principle, they can choose, in a competitive environment, the providers with whom they want to deal. Furthermore, in theory, competition places a pressure to improve performances.

This does not mean, however, that competition solves all issues encountered by consumers in markets. The question may be whether it even solves any of these difficulties. Let us remember the example given above of that consumer receiving an erroneous telephone bill. To such a consumer, competition grants a right to shift

---

and on universal service for telecommunications in a competitive environment [1998] OJ L 101/24; European Parliament and Council Regulation (EC) 2887/2000 on unbundled access to the local loop [2000] OJ L 336/4.

86 Although they probably gave rise to contacts and discussions between these various institutions.

87 Another instrument adopted by the Commission and introducing competition in the telecom sector continues to apply: Commission Directive 88/301 of 16 May 1988 on competition in the markets in telecommunications terminal equipment [1988] OJ L 131/73, amended.

88 Introduction of competition, limitation of the legislative power of the Member States, organisation of access to network, creation of users' rights, establishment of an administrative framework.

to another supplier. This does not mean, however, that the erroneous bill will not have to be paid ('Problems of the past').Similarly, competition does not, by itself, avoid all possible issues of arising in the relations between consumers and firms. On the contrary, in a competitive environment, firms are sometimes inclined to adopt reproachable behaviour in an attempt to survive when they feel threatened ('Problems in the future').

The process of liberalisation

The concept of liberalisation was first introduced, in the second half of the twentieth century, in one Member State: the United Kingdom.[89] Through a variety of circumstances, these principles inspired several proposals made by the European Commission in the context of public utilities. One reason was that these national utilities were performing poorly.

The change was initiated when the Commission adopted, at the end of the 1980s, in the telecom sector, the two already presented liberalisation directives.[90] These instruments abolished the monopoly earlier granted to telecom operators on national territories.[91] They angered national governments, which did not want any interference by the Commission in the regulation of their national public utilities. The validity of the directives was challenged before the Court of Justice – but the challenge failed: the Court ruled in favour of the Commission.

As its policy was upheld, the Commission adopted other 'liberalisation' directives in the telecom sector. Through these instruments, competition was introduced in other, until then spared, markets belonging to the telecom sector.[92] The Commission also envisaged the extension of liberalisation to other areas. But the movement was halted. One reason was the adoption of parallel legislative

---

89   As the prime minister of that country, M. Thatcher, once stated:
     There is no such thing as 'Society'. Economic activities should be carried out by individuals and undertakings acting autonomously in a context deprived of rules – or containing as little of them as possible. The size of public authorities and their scope of intervention should be reduced, where these authorities are not eliminated altogether. Public undertakings should be sold to private shareholders. Monopolies should be abolished. Only then would the huge creativity, and energy, of business actors, be unleashed – and efficiency would reach its maximum level.

90   Commission Directive 88/301 of 16 May 1988 on competition in the markets in telecommunications terminal equipment and Commission Directive (EEC) 90/388 on competition in the markets for telecommunications services [1990] OJ L 192/10. For a general presentation of liberalisation in Europe, see the references quoted in n. 1.

91   For instance, it was established that the rules applicable in the markets concerned, particularly the technical specifications to be complied with by firms, should be set by neutral bodies, and not longer by instances also carrying out economic activities.

92   Through these directives, liberalisation was extended to the provision of networks as well as to mobile telephony. The directives also organised the markets on which competition had been introduced.

measures, in the telecom sector, by the Council, later the Parliament and Council. This action was a way, for these latter institutions, to assert their power on the sectors concerned. An unusual situation was created, where the same activities were regulated, in the same sector, by concurrent sets of rules, adopted by different institutions.[93] That situation was detrimental to legal certainty and institutional clarity.[94] To put an end to it, the three institutions (Parliament,[95] Council, Commission) prepared a common set of rules, which was adopted in 2002.

A second reason for the halt given to liberalisation was the adoption, by the Court, of a more reserved position in subsequent liberalisation cases. These cases concerned electricity markets. In the early 1990s, these markets were still organised in the form of national monopolies. For reasons mentioned above, that form of market organisation was not found appropriate by the Commission.[96] For that institution, competition had to be introduced in these markets as well. But the strategy to be used to that effect remained unclear. The unilateral adoption of liberalisation directives would have prompted, probably, a legislative reaction on the part of the Parliament and the Council, as these latter institutions had done in the telecom sector. The undesirable situation mentioned for telecom would have extended, then, to energy markets. The Commission did not want to pursue that path and decided to negotiate with the Parliament and the Council the adoption of a common set of rules.

However, the discussions proved long, and difficult.[97] To accelerate the mechanism, the Commission decided to bring the matter again to the Court of Justice. The hope was that the Court would adopt the same attitude as in 1991 and 1993, when the power of the Commission to act in the sectors concerned had been confirmed by that institution.

This time, however, the Court did not follow the Commission. The Court considered that the Commission had not demonstrated that a violation had been committed by the Member States.[98] In the light of that change in position, the

---

93 The liberalisation directives were adopted by the European Commission and were based on Article 86 (formerly Article 90) EC. The directives adopted by the Council, and later by the Parliament and the Council, are called harmonisation directives. They were based on Article 95 EC and aimed at approximating the national legislation, the disparity of which was experienced as threatening the realisation of the common market.

94 Some provisions in the two concurrent set of legislations were indeed different and even contradictory – thereby submitting undertakings to conflicting obligations.

95 In between, the Parliament had been fully associated in the legislative procedure which had become a co-decision.

96 Bad management, lack incentive for the firm to improve its performance.

97 The Council is made of representatives of the Member States. A majority of them did not want to change the organisation of electricity markets. They were satisfied with the persistence of national monopolies in that sector.

98 For the Court, the Commission did not convincingly rebut the arguments put forward by the defendants to demonstrate that, absent monopolies, public policy objectives

Commission abandoned plans to act unilaterally. Negotiations were reinitiated and, after some time, directives were adopted by the Parliament and the Council. These instruments introduced competition in postal services as well as in energy markets. They further organised these markets along the principles: authorisations, access to network, universal service and administrative framework.

Two approaches

As appears from these discussions, two approaches may be adopted regarding the relationship between liberalisation and consumers.

One approach is to consider that liberalisation may be equated with introduction of competition. Then, we have to consider that liberalisation must be limited to the directive adopted by the European Commission. The instruments enacted by the Council, later the Parliament and Council, may also be taken into account – only, however, to the extent they abolish monopoly and organise competition. On that interpretation of the notion of liberalisation, the rest of the provisions contained in these instruments should not be regarded as being part of the process.

In that first approach, liberalisation may not be considered as entailing a definitive improvement in the legal protection granted to consumers. Of course, consumers receive, through competition, the possibility of choosing among suppliers the one or those which, on the basis of received information, they consider as best suiting their needs. The situation of consumers is thereby improved to a significant extent. However, that measure, by itself, does not improve the position of consumers in their past or future situation with the firms.

Another approach is to deem that liberalisation encompasses the totality of the process. In that conception, liberalisation is not limited to the introduction of competition. It covers the five principles mentioned above while presenting the reform. Then, the social provisions, the establishment of a universal service and the creation of rights for users are considered part of the phenomenon. These various aspects have been analysed throughout the article. I have stated that the measures concerned improved, in law, the situation of consumers, while stressing the continuous ambiguity surrounding the intentions of the EC legislator.

Conclusion: A Real Protection?

In conclusion, I can say that the directives in the European Union associated with liberalisation, have affected considerably the position of consumers.

Change 1, competition was introduced in various markets. As a result of competition, consumers were granted the right, and the opportunity, to make selections among products and services. This is an important development for

---

relating to the availability of energy throughout the national territory could not be implemented.

consumers, as it considerably changes their position in markets. Beforehand, consumers had to support bad service, inadequate goods, without real, effective possible reaction. Now, they can shift to another supplier.

In some aspects, the European liberalisation has, however, gone further. The action of markets has been completed by specific measures. These measures have been developed more extensively in the sector of electronic communications – hence my emphasis on that sector in the current article. They introduce two forms of change.

Change 2, social provisions were enacted and a universal service was established. In these two cases, consumers were taken into account. An access to fundamental services was opened to specific categories of the population with social or geographic needs. However, a doubt remains about whether these measures can be considered to provide adequate protection to consumers. These measures must indeed be financed – and the system established to that effect consists of sharing among consumers the cost induced by these measures. Can we speak of consumer protection where some consumers support the cost of providing services to others?

Change 3, rights were granted to users in transactions with operators and service providers. These rights are in line with traditional consumer policy within the European Union (provision of information, organisation of alternative dispute resolution mechanisms ADRs). Again, however, there is a certain ambiguity in the process.

First, some of these rights appear related to the competitive process rather than constitute a real protection for users (number of portability, selection or pre selection of carriers). In the absence these rights, competition would not function properly in the markets concerned. For that reason, the provisions introducing these rights may be considered as an accessory to those introducing competition. These provisions do not, strictly speaking, create rights: they organise competition.

Second, the other provisions associated with users' rights are meant for undefined beneficiaries. On the basis of the directives involved, it remains difficult to identify the category of users that the EC legislator has intended to protect. The measures certainly benefit consumers. But, more generally, they can be extended to all final users.

In all these remarks, I have talked of 'doubt' and 'ambiguity'. These terms should not take away the benefits deriving, for users, from competition, or give the impression that the advantages provided by that form of market organisation are being neglected. They are used to stress that, currently, a debate rages about how consumers should be protected. That debate goes as follows. Should authorities grant specific protection to consumers? Or are consumers sufficiently protected by the introduction of competition?

In my view, the two options must be considered. Competition, or at least a certain dose of it, is necessary for consumers to enjoy the right of choosing their business partners. The introduction of competition does not imply, however, that problems cease to appear in relations between firms and consumers. These problems must be addressed through specific protective measures. In the absence of such measures, 'bad' firms may be tempted to cheat more often; the confidence of consumers may drop; and 'good' firms may suffer from it.

3   The Impact of the European Union on Consumer Policy in Malta: A Mixed Blessing?

Paul Edgar Micallef

A Historical Chronology of Consumer Policy in Malta

Consumer policy in Malta is driven primarily by two considerations. One is obvious: the need to ensure that the rights of consumers are adequately protected by finding an equitable balance between the legitimate rights and expectations of consumers on the one hand and of traders on the other. The presumption, in the early years of the formulation of consumer policy in Malta, was that there was a deficit of rights which was prejudicial to consumers, and that this somehow had to be addressed through the gradual enactment of measures relating to the different areas of consumer protection.[1] This process was initiated in the early 1980s with the enactment of various laws aimed at dealing with specific consumer issues and continued, in a somewhat haphazard fashion, until 1991 when the Government undertook a fairly wide-ranging public consultation outlining its proposals to have in place a comprehensive consumer protection regulatory framework.[2] The other consideration, consequential to the membership of Malta in the European Union,[3] is the onerous requirement for Malta to implement the EU *acquis* on consumer protection.[4] This latter consideration led to the enactment of various laws related to

*   Dr. Paul Micallef is a member of *l-Ghaqda tal-Konsumaturi* and is the Chief Legal Adviser to the Malta Communications Authority. The views in this chapter are strictly those of the author and the chapter reflects the position under Maltese law as it was on 31 December 2007. Separately, amendments enacted early in 2008 are commented on at p. 303–309.

1   See White Paper entitled 'Rights for the Consumer', August 1991, pp. 5–7.
2   *Ibid.*
3   Malta became a member of the EU on the 1 May 2004. The membership of Malta was for some years a hot political issue that was only definitively settled with the referendum and general election results of 2003, which paved the way for EU membership.
4   The Commission, in a report it issued in 1993 on the application of Malta to join the EU, had observed that the Maltese legislator then needed to introduce various laws to implement the *acquis* in relation consumer safety, transactions and consumer information. See Bulletin of the European Communities Supplement 4/93 at p. 26.

matters that were not regulated at the time when Malta decided to seek membership. In enacting these laws, in some instances, the Maltese authorities chose to go beyond the minimum measures provided for in the applicable EU directives,[5] providing for a higher level of consumer protection, even if these instances were, admittedly, few and far between.[6]

Maltese consumer policy does not go far back in time. Until the 1980s, the term 'consumer' was practically unknown in Maltese law. The Maltese Civil Code, enacted in the latter part of the nineteenth century, dealt with the rights and obligations of buyers and sellers, providing for civil remedies if there is breach of contract, a tort or quasi-tort.[7] The Code does not deal with the figure of the 'consumer', the legislator preferring to enact specific laws to deal with consumer issues rather than amending the Civil Code to deal with new consumer protection related issues.[8]

In the early 1980s, the Government started to enact laws addressing specific consumer issues. Until then there were laws that dealt with different aspects relating to consumer protection though, in most instances, these laws were not enacted with the prime purpose of consumer protection. These included the former Weights and Measures Ordinance,[9] various food safety laws,[10] laws regulating the sale of certain goods and services[11] and laws on standards.[12]

The first law dealing explicitly with consumer protection was the Consumer Protection Act enacted in 1981. The title of this law was somewhat of a misnomer as this was actually a very short law enacted for the sole purpose of encouraging the setting up of consumer associations by giving those associations recognised by Government, protection at law when making public statements in good faith about

---

5   Many of the EU consumer protection directives include a minimum harmonisation clause enabling Member States to adopt more stringent provisions, which go beyond the measures stated in the directives, thereby providing consumers with a higher level of consumer protection.

6   These exceptions include the laws implementing the Unfair Terms Directive and, to a lesser extent, the Sale of Consumer Goods Directive.

7   Civil Code, Articles 959–1051A which articles deal with contracts, quasi-contracts, torts and quasi-torts, and Articles 1346–1484 which with sale.

8   Such as the use of unfair terms in contracts or the protection of consumers when buying goods which, rather than being dealt with under the Civil Code, are regulated under the Consumer Affairs Act.

9   This law was enacted in 1920s and has since been repealed and replaced by the Metrology Act.

10   These included the Food, Drugs and Drinking Water Act 1972. This law has since been supplemented with the Food Safety Act 2002 which latter law set up the Food Safety Commission whose remit includes monitoring and dealing with food safety issues.

11   See Control on the Sale of Commodities Regulations, 1972 (Subsidiary Legislation 117.15).

12   The former Quality Control (Exports and Imports and Local Goods) Act 1971.

goods.[13] Though this law did not achieve much, other than encourage the setting up of a consumer association in the early 1980s, it does serve to demonstrate that the Maltese authorities, at a relatively early stage in the history of consumer policy in Malta, wanted to give special importance to the role of consumer associations. The Consumer Protection Act was followed in 1986 by the Trade Descriptions Act[14] and in 1987 by the Door-to-Door Salesmen Act.[15] The latter law was enacted primarily to deal with aggressive unfair practices conducted by certain firms engaging in door-to-door marketing, whereby a substantial number of consumers were being hoodwinked into buying products they did not really want or need.[16] Significantly, this law was the first law dealing with consumer protection, influenced, in part, by EU legislation – in this case the Doorstep Selling Directive[17] – this at a time when the Government of the day had no declared intention of joining the EU.[18]

The early 1990s heralded what is, to date, the main period of activity in so far as Government initiatives on consumer policy are concerned. The first major development during this period was the publication by the Government, in August 1991, of a White Paper entitled 'Rights for the Consumer' ('1991 White Paper'), whereby a review of the existing laws that directly or indirectly impacted on consumer protection was undertaken. In doing so, the Government proposed the creation of a 'Consumer Protection Council' to promote and protect the interests of consumers, proposing that this Council should have executive powers to curb practices or activities of harm to consumers.[19] Significantly, the proposals in the

---

13 This law was repealed in 1996. Significantly, however, the provisions giving recognised consumer associations protection at law when making public statements in good faith were improved upon and extended to all activities conducted by traders. See Consumer Affairs Act, Article 36. See also P.E. Micallef, 'The Malta Consumer Affairs Act 1994 – Setting up the Foundations for a Comprehensive Framework to Protect Consumers', *Consumer Law Journal*, 5/1 (1997): 24–5.

14 See Cap. 313 of the Laws of Malta. The Trade Descriptions Act is modelled on the United Kingdom Trade Descriptions Act 1968. The purpose of this law is primarily to prohibit misleading descriptions of goods and services.

15 See Cap. 317 of the Laws of Malta.

16 There was one particular firm engaged in selling dated encyclopaedias that engaged in some rather dubious marketing practices. This law was, in part, drafted in reaction to the practices of this firm.

17 Council Directive 85/577/EEC to protect the Consumer in respect of Contracts Negotiated away from Business Premises.

18 The extent of the problem then was demonstrated by the fact that Government had, in the original Bill, proposed a cooling off period whereby a door-to-door sale would only be valid if within 15 days from the date of agreement entered into, the agreement was formally confirmed by the consumer. This measure, however, was not carried through and was substituted with a cooling off period whereby a consumer has 15 days to cancel the agreement.

19 See 1991 White Paper at p. 7 onwards, wherein it was proposed that the Council would have a remit to educate consumers, promote voluntary consumer associations and monitor and review all commercial activities that might impact on consumers.

1991 White Paper were also influenced by developments in the EU.[20] Malta had, a few months earlier, applied to become a member of the EU.[21] Consequently, Malta had to start implementing the various EU consumer protection directives then in place as part of its consumer policy. Proposals featured in the 1991 White Paper included measures relating to advertising, the use of unfair terms in consumer contracts, product liability and product safety, pricing, labelling and marking of products, protection of consumers when purchasing or hiring goods or services, and the establishment of a small claims tribunal to determine consumer versus trader disputes involving relatively small pecuniary values.

In November 1993 the Government issued another White Paper entitled 'Fair Trading: the next step forward ...' (the '1993 White Paper') which included two draft laws entitled respectively the Consumer Affairs Act and the Competition Act. The draft Consumer Affairs Act focused primarily on the establishment of the entities responsible for consumer affairs, proposing the establishment of the post of a Director of Consumer Affairs and of a Consumer Affairs Council, on the recognition and regulation of consumer associations and the rights these should have at law, and on the establishment of a consumer claims tribunal. In this draft law, the Government diverged substantially from its proposals in the earlier 1991 White Paper, as it now advocated the creation of an executive director responsible for consumer affairs, with the proposed Consumer Affairs Council enjoying a consultative role with a very restricted executive role. This meant a notable shift from the collective decision making body as originally proposed in 1991 to a new structure whereby most of the executive powers resided in the person of the Director of Consumer Affairs. No reasons were given in the 1993 White Paper why there was a change from what was proposed two years earlier. Regrettably then, the only discussion over the regulatory structures to be adopted in dealing with consumer protection issues was limited to the Government proposals in the 1991 and 1993 White Papers. Had there been more meaningful and participative discussion then, perhaps, a more co-ordinated and focused approach might have been taken, to ensure that consumer affairs were more effectively monitored and regulated. As things evolved, the measures taken through the years were, in many instances, more the result of a reactive response to the need to comply with new incoming EU directives, rather than the result of a structured evolution of a responsive and comprehensive regulatory structure.

---

20   The 1991 White Paper does, in the context of different areas, refer to some of the then applicable EU consumer policy related directives such as the Product Liability Directive. It is to be borne in mind that in 1991 some of the more important EU directives notably those on unfair terms and sale of goods to consumers had not as yet been enacted and therefore in these and other important areas of consumer law the Maltese legislator could not as yet refer to EU direction on consumer policy.

21   Malta applied to join the EU on the 16 July 1990. Malta and nine other countries became members on 1 May 2004.

Progress from the purely structural side proceeded at a smooth pace and, in 1994, a Bill entitled the Consumer Affairs Act was published and approved by Parliament, which Act came into force on 23 January 1996. This Act, in substance, replicated most of the legislative provisions as proposed in the draft Bill published in the 1993 White Paper. The main focus of the Act was the creation of the executive post of the Director of Consumer Affairs with responsibility for the enforcement of various consumer related laws,[22] the setting up of an advisory council called the Consumer Affairs Council, the regulation of the role of consumer associations and establishment of a tribunal to deal with minor consumer versus trader disputes.[23] In October 1996 there was a change of Government.[24] The new administration, in line with its electoral programme, in August 1998 prepared a draft law[25] proposing the setting up of an Authority for Fair Trading and Consumer Affairs which would broadly assume the functions of the Director of Consumer Affairs and of the Director of Fair Competition thereby creating one comprehensive body responsible for consumer and competition issues. However, the proposals in this draft law were not taken forward as a snap election was held a few months later, leading to another change in government in 1998.

Whilst the new incoming administration[26] opted not to take forward the proposed amendments of the previous administration, it decided actively to undertake a legislative programme to transpose most of the then existing EU consumer protection directives. In 1999 a small team of experts was appointed to take this task forward and, in 2000, amendments[27] to the Consumer Affairs Act and to the Door-to-Door Salesmen Act[28] were enacted with the purpose of

---

22 These laws included the Weights and Measures Ordinance, the Trade Descriptions Act and the Door-to-Door Salesmen Act.

23 See Micallef, 'The Malta Consumer Affairs Act 1994 – Setting up the Foundations for a Comprehensive Framework to Protect Consumers': 19–31.

24 The new Labour administration had frozen the application of Malta to join the EU. This measure, in part, meant that the former impetus to transpose the existing EU consumer protection directives lost some momentum, even though the new administration was, in the sphere of consumer protection, strongly committed to the introduction of new laws to protect consumers.

25 This draft was not formally published for public consultation. In August 1998 Government chose to circulate the draft informally with the various social stakeholders including business and consumer lobbies before deciding to formally publish its final proposals.

26 The new Nationalist administration, on being elected to Government in October 1998, re-activated the application of Malta to join the EU. This consequently meant that the transposition of the EU *acquis* now had to be pursued in earnest.

27 The various amendments to the Consumer Affairs Act and to the Door-to-Door Salesmen Act came into force at different stages.

28 Later renamed the Doorstep Contracts Act.

implementing the EU Directives on product liability,[29] misleading and comparative advertising[30] ('Misleading and Comparative Advertising Directive'), unfair terms in consumer contracts[31] ('Unfair Terms Directive'), sale of consumer goods and associated guarantees[32] ('Sale of Consumer Goods Directive'), injunctions for the protection of consumers' interests ('Injunctions Directive'), and doorstep selling ('Doorstep Selling Directive'). These amendments also catered for the insertion of a new part in the Consumer Affairs Act, outlining the principles to be adhered to in the interpretation and implementation of the Act and of any regulations made thereunder.[33]

The year 2000 also witnessed the enactment of consumer laws in the travel and tourism sector with the enactment of the Package Travel, Package Holidays and Package Tours Regulations ('Package Travel Regulations') and the Protection of Buyers in Contracts for Time Sharing of Immovable Property Regulations ('Time Share Regulations')[34] which laws implement respectively the Package Travel Directive[35] and the Timeshare Directive.[36] In 2004 the Time Share Regulations were complemented by a separate set of regulations: the Timeshare and Timeshare-like Products Promotion (Licensing of OPC Representatives) Regulations ('Timeshare Promotion Regulations')[37] to regulate the marketing of timeshare with the purpose of curbing certain malpractices. Related to this sector are the Civil Aviation (Denied Boarding, Compensation and Assistance to Passengers) Regulations, 2005, which

---

29   Council Directive 85/374/EEC of 25 July 1985 on the approximation of the laws, regulations and administrative provisions of the Member States concerning liability for defective products.

30   Council Directive 84/450/EEC of 10 September 1984 relating to the approximation of the laws, regulations and administrative provisions of the Member States concerning misleading and comparative advertising as amended by Directive 97/55/EC of the European Parliament and of the Council of 6 October 1997.

31   Council Directive 93/13/EEC of 5 April 1993 on unfair terms in consumer contracts.

32   Directive 1999/44/EC of the European Parliament and of the Council of 25 May 1999 on certain aspects of the sale of consumer goods and associated guarantees.

33   See Consumer Affairs Act, Part V. The principles broadly reflect the Guidelines for Consumer Protection adopted by the United Nations General Assembly on 9 April 1985 and are not directly enforceable in any court or tribunal.

34   These Regulations were enacted by the Minister responsible for tourism on the recommendation of the Malta Tourism Authority acting by virtue of the powers to make regulations granted to the Minister under the Malta Travel and Tourism Services Act (Cap. 409 of the Laws of Malta).

35   Council Directive 90/314/EEC of 13 June 1990 on package travel, package holidays and package tours.

36   Council Directive 94/47/EC of the European Parliament and the Council of 26 October 1994 on the protection of purchasers in respect of certain aspects of contracts relating to the purchase of the right to use immovable properties on a timeshare basis.

37   See Legal Notice 299 of 2004.

establish that non-compliance with the EU Denied Boarding Regulations[38] is an offence under Maltese law punishable by a maximum fine of 1,000 Maltese liri.[39]

In 2001 Government took the administrative measure of placing the office of the Director of Consumer Affairs and the office of the Director of Fair Competition under one unified office called the Consumer and Competition Division with the Director General of this division assuming the roles of both the Director of Consumer Affairs and the Director of the Office of Fair Competition. During 2001 another two important consumer related laws were enacted: the Product Safety Act primarily falling within the remit of the Director of Consumer Affairs,[40] which law implements the Product Safety Directive,[41] and the Distance Selling Regulations[42] which implements the Distance Selling Directive.[43] In 2002 the Consumer Affairs Act (Price Indication) Regulations ('Price Indication Regulations') were enacted[44] implementing the Price Indication Directive,[45] followed in 2005 by Consumer Credit Regulations[46] implementing the Consumer Credit Directive.[47] 2005 also saw the enactment of the Distance Selling (Retail Financial Services) Regulations under the Malta Financial Services Authority Act implementing the Directive on

38   Regulation (EC) No. 261/2004 of the European Parliament and of the Council of 11 February 2004 establishing common rules on compensation and assistance to passengers in the event of denied boarding and of cancellation or long delay of flights. This Regulation repealed the previous Regulation (RRC) No. 295/91.

39   Legal Notice 63 of 2005 designates the Director of Civil Aviation as the person responsible for the enforcement of the EU Denied Boarding Regulations.

40   In certain instances the Director of Consumer Affairs is required to act with the concurrence of the Director responsible for Market Surveillance, such as when issuing a public warning statement under the Product Safety Act.

41   Council Directive 92/59/EEC of 29 June 1992 on General Product Safety.

42   As per Legal Notice 186 of 2001 enacted by the Minister responsible for consumer affairs after consultation with the Consumer Affairs Council in accordance with his powers under the Consumer Affairs Act, Article 7.

43   Directive 97/7/EC of the European Parliament and of the Council of 20 May 1997 on the protection of consumers in respect of distance contracts.

44   The Price Indication Regulations were enacted as per Legal Notice 283 of 2002 by the Minister responsible for consumer affairs after consultation with the Consumer Affairs Council in accordance with his powers under the Consumer Affairs Act, Article 7.

45   Directive 98/6/EC of the European Parliament and of the Council of 16 February 1998 on consumer protection in the indication of the prices of products offered to consumers.

46   The Consumer Credit Regulations were enacted as per Legal Notice 84 of 2005.

47   Council Directive 87/102/EEC of 22 December 1986 for the Approximation of the Laws, Regulations and Administrative Provisions of the Member States concerning consumer credit as amended by Council Directive 90/88EC of 22 February 1990 and Directive 98/7/EC of the European Parliament and of the Council of 16 February 1998.

distance marketing of consumer financial services.[48] Of importance, given also the increasing use of online services to make transactions, was the enactment of the Electronic Commerce (General) Regulations in 2006 ('E-Commerce Regulations'), which complement the measures enacted under the Electronic Commerce Act.[49] The Regulations together with the Act implement the E-Commerce Directive[50] focusing on the protection of consumers who use information society services.

Amongst the more recent legislative measures relating to consumer protection are the implementation of the Injunctions Directive and the compliance with the procedural requirements under the EU Regulation on consumer protection co-operation.[51] The first measures to implement the Injunctions Directive were taken following amendments to the Consumer Affairs Act in 2000.[52] At that juncture, the measures transposing the Injunctions Directive applied only to some of the directives listed in the Annex thereto.[53] Subsequently to ensure full transposition other laws were enacted in 2005 and 2006.[54] Amendments to the Consumer Affairs Act[55] were also enacted to comply with the certain procedural requirements of the Regulation on consumer protection co-operation.[56] Finally there is currently a Bill

---

48 Directive 2002/65/EC of the European Parliament and of the Council of 23 September 2002 concerning the distance marketing of consumer financial services. The Regulations also implement the Injunctions Directive given that Directive 2002/65/EC is also listed in the Annex to the Injunctions Directive as amended.

49 See Electronic Commerce Act, Cap. 426 of the Laws of Malta.

50 Directive 2000/31/EC of the European Parliament and of the Council of 8 June on certain legal aspects of information society services, in particular electronic commerce, in the internal market.

51 See Regulation (EC) No. 2006/2004 of the European Parliament and of the Council of 27 October 2004 on cooperation between national authorities responsible for the enforcement of consumer protection laws.

52 See Act XXVI of 2000 entitled 'An Act to amend the Consumer Affairs Act, Cap. 378, and to provide for other matters ancillary and consequential thereto'.

53 It is pertinent to note that since 2000, the EU has added other directives to the directives listed in the Annex to the Injunctions Directive, including notably the Sale of Consumer Goods Directive, the E-Commerce Directive, the Directive on distance marketing of consumer financial services and the Unfair Commercial Practices Directive.

54 The consumer laws transposing the directives mentioned in the Annex to the Injunctions Directive are administered by different public authorities under different laws. This situation led to the implementation of the Injunctions Directives under different laws administered by different public authorities. See below at p. 132 on 'The Injunctions Directive'.

55 As per Act XV of 2006 which amended the Consumer Affairs Act and other laws.

56 This Regulation sets down the conditions which consumer protection authorities in the different Member States are to follow in cooperating with each other and with the EU Commission to ensure that there is compliance with the requirements of the various directives and regulations related to consumer protection as listed in the Annex to the Regulation. The Consumer Affairs Act and other laws were amended in 2006

before Parliament,[57] the purpose of which is to transpose the Unfair Commercial Practices Directive, to implement certain wide-ranging measures relating to enforcement and to establish a new appeals tribunal. It is envisaged that this Bill will become law in the very near future.[58]

Travel and Tourism Services

The main impact of the EU in relation to this sector has been through the measures taken by the Maltese authorities to implement the Package Travel Directive and the Timeshare Directive by their transposition under Maltese law and, in the case of the Denied Boarding Regulation,[59] by direct application of this EU regulation. The sum of these measures has been the introduction of beneficiary measures that have served to enhance consumer protection in areas where previously there were no specific norms to protect the rights of consumers, whether these consumers were outgoing or incoming tourists or travellers. In general, the approach taken by the Maltese legislator in this sector has, with some minor variations, been to implement the minimum measures established by EU law, with, however, the significant exception of timeshare, where problems specific to the Maltese situation relating to aggressive marketing practices have also been addressed.[60]

Package travel

The first measures to implement the Package Travel Directive under Maltese Law were taken with the enactment of the Malta Travel and Tourism Services Act ('MTTS Act') in 1999. These measures included a definition of 'travel package' modelled on the definition of 'package' in the Directive, a provision obliging every travel agent licensed under the Act to have a policy of third party liability

---

precisely to comply with the requirements of this Regulation. See Act XV of 2006 which amended respectively the Consumer Affairs Act, the Civil Aviation Act and the Broadcasting Act. Separately other consumer protection laws, enforced by other public authorities, were enacted to comply with the requirements of this Regulation.

57 See Bill Number 112 published in the Government Gazette on the 16 November 2007. At the time of writing, the Bill has yet to be approved by Parliament.

58 Article 19 of the Unfair Commercial Practices Directive requires Member States to apply the measures contained in that Directive by the 12 December 2007.

59 Regulation (EC) No 261/2004 of the European Parliament and of the Council of 11 February establishing common rules on compensation and assistance to passengers in the event of denied boarding and of cancellation or long delay of flights, and repealing Regulation (EEC) No 295/91.

60 See P.E. Micallef, 'The Regulation of Timeshare under Maltese Law', *International Travel Law*, (2005): 76–84, and also the EC 'Consumer Law Compendium – Comparative Analysis' December 2006, prepared for the European Commission, available at: www.eu-consumer-law.org/consumerstudy_part3b.pdf.

insurance and, if required by the Malta Tourism Authority ('MTA'), an additional policy of professional indemnity insurance.[61] The MTTS Act also empowers the Minister responsible for tourism, on the recommendation of the MTA, to make regulations on package travel services and on the provision of timeshare.[62]

In 2000 the Package Travel Regulations[63] were enacted implementing the Package Travel Directive with practically no significant variations from that Directive. The Regulations focus on two important consumer rights, namely the right to information and the right to redress where the services paid for are not provided. The information rights include provisions about the information that must be provided in a brochure if a brochure has been issued,[64] the information that must be provided before the contract is concluded, information that must be provided in good time before the start of the journey and the essential terms that must be included in the contract.[65] The Regulations detail the remedies that a consumer has if there is a cancellation of the package by the organiser or when a significant proportion of the services contracted for are not provided.

In line with the Package Travel Directive, other aspects regulated under these Regulations include the faculty of a consumer to transfer his booking to a third party,[66] price revision,[67] and significant alterations to essential terms in the contracts and the rights that a consumer has in such instances.[68] A breach of these Regulations is an offence and the offending party may face a fine of up to

---

61 MTTS Act, Article 31. The requirement is onerous on what are described under the Act as 'tourism operations' which term includes travel or tourism agencies. Regulation 15.8 of the Package Travel Regulations further provides that the provisions of Article 31 of the Act apply to any organiser or retailer to whom the Regulations may apply, even if they do not operate a tourism operation as defined under the MTTS Act. See also P.E. Micallef, 'The Outgoing Tourist – Rights and Remedies under Maltese Law', *International Travel Law Journal*, Issue Two (2004): 96.

62 MTTS Act, Article 47. It is interesting to note that as worded the Minister is not empowered of his own initiative to made regulations relating to timeshare or package travel, but can only make such regulations acting on the recommendation of the MTA.

63 As per Legal Notice 157 of 2000 as amended by Legal Notice 258 of 2001.

64 There is no obligation per se to provide a brochure. However if a brochure is provided then it must abide with the requirements under the Package Travel Regulations, regulation 5(1).

65 Package Travel Regulations, regulations 5.1, 6.1, 7.1 and 8.1. These broadly reflect Articles 3, 4.1 and 4.2 of the Package Travel Directive.

66 *Ibid.*, regulation 10.1.

67 *Ibid.*, regulation 11.1. Price revision can only take place if stated in the contract and then only in the instances stated under the Regulations. Furthermore, the Regulations prohibit any increase in price prior to twenty days before the departure date.

68 *Ibid.*, regulation 12.1. If the package organiser has to alter 'significantly' an essential term then he is required to notify the consumer to enable him to take his decision including the opportunity to withdraw from the contract.

a maximum of 1,000 Maltese liri[69] and a daily fine of up 50 Maltese Liri for each day during which the offence continues.[70] The MTA, as the competent authority responsible for ensuring compliance with these Regulations, also has the faculty of suspending or declining to renew the licence of an offending package organiser to operate as a travel agent under the MTTS Act for a period not exceeding one year.[71]

The sanctions available under these Regulations are without prejudice to the right of aggrieved consumers to seek civil redress against the offending party. In practice, in the overwhelming majority of cases, consumers, rather than reporting any alleged non-compliance with the Regulations to the MTA, opt to seek civil redress in accordance with the remedies granted to them under the Package Travel Regulations. In most cases, consumers seeking civil remedies refer their case to the Director of Consumer Affairs who endeavours to mediate between the parties concerned. If mediation does not succeed then the aggrieved consumer has the option of filing a dispute before the Consumer Claims Tribunal if he is seeking compensation or some form of other civil redress.[72] It is relevant to note that under the Consumer Claims Tribunal procedure, before a claim is filed, consumers are first required to refer their case to the Director of Consumer Affairs[73] or to a registered consumer association.[74]

The role of the MTA, within the context of these Regulations, is effectively a very limited one since in most instances what most consumers seek is compensation rather than the initiation of enforcement proceedings by the MTA.[75] Understandably, what consumers are interested in is not the imposition of fines or of other punitive sanctions on offending package organisers or retailers, but substantive redress of their grievances. In such circumstances, it is legitimate to ask whether the MTA is effectively the public authority best suited to enforce compliance with these Regulations. It makes more sense to empower the Director

---

69   The Maltese lira is equivalent to approximately 2.32 Euros.
70   Package Travel Regulations, regulation 16.1.
71   *Ibid.*, regulation 16.2.
72   The Consumer Claims Tribunal can, however, only determine disputes where the amount being claimed does not exceed 1,500 Maltese liri.
73   See Consumer Affairs Act, Article 23(4), which requires that a claim, before being presented, must be referred by the consumer to the Director of Consumer Affairs or to a registered consumer association who in turn are required to try and bring the parties to agreement. If no agreement is reached within fifteen working days, then the consumer may file his claim directly with the Consumer Claims Tribunal.
74   Consumer Affairs Act, Part IV deals with the registration of consumer associations, establishing the criteria for such registration and the rights and obligations that such associations have at law. See also P.E. Micallef, 'Making Consumer Redress a Reality', *New Zealand Business Law Quarterly*, 8/4 (2002): 441–8 for a description of the rights that such associations have under Maltese law.
75   To date the MTA, as the competent enforcement authority, has never initiated any court action for any alleged breach of the Package Travel Regulations.

of Consumer Affairs to assume the role of the MTA in context of these regulations given that, to date, the Director has been actively involved in many of the cases that consumers have brought before the Consumer Claims Tribunal in relation to alleged non-compliance with, or disputes arising under, the Regulations. The Director would be in a better position to fulfil his role of ensuring that consumers are given their dues if he is also empowered to undertake the appropriate regulatory measures against a package organiser who fails to comply with the Regulations. There is also the practical consideration that a non-compliant package organiser or retailer may be acting in breach both of the Package Travel Regulations and of laws directly enforced by the Director of Consumer Affairs.[76] In such circumstances, it makes more sense to have one enforcement authority proceeding against the non-compliant package organiser rather than have two different authorities acting under two different legal regimes with the attendant problems that the duplication of processes can lead to.

Timeshare

Though the timeshare industry has been operating in Malta since at least the early 1980s, the first law regulating timeshare was only introduced in 2000 with the enactment of the Time Share Regulations. The legislator, in enacting these regulations, implemented the Timeshare Directive with some minor variations intended to provide more extensive protection to consumers.[77] The Regulations cover the various aspects relating to timeshare as provided for in the Timeshare Directive, including the information requirements onerous on the seller of timeshare, the language in which a timeshare contract must be written, and the right of the timeshare purchaser to withdraw from or cancel a contract in accordance with the minimum periods stipulated in the Directive.

The legislator, in these Regulations, failed to address what was, and probably still is, one of the major abuses relating to the marketing of timeshare in Malta, namely the aggressive marketing practices which time and again have been the cause of serious complaints by tourists visiting Malta. Initially the approach taken by the legislator was primarily to ensure that the minimum EU legislative requirements were satisfied, without concurrently addressing other issues specific to the timeshare industry in Malta. Fortunately, even if somewhat late in day, the need to curb aggressive marketing practices was finally addressed following the enactment of the Timeshare Promotion Regulations in 2004.[78] The object of these latter regulations is to provide for the licensing of OPC (so-called 'outside

---

76   For example the use of an unfair term in the package contract.
77   One such variation is that under regulation 4.5 of the Time Share Regulations whereby the seller is required to ensure that a period of at least seven consecutive days in each calendar year is reserved for the upkeep of the timeshare property.
78   As per Legal Notice 299 of 2004 as amended by Legal Notice 151 of 2006.

promotional contacts') representatives and to regulate their conduct when promoting the sale of timeshare.[79]

The failure, in 2000 when the Time Share Regulations were enacted, to deal with specific domestic mal-practices that, at the time, undermined timeshare in Malta, reflected a mistaken approach by the competent authorities. Consumer protection measures should not be taken solely to comply with international obligations – in this case the requirements of the EU *acquis* – but should also ensure that the interests of consumers are adequately protected, taking into account the specific domestic circumstances applicable to the Maltese market. Regrettably, time and again the legislator has opted merely to transpose the minimum EU requirements leaving consumers exposed to certain mal-practices.

The responsibility of ensuring compliance with both the Time Share Regulations and the Timeshare Promotion Regulations falls within the remit of the MTA. Non-compliance with the Time Share Regulations is an offence and those found guilty face a penalty of a maximum of 1,000 Maltese Liri, and a daily fine of up to 50 Maltese Liri for each day of non-compliance.[80] Such sanctions are without prejudice to the right of consumers to seek civil redress. Unlike what happens in the case of the Package Travel Regulations, consumers who seek redress under the Time Share Regulations, in many instances, first refer their complaints to the MTA. One should remember that in context of timeshare, many of the complainants are tourists who invariably are referred to the MTA if they have complaints concerning timeshare. Moreover the MTA does perform a fairly active enforcement role in so far as timeshare is concerned, given also that timeshare is considered to be an important segment of the tourist industry in Malta. There is also the practical consideration that few tourists are in position to initiate court proceedings in Malta to seek redress in accordance with the Time Share Regulations. In many cases, the best solution is for the aggrieved tourist to seek the intervention of the MTA to bring pressure on the timeshare seller to rectify matters and, where justified, require the seller to provide adequate redress to the tourist concerned.

Denied boarding

Prior to the accession of Malta as a member state in the EU on the 1 May 2004, denied boarding was regulated by Civil Aviation (Denied Boarding Compensation) Regulations, 2001[81] which regulations were modelled on the former EC Regulation on denied boarding.[82] As result of the membership of Malta within the EU,

---

79   See Micallef, 'The Regulation of Timeshare under Maltese Law': 81.
80   Time Share Regulations, regulation 13.1.
81   These regulations were enacted as per Legal Notice 78 of 2001. See also Micallef, 'The Outgoing Tourist – Rights and Remedies under Maltese Law, Part One': 102–3.
82   Council Regulation (EEC) No. 295/91 of 4 February 1991 establishing common rules for a denied-boarding compensation system in scheduled air transport. Prior to Malta's entry in the EU, EC Regulations could not be applied directly. The Maltese

these Regulations no longer apply. Instead, denied boarding is regulated by the EC Denied Boarding Regulation which applies directly to Malta and does not necessitate any substantial national legislation to transpose the provisions in the EC Regulation.[83] The intervention by the Maltese legislator has been restricted to two short legal notices. The purpose of the first legal notice[84] was to designate the Director of Civil Aviation as the competent national authority responsible for the enforcement of the provisions of the EC Regulation as regards flights from airports situated in Malta and flights from a third country to Malta.[85] The second legal notice[86] provides for the penalties that an operating air carrier incurs if it fails to comply with any obligation under Articles 4–6, 10, 11 and 14 of the EC Regulation.[87] The same legal notice states that it is a defence from liability under the EC Regulation if an operating air carrier shows that it took all reasonable steps and exercised all due diligence to avoid committing a breach of the above mentioned articles under the EC Regulation.[88]

As with the Package Travel Regulations and the Time Share Regulations, the issue arises whether the Director of Civil Aviation should be the public authority empowered to ensure compliance with the EC Denied Boarding Regulation. If a passenger is seeking civil remedies then, in many instances, as a consumer he is entitled to seek redress by filing a claim before the Consumer Claims Tribunal. Following such a route would invariably mean that the passenger will probably, at some stage, have to refer his complaint to the Director of Consumer Affairs. In such circumstances, it would be more practical if the Director of Consumer Affairs is designated as the competent regulatory authority responsible for ensuring compliance with the EC Denied Boarding Regulation. Such a measure would enable the Director of Consumer Affairs to intervene directly in cases involving an alleged breach of non-compliance with the EC Regulation, rather than simply

---

legislator in the case of the former EC regulations on denied boarding, choose to enact regulations based on the then existing EC regulations.

83   The national legislation in place relates to the designation of the national competent regulatory authority and the exercise of its enforcement powers where applicable.

84   See Legal Notice 63 of 2005 entitled 'Civil Aviation (Denied Boarding Compensation and Assistance to Passengers) (Designation of Competent Authority) Regulations'.

85   Regulation 16 of the EC Regulation on Denied Boarding requires each Member State to designate a body responsible for the enforcement of the said Regulation.

86   See Legal Notice 297 of 2005 entitled 'Civil Aviation (Denied Boarding, Compensation and Assistance to Passengers) Regulations'.

87   These are the substantive provisions of the Regulation and deal respectively with denied boarding, cancellation, delay, upgrading and downgrading, the rights of persons with reduced mobility or special needs, and the obligation to inform passengers of their rights.

88   See Legal Notice 297 of 2005, regulation 4. Article 16.3 of the EC Regulation requires Member States to ensure that the sanctions laid down for infringement of the EC Regulation are 'effective, proportionate and dissuasive'. L.N. 297 of 2005 was enacted to comply with this EU requirement.

act as a mediator between the dissatisfied consumer and the operating air carrier. Moreover consumers should, where possible, have one focal point to address their complaints to rather than, as is the case at present, deal with two, possibly even three, different public authorities: the Director of Consumer Affairs in seeking civil redress before the Consumer Claims Tribunal, the Director of Civil Aviation in requesting the initiation of regulatory sanctions following an alleged breach of the EC Regulation and the MTA if the complaint involves a breach of the Package Travel Regulations.[89] Clearly, the correct approach should be to simplify matters for the aggrieved consumer and avoid situations where the consumer has to determine which regulatory authority is best suited to address his complaint or worse deal with various authorities on the same issue.

One direct intervention by the EU Commission, that may serve partially to address the lack of a single focal point insofar as the handling of consumer issues in the travel and tourism is concerned, was the commencement of operations in September 2007 of the European Consumer Centre of Malta ('Ecc-net').[90] Though this office does not have any enforcement powers at law and is not exclusively focused on tourism or travel issues, it can serve as a useful focal point to assist consumers in resolving disputes they may have relating to travel or tourism services, irrespective of the nature of the issue and whether the issue in question involves one or more regulatory authorities.

The Sale of Consumer Goods

One of the most important measures in the context of consumer protection introduced into Maltese law as a direct result of the EU consumer *acquis*, is the amendment to the Consumer Affairs Act whereby Part VIII entitled 'Sale of Goods to Consumers' was added to that Act.[91] Until these amendments sale of goods to consumers was regulated in accordance with the general provisions under the Civil Code.[92] The need to review the regime dealing with the sale of goods to consumers was discussed at some length in the 1991 White Paper. Among the changes proposed in that paper was an amendment to the Civil Code to lengthen

---

89   For a further discussion on this point see also S. Grech, *Consumers' Rights in the Travel and Tourism Industry*, Law Thesis University of Malta (2006), p. 131 onwards.

90   ECC-net Malta was established on the 10 September 2007 and shares an office with the Ghaqda tal-Konsumaturi. At this juncture it is still too early to comment on the effectiveness of this new office, however with adequate and continued publicity this office should have a pivotal role in assisting consumers in seeking information about their rights.

91   See Consumer Affairs Act, Articles 72–93. These provisions were enacted under Act XXVI of 2000.

92   See Civil Code Title VI of Sale, more specifically Articles 1378–1432 and 1433–1439 which deal respectively with the obligations of the seller and of the buyer.

the period of forfeiture when the buyer of a product with a latent defect could initiate court proceedings, from one month to six months.[93] This amendment was enacted in 1994 together with the legislation enacting the Consumer Affairs Act.[94] Interestingly the 1991 White Paper also proposed changes to the law to deal with after-sales services and the prohibition of clauses attempting to reduce the legal warranty established by law. Significantly, this was at a time when the EU was still some way off in the issuance of a directive on the sale of goods to consumers.[95]

The enactment of Part VIII entitled 'Sale of Goods to Consumers'[96] reflects the provisions of the Sale of Consumer Goods Directive with, however, certain notable variations which go beyond the minimum requirements of this Directive or else include measures which are not dealt with under the Directive. The transposition of this Directive reflects one of the few instances where the Maltese legislator, in implementing the EU consumer *acquis*, opted to include measures giving consumers more extensive protection. The main innovations introduced as a result of the transposition of the requirements of the Directive relate to the introduction of the concept of 'conformity with the contract'[97] which goes beyond the notion of liability for latent defects under the Civil Code,[98] and the inclusion of new remedies in addition to those which exist under the Civil Code namely the legal right to ask for a replacement of the good which is not in conformity with the contract or else to have it repaired free of charge.[99]

In line with the Directive, Part VIII of the Consumer Affairs Act also regulates what is described as a 'commercial guarantee', namely a voluntary undertaking given by the trader or producer of the goods to compensate, replace, repair or handle the goods if these do not meet the specifications that the trader or producer as the case may be, voluntarily gives to the consumer.[100] The applicable provisions under the Act go beyond the minimum requirements of the Directive, by requiring more detailed information,[101] stipulating additional rights to protect those consumers who are given such a guarantee.[102] The Consumer Affairs Act further provides that a consumer may institute civil proceedings requiring the person responsible for

---

93   See 1991 White Paper, pp. 18–20.
94   See Act XXVIII of 1994, Article 45. This amendment came into force on 23 January
      1996.
95   The Sale of Goods to Consumers Directive was enacted on 25 May 1999.
96   See Consumer Affairs Act, Articles 72–93.
97   *Ibid.*, Article 73. This Article closely reflects Article 2 of the Directive.
98   See Civil Code, Article 1424 onwards.
99   See Consumer Affairs Act, Article 74.
100   *Ibid.*, Article 72(1) interpretation of the term 'commercial guarantee'.
101   See Sale of Consumer Goods Directive, Article 6 and Consumer Affairs Act, Articles
      82–90.
102   These include provisions whereby the guarantor of the commercial guarantee cannot
      ask the consumer for any fee unless this is expressly stated in the guarantee, and
      that the guarantor is responsible for the cost of carriage in the performance of the
      guarantee unless the contrary is stated in the guarantee.

the execution of the guarantee[103] to take such remedial action as may be necessary to observe the terms of the guarantee. In doing so the court may order that person to pay a sum not exceeding 50 Maltese liri for each day of default in failing to comply with any court order requiring performance of his obligations under the guarantee.[104]

One measure that is not specifically dealt with under the Directive, but is of considerable importance, is the requirement introduced with the provisions amending the Consumer Affairs Act implementing the Directive, whereby replacement parts or appropriate repair service 'must be available for a reasonable time from the date of the delivery of the goods by the trader to the consumer'.[105] A trader can, however, release himself from such a requirement if he expressly warns the consumer in writing before the contract to purchase the goods is entered into, that he does not supply replacement parts or provide repair service. Regrettably this provision does not go far enough in dealing with what in Malta is historically an 'old' outstanding concern for many consumers, namely the quality of and failure to provide adequate after-sales services. Apart from the possibility that under the present norms a trader can easily avoid any responsibility by simply informing the consumer that he does not provide such services, the failure to define precise periods during which replacement parts and after-sales services are to be provided gives room to conflicting interpretations as to what constitutes a 'reasonable time'. Even the civil sanction of incurring a maximum of 50 Maltese liri for each day of non-compliance in cases involving a costly product such as a car may be inadequate to compensate the consumer. In Malta, perhaps even more than in most other Member States, the issue of having in place measures regulating after-sales services is of paramount importance given that many goods are imported from abroad and that time and again many consumers have to go to considerable lengths in order to rectify matters at times even communicating directly with the producers abroad.

Tackling such an issue is understandably complex given that one must consider the nature of the goods concerned, the costs involved and the replacement parts or services required. However if there is to be a comprehensive regime to protect consumers in so far as the sale of goods is concerned, then the issue of having in place a regime dealing with after-sales services should be a top priority for the EU. One of the goals of the internal market is to promote consumer confidence in the single market. Having in place such a regime would go some way towards achieving such a goal. The continued failure to cater adequately for such a regime means that there will continue to remain a serious lacuna in the comprehensive framework to protect consumer rights. In a local context, given the probable outcry that any decisive measures by Government to regulate after-sales services

---

103 Such a person is under the Act described as a 'guarantor'. See Consumer Affairs Act, Article 72(1).
104 *Ibid.*, Article 91.
105 *Ibid.*, Article 93.

will lead to, it is highly unlikely that, in the near future, any further initiatives by the Maltese legislator will be undertaken if not prompted by an unequivocal EU requirement laying down clear consumer rights in relation to the provision of after-sales services.

Unfair Commercial Practices

The EU consumer *acquis* has been the main source in shaping Maltese consumer policy and for the enactment of various laws to curb diverse unfair commercial practices. Some of first laws enacted by the Maltese legislator in the field of consumer affairs, notably the Trade Descriptions Act and the Doorstep Contracts Act, focused on the regulation of trade practices, the former on trade practices in general and the latter on a specific practice. The bulk of existing legislation was, however, enacted in the late 1990s to implement the various directives on diverse unfair commercial practices. At the present time there is no express provision regulating unfair commercial practices generally. This lacuna under Maltese law should shortly be addressed as Parliament is currently discussing a Bill[106] to transpose the Unfair Commercial Practices Directive. Once approved, this law will serve to have in place a fairly comprehensive regime prohibiting unfair commercial practices.

Advertising and unfair terms

The main provisions implementing the Unfair Terms Directive and the Misleading and Comparative Advertising Directive are in Part VI of the Consumer Affairs Act entitled 'Unfair practices'.[107] Whereas the provisions regulating misleading and comparative advertising[108] implement, without any significant variations, the Misleading and Comparative Advertising Directive, the provisions implementing the Unfair Terms Directive go beyond the minimum requirements of that Directive.[109] Part VI also includes provisions that prohibit specific practices such as the so-called pyramid selling schemes.[110]

---

106 On 16 November 2007 the Government published Bill Number 112 amending the Consumer Affairs Act, the Commercial Code and the Doorstep Contracts Act with the main object of this Bill being the transposition of the Unfair Commercial Practices Directive.

107 Consumer Affairs Act, Articles 44–55.

108 *Ibid.*, Articles 48–50.

109 *Ibid.*, Articles 44–7.

110 *Ibid.*, Articles 51–3 which deal respectively with malpractices relating to the offering of gifts or prizes in connection with the supply of goods or services, pyramid selling schemes and misleading representations about certain other schemes such as the so-called work from home schemes.

The Unfair Terms Directive protects consumers where a contractual term has not been individually negotiated.[111] Maltese law, in contrast, applies to all contractual terms including those terms that may have been individually negotiated by the trader and the consumer.[112] The provisions under Part VI of the Consumer Affairs Act also include a black list of terms which are prohibited and therefore cannot be enforced against consumers and, as is the case with the Directive, establish the factors that are to be taken into account in determining whether a term is unfair or not.[113] Another significant difference under Maltese law, which again is intended to give wider protection to consumers than that provided for under the consumer *acquis*, is the power of the Director of Consumer Affairs to issue compliance orders requiring any person to delete or alter terms in a contract which the Director considers to be unfair to consumers, and to incorporate such terms in a contract which the Director considers necessary for the better information of consumers or for preventing a significant imbalance between the rights of and obligations of the parties provided this is to the benefit of consumers.[114] To this extent consumers are protected on two fronts, first by the fairly wide-ranging approach adopted by the legislator in that all terms which are unfair cannot be enforced against consumers, and second that the Director of Consumer Affairs can intervene to curb the use of unfair terms.[115] These measures are intended also to give maximum effect to the requirement under the Unfair Terms Directive whereby Member States are required to ensure in the interests of consumers and of competitors that 'adequate and effective means exist to prevent the continued use of unfair terms in contracts concluded with consumers by sellers or suppliers'.[116]

With regard to the existing provisions on misleading and comparative advertising,[117] Bill Number 112, currently before Parliament for discussion, proposes significant amendments to the existing provisions. In substance, in this Bill the Government is proposing that the remedies applicable where there is non-compliance with the new norms on misleading and comparative advertising will be of a purely civil nature, whereby an injured trader can seek civil damages before

---

111 Unfair Terms Directive, Article 3.1.

112 Consumer Affairs Act, Article 44(1).

113 *Ibid.*, Article 45.

114 *Ibid.*, Article 94(1)(a). See also I.Vella Galea, *Unfair Terms in Standard Form Contracts under Maltese Law*, University of Malta Law Thesis (2005), pp. 88–95.

115 The Director may also be requested by bodies such as recognised consumer associations and which, for the purposes of the Consumer Affairs Act, qualify as 'qualifying bodies' to issue a compliance order. See Consumer Affairs Act, Articles 94–101 and also Article 2 for a definition of 'qualifying body'.

116 Unfair Terms Directive, Article 7.1 paragraph 2, further requires that there should be provisions whereby persons or organisations having a legitimate interest under national law to protect consumers, may apply to the appropriate authorities to prevent the continued use of unfair terms.

117 Consumer Affairs Act, Articles 48–50.

the courts of civil jurisdiction.[118] If these amendments are approved as proposed this will signify that, in contrast with the existing situation where the Director can undertake regulatory action, if there is non-compliance with the norms on misleading or comparative advertising then the only effective intervention will be incumbent on an aggrieved competing trader to seek civil damages.[119] This proposal is of some concern. Whilst conceivably the Director of Consumer Affairs may be able to intervene in the case of misleading advertising if this is construed as being an unfair commercial practice,[120] the Director will have no regulatory role if there is a breach of the provisions regulating comparative advertising if such advertising impacts negatively on consumer behaviour. Moreover, one negative result of the fact that the Unfair Commercial Practices Directive is a maximum harmonisation directive is that Members States cannot provide more extensive protection to their consumers if the Member State wishes to extend the applicability of the revised norms on comparative and misleading advertising to instances where non-compliance influences negatively consumer behaviour.[121]

Doorstep selling

One of the first laws expressly enacted with the intention of protecting consumers was the Door-to-Door Salesmen Act in 1987.[122] The intention of the legislator was primarily to deal with certain abusive practices relating to doorstep marketing then rampant in Malta. Though Government at the time had no declared intention of joining the EU, the Doorstep Selling Directive was used as the basis to regulate doorstep selling. In doing so, the Government enacted various measures that are in still in place which went well beyond the minimum requirements under that Directive, notably a cooling off period of 15 days during which consumers can withdraw from a doorstep contract and a requirement that doorstep salespersons

---

118   See Commercial Code Cap.13 of the Laws of Malta and Bill No. 112, clauses 56–8.

119   See Bill No. 112, the amendments to the Commercial Code amending Article 37 thereof.

120   See Bill No. 112 clause 26, proposing new Articles 51B onwards.

121   See Unfair Commercial Practices Directive, Article 14 amending Article 1 of the Misleading and Comparative Advertising Directive which clearly states that the purpose of the latter Directive 'is to protect traders against misleading advertising and the unfair consequences thereof and to lay down the conditions under which comparative advertising is permitted'. Furthermore, Article 7(1) of the Misleading and Comparative Advertising Directive permits Member States to retain or adopt provisions with a view to ensuring more extensive protection with regard to misleading advertising only 'for traders and competitors'. The said directive does not allow Members States to provide more extensive protection insofar as comparative advertising is concerned.

122   Following amendments introduced in 2000, the Act was renamed the 'Doorstep Contracts Act'.

provide consumers with a cancellation form.[123] Other measures enacted include a requirement that a person, in order to act as a door-to-door seller, must be licensed as such by the Director of Consumer Affairs. If a door-to-door salesman does not have such a licence, he will be acting in breach of the law.[124] Moreover, a doorstep contract concluded with a person who is not duly licensed is, at the option of the consumer, annullable. This measure was included to enable the competent authorities effectively to curb malpractices in so far as doorstep selling is concerned, whilst giving consumers additional protection. In 2000 amendments were enacted with the dual scope of bringing the then existing legislation in line with the Directive[125] and to deal with some shortcomings that had become evident through the years following the enactment of the Act in 1987.[126]

Distance selling

Distance Selling is regulated by two sets of regulations, the Distance Selling Regulations transposing the Distance Selling Directive covering all products and services other than financial services, and the Distance Selling (Retail Financial Services) Regulations transposing the Distance Marketing of Consumer Financial Services Directive. The Distance Selling Regulations are enforced by the Director of Consumer Affairs and impose similar information and transparency requirements to the Distance Selling Directive. The Regulations provide protection to consumers with regard to inertia selling and unsolicited communications whilst prohibiting the conclusion of distance contracts with minors. The major difference between the Regulations and the Directive is that the Regulations provide for a 15 day cooling off period, which exceeds the seven day period provided for under the Directive.[127] Breach of these regulations constitutes a criminal offence.[128]

The Distance Selling (Retail Financial Services) Regulations are enforced by the Malta Financial Services Authority ('MFSA'), establish a cooling off period of 14 days, provide for protection against unsolicited services and communications and impose information requirements in respect of distance selling of financial services in line with the Distance Marketing of Consumer Financial Services

---

123 Doorstep Contracts Act, Article 8.

124 *Ibid.*, Articles 4 and 5.

125 Primarily this related to the extension of the protection under the Act to contracts negotiated away from the business premises of the seller. Previously the focus of the law was limited to contracts negotiated at the consumer's home.

126 The main change in this context was to enable consumers to cancel a doorstep contract even by word of mouth. Previously cancellation could only be effected using the cancellation form that sellers were obliged to provide to consumers. The problem was that, in some instances, such forms were not being provided and consumers were consequently unaware of their rights at law.

127 Distance Selling Regulations, regulation 6.

128 *Ibid.*, regulation 17.

Directive.[129] In the event of non-compliance with these regulations, the MFSA is empowered to impose administrative penalties.[130] The MFSA is, furthermore, empowered to issue compliance orders whereby it may order the deletion or alteration of clauses in distance contracts considered to be unfair to consumers; require the inclusion of certain terms for the better information of consumers; the taking of certain measures or the cessation from the commission of a breach of the regulations.[131] A qualified entity, including a consumer association recognised under the Consumer Affairs Act, has the right to request the MFSA to issue such an order, and if the MFSA refuses to do so such an entity has the right to request the Financial Services Tribunal to order the MFSA to issue such an order.[132]

A general clause prohibiting unfair commercial practices?

In 2000 when the Consumer Affairs Act was extensively amended in part to transpose various directives, a declaratory but unenforceable provision was included as part of a declaration of principles, stating that consumers are entitled 'to protection from unlawful or unfair trading practices'.[133] The opportunity then was not taken to go beyond such a declaration and provide for a substantive provision establishing a general norm prohibiting unfair practices, therefore leaving a lacuna in the general regulatory framework.

The need for a general clause prohibiting unfair trading practices is an imperative requisite if there is to be in place a comprehensive framework to protect consumers. One can never, in absolute terms, exclude the possibility that some unfair practice may emerge which is not expressly regulated at law and which may cause severe hardship to consumers. Time and again, in a local context, there have been instances where effectively direct regulatory intervention was not possible simply because there was no evident provision at law which could be availed of to control such a practice. Repeatedly the Maltese legislator had to react by introducing specific rules to curb such practices[134] with the consequence that the belated introduction of such laws was not always timely enough to protect those consumers who had already fallen victim to such practices.

---

129 See Distance Selling (Retail Financial Services) Regulations, regulations 5, 6 and 7.

130 *Ibid.*, regulation 25.

131 *Ibid.*, regulations 13 and 14.

132 *Ibid.*, regulation 15. Such qualified entities have similar rights under the Consumer Affairs Act.

133 Consumer Affairs Act, Article 43(2)(e).

134 Typical instances include the Door-to-Door Salesmen Act 1987, which was purposely introduced to deal with the blatantly unfair conduct of a particular doorstep selling trader and, more recently, the Timeshare Promotion Regulations 2004 enacted to deal with aggressive marketing practices by marketing people employed by certain timeshare businesses.

The need for regulatory measures to prohibit unfair commercial practices at a European level has long been recognised, even if initially the undertaking of such a project was seen as too ambitious an initiative to be taken on such a wide-ranging scale.[135] This notwithstanding, perhaps in part conditioned by the need to have a 'proper functioning of the internal market and to meet the requirement for legal certainty',[136] in May 2005 the EU enacted the Unfair Commercial Practices Directive providing for a general clause prohibiting unfair commercial practices and requiring Members States to enact the laws implementing this Directive by not later than the 12 June 2007.[137] For the purposes of assessing whether a practice is unfair, the Directive sets down two criteria: namely whether the practice is contrary to the requirements of professional diligence and if it materially distorts or is likely to materially distort the economic behaviour of the average consumer.[138]

In May 2007 Government undertook the first steps for the transposition of this Directive under Maltese law, when it published for public consultation its legislative proposals to implement the Directive.[139] This was followed, on 16 November 2007, by the publication of a Bill entitled the Consumer Affairs (Amendment) Act, incorporating most of the proposals made in the public

---

135 See G. Howells and T. Wilhelmsson, *EC Consumer Law* (Aldershot, 1997), pp. 165–6 and 186–7.

136 See Directive 2005/29/EC of the European Parliament and of the Council of 11 May 2005 concerning unfair business-to-consumer commercial practices in the internal market, preamble (5) thereof.

137 See Unfair Commercial Practices Directive, Article 19.

138 *Ibid.*, Article 5.2. Protection is also extended to the 'average member' of a group to whom the practice is directed and, in certain circumstances, such protection is extended to consumers who are considered to be vulnerable to the practice 'because of their mental or physical infirmity, age or credulity'. The use of the term 'average' and the qualifications to that term in the Directive has been widely criticised more so as the Directive is a maximum harmonisation directive which, therefore, does not permit Member States to have in place provisions which may give more protection to consumers avoiding the limitations inherent in the use of the term 'average consumer'. See also T. Wilhelmsson, 'The Informed Consumer v. the Vulnerable Consumer in European Unfair Commercial Practices Law – A Comment', in G. Howells *et al.* (eds), *The Yearbook of Consumer Law 2007* (Aldershot, 2007), pp. 211–28.

139 The public consultation was undertaken by the Consumer and Competition Division within the Ministry for Competition and Communications and was initiated on 10 May 2007. The documentation included a brief summary on the measures being proposed and a Bill proposing amendments to the various existing laws including the Consumer Affairs Act and the Commercial Code and the enactment of two new laws entitled respectively the Unfair Commercial Practices Act and the Product Liability Act. Regrettably, there was scarce public debate on the proposed amendments even if responses were made by different lobby groups and individuals to the proposed amendments.

consultation issued in May.[140] The Bill substantially amends the Consumer Affairs
Act, including a specific part implementing the Unfair Commercial Practices
Directive that transposes the measures in that Directive.[141] Other salient measures
include the establishment of a regime of administrative fines,[142] a new adjudicative
tribunal – the Consumer Affairs Appeals Board – to hear and determine appeals
from regulatory decisions taken by the Director of Consumer Affairs,[143] a new
section on illicit schemes[144] and amendments to the Commercial Code whereby
the existing provisions on misleading and comparative advertising are removed
from the Consumer Affairs Act and instead new provisions on advertising inserted
in the Commercial Code.[145] These amendments, once enacted, should overall
be a welcome measure in protecting consumers since they provide for various
important measures, notably the prohibition of unfair commercial practices
in general, thereby addressing a long outstanding lacuna in Maltese law given
that currently there is no provision prohibiting unfair commercial practices not
specifically regulated under any of the various consumer laws enacted to date
dealing with particular commercial practices.

Consumer Credit

Consumer Credit is one of the more recent areas of Maltese consumer law with
the Consumer Credit Regulations being enacted in 2005.[146] Until the enactment
of these regulations, consumer credit was never really given the importance
that it warranted. Indeed, to some extent consumer credit still does not feature
as prominently as it should in the priorities of Government consumer protection
policies. To date Government has failed to appoint specialised public officers
within the office of the Director of Consumer Affairs to deal exclusively with
consumer credit related issues and consumer credit remains one area in relation to

---

140 Important changes from what was proposed in May is the inclusion of the provisions
      regulating unfair commercial practices as part of the Consumer Affairs Act rather
      than under a separate new law, and the extension of the remit of the Appeals Board as
      proposed from one limited to decisions taken relating to unfair commercial practices
      to a wider remit that encompasses regulatory decisions taken on consumer laws
      enforced by the Director of Consumer Affairs.
141 Bill No. 112 of 2007, clause 26 which proposes the inclusion of new Articles 51A to
      51J.
142 *Ibid.*, clause 47 which proposes the inclusion of a new Article 106A on administrative
      fines.
143 *Ibid.*, clause 52 which amends the Consumer Affairs Act by including a new Part XII
      entitled 'Consumer Affairs Appeals Board.
144 *Ibid.*, clauses 27 to 33.
145 *Ibid.*, clauses 56 to 58.
146 Consumer Credit Regulations were enacted as per Legal Notice 84 of 2005, with the
      Regulations coming completely into force on 1 October 2005.

which minimal regulatory activity has been undertaken.[147] One can go as far as to say that, until a few years ago, consumer credit was not even perceived as a prime consumer problem area necessitating some form of active regulatory supervision. Even the 1991 White Paper barely mentioned consumer credit and the need to regulate such a sensitive area.

The Consumer Credit Directive, if anything, has had the merit of ensuring that the Maltese legislator enacts laws to provide some minimal protection to consumers entering into credit agreements. The Consumer Credit Regulations, in substance, do not go beyond the implementation of the minimum requirements of the Directive, other than with the significant exception of home loan agreements. In this context, the Regulations require a creditor to provide the consumer with general pre-contractual information together with a completed personalised standard information sheet in accordance with the format established in the Regulations. The creditor is also required to abide with certain requirements in relation to home loan agreements, notably that of providing a clear description of the security being provided to the creditor, a clear indication of the costs that the consumer has to pay if there is a breach of his contractual obligations and a clear statement of any fees payable in respect of an application for such a loan, the valuation of the security provided and the costs of legal services payable to the creditor.[148]

One issue which impacts significantly on the effectiveness of these Regulations is that the legislator opted to give the responsibility of administering these regulations to the Director of Consumer Affairs without, at the same time, ensuring that his office is adequately staffed to undertake such a task. At present, the Director has no in-house expertise to monitor effectively and ensure compliance with these Regulations. This has, to some degree, impacted negatively on the effectiveness of the Regulations as a tool to provide some protection to consumers in what is a fairly complex branch of consumer law. A better option would have been to designate the MFSA as the competent regulatory authority. The MFSA is much better resourced to ensure compliance with these Regulations, given its long standing regulatory role and in-house expertise in the banking and financial credit sectors. The MFSA is responsible at law for the supervision of credit institutions, the protection of the general interests and legitimate expectations of consumers of financial services, and the monitoring of the working and enforcement of laws that directly or indirectly affect consumers of financial services, whereas the office

---

147 The main initiatives undertaken to date were the publication of a series of information leaflets and the organisation, in 2007, of a conference on consumer credit.

148 Consumer Credit Regulations, regulation 5. See also the Second and Third Schedules to the Regulations which respectively establish the general information on credit for home loans to be provided to the consumer, and the information to be presented in the Standardised Information Sheet that creditors are required to provide to consumers taking home loans.

of the Director is expected to deal with a myriad of consumer issues of which consumer credit is just one more area of responsibility.[149]

Though legally the MFSA does not have a remit to intervene directly in consumer credit issues, the fact that the MFSA is responsible for monitoring and licensing banks and other credit institutions does give the MFSA an effective tool in regulating the conduct of such entities in relation to consumer credit issues. Logically it makes more sense to have the MFSA assume the mantle of supervising compliance with the Consumer Credit Regulations. It is suggested that the legislator should actively re-examine the roles of the Director of Consumer Affairs and of the MFSA in so far as consumer credit is concerned. The guiding criteria should be to identify and empower that public authority that has the required expertise and resources to ensure effective compliance with the Consumer Credit Regulations. In the present circumstances the MFSA effectively is in a much better position to undertake this mandate. Delay in addressing this administrative shortcoming will only prolong an unacceptable regulatory situation where the current competent regulatory authority is not adequately equipped to ensure compliance with the applicable regulations.

The Injunctions Directive

The importance of having effective procedures to protect the interests of consumers, whether collectively or individually, has always been a consideration in the consumer policies adopted by the Maltese authorities, with a mix of public and private law enforcement measures being introduced through the years. Unfortunately, there has not always been the desired level of discussion on this practical aspect of consumer affairs. What little discussion that there has been, has always tended to focus on substantive law issues and scarce attention has been given to procedural law issues. This, however, has not deterred the Maltese legislator from taking various interesting measures aimed at having in place effective processes to protect the consumer interest, particularly in enhancing the role of consumer associations.[150] It is in this context that the implementation of the Injunctions Directive must be considered.

One of the first laws specifically targeted at consumer protection – the Consumer Protection Act of 1981[151] – exclusively dealt with the protection of consumer

---

149 See Malta Financial Services Authority Act, Article 4. The Minister responsible for finance can extend the remit of the MFSA to other areas of financial activities or services as he may deem appropriate.

150 See also Micallef, 'Making Consumer Redress a Reality': 441–51.

151 This Act was subsequently repealed by Act XXVIII of 1994. The measures therein included were improved upon following the enactment of Part IV of the Consumer Affairs Act in 1994, which paved the way for more tangible rights in favour of consumer associations.

associations when making public statements in good faith. Subsequent legislative measures were enacted with the purpose of promoting a pro-active role for consumer associations, culminating in the measures adopted when the Consumer Affairs Act was originally enacted in 1994 whereby recognised consumer associations[152] were given the right to make complaints to the competent enforcement authorities and to participate in the prosecution of any offences subsequent to such complaints.[153] Other procedural measures, as part of a strategy to have in place an effective regulatory regime, included the introduction of a Consumer Claims Tribunal as an alternative means of adjudicating consumer versus trader disputes involving relatively small pecuniary values and the introduction of enforcement tools to enable the Director of Consumer Affairs to ensure compliance with consumer laws falling under his remit. These tools include the faculty to issue public warning statements,[154] to require undertakings in writing from traders acting in breach of certain consumer laws[155] and to request the issue of compensation orders.[156] All these enforcement tools remain in place even if, in practice, there has been very limited recourse to them as a means of protecting consumers and ensuring compliance with the law.[157]

The Injunctions Directive is unique amongst the various consumer protection directives enacted by the EU since it focuses exclusively on procedure, requiring Member States to have in place laws that enable the competent consumer authorities and consumer groups to request the issue of injunction orders to protect the collective interests of consumers. This EU requirement, in turn, provided

---

152 Consumer associations that fulfil certain requirements under the Consumer Affairs Act can apply to be recognised as 'registered consumer associations'. Such associations are then entitled to certain rights at law. See Consumer Affairs Act, Part IV.

153 See Consumer Affairs Act, Part III. Recognised consumer associations are also granted rights under the Trade Descriptions Act and the Competition Act. See Micallef, 'Making Consumer Redress a Reality': at 441 onwards.

154 The Consumer Affairs Act, Article 8, empowers the Director of Consumer Affairs, with the concurrence of the Consumer Affairs Council, to issue public warning statements about goods or services that are unsatisfactory. In doing so the Director is exempt from liability at law provided such statements are made in good faith.

155 The Consumer Affairs Act, Article 12, gives the Director of Consumer Affairs the faculty of requiring a written undertaking from a trader whereby the latter agrees to desist from any abusive conduct described in the undertaking under such conditions as the Director may impose.

156 The Director, in the conduct of a prosecution for a breach of a law that he administers, may of his initiative or at the request of a consumer request the court to issue a compensation order in favour of the aggrieved consumer who has been adversely affected as a result of the illegal act or omission of the trader concerned. See Consumer Affairs Act, Article 14.

157 For example, though the faculty to request compensation orders has been in place since 1996, no requests, whether by the Director of Consumer Affairs or by aggrieved consumers, have ever been made for the issue of such orders.

the Maltese legislator with a golden opportunity to improve upon the various enforcement tools available. To some degree this opportunity was availed of by the Maltese legislator even if *per se* implementation of the Injunctions Directive has been undertaken in a somewhat particular and disjointed fashion.

Rather than enacting a single law introducing a uniform procedure, different laws have been enacted in order to transpose this Directive.[158] This route was taken primarily because the laws transposing the directives listed in the Annex to the Injunctions Directive are enforced by different public regulatory sectoral authorities thereby leading to a situation where the legislator opted to enact separate laws to transpose into Maltese law the requirements of the Injunctions Directive, giving rise to different processes administered by different authorities[159] and subject to review by different adjudicative tribunals.[160] This is hardly the best of solutions to guarantee uniformity of procedure in what is, after all, a relatively novel means of safeguarding consumer rights in Malta.

The first law enacted to implement the Injunctions Directive was Act XXVI of 2000, which amended the Consumer Affairs Act, adding a new Part IX entitled 'Compliance Orders'.[161] The injunctions procedure under Part IX applies only to those laws that implement the directives listed in the Annex to the Injunctions Directive, which laws form part of the Consumer Affairs Act,[162] or are made

---

158 See also EC 'Consumer Law Compendium – Comparative Analysis', December 2006, prepared for the European Commission at pp. 586–8 and 606, available at: http.//ec.europa.eu/consumers/cons_int/safe_shop/acquis/comp_analysis_en.pdf.

159 These authorities include: the Director of Consumer Affairs who enforces the Consumer Affairs Act and all the regulations made thereunder including notably the Distance Selling Regulation, the Price Indication Regulations and the Consumer Credit Regulations; the MFSA which enforces the Distance Selling (Retail Financial Services) Regulations; the MTA which enforces the Package Travel Regulations and the Time Share Regulations; the Malta Broadcasting Authority which enforces the provisions of the Broadcasting Act which transpose the Television without Frontiers Directive); and the Malta Communications Authority which enforces the E-Commerce Regulations.

160 These include the Court of Magistrates under the Consumer Affairs Act and under the Injunctions for the Protection of the Interests of Consumers (Package Travel and Protection of Buyers in Contracts for Time Sharing of Immovable Property) Regulations, 2006, the Financial Services Tribunal under the Distance Selling (Retail Financial Services) Regulations, 2005, the Court of Appeal under the Advertising, Sponsorship and Teleshopping (Protection of Consumers' Interest) (Television Broadcasting Injunction) Order, 2005, and the Communications Appeals Board under the E-Commerce Regulations.

161 The Maltese legislator in all instances when implementing the Injunctions Directives choose to use the term 'compliance order' to describe injunctions orders.

162 These include the Unfair Terms Directive and Misleading and Comparative Advertising Directive implemented under Part VI of the Act and the Sale of Consumer Goods Directive implemented under Part VIII of the Act.

by regulations under the aforesaid Act,[163] or else are laws in relation to which the Minister responsible for consumer affairs has issued an order declaring that Part IX applies thereto.[164] The issuance of compliance orders under Part IX is the responsibility of the Director of Consumer Affairs. Until the enactment of these amendments to the Consumer Affairs Act in 2000, the Director of Consumer Affairs did not have regulatory tools, other than initiating court proceedings, which effectively empowered him to prohibit any practices that were or might be harmful to consumers. Hence, the addition of Part XI to the Consumer Affairs Act to some extent rectified this situation.[165]

What is noteworthy is that in the exercise of his powers to issue such orders, the Director of Consumer Affairs is not restricted to the issuance of orders requiring the cessation or prohibition of any infringement of the laws that he enforces. The Director also has the authority to take a pro-active role in that he may, in the context of the use of unfair terms, require the incorporation of terms in a consumer contract if he considers such a measure to be 'necessary for the better information of consumers, or for preventing a significant imbalance between the rights and obligations of the parties, and this to the benefit of consumers'.[166] This faculty of empowering the Director to require the taking of corrective measures, rather than simply ordering a person to desist from infringing the law, is also reflected in another fairly wide-ranging power whereby the Director may require a person to 'take any measures specified in the compliance order, within the time specified in the compliance order' to ensure that the obligations at law are complied with.[167] Strictly speaking, these measures go beyond what is required under the Directive since Member States are only required to ensure that injunction orders may be issued requiring the cessation or prohibition of the infringement of consumer

---

163 These regulations include the Distance Selling Regulations, the Price Indication Regulations and the Consumer Credit Regulations which respectively transpose the Distance Selling Directive, the Price Indication Directive and the Consumer Credit Directive.

164 The Minister in issuing such an order is required to consult the Consumer Affairs Council. The order must then be published in the Government Gazette. To date only the Doorstep Selling Act has been designated by the Minister in accordance with this faculty granted to the Minister. See Consumer Affairs Act, Article 94(1)(c) and (d).

165 See Consumer Affairs Act, Articles 94–101 which implement the Injunctions Directive in so far as this relates to the consumer laws enforced by the Director of Consumer Affairs. Bill No. 112 envisages procedural amendments to the existing provisions dealing with Compliance Orders and Enforcement including notably the imposition of administrative fines in case of non-compliance and the right to contest any compliance orders before a new adjudicative tribunal in lieu of having recourse to the ordinary courts as is currently the situation. See Bill No. 112 clauses 47 and 52.

166 *Ibid.*, Article 94(1)(a)(ii).

167 *Ibid.*, Article 94(1)(c). This power applies only to the Consumer Affairs Act, the regulations made thereunder or any other consumer protection law designated by the Minister responsible for consumer protection.

protection directives listed in the Annex to the Directive. It is up to the Member State to determine whether such measures should be complemented by other powers.[168] The legislator opted to introduce more wide-ranging powers, though to date such powers have not actually been used.[169]

The 2000 amendments to the Consumer Affairs Act did not fully transpose the Injunctions Directive since the measures in that Act were not applicable to all the Maltese laws transposing the directives listed in the Annex to the Injunctions Directive.[170] The Consumer Affairs Act does empower the Minister responsible for consumer affairs to extend the application of the injunctions procedure under that Act to 'any other law dealing with consumer rights and protection'.[171] The main obstacle in pursuing such a route is that all the other consumer protection laws implementing the other directives listed in the Annex to the Injunctions Directives are laws which are administered by public authorities other than the Director of Consumer Affairs who, under the Consumer Affairs Act, is the only authority empowered to issue compliance orders. Faced with this procedural difficulty, the route chosen by the legislator was to enact mirror provisions similar, but not identical, to those enacted under Part IX of the Consumer Affairs Act.

It is pertinent to note that when Part IX of the Consumer Affairs Act was enacted in 2000, there was no declared policy by the legislator of following the route of having diverse laws implementing the Injunctions Directive. If anything the wording used in Part IX of the Consumer Affairs Act indicates that the intention of the legislator in 2000 was to have one single uniform injunctions process.[172] The entry of Malta in the EU in May 2004, added more urgency to the need to implement fully the Injunctions Directive. At that time, the only measures in place implementing the Injunctions Directive were those enacted under the Consumer Affairs Act and the Injunctions Directive had still not been implemented with regard to many of the directives listed in the Annex thereto. Legislative amendments to rectify this were then taken in short order. In 2005 the Distance Selling (Retail Financial Services) Regulations were enacted. These Regulations include specific provisions implementing the Injunctions Directive

---

168 The Directive does, by way of example, state that where appropriate there should be recourse to measures such as the publication of the decision reflecting the issue of the order or the publication of a corrective statement with a view to eliminating the continuing effects of the infringement. See Injunctions Directive, Article 2.1(b).

169 Bill No. 112 proposes an even more wide-ranging role for the Director in that the Director may also require the offending party to make a corrective statement in relation to alleged non-compliance. See Bill No. 112 clause 39, amending Article 94 of the Consumer Affairs Act.

170 See Injunctions Directive, Article 1 and the list of Directives as amended in the Annex thereto.

171 See Consumer Affairs Act, Articles 94(1)(c) (d) and 100.

172 At that time the only laws transposing the directives listed in the Annex to the Injunctions Directive were all enforced by the Director of Consumer Affairs.

limited to distance selling in retail financial services.[173] These Regulations were followed by the Advertising, Sponsorship and Teleshopping (Protection of Consumers' Interest) (Television Broadcasting Injunction Order) of 2005, which extend the injunctions procedure to the national legislation implementing the Television without Frontiers Directive,[174] the E-Commerce Regulations[175] which apply the injunctions procedure to the national legislation implementing the E-Commerce Directive and, more recently, the Injunctions for the Protection of the Interests of Consumers (Package Travel and Protection of Buyers in Contracts for Time Sharing of Immovable Property) Regulations.[176] The provisions of these laws implementing the Injunctions Directive are, with some variations, similar to the provisions of Part IX of the Consumer Affairs Act. The main variations primarily relate to the public authority responsible for enforcement and to the review tribunal before which an interested party may contest a decision taken by the public authority in issuance of a compliance order.

The approach taken by the Maltese legislator in transposing the Injunctions Directive has led to a profusion of procedures and a right of review before different adjudicative tribunals depending on which public authority took the decision and under which law. This is not necessarily the best of solutions. It is perhaps premature to criticise outright the approach taken. Whilst perhaps one can understand the rationale of empowering a specialised public authority to have jurisdiction to issue compliance orders to prohibit or restrain a breach of the law it enforces, on the other hand, it is equally important to ensure that there is some degree of uniformity in application of the various processes implemented. One measure that even now should be actively considered is to have a single specialised review tribunal rather than different tribunals depending on which law is being applied. Such a measure would at least serve to ensure some consistency in the application of the injunctions procedure under Maltese consumer law. One possible solution in ensuring uniformity in the application of these various processes may lie in the proposal made in Bill Number 112 currently being discussed before Parliament that envisages the establishment of a 'Consumer Affairs Appeals Tribunal' with jurisdiction to hear and determine appeals from any decisions taken by the Director of Consumer Affairs.[177] One should actively consider extending the jurisdiction of

---

173 See Distance Selling (Retail Financial Services) Regulations, regulations 3, 15–23. The Regulations also transpose the Directive on distance marketing of consumer financial services.

174 Council Directive 89/552/EEC of 3 October 1989, on the coordination of certain provisions laid down by law, regulation or administrative action in Member States concerning the pursuit of television broadcasting activities.

175 The E-Commerce Regulations also transpose into Maltese law certain provisions of the E-Commerce Directive.

176 As per Legal Notice 282 of 2006.

177 See Bill No. 112 clause 52 which proposes the inclusion of new part entitled 'Consumer Affairs Appeals Board' to the Consumer Affairs Act.

this new tribunal to decisions taken by other regulatory authorities insofar as these decisions relate to consumer laws that are enforced by these authorities. Such a measure would have the benefit of having a single focused review tribunal dealing with most consumer law issues insofar as these relate to regulatory measures. Possibly, in order to enable this tribunal to undertake such a task with greater competency, the composition of the membership of the tribunal[178] could be varied by having a panel consisting of experts from different spheres of responsibility falling within the remit of the tribunal. The composition of the tribunal would be formed according to the nature of the each appeal lodged, with the chairman of the tribunal choosing from this panel two other members who he considers to be most knowledgeable of the issues in the dispute. This tribunal would, over time, accumulate expertise in the various consumer laws enforced by the different public authorities and fulfil the role of an effective adjudicative review body.

Sanctions

The EU, in some of the consumer protection directives that it has enacted, requires Member States to have in place penalties that are effective, proportionate and dissuasive in ensuring compliance with the national provisions applying the applicable directive. Member States are further required to ensure that 'all necessary measures' are taken to ensure that the aforesaid national provisions are enforced.[179] The existing regulatory regime under the Consumer Affairs Act does not appear to fulfil the above requirement, given that the existing sanctions available to the Director of Consumer Affairs do not appear to constitute an effective and practical deterrent. Whilst the Director does have access to various regulatory tools, non-compliance with any orders that the Director may issue is a criminal offence punishable, if found guilty, by the imposition of a fine which, in the case of a breach of a provision of the Consumer Affairs Act, cannot exceed the sum of 10,000 Maltese liri; whereas in the case of regulations[180] made under the said Act the fine cannot exceed 2,000 Maltese liri. The present maximum penalties that may ultimately be imposed are certainly not an effective deterrent for all

---

178 The Bill envisages a board composed of three members: an advocate of at least seven practice who presides and two other members 'who because of their experience, qualifications or activities are considered by the Prime Minister as able to properly assess the fairness or otherwise of commercial practices from a consumer's and a trader's perspective'. See Bill No. 112, clause 52 which proposes the addition of new Article 110A.

179 See for example Unfair Commercial Practices Directive, Article 13. Other Directives have similar if not identical Articles that in substance require Member States to have in place effective sanctions.

180 Regulations enacted under the Consumer Affairs Act include the Distance Selling Regulations, the Price Indication Regulations and the Consumer Credit Regulations.

possible infringements that may occur under the Consumer Affairs Act. Moreover the procedure of having recourse to the initiation of criminal proceedings before the competent Courts is, in many instances, characterised by lengthy proceedings that may make it difficult to ensure compliance in good time so as to minimise the harmful effects of any infringements on consumers.

Bill Number 112 currently before Parliament attempts to address some of these concerns. One of the most notable changes being proposed in this Bill is the creation of an administrative fines regime whereby administrative fines[181] may be imposed by the Director in cases of non-compliance with the provisions of the Consumer Affairs Act or of any regulations made under that Act.[182] The Bill envisages a maximum fine of 20,000 Maltese liri and/or a maximum daily fine of 100 Maltese liri. In determining the amount to be imposed in relation to a specific infringement, the Bill lays down a series of rules to guide the Director.[183] Decisions taken by the Director imposing such fines can then be contested before the proposed Consumer Affairs Appeals Tribunal.

The proposed measures introducing this new administrative fines regime are welcome and overdue. The current situation of equating non-compliance of existing consumer law provisions as criminal offences is, in most instances, an inappropriate and disproportionate measure.[184] In practice such measures have failed to ensure that there is in place an effective sanctions regime. It does not really make sense to equate all infringements of consumer law as criminal offences. One questions, for example, whether it is an equitable measure that the use of unfair term in a consumer contract, a misleading promotion that influences consumer choice or the failure to comply with information requirements in a distance selling contract should be considered as criminal offences. In such instances the more appropriate sanction is the imposition of an administrative fine, doing away with the mistaken concept that non-compliance with consumer law should invariably be equated to a criminal offence. What are of concern are the very low maximum administrative fines that can be imposed. The proposed maximum amounts are expected to be an effective deterrent for all foreseeable infringements of most extant consumer legislation. One asks whether the proposed maximum amounts will, in practice, be adequately dissuasive in all instances of non-compliance, bearing in mind that some cases may involve substantial sums whereby people will be prepared to run the risk of acting in blatant breach of their obligations at law with the knowledge that the profit to be made will excessively surpass the punitive fines laid down at law. It is suggested that the amounts of a 100,000 Maltese liri and of a maximum

---

181 Such fines would be recoverable as civil debts.

182 Bill No. 112 Article 106A being proposed under clause 47.

183 *Ibid.*, proposed Second Schedule under clause 54.

184 There are of course specific instances such as non-compliance with product safety laws or the threatening of public offices enforcing consumer laws, where sanctions of a criminal nature are more appropriate and therefore should not be substituted by sanctions of an administrative nature.

daily fine of a 1,000 Maltese liri are more realistic amounts if the legislator really intends to have in place sanctions that may serve to dissuade traders from not complying with their obligations at law.

Another positive measure in the Bill, which serves to address a lacuna in the current law, is the proposed insertion of a series of norms to guide the Director in establishing the quantum of the fine to be imposed, identifying clearly those aggravating or mitigating circumstances which justify an increase or decrease. At present there is no clear guidance as to what fine should actually be imposed. The inclusion of these rules will serve to provide some clarity and precision as to the quantum of the fine that may be imposed in any given circumstance. The enactment of a regime of administrative fines commensurate with the gravity of the infringement whereby the Director of Consumer Affairs is empowered to impose such fines subject to the right of appeal before an independent tribunal, specialised in consumer protection issues, has the benefit of immediacy of action and should be conducive to more effective compliance with any orders that the Director may issue, without compromising the right to contest both the order and the sanction imposed before an independent tribunal.

Conclusion

Has the impact of the EU been a mixed blessing on consumer policy in Malta? To answer this question I must differentiate between, on the one hand what has happened until the recent past, and on the other hand, developments in the EU of the past three years and how these augur for the future.

Examining the consumer policies and the consequential measures introduced in the past as a direct result of Malta's membership within the EU, in relation to the measures implemented until a few years ago, the EU has had a positive impact overall on Malta.[185] There are two considerations that lead me to reach this conclusion. First a substantial number of the measures introduced by Malta both before and after Malta joined the EU, would possibly either not have been implemented or else would have implemented in a much milder form, were it not that Malta, as a member of the EU, was required to transpose the EU consumer *acquis* as reflected in the various consumer protection directives. Various instances come to mind including notably the timeshare, unfair terms, distance selling and consumer credit directives whereby, consequential to their transposition into Maltese law, consumers in Malta have rights which they previously did not have.

The second consideration is that, until at least very recently, most of the EU consumer protection directives were minimum harmonisation directives. This meant that Malta could, when transposing a directive, introduce or retain measures

---

185 I expressly qualify this since the Unfair Commercial Practices Directive enacted in May 2005 marks the beginning of a new approach requiring most consumer policy directives to be maximum harmonisation directives.

that went beyond the minimum stated in the directive provided the implementing national law gave consumers more extensive protection. This happened in a few instances including, notably, with the transposition of the unfair terms and timeshare directives and, to a lesser extent, with the sale of consumer goods directive. The combination of these two considerations served to ensure that, whilst the consumer *acquis* spurred the Maltese Government to undertake measures in the sphere of consumer protection which perhaps in other circumstances it would not have readily undertaken, the consumer *acquis* also afforded the Maltese Government some flexibility in applying measures beyond the minimum required where the introduction of such measures was considered to be imperative in order to protect consumers from certain abusive practices particular to the local market.[186]

Had the EU maintained its former policy of enacting minimum harmonisation directives then my verdict would be that the impact of the EU has been an unqualified blessing on Maltese consumer policy. Developments in the past few years however strongly indicate a change in approach by the EU, from a position whereby Member States could enact measures beyond those provided in a given directive, to a new position whereby there can be no substantial variation from the measures laid down in a directive, even if such measures give consumers more rights under national law. Moreover, in evaluating this change in approach one must bear in mind that some Member States, Malta included, may actually be required to review existing laws if their laws provide consumers with more rights than those established under a maximum harmonisation directive. This leads me to re-assess my evaluation as to whether the EU has impacted positively on Maltese consumer policy.

If one considers only the Unfair Commercial Practices Directive which has been enacted in line with this new approach, Malta will probably not need to make amendments to its existing consumer laws that may actually lessen any of the rights that consumer enjoy.[187] However, what if this approach is extended to other existing directives that have been implemented under Maltese law and where, under the transposing Maltese law, consumers enjoy rights exceeding the minimum established in the directives? For example would it be beneficial to consumers if the more wide-ranging rights they enjoy in relation to the regulation of unfair terms under Maltese law had to be amended to reflect a lower degree of protection imposed because the minimum harmonisation clause in the Unfair Terms Directive is deleted or amended in accordance with the new maximum harmonisation approach.[188]

---

186 One instance is in timeshare whereby Government had to enact specific measures to curb certain marketing practices undertaken by timeshare salespersons which were irreparably harming the tourism industry in Malta.
187 Bill No. 112 which transposes this directive does not appear to detract from any existing rights at law which consumers enjoy.
188 Unfair Terms Directive, Article 8.

The EU, in taking forward a maximum harmonisation approach, contends that such an approach is necessary in order to counter the difficulties consequential to what has been described as the 'fragmentation' of EU consumer protection rules once Member States, in many extant directives, are allowed to adopt more stringent rules in their national laws to ensure a higher level of consumer protection. The EU argues that such fragmentation is of detriment to the internal market, both because it serves to discourage cross border sales as businesses incur extra costs of compliance with different national laws regulating consumer transactions, and because it undermines consumer confidence in cross-border purchases given that the laws of Member States may differ.[189] The reasoning of the EU is aptly reflected in the preamble to the Unfair Commercial Practices Directive where the EU emphasises what it describes as the 'disparities' between the laws of the Members States relating to unfair commercial practices and the 'marked differences which can generate appreciable distortions of competition and obstacles to the smooth functioning of the internal market'.[190] In an attempt to eliminate such differences the EU has embarked on a process whereby the obstacles to the internal market caused by such differences are eliminated by:

> establishing uniform rules at Community level which establish a high level of consumer protection and by clarifying certain legal concepts at Community level to the extent necessary for the proper functioning of the internal market and to meet the requirement of legal certainty.[191]

One cannot discount the concerns raised by the EU, but the question whether ultimately consumers should lose rights they may have under national law so as to ensure uniformity of consumer protection rules throughout the single market remains an important consideration. Should uniformity of rules throughout the single market prevail over more stringent national consumer protection regimes even if the former entails a lower level of protection? My view would be to go for a compromise solution that attempts to cater for the need to ensure some degree of uniformity, whilst affording Member States sufficient flexibility to deal with problems that may be specific to that Member State. This would be in line with the mixed approach suggested by the EU Commission, endeavouring, as it were, to retain the best of both worlds whereby a degree of uniformity is introduced whilst leaving some flexibility at a national level where each Member State can address circumstances that may be particular to that State.[192] In taking forward such a solution, a distinction should be drawn between substantive law and procedural law whereby the thrust in ensuring uniformity should focus on substantive law

---

189 See Green Paper on the Review of the Consumer *Acquis*, issued by the Commission on 8 February 2007.
190 Unfair Commercial Practices Directive, preamble para. (3).
191 *Ibid.*, preamble para. (5).
192 See Green Paper on the Review of the Consumer *Acquis*, p. 8.

issues whilst giving Member States more leeway on procedural law. A case in point that illustrates this and directly relates to Malta, is the power given to the Director of Consumer Affairs under Maltese law where, if an unfair term is used, a defaulting party may be required to include terms which the Director considers to be for 'the benefit of consumers' rather than simply deleting or altering the term objected to.[193]

Allowing Member States flexibility in dealing with processes underlying the application of the consumer *acquis* should, however, be accompanied by a more robust approach by the EU, giving more direction to the principles that should govern the role of the competent national regulatory authorities. To date the EU has limited itself to somewhat generic provisions requiring Member States to ensure that such authorities are composed in such a manner so as not to cast doubt on their impartiality.[194] In a national context, the office of the Director of Consumer Affairs operates as part of a government department subject to Ministerial supervision.[195] Though, in practice, there is minimal interference in day-to-day administration, the existing regulatory structure is not conducive in guaranteeing the desired level of autonomy of action in every circumstance. In an administrative set-up subject to Ministerial control, the temptation, at a political level, to interfere remains. The recent proposals by the Commission, in the context of the electronic communications regulatory framework, may indicate the way forward for similar initiatives by the Commission in the realm of consumer protection. In electronic communications the Commission is proposing that Member States be required ensure that the competent national regulatory authorities exercise their powers 'independently, impartially and transparently'.[196] Even more significant is the proposal whereby the head of a national regulatory authority can be dismissed only in given circumstances and after a public statement as to why he was dismissed. It is suggested that the Commission should actively consider similar measures *vis-à-vis* the consumer *acquis*, more so if, for the foreseeable future, the required impetus at a national level to have in place a more effective and autonomous regulatory authority remains somewhat of a forlorn hope.

---

193 Consumer Affairs Act, Article 94(1)(a).

194 See, for example, Unfair Commercial Practices Directive, Article 11.

195 The Director-General of the Consumer and Competition Division performs the functions of the Director of Consumer Affairs.

196 Commission's 2007 Reform Proposals on electronic communications issued on 13 November 2007, the amendments proposed to the Directive 2002/21/EC, Article 3 thereof.

4 The Limits of Competition: Reasserting a Role for Consumer Protection and Fair Trading Regulation in Competitive Markets

Nicola Howell[1] and Therese Wilson[2]

Introduction

In this chapter we advocate for the continued need for consumer protection and fair trading regulation, even in competitive markets. For the purposes of this paper a 'competitive market' is defined as one that has low barriers to entry and exit, with homogenous products and services and numerous suppliers. Whilst competition is an important tool for providing consumer benefits, it will not be sufficient to protect at least some consumers, particularly vulnerable, low income consumers. For this reason, we argue, setting competition as the 'end goal' and assuming that consumer protection and consumer benefits will always follow, is a flawed regulatory approach. The 'end goal' should surely be consumer protection and fair markets, and a combination of competition law and consumer protection law should be applied in order to achieve those goals.

We begin by describing the relationship between competition law and consumer protection law in the Australian regulatory context. This is demonstrated, for example, by the enactment of the Trade Practices Act 1974 (Cth) and the establishment at the time of the Trade Practices Commission, now the Australian Competition and Consumer Commission, which has regulatory responsibilities for both competition and consumer protection.

Our chapter then explores the role often accorded to consumer protection law, limiting it to intervening where there is a market failure. We argue, however,

1   Director, Centre for Credit and Consumer Law, Griffith University. The Centre for Credit and Consumer Law is funded by the Queensland Government's Consumer Credit Fund (administered by the Office of Fair Trading) and Griffith University.
2   Senior Lecturer, Griffith Law School and Member, Socio-Legal Research Centre, Griffith University. An earlier version of this chapter was presented to the International Association of Consumer Law Conference, April 2007. Thanks to the anonymous referee for very helpful comments.

that the intervention of consumer protection law is appropriate not only in the case of market failure, but also in the case of competition failure. To explain, 'competition failure' is the term we will use to describe the phenomenon that occurs where competitive markets fail consumers in ways that might not strictly be regarded as market failure. We give examples of this, including a failure to protect disadvantaged or marginalised consumers whose preferences are not seen as priorities for traders. The point is made that competition creates both winners and losers, and that whilst competition is an important tool to use in generating good consumer outcomes, it is not sufficient to protect the losers of competition – those consumers not regarded as profitable targets.

We recognise that aspects of failures that we define as 'competition failures', such as a failure to serve low income consumers, may also be attributable to factors recognised under the umbrella of market failures. This includes information asymmetry, where lenders may lack information about lending to this sector of the community.[3] However, we consider it useful to maintain the distinction between 'market' and 'competition' failures to illustrate our point that some failures seem to be regarded as grounds for intervention by the Australian government, while others do not seem to be so regarded.

The Australian consumer credit market will be presented as a case study, where low income consumers pay more for credit services than more affluent and profitable consumers, and where they may have no alternative but to access credit products which are unfair in their terms and in many respects unsafe.

In 2007, Australian government policy does not currently reflect an understanding or acknowledgement of the ways in which competitive markets might fail consumers. We argue that the role of competitive markets has been over-valued in Australian government policy, with an emphasis on removing red tape and regulatory burdens, at the risk of reducing consumer protection. There is a reluctance to impose new regulatory burdens on business in order to protect consumers, for example through the enactment of nationally consistent legislation to prohibit unfair terms in consumer contracts.

Our chapter will conclude by arguing that consumer protection law should be a priority for regulators in its own right, and that ensuring competitive markets will not always be the answer.

Relationship between Competition Law and Consumer Protection Law

In this part of the chapter, we summarise the links between competition and consumer protection. In Australia, consumer protection law and competition law came into their own in the 1970s, with the introduction of the Trade Practices Act 1974 (Cth) and the establishment of the (then) Trade Practices Commission (now

---

3   I. Ramsay, *Consumer Law and Policy: Text and Materials on Regulating Consumer Markets*, 2nd edn (Oregon, 2007), pp. 70–71.

the Australian Competition and Consumer Commission). Consumer protection law and competition law were seen as complementary, and were therefore both included within the one piece of legislation and the one regulatory agency. This complementary nature was also expressed in the object of the Act, which is described as being 'to enhance the welfare of Australians through the promotion of fair trading and competition and provision for consumer protection'.[4]

In this object, the reference to 'welfare' reflects a concept of *economic* welfare,[5] rather a broader idea of social or community welfare. According to the Dawson Review of the competition provisions of the Trade Practices Act:

> In economic terms, welfare will be enhanced by rising living standards in the form of higher incomes in real terms and an increase in consumer choice, by sustainable high economic growth, and by a lower unemployment rate. These benefits flow when human and other resources are used more efficiently to increase productivity and to maximise returns on investment. Competitive markets are the key to economic efficiency.[6]

From this perspective comes the repeated assertion that competition law and competition policy are not ends in themselves; they are simply mechanisms to achieve economic efficiency, which in turn is the vehicle for generating improved consumer (economic) welfare.[7]

There is broad agreement that competition policy and competitive markets benefit consumers by driving greater choice, lower prices and better quality from producers and suppliers. Those traders who meet the expressed preferences of consumers will do well; those who do not offer a competitive product or service will lose business. A competitive market is, for the most part, more beneficial to consumers than a monopolistic market. While some (including ourselves) might quibble with those statements as they apply to particular sectors in detail, few would disagree with these statements in broad principle.

Commentators have therefore suggested that competition law and consumer law 'should be seen as one subject not two';[8] that competition law is 'the cornerstone of consumer protection';[9] and that 'robust competition in a strong market is the primary bulwark of consumer protection'.[10] For these and other commentators,

---

4   Trade Practices Act 1974 (Cth) s. 2.
5   D. Dawson, *Review of the Competition Provisions of the Trade Practices Act* (2003), p.29.
6   *Ibid.*
7   *Ibid.*, p. 32.
8   J. Vickers, 'Economics for Consumer Policy', British Academy Keynes Lecture, 29 October 2003, p. 4.
9   J. Stuyck, 'EC Competition Law After Modernisation: More Than Ever in the Interests of Consumers', *Journal of Consumer Policy*, 28 (2005): 1–30, at 27.
10   T. Muris, *The Federal Trade Commission and the Future Development of US Consumer Protection Policy*, George Mason Law and Economics Research Paper No. 04–19 (2004), p. 4; available at: http://ssrn.com/abstract=545182.

competition law and consumer law are closely related, even intertwined, in their goals, objectives and outcomes.

For example, Neil Averitt and Robert Lande described the relationship in the following way: competition law and policy ensures that 'the marketplace remains competitive, so that a meaningful range of options is made available to consumers',[11] and consumer laws are designed to 'ensure that consumers can choose effectively from among those options with their critical faculties unimpaired by such violations as deception or the withholding of material information'.[12] On this analysis, grounds for intervention in markets should be restricted to the cases where there is anti-competitive conduct (competition law is the solution) and/or market failure (consumer protection law is the solution).

In this chapter, we will not focus on the detail of interventions to prevent anti-competitive conduct; this is the subject of many other texts. Instead, in the next part of our paper, we focus on consumer protection interventions to overcome market failures and what we have termed 'competition failures'.

Market Failures, Information Asymmetry and Consumer Literacy

From a theoretical, economic perspective, consumer protection legislation is seen as an appropriate response to 'market failure', that is, to situations where the competitive market process is not working as it should. For example, Chris Field suggests that:

> ... [consumer protection] regulation is needed, and justified, where: (1) there is a demonstrable market failure (for example, what economists refer to as information asymmetries); (2) the regulation proposed is directed to addressing the market failure; (3) the regulation is the least restrictive way of achieving its remedial purpose; and (4) the regulation does not create more costs than then benefits that it seeks to achieve.[13]

The main market failure for consumers is often seen to be 'information asymmetry', when consumers do not have accurate, sufficient, or effective information to make an effective and informed choice between products/services and suppliers, should they wish to take up that opportunity.[14] Consumer protection regulation to address this market failure includes prohibitions against misleading or deceptive

---

11   N. Averitt and R. Lande, 'Consumer sovereignty: A unified theory of antitrust and consumer protection law', *Antitrust Law Journal*, 65 (1997): 713–56, at 713.

12   *Ibid.*, 713–4.

13   C. Field, 'Competition, Consumer Protection and Social Justice – Providing a Consumer's Voice', *Australian Business Law Review*, 33(1) (2005): 51–4, at 52.

14   Averitt and Lande: 717: 'We ask that consumers be enabled to make rational choices to the extent that they wish to concentrate on doing so.'

conduct;[15] as well as specific obligations to disclose certain information, often in a particular form and at a particular time. Australian examples include requirements for financial services licensees to provide written financial services guides; product disclosure statements; statements of advice to retail clients;[16] and requirements for credit providers to provide pre-contractual statements, information statements and written contracts that contain specified information.[17]

This focus on reducing information asymmetries through mandated information disclosure dovetails neatly with the project to develop empowered and financially literate consumers. Governments in Australia now devote significant resources to financial literacy and consumer education. In 2005, the Commonwealth Government established the Financial Literacy Foundation, with a remit to 'give all Australians the opportunity to better manage their money'.[18]

The Foundation's activities include raising awareness through media campaigns, working with education authorities to have financial literacy included in the school curriculum, research (a national study to set a benchmark of financial literacy), working with employers to increase access to financial literacy in the workplace and developing a web-based catalogue of financial literacy projects and resources.[19]

The joint Australian/State/Territory Ministerial Council on Consumer Affairs also has an education strategy, with two current projects: financial and consumer education for young people and a National indigenous consumer strategy, launched in 2005.[20] And individual government agencies at all levels have also developed their own programs and initiatives.[21] However, this commitment to financial

---

15 See, for example, Trade Practices Act 1974 (Cth), ss. 52, 53.

16 See, for example, Corporations Act 2001 (Cth), ss. 941A, 941B (Financial Services Guide); s. 946A (Statement of Advice); ss. 1012A, 1012B, 1012C (Product Disclosure Statement).

17 See, for example, Consumer Credit Code ss. 12, 15, 16 (written contract document); s. 14 (precontractual disclosure).

18 See http://www.understandingmoney.gov.au/Content/Consumer/AboutUs.aspx, viewed 31.1.2007.

19 See http://www.understandingmoney.gov.au/Content/Consumer/AboutUs.aspx, viewed 29.8.2007.

20 Ministerial Council on Consumer Affairs Strategic Agenda September 2005, items 3.1 and 3.2, see http://www.consumer.gov.au/html/mcca_projects.htm#P268_12056; viewed 31.1.2007.

21 See, for example, the Australian Securities and Investments Commission's work on financial literacy (http://www.fido.gov.au/fido/fido.nsf/byheadline/Financial+lit eracy?openDocument) and consumer education: http://www.fido.gov.au/fido/fido. nsf/byheadline/Consumer+education+strategy+2001+to+2004?openDocument); the Australian Competition and Consumer Commission'sScamwatch: (http://www. scamwatch.gov.au/content/index.phtml/itemId/693900); ConsumerAffairs Victoria research papers on Consumer Education in Schools, Information Provision and Education Strategies, and Social Marketing and Consumer Policy available at: (http://

literacy and consumer education is not without its critics[22] and we discuss some of the limitations of financial literacy and consumer education initiatives below.

The discussion above relates to demand-side information problems. There are also information asymmetry problems on the supply side, where consumers have more information than traders about factors relevant to cost or risk. For example, consumers normally know more about their personal factors relevant to credit risk or insurance risk than do credit providers or insurers.

Asymmetric information is not the only example of a market failure that might justify intervention. Others include negative externalities, where the true costs of products or services are not reflected in their price (for example environmental costs). Although negative externalities are treated as market failures in economic theory, in practice, it seems that these externalities are rarely factored into the pricing of goods and services.

Other market failures include situations involving public goods (unlikely to be provided by the market) and free riders; 'lemons'; and transaction and switching costs (a subset of the information asymmetry problem).[23] Rhonda Smith gives an example of this latter market failure in a paper published in 2000. Smith refers to litigation by the then Trade Practices Commission in the newly deregulated and highly competitive telecommunications industry. Misleading advertisements by Telstra regarding the pricing of local calls could not be deciphered by consumers because of the significant transaction and search costs:

- ... the pricing plans for the products were complex and so more search yielded little benefit
- this difficulty was compounded by the rapid rate of change in the industry – both technology and price offerings – so that data obtained was quickly outdated, sometimes before comparisons could be made
- the position was worsened by the type of sale involved. Consumers were entering into a contract and so their ability to respond to new or more accurate information in the future was reduced, at least for some time. This locked them into their current supplier and locked them away from alternative suppliers. In a competitive market, this reduced the incentive of suppliers to fully inform potential customers.[24]

---

www.consumer.vic.gov.au/CA256EB5000644CE/page/Listing-Resource-Reports+&+Gui delines?OpenDocument&1=Home~&2=~&3=~&REFUNID=~#Research,viewed 12.12.2007).

22   Consumers Federation of Australia, *Submission to the Consumer and Financial Literacy Taskforce Discussion Paper 'Australian Consumers and Money'* (2004), available   at   http://www.consumersfederation.com/documents/CFAresponse-CFLTaskforceDiscussonPaperfinal_001.pdf.

23   Averitt and Lande: 724–6.

24   R.L. Smith, 'When competition is not enough: Consumer protection', *Australian Economic Papers* (2000): 408–25, at 416.

In this case, even in the absence of misleading advertising, we suspect that consumers would have found it difficult, if not impossible, to identify the most beneficial call plan.

In this same paper, Smith also suggests that a disparity in bargaining power between consumers and traders can also be considered to be a market failure, as it leaves consumers open to exploitation.[25] She suggests that this disparity in bargaining power 'generally results from a lack of consumer choice or some incapacity on the part of the consumer'.[26]

A disparity of bargaining power is often given as a justification for consumer protection measures. However, we are not convinced that a disparity of bargaining power should strictly be considered as market failure in the economic sense. On the contrary, a disparity in bargaining power is the natural outcome of consumer transactions in the twenty-first century markets. Markets do not have a conscience; they are not interested in ideals of distributive or social justice or fairness.[27] Most of the major consumer transactions today pit an individual consumer against a large and well-resourced business, often operating at least nationally, if not globally. Even if the trader is a small business, that trader will have more experience of the transaction in question than an individual consumer. In this context, the notion of an equality of bargaining power is more illusory than real. If a disparity in bargaining power amounts to a market failure, then, almost by definition, most consumer markets in Australia would show signs of market failure.

Competition Failures

It is clear that from an economic perspective, market failures occur. In these circumstances, classical economists might concede that consumer law is an appropriate response. However, from a broader social or community welfare perspective, it is equally clear that competition and competitive markets can fail consumers. Some examples follow.

First, competitive markets, exhibiting high levels of rivalry between participants, can take advantage of confusion and, what some commentators have referred to

---

25 *Ibid.*, 408–409.

26 *Ibid.*, 409.

27 For example, a submission by the Australian Chamber of Commerce and Industry to the National Competition Policy Review criticises any suggestion that markets should take into account social equity: 'Where governments seek to achieve some social equity or other (re)distributional outcomes on the basis of 'public interest' or 'public benefit', these [should] be pursued through other policy channels, such as taxation and/or public expenditure.' *ACCI Submission to the Productivity Commission Review of National Competition Policy and Arrangements*, Australian Chamber of Commerce and Industry, (2004), p. 10, available at: http://www.pc.gov.au/inquiry/ncp/subs/sub110.pdf, viewed 14.12.2007.

as 'confusopoly'.[28] The telecommunications sector has been a key example of this problem, as highlighted above. Competitive financial services, electricity and gas markets can also exhibit similar characteristics.[29] In these markets, a prohibition of misleading or deceptive conduct will not necessarily solve consumer problems, nor will mandatory disclosure of information.

Competitive markets can also fail consumers when policy makers are too optimistic about the benefits of disclosure regulation. For example, whilst acknowledging the importance of information disclosure initiatives, Geraint Howells cautions against over-reliance on the information initiatives, highlighting the following limitations:[30]

- consumers are burdened by a lack of time, and 'it would be wrong to assume that all information was actually being read';
- information disclosure benefits middle-class consumers, and in segmented markets, any increase in standards from informed consumers is likely to have little impact on poorer consumers;
- consumers can have a lack of alternatives (real or perceived), and in this circumstance, consumers 'may rationally decide not to make use of information';
- there may be market impediments to acting on the information by switching;
- behavioural economics provides some insights into the 'irrational' responses of consumers, which suggest that the consumer who is 'reasonably well informed and reasonably observant and circumspect' is in fact the atypical consumer.

Joshua Gans also uses behavioural economics to illustrate a failing of competition. He suggests that consumers' lack of self-control and naivety will lead consumers to purchase too much of a product at a given price, and that: 'this gives rise to welfare reductions even in competitive markets and ... these things are exacerbated

---

28   This concept is referred to in Organisation for Economic Co-operation and Development, *Roundtable on Demand-side Economics for Consumer Policy, Summary Report*, Directorate for Science, Technology and Industry, Committee on Consumer Policy, DSTI/CP(2006)3/FINAL, p. 11, available at: http://www.oecd.org/dataoecd/31/46/36581073.pdf.

29   L. Sylvan, 'Activating competition: The consumer–competition interface, *Competition and Consumer Law Journal*, 12 (2004): 191–206, at 196.

30   G. Howells, 'The Potential and Limits of Consumer Empowerment by Information', *Journal of Law and Society*, 32(3) (2005): 349–70, at 356–62. See also T. Wilhelmsson, 'The Informed Consumer v. the Vulnerable Consumer in European Unfair Commercial Practices Law – A Comment', in G. Howells et al (eds) *The Yearbook of Consumer Law 2007* (Aldershot, 2007), p. 211, at pp. 214–5.

by the strength of competition.'[31] He notes: 'Competition is good at providing what consumers demand and not what they would otherwise want, so welfare may be harmed.'[32] Here, he distinguishes between what consumers demand, as demonstrated through their purchasing activity, and what they would in fact want if behavioural biases and short-comings had no impact on their decision-making. By implying that consumer demands, through their purchasing practices, are not necessarily reflective of actual wants; Gans appears to be questioning the reliance on competition as an efficient market mechanism.[33] Gans shows support for more interventionist forms of regulation that might, for example, regulate disconnection fees, automatic contract renewal and switching costs.[34] In contrast, the traditional information disclosure response would not restrict the imposition of those fees and costs, but would simply require their disclosure.

The findings of behavioural economists highlight the numerous ways in which consumer behaviour and decision making processes diverge from that expected of the 'economically rational' consumer. Under the model used by traditional economists:

> consumers who individually may not always be rationally calculating, *en masse* and in general can be modelled as if they behave rationally. Preferences are determined on the basis of maximised self-interest. And preferences in the short-term are stable; consumers approach markets with given preferences.[35]

However, studies in behavioural economics suggest the existence of a range of biases that are inconsistent with 'rational' behaviour of consumers. These biases have been summarised by the Organisation for Economic Co-operation and Development[36] as included the following:

- Behaviour and decisions can be influenced by the way in which choices are framed: 'If options are framed in terms of possible losses, risk aversion tends to dominate; if options are framed in terms of possible gains people are more likely to take up those options.'
- Some behaviours depend upon the way in which choices are framed (suggesting that consumer preferences are not stable).

---

31 J.S. Gans, '"Protecting consumers by protecting competition": Does behavioural economics support this contention?', *Competition and Consumer Law Journal*, 13 (2005): 1–11, at p. 2.

32 *Ibid.*, at p. 3.

33 *Ibid.*, at p. 10: 'While I would hesitate to say that a move away from competition would be similarly desirable, there is at least a case to be made here'.

34 *Ibid.*, at p. 11.

35 Organisation for Economic Co-operation and Development, *Roundtable on Demand-side Economics for Consumer Policy, Summary Report*, p. 13.

36 *Ibid.*, pp. 39–41.

- People find it very difficult to estimate probabilities, and have a general difficulty in assessing the risk of very low probabilities.
- People are reluctant to sell or give up a good that they already own (endowment, or status quo bias).
- In the face of many choices, people can choose not to choose, and opt out of search and comparison activities.
- The order in which options are presented can influence choice (default bias).

Space considerations prevent us from exploring and applying the findings of behavioural economics in more detail. However, these and other findings support our argument that undue reliance on disclosure to protect consumers can result in poor outcomes.

The broad insights offered by behavioural economics can provide a useful supplement to the more traditional economics/market analysis used by policy makers. However, these insights are yet to permeate consumer policy in Australia to any significant extent. The key focus of policy makers in this country continues to be on competition, information disclosure and financial literacy.

Highly competitive markets may also fail consumers by facilitating the business of rogue and fraudulent traders. As noted above, the theoretical perfectly competitive market is one that has low barriers to entry and exit, with homogenous products/services, and numerous suppliers. However, markets with low barriers to entry and exit can also attract unscrupulous operators, who may have no reputation to protect. In at least some jurisdictions in Australia, there are no licensing, registration, or accreditation requirements for credit providers and very few limits on product cost.[37] As a result, lenders (including lenders offering very high cost credit) can readily establish operations. If lenders are particularly targeting consumers excluded from mainstream finance, and who are likely to be desperate for finance, reputation concerns may not be a high priority.

The phenomena of 'reverse competition', where suppliers compete to encourage brokers or advisers to recommend their products over others, can also result in higher prices to consumers, and/or poor recommendations.[38]

---

37 The State of Queensland provides one example. Under the Consumer Credit (Queensland) Act 1994 (Qld), there are no requirements that must be met before a business seeks to provide consumer credit, although, on the application of the relevant government official, the Court can make an order prohibiting or restricting a person from providing consumer credit (s. 23). Unlike some other Australian jurisdictions, there is no ceiling on interest rates or fees and charges for consumer credit in Queensland. Office of Fair Trading, Queensland, *Managing the Cost of Consumer Credit in Queensland Discussion Paper* (2006), p. 14.

38 See, for example, J. Hunter, *Testimony before the House Committee on Financial Services Subcommittee on Housing and Community Opportunity: Title Insurance Cost and Competition*, Consumer Federation of America, pp. 4–5; available at: http://www.consumerfed.org/pdfs/Title_Insurance_Testimony042606.pdf, viewed   14.2.2007;

Finally, competitive markets can particularly fail disadvantaged or marginalised consumers, whose preferences are not seen as priorities for traders. Competition and competitive markets do not require business to provide goods or services to all consumers or to provide products or services that are unprofitable. Businesses do not compete for the custom of those who are not seen as attractive or profitable customers, and competition does not necessarily do anything to ensure that all consumers have a range of options, at appropriate pricing levels.[39] As Peter Cartwright notes, an absence of choice can result 'not from inadequate competition, but from a competitive financial services industry taking an economic decision only to offer more profitable products ...'.[40]

As we noted earlier, markets are not interested in social justice or equity, even though these matters might be important for consumers.[41] And clearly, the benefits of competitive markets are not evenly spread amongst consumers – competition creates both winners and losers.

Competition, then, is often (but not always) needed to generate good consumer outcomes, but it is not sufficient.[42] Where competition fails to benefit or protect consumers, consumer protection interventions may also be needed.

The Consumer Credit Market – A Case Study

In this part of the chapter, we will examine the consumer credit market in Australia as a case study. We will argue that that market has failed low income consumers who have not benefited from competition within it, thus demonstrating a need for consumer protection to be given priority by policy makers.

The Australian consumer credit market is generally regarded as a competitive one, at least with regard to housing and personal loans. A study published by Justin Malbon in 1999 noted of the housing and personal loans market that: 'There are a large

---

also *Call for new laws to protect against unhealthy competition*, Radio National AM transcript 29 March 2004, available at: www.abc.net.au/am/content/2004/s1076015. htm, viewed 14.2.2007.

39 In the financial services sector, this leads to the phenomena of financial exclusion – see N. Howell and T. Wilson, 'Access to consumer credit: the problem of financial exclusion in Australia and the current regulatory framework', *Macquarie Law Journal*, 5 (2005): 127–48, at 132–3.

40 P. Cartwright, *Banks, Consumers and Regulation* (Oxford, 2004), p. 212.

41 Organisation for Economic Co-operation and Development, *Roundtable on Demand-side Economics for Consumer Policy, Summary Report*, pp. 17 and 40. See also R. Smith and S. King, 'Insights into consumer risk: Building blocks for consumer protection policy' (2006), cited *ibid.*, p. 59.

42 A. Fels, 'Reflections of a former regulator on the consumer affairs scene', in Consumer Affairs Victoria, *Essays in Australian Consumer Affairs: An occasional series*, March (2005), pp. 51–7 at p. 51.

number of lenders, there is visible and aggressive advertising on interest rates and most consumers shop around for their loans before deciding to make a purchase.'[43]

Even in relation to personal loans, however, the consumer credit market in Australia has failed low income consumers in three key ways. First, there is a general lack of competition when it comes to 'unprofitable consumers', who as a result pay higher prices for products and services than more affluent and 'profitable' consumers; second, one consequence of that lack of competition is that products targeted at low income consumers in this market have been found to contain unfair contract terms, including terms as to price; and thirdly, these products are often unsafe in the sense that they can result in substantial detriment to consumers.

The losers of competition – the unprofitable consumers

Chris Field has noted that low income consumers tend to be the 'losers' of competition, given the distributional effects of markets.[44] This group is likely to grow as the income divide in Australia grows at a rate exceeding that of other OECD countries.[45]

Whilst economic growth is said to be a benefit of competition policy, that growth is of no benefit to many low income consumers. This highlights the essential nature of effective consumer law in protecting the interests of those consumers, notwithstanding the appearance of a competitive market. As Field puts it: 'The poor can never be an inconvenience to the greater good. Consumer organisations must be a voice, when others are too often silent, for a fair distribution of the great dividends that our open and free market creates.'[46] This reflects a Rawlsian approach that 'The outcomes of markets are only justified to the extent that they benefit the least-advantaged group in society in the long run'.[47]

The example that Field gives of low income consumers as 'losers' of competition is in relation to bank fees, which tend to be lower for those customers

---

43		J. Malbon, *Taking Credit: A Survey of Consumer Behaviour in the Australian Consumer Credit Market* (1999), p. 9. There was found to be substantially less competition in the credit card market and in the linked credit market where credit is offered on the purchase of goods with an interest free period.

44		Field, 'Competition, Consumer Protection and Social Justice – Providing a Consumer's Voice': 54.

45		See, for example, 'Income and Income Distribution Australia 2005–2006', released 2 August 2007, viewed 16.10.2007 at http://abs.gov.au/AUSSTATS, Australian Bureau of Statistics; S. Ziguras, 'Measuring the income divide: How does Australia compare?', (2002), viewed 16.10.2007 at: http://www.onlineopinion.com.au/view.asp?article=1868.

46		Field, 'Competition, Consumer Protection and Social Justice – Providing a Consumer's Voice': 54.

47		Ramsay, *Consumer Law and Policy: Text and Materials on Regulating Consumer Markets*, p. 34 referring to J. Rawls, *A Theory of Justice* (Cambridge Massachusetts, 1971), pp. 100–108.

with residential mortgages, but higher for those customers 'without a loan, who have low balances and have a high-volume of transactions'.[48] This seems to confirm Connolly and Hajaj's observation in their report on financial services and social exclusion in 2001, that despite the prediction of the Wallis Inquiry[49] that increased competition in the financial services market would bring about affordable financial services for all Australians, no such competition has emerged for low income consumers.[50]

The consumer credit market in Australia, which is the focus of this part of our chapter, is another example of the failure of competition to benefit low income consumers. An inability to access small, short-term loans on reasonable terms by people on low incomes is one aspect of the phenomenon described as 'financial exclusion', defined more broadly in the Australian context as: 'The lack of access by certain consumers to appropriate low cost, fair and safe financial products and services from mainstream providers.'[51]

Where people are excluded from accessing credit from 'mainstream' credit providers such as banks and credit unions in order to acquire essential household items or to meet emergency bills, they have the options of seeking credit from the not-for-profit sector through No Interest Loans Schemes (NILS) or Low Interest Loans Schemes (LILS),[52] or from the high cost, fringe credit sector.[53] Whilst NILS and LILS programs are currently offered on a relatively small scale in Australia, there is evidence that high cost fringe lending is growing rapidly[54] and that this is likely to be the primary source of small loans for people on low incomes.

The financial exclusion of low income consumers as it relates to an inability to access small, short-term credit at reasonable rates and on reasonable repayment terms, is a failure of competition. We define the term 'low income consumer' in this context flexibly enough to include those individuals who are denied access to mainstream financial services because of their income level, without stipulating what that income level must be. Current definitions used elsewhere seem to set the bar very low. For example, in seeking to qualify for a Centrelink (Australian Social Security) health care card, a single person with no dependants is regarded as an eligible, low-income earner where he or she earns a gross annual income of no

48   Field, 'Competition, Consumer Protection and Social Justice – Providing a Consumer's Voice': 54, quoting from *Banking Fees in Australia*, Reserve Bank Bulletin, April 2003.
49   S. Wallis, *Financial Systems Inquiry Final Report* ('Wallis Inquiry Report') (1996).
50   C. Connolly and K. Hajaj, *Financial Services and Social Exclusion*, Financial Services Consumer Policy Centre, University of NSW, Chifley Research Centre (2001), p. 33.
51   *A Report on Financial Exclusion in Australia, ANZ*, Chant Link and Associates (2004), p. 58.
52   For an explanation of NILS and LILS schemes in Australia, see Consumer Affairs Victoria, *The Report of the Consumer Credit Review* (2006), pp. 90–91.
53   See discussion, *ibid.*, p. 37.
54   Again, see discussion *ibid.*, p. 37; and also *Managing the Cost of Consumer Credit in Queensland Discussion Paper*, p. 12.

more than AUD$ 21,840.[55] This is also the standard adopted by National Australia bank in offering its 'Step Up Loan', a low interest loan for amounts between $800 and $3000 at a rate of 6.99 per cent per annum, offered in partnership with Good Shepherd Youth and Family Service.[56] This is likely to fall short of the income level at which consumers might resort to high cost fringe credit, for example a small quantitative study conducted in Victoria in 2002 found the average income of fringe credit borrowers to be in the vicinity of $24,000 per annum.[57]

Some indication of the income level at which people face financial stress and indebtedness (and, given the links between indebtedness and financial exclusion,[58] then impliedly financial exclusion) can be derived from statistics compiled by the Australian Bureau of Statistics in 2003 and 2004.[59] Those statistics were used to divide income levels in Australia into deciles, the lowest three deciles being comprised of people whose median disposable weekly incomes were $262 (or $13,624 per annum).

This group is described as 'low economic resources households', of which 78 per cent derive their income from government pensions and allowances. They are characterised by higher probabilities of financial distress indicators in that only 13 per cent of these households have an ability to save, compared with 37 per cent of other households; 28 per cent of these households spend more than they receive compared with 16 per cent of other households; 12 per cent of these households report going without meals compared with 2 per cent of other households; and 52 per cent report an inability to raise $2000 to meet an emergency expense compared with 9 per cent of other households.[60] This final indicator is, of course, highly indicative of financial exclusion.

Whilst those in the 'low economic resources households' group would have to be regarded as low-income consumers for the purposes of this chapter the point needs to be made that these income levels set the bar low, and would not accommodate all of those who have been found to turn to alternative credit providers to meet their credit needs due to a lack of access to mainstream credit providers.[61] There is therefore a 'gap' in the market in relation to which there is currently not even an attempt to provide alternative forms of credit to exploitative fringe credit.

---

55   Centrelink, http://www.centrelink.gov.au/internet/internet.nsf/payments/conc_cards_ iat.htm#qualify, viewed 13.12.2006.
56   National Australia Bank, available at: http://www.national.com.au/About_ Us/0,,82040,00.html, viewed 13.12.2006.
57   D. Wilson, *Payday Lending in Victoria – A Research Report* (2002), Consumer Law Centre Victoria.
58   Department of Trade and Industry (U.K.), *Fair, Clear and Competitive: the Consumer Credit Market in the 21st Century* (2003), p. 77.
59   *Australian Social Trends*, Australian Bureau of Statistics (2007).
60   Australian Bureau of Statistics 2007.
61   Wilson, *Payday Lending in Victoria – A Research Report*. Unfortunately there has been no more recent or more comprehensive quantitative study of fringe credit borrowers in Australia.

The growth in the fringe credit market has been linked to a failure on the part of mainstream credit providers such as banks to serve the needs of low income consumers.[62] This failure is no doubt due to perceptions of risk and lack of profitability in this market due to the costs of providing small personal loans. Earlier in this decade in Australia we have seen closures of banks in low income areas and banks trying to attract and retain a 'more profitable' group of customers.[63] Iain Ramsay's observations in relation to banks in Canada seem equally apt in the Australian context:

> There is evidence that banks, notwithstanding their public relations efforts, are not strongly committed to cultivating lower income clients or branches which serve lower income areas which do not generate sufficient profits in this age of shareholder-driven capitalism.[64]

Some Australian banks have certainly embraced the concept of corporate social responsibility, extending to meeting the credit needs of low income consumers, more readily since a report by the Parliamentary Joint Committee on Corporations and Financial Services in 2004, which stated amongst other things that: 'the Government has an obligation to intervene should the market fail to look after the needs of consumers especially in the area of access to banking and financial services'.[65]

That same report also recommended that the Australian Department of Treasury consider the enactment of legislation such as the Community Reinvestment Act 1975 (USA), which effectively links banking licences to investment in and service provision to low and moderate income communities, in the event that Australian banks did not meet their social obligations on a voluntary basis.[66]

Following this there has been support for NILS programs by both Westpac[67] and National Australia Bank,[68] and LILS programs introduced by both ANZ[69]

---

62   Ministerial Council on Consumer Affairs, *Long Term Regulation of Fringe Credit Providers Discussion Paper* (2003), p. 5.
63   Connolly and Hajaj, *Financial Services and Social Exclusion*, pp. 13 and 16.
64   I. Ramsay, *Access to Credit in the Alternative Consumer Credit Market* (British Columbia, 2000), p. 5.
65   Parliamentary Joint Committee on Corporations and Financial Services, *Money Matters in the Bush: Inquiry into the Level of Banking and Financial Services in Rural, Regional and Remote Areas of Australia* (2004), p. 307.
66   *Ibid.*, p. 304. To date, there has been no Australian government response to this report, nor its recommendations.
67   *Pressing On: 2004 Social Impact Report*, Westpac (2004).
68   National Australia Bank, available at: http://www.national.com.au/About_Us/0,,81306,,00.html, viewed 13.12.2006. In April 2006 NAB announced a $30 million commitment over 3 years to both NILS and LILS programs.
69   ANZ (2006) available at: http://www.anz.com/aus/values/community/progress_loans.asp, viewed 13.12.2006.

and National Australia Bank[70] in partnership with community organisations. Unfortunately, these schemes currently operate on a small scale and primarily in the state of Victoria.[71] This leaves low income consumers, seeking small loans to acquire essential household items or to meet emergency bills, in a situation where they are left with no choice but to pay exorbitant fees[72] for credit, with the perverse result that those consumers are paying more for credit services than more affluent consumers. Ramsay notes that: 'individuals are paying too much for services in these markets compared to consumers in middle income markets and that this is unfair.'[73]

Within the fringe credit market itself there seems to be no incentive to compete for business by offering reasonable rates. Low income consumers are in poor bargaining positions, and, in any event, the fringe credit industry has submitted that it is unable to operate at what more affluent consumers might regard as reasonable rates, due to its members' own operating costs and the nature of small amount lending which lacks economies of scale.[74] It may be that the fringe credit industry is simply not one that can be conducted both profitably and justly. There is a clear case for regulatory intervention in this market to protect low income consumers, by encouraging and facilitating non-exploitative lending to meet the demand for small loans.

Despite an obvious market, competition has failed to provide low-income consumers with short-term credit at rates comparable to those for more affluent consumers. Low-income consumers have identified the sort of financial product they require. It is a matter of social equity, that it is provided to them at a fair and just price.[75]

Unfair contract terms

As stated above, a low income consumer in need of small amount, short-term credit is not in a strong bargaining position. Such a consumer may fall prey to

---

70 National Australia Bank, available at: http://www.national.com.au/About_ Us/0,,82040,00.html, viewed 13.12.2006.

71 Consumer Affairs Victoria, *The Report of the Consumer Credit Review*, Office of Fair Trading, Queensland, *Managing the Cost of Consumer Credit in Queensland Discussion Paper.*

72 When converted to annual percentage rates the fees charged on payday loans, a form of fringe credit, can range from 235 per cent to 1300 per cent or more per annum. See *Payday Lending – A Report to the Minister of Fair Trading*, Office of Fair Trading, Queensland (2000) and *Submission to Office of Fair Trading, Queensland: Managing the cost of consumer credit in Queensland, discussion paper*, Centre for Credit and Consumer Law (2006).

73 Ramsay, *Access to Credit in the Alternative Consumer Credit Market*, p. 20.

74 Consumer Affairs Victoria, *The Report of the Consumer Credit Review*, p. 108.

75 Wilson, *Payday Lending in Victoria – A Research Report*, p. 82.

unfair contract terms. An example of such a term given in the recent Victorian Credit Review was:

> As continuing security for the payment of all debts, liabilities and obligations of the borrower to [credit provider], the applicant grants a security interest to and in favour of [credit provider] in all of my present or after acquired personal property and proceeds there from including, without limitation the vehicle as described in Schedule "A".

One study demonstrated that a low income consumer seeking credit in the fringe market will be primarily concerned with accessing loan moneys from any credit provider willing to lend to them, and will not regard himself or herself as having any choice but to borrow on the terms offered.[76] This is particularly the case given that standard form contracts are likely to be offered on a 'take it or leave it basis' and are likely to be favourable to the credit provider.[77] Noting that many contracts used in the fringe credit industry: 'contain terms and conditions heavily biased in favour of the credit provider', the Victorian credit review report went on to note further that 'vulnerable and disadvantaged consumers have a limited capacity to read and understand the full implications of terms and conditions and this enables credit providers to exploit weaknesses in current regulation'.[78]

There are mechanisms under the Australian Uniform Consumer Credit Code enabling consumers to apply to the court to reopen unjust transactions or review unconscionable or other interest charges under hardship or unconscionability provisions.[79] It is unlikely, however, that low income consumers will have the resources or inclination to bring applications before the court. A research study undertaken in the United Kingdom demonstrated that low income consumers are unlikely to take legal action in relation to a loan dispute, on the basis of factors such as cost, a sense of powerlessness, and a fear of acrimonious disputes.[80] A more recent New South Wales study of responses to legal problems in disadvantaged areas found that, of a range of civil, criminal and family problems, credit/debt problems had one of the highest rates of inaction for survey participants.[81]

---

76 Malbon, *Taking Credit: A Survey of Consumer Behaviour in the Australian Consumer Credit Market*, p. 78.
77 G. Hadfield, R. Howse and M.J. Treblicock, Information-based principles for rethinking consumer protection policy', *Journal of Consumer Policy*, 21 (1998): 131–69, at 142.
78 Consumer Affairs Victoria, *The Report of the Consumer Credit Review*, p. 183.
79 Sections 70(1), 70(2)(1) and 72, Uniform Consumer Credit Code.
80 H. Genn, *Paths to Justice: What People Do and Think About Going to Law* (Oregon, 1999), p. 101.
81 C. Coumarelos, Z. Wei and A. Zhou, *Justice Made to Measure: NSW Legal Needs Survey in Disadvantaged Areas*, Law and Justice Foundation of NSW, Access to Justice and Legal Needs, Volume 3 (2006), p. 99, although the sample size for credit/debt matters was only 26.

Further, borrowers in the fringe credit market do not have access to alternative dispute resolution, such as exists for borrowers from mainstream lenders under the Banking and Financial Services Ombudsman scheme and other similar schemes.[82] The Victorian Credit Review commented that:

> There is no requirement for small amount lenders to have any external dispute resolution. Many consumer advocates recommended that commercial small amount credit providers be required to belong to an accredited alternative dispute resolution scheme.[83]

Even in the event that a complaint concerning unfair contract terms in the fringe market gets to court, the courts have tended to require evidence of procedural unfairness (concerned with 'the circumstances under which the transaction came about'[84]) in order to grant relief. As one of us has noted elsewhere, substantive unfairness, being related to the terms of the contract themselves, has in practice only led to relief being granted in a small number of cases.[85]

The presence of unfair contract terms and the lack of effective mechanisms for complaint about those terms by low income consumers are again indicative of the need for strong consumer protection regulation in this area, involving legislation to prohibit unfair terms in consumer contracts.[86]

---

82   There are currently in Australia, eight industry based external dispute resolution services, including the BFSO but also, for example, the Credit Ombudsman Service, the Credit Union Dispute Resolution Centre, and the Financial Cooperative Dispute Resolution Scheme. See C. Pearce, 'Opening Address to the Financial Industry Complaints Service Annual Conference' (Speech delivered 6 March 2007), available at: http://www.treasurer.gov.au/cjp/content/speeches/2007/002.asp.

83   Consumer Affairs Victoria, *The Report of the Consumer Credit Review*, p. 94. This is because the obligation to belong to an approved External Dispute Resolution scheme is imposed only upon holders of an Australian Financial Services licence. Unless a credit provider also offers other retail financial services (deposit-taking, insurance, and so on), it is not required to obtain an Australian Financial Services Licence. See Corporations Act 2001 (Cth) s. 911A (need for an Australian financial services licence); s. 912A(g) (licence obligation to have a dispute resolution system); s. 766A (definition of financial service) and s. 765A (credit is not a financial product).

84   N. Howell, 'Catching up with consumer realities: The need for legislation prohibiting unfair terms in consumer contracts', *Australian Business Law Review*, 34(6) (2006): 447–66, at 448.

85   See discussion *ibid*. It is suggested that this judicial reluctance to intervene in relation to substantive unfairness is largely attributable to concerns about upholding the notion of freedom of contract.

86   See discussion *ibid.*, at 463–4.

Unsafe products

There is evidence of substantial detriment being suffered by low income consumers who have accessed credit from the fringe market.[87] There are five key problems that have been identified in relation to fringe credit, that make these products unsafe.[88] These are loan 'rollovers'; debt collection methods; taking household items as security; failure to assess capacity to repay; and avoiding the operation of the Uniform Consumer Credit Code. We will focus here on debt collection methods, the loan 'rollovers' and a related issue of failure to assess capacity to repay, which seem particularly hazardous.

Examples given of debt collection methods employed by fringe credit providers include threatening to access social security benefits, threatening to repossess goods which are not actually the subject of a formal security arrangement, contacting a borrower's employer direct seeking payment of wages to the credit provider and general harassment and coercion.[89] The taking of security over household items has been described as 'blackmail security' in that its only purpose is to provide some threat to ensure repayment.

> Consumer organisations have reported that some fringe credit providers use the threat of repossession to create a sense of fear for some borrowers. This can then give the fringe credit provider an effective priority over other lenders as borrowers maintain payment to the fringe credit provider for fear of having their essential household goods repossessed, even if they declare themselves bankrupt.[90]

'Rollovers' are a feature of payday loans, which are one category of fringe credit. They are short-term loans, usually for a period of approximately 14 days, for small amounts in the vicinity of $250.00.[91] Of great concern is the practice of allowing borrowers to 'rollover' the loan on payment of an additional loan fee, which is said to be 'the beginning for many of an uncontrollable debt spiral'[92] wherein borrowers pay, over a period of time, an amount well in excess of the original loan amount often without reducing the principal amount owed.[93] Given the very short time period allowed for loan repayment in the case of a payday loan, it is likely that many low income consumers will not have the necessary lump sum

---

87   Consumer Affairs Victoria, *The Report of the Consumer Credit Review*, pp. 119–20, and Office of Fair Trading, Queensland, *Managing the Cost of Consumer Credit in Queensland Discussion Paper*, p. 13.

88   Consumer Affairs Victoria, *The Report of the Consumer Credit Review*, p. 119.

89   *Ibid.*, p. 121.

90   *Ibid.*, p. 122.

91   T. Wilson, 'The inadequacy of the current regulatory response to payday lending', *Australian Business Law Review*, 32 (2004):159, at 160.

92   P. Syvret, 'The Quick and the Debt', *The Bulletin*, 6 February (2001): 30.

93   Wilson, 'The inadequacy of the current regulatory response to payday lending': 160.

to repay the loan in full on the due date, and will need to take up the 'rollover' option. The 'rollover' has been described as: 'one of the most controversial features of payday loans because it carries great financial risk for consumers and is perhaps the key to the lucrative nature of the business for lenders',[94] and is a feature which pulls borrowers 'into a series of repeated loan transactions that may be financially devastating to the borrower'.[95]

There is evidence indicating that payday lenders actively target those on low incomes who will be unable to make due payments and will need to roll loans over. This has in fact been described in a recent study in the U.S. as 'the foundation of the payday lending business model'.[96] That same report noted that 'the profitability of payday lending is driven by volume, which is in turn driven by rollovers'.[97] Evidence of this 'business model' in Australia includes the opening of payday lending outlets in predominantly low income suburbs, and experiences reported by financial counsellors.[98] Further, research conducted in Australia in 2002 showed that a large number of payday borrowers earned less than $401.00 per week.[99]

Closely related to the question of 'rollovers' is the failure on the part of fringe lenders to assess borrowers' capacities to repay 'so the credit does not place them in financial hardship'.[100] A failure to assess capacity to repay within the loan term has been found to 'contribute to real financial distress'[101] which can only exacerbate problems of over-indebtedness and poverty in the Australian community. Competition, in the sense of having many players in the market, has not protected consumers.

At the very least there is a role for consumer protection regulation to prohibit the use of the 'rollover' mechanism; to require lenders to properly assess borrowers' capacities to repay; and to give borrowers reasonable periods of time to repay loans in accordance with their capacities, without payment of additional fees. More generally, the hazards of fringe credit referred to above would arguably justify a significant interference with the free running of this market, in order to protect vulnerable consumers.

---

94   S. Lott and M. Grant, *Fringe Lending and 'Alternative' Banking: The Consumer Experience. Public Interest Advocacy Centre* (Canada, 2002), p. 22.

95   *Ibid.*, p. 13.

96   U. King, L. Parrish and O. Tanik, *Financial Quicksand: Payday lending sinks borrowers in debt with $4.2 billion in predatory fees every year*, Center for Responsible Lending (2006), p. 3.

97   *Ibid.*, p. 8.

98   C. Field, 'Payday Lending – an Exploitative Market Practice', *Alternative Law Journal*, 27(1) (2002): 36, at p. 37.

99   Wilson, *Payday Lending in Victoria – A Research Report*, p. 9.

100 Consumer Affairs Victoria, *The Report of the Consumer Credit Review*, p. 92.

101 King, Parrish, Tanik, p. 8.

Rationale for Consumer Protection Interventions

The limitations of competition and competitive markets demonstrated by this case study as well as examples given earlier in this chapter, give rise to alternative theories for consumer protection regulation, which do not rely solely on the classical ideas of market failure.

However, these alternative rationale(s) for consumer protection interventions are not always easy to articulate and do not necessarily form a coherent picture. As Louise Sylvan has noted, with the exception of regulation to stop consumers being misled: 'Other consumer protection regulation, while plentiful and much of which is crucial, is not woven together into a well-structured pattern.'[102]

Commentators have therefore struggled to define consistent and comprehensive categories for consumer law. In part this may be because consumer problems cover all aspects of the economy, have elements of civil, criminal, contract, tort and other laws, and are often 'on the border line of private/public and social/commercial problems'.[103] By way of illustration, some categorisations of consumer law suggested by others are provided below:

- Anthony Duggan has suggested that consumer protection interventions are made on the basis of economic efficiency considerations, loss distribution considerations, and/or paternalistic concerns.[104]
- Geraint Howells suggests that consumer protection interventions should focus on promoting competition, achieving individual justice, and realising social justice.[105]
- John Vickers talks of consumer regulation in terms of the problems that it is seeking to address – duress and undue pressure; information problems pre-purchase; and undue surprises post-purchase.[106]
- In contrast, Iain Ramsay suggests a 'third way' approach to consumer credit regulation, one that both recognises the importance of the market, and of empowering consumers within that market, and also focuses on the relevance of social policy in achieving goals that cannot be met relying on the market alone.[107]

---

102 Sylvan, 'Activating competition: The consumer – competition interface': 193.
103 G. Howells and S. Weatherill, *Consumer Protection Law* (Aldershot, 2005), p. 660.
104 A. Duggan, 'Saying Nothing with Words', *Journal of Consumer Policy*, 20 (1997): 69–88, at p. 73.
105 G. Howells, 'Contract Law: the Challenge for the Critical Consumer Lawyer', in T. Wilhelmsson, (ed.), *Perspectives of Critical Contract Law* (Aldershot, 1993), p. 335.
106 Vickers, 'Economics for Consumer Policy', p. 3.
107 I. Ramsay, 'Consumer Credit Regulation as "The Third Way"'?, Speech delivered at the Australian Credit at the Crossroads Conference, Melbourne Australia, 8 November 2004, p. 5.

These categories are not necessarily comprehensive. Interestingly, for some commentators, including Howells, it appears that the categorisation of consumer law incorporates broader community or social ideals that may require intervention even in a competitive market that provides for overall consumer (economic) welfare. This suggests that consumer law should do more than perfect the functioning of the market; it should have more distributive goals.[108]

There is another argument that equity or distributive justice is not an appropriate goal for markets, and/or that market regulation is not effective in achieving equitable goals. An example relevant to this paper is that of interest rate ceilings, with some commentators of the view that such mechanisms introduce credit rationing and do not ultimate benefit consumers on low incomes.[109]

One of the more recent classifications in Australia is provided by Sylvan, who suggests that regulation to protect consumers takes one of three forms:

i.   Competition-enhancing rules (for example, information disclosure requirements, prohibitions against misleading conduct);
ii. Rules to minimise harm in the provision of goods and services (for example, product safety); and
iii. Rules to protect consumers from inappropriate behaviour of traders (for example, prohibitions against undue coercion, or unacceptable disconnection from essential services).[110]

Again, however, this classification is only a starting point, as Sylvan herself effectively acknowledges.[111] It raises more questions than it answers. For example, how much harm can/should be minimised? When is behaviour to be deemed inappropriate or unacceptable, rather than simply a consequence of a market system that is based on parties utilising their own strengths and preferences to get the most favourable outcome and/or seeking to enforce contract terms 'agreed upon' in advance.

An added complication is the fact that consumers are not homogenous in their preferences, skills, ability, socio-economic status and other characteristics. It may not be possible to design consumer policy that meets the needs of all consumers,

---

108 Howells, 'Contract Law: the Challenge for the Critical Consumer Lawyer', p. 298.
109 For example, T. Durkin, 'An economic perspective on interest rate limitations', *Georgia State University Law Review*, 9 (1993) 821–38, at 824–5; K. Engel, and P. McCoy, 'A tale of three markets: the law and economics of predatory lending', *Texas Law Review*, 80 (2002): 1255–366, at 1313.
110 Sylvan, 'Activating competition: The consumer – competition interface': 194. In an earlier paper, Sylvan categorises consumer protection rules as Market conduct and information rules (competition enhancing); sensible society rules; and equitable rules (L. Sylvan, 'A Global View of Consumer Issues: Then and Now' (Speech delivered at the American Council on Consumer Interests 50th Anniversary Conference, 1 April 2004, Washington, USA), p. 6.
111 Sylvan 'Activating competition: The consumer – competition interface': 205.

including the marginalised and the vulnerable.[112] If this is the case, there are difficult issues to grapple with in a policy sense, including whose interests should prevail if a proposed policy response benefits one group of consumers, but does not benefit, or even harms, another. Sylvan illustrates this point by asking: 'How does a regulator handle situations where different subsets of consumers are likely to have outcomes in different quadrants – some are disadvantaged by an intervention while others are unaffected or better off?'[113]

These considerations highlight the difficulties and complexities associated with designing effective consumer policy. It is not within the scope of this chapter to come up with a consistent and comprehensive rationale for consumer protection interventions; this is the topic for another day.[114] However, this discussion illustrates the support amongst commentators for interventions in consumer markets in circumstances that may not equate to market failure from an economic perspective.

Australian Government Approach – Rhetoric versus Reality

Unfortunately, this general acknowledgment amongst many academics, and consumer advocates,[115] of the ways in which competitive markets can fail consumers does not seem to be reflected in Australian government policy and practice in 2007.[116] Advocates for changed or increased consumer protection mechanisms designed to meet the complexities and challenges of consumer markets are finding their calls for intervention ignored or pilloried as unnecessary and/or paternalistic. Instead, the government perspective appears to be that competitive markets are the true goal and that: '… confident consumers know they have real power – the power of choice. And they know how to use that power'.[117]

---

112 Although another perspective is that 'most consumers are vulnerable in at least some situations', Wilhelmsson, 'The Informed Consumer v. the Vulnerable Consumer in European Unfair Commercial Practices Law – A Comment', p. 213.

113 Sylvan 'Activating competition: The consumer – competition interface': 204.

114 However, it may be that the current Productivity Commission Inquiry into Australia's Consumer Policy Framework will tackle this task. See Productivity Commission, Consumer Policy Framework, Productivity Commission Issues Paper, January 2007, pp. 14–15.

115 See for example, D. Tennant, 'The dangers of taking the consumer out of consumer advocacy', speech to the National Consumer Congress, Melbourne, March 2006, pp. 4–5, available at: http://www.carefcs.org/srcfiles/The-dangers-of-taking-the-consumer-out-of-consumer-advocacy---16-March-2006.doc.

116 The Liberal/National coalition was in government from 1996 to November 2007.

117 C. Pearce, 'Opening Address to Consumer Representatives' Forum' (Speech delivered at the Consumer Representatives' Forum, Melbourne Australia, 15 June 2005), available at: http://parlsec.treasurer.gov.au/cjp/content/speeches/2005/010.asp.

The government appears to take a narrow approach to the concept of market failure, and tends to give little weight to what we have termed 'competition failure' as a justification for market intervention.

This trend of overvaluing the role of competitive markets is manifested in government policy and practice in a number of ways.

The first is the National Competition Policy's legislative review program. The Competition Principles Agreement, signed in 1995, committed the Australian, State and Territory governments to 'list, review, and where appropriate, reform all legislation which restricts competition'.[118] While legislation that has overall benefits for the community can pass the legislative review hurdles, the review program effectively reverses the onus of proof. Advocates for the retention of legislation with anti-competitive effects have to demonstrate that the removal of the restrictions would not be in the interests of the community.[119]

The second is an almost zealous concern about eliminating red tape and reducing regulatory burdens on business.[120] Consumer protection legislation is often a target of these initiatives.[121]

Of course, implementing a rigorous legislative review program and reducing *unnecessary* red tape and regulatory burdens are laudable goals. Ineffective regulation imposes costs on the whole community.[122] Our concern is, however, that these programs too strongly emphasis the merits of unfettered markets and the costs of regulation. It appears that reviewers focus on questions of 'How does this legislation impede competition?' and 'How much does it cost business?'. For consumer protection matters, we suggest that it would be more appropriate to first ask 'What are the consumer problems and what is the fairest, most efficient and effective solution or solutions?'.

Third, there appears to be a retreat from a focus on legislation, regulation and enforcement to deal with consumer issues. The proposal for nationally consistent legislation to prohibit unfair terms in consumer contracts has apparently stalled and there is some suggestion that it has stalled at the national level.[123] Despite a Parliamentary Joint Committee report recommending federal regulation of the property investment market, the Australian Government 'wishes to continue to

---

118 Productivity Commission, *Review of National Competition Policy Reforms*, Report No. 33, 28 February (2005), p. 16.

119 *Ibid.*

120 The most recent review being G. Banks, *Rethinking Regulation: Report of the Taskforce on Reducing Regulatory Burdens on Business* (2006).

121 See, for example, *ibid.*, pp. 51, 106.

122 *Ibid.*, p. 12.

123 See for example, Standing Committee on Law and Justice, *Unfair terms in consumer contracts*, Report 32, November (2006), NSW Legislative Council, pp. 54–5. It is also worth noting that the Ministerial Council on Consumer Affairs' regular Communiqués refer only to the possibility of State and Territory legislation, see Joint Communiqué Ministerial Council on Consumer Affairs Meeting Tuesday 16 and Wednesday 17 May 2006, Ministerial Council on Consumer Affairs.

investigate all options'.[124] Similarly, it seems that calls for nationally uniform legislation for finance and mortgage brokers will not necessarily result in federal legislation, despite the obvious parallels between financial advisers (regulated by the Corporations Act 2001 (Cth)) and credit advisers.[125]

Part of the problem may be attributed to the now pervasive requirement that new regulatory proposals must undergo a regulatory impact assessment. This process requires an assessment of the costs and benefits of legislation and any alternatives to legislation. We agree that this is an important process. However, in practice, given the difficulties of quantifying diffuse benefits that are not necessarily economic, this cost–benefit analysis can almost set social regulation (including consumer protection regulation) up to fail. We suspect that it will be relatively easy for business to quantify the costs of new legislation (for example, of meeting new information disclosure requirements), but describing and costing consumer benefits is much more difficult. As the Productivity Commission notes: 'Often, the benefits of government intervention in promoting the interests of consumers and efficient market outcomes are widely spread and difficult to quantify.'[126]

Finally, it seems fair to say that in recent times, the Australian Government has failed to provide national leadership on consumer policy,[127] perhaps reflecting the lack of priority that this area seems to merit within the Government.

We hope that the Government's current inquiry into national consumer policy will start to reverse this trend. However, phrases such as 'unnecessary regulation', 'promoting certainty and consistency for business and consumers' and 'the extent to which more effective use can be made of self-regulatory, co-regulatory, consumer education and consumer information approaches' are prominent in the terms of reference for the inquiry.[128] These issues should be important considerations in any review of national consumer policy and administration. However, our concern is that a focus on red tape and regulatory burdens is looking in the wrong direction.

---

124 Joint Communiqué Ministerial Council on Consumer Affairs Meeting Tuesday 16 and Wednesday 17 May 2006, Ministerial Council on Consumer Affairs.

125 One industry member has suggested that: 'Common sense would see the Federal Government resolve the issue by an extension of its existing financial service laws, some of which already impact on the day-to-day activities of finance brokers. However, it would appear that considerably more consumer blood will need to be let before it becomes an imperative of the Federal Government.' See http://www.mortgagemagazine.com.au/detail_article.cfm?articleID=659, viewed 14.2.2007.

126 Productivity Commission, *Consumer Policy Framework*, Productivity Commission Issues Paper, (2007), p. 23. See also J. Goldring, 'Consumer Law and Legal Theory: Reflections of a Common Lawyer', *Journal of Consumer Policy*, 13(2) (1990): 113–32, at 128, who notes in relation to wider social costs and benefits, that 'such costs and benefits are notoriously difficult to quantify'.

127 Fels, p. 56 suggesting that their involvement is 'a little bit reluctant and limited'.

128 The terms of reference for the review are available at: http://www.pc.gov.au/inquiry/consumer/tor.html, viewed 14.2.2007.

Instead, there should be a more proactive aim to: 'get the right consumer policies in place, and then minimise regulation to achieve them.'[129]

Fortunately, the Productivity Commission's Issues Paper for this inquiry seems to take a more nuanced approach,[130] although the difficulties of balancing the competing priorities in the terms of reference for the inquiry should not be underestimated.

Interestingly, this attitude of the Australian Government and the positioning of consumer policy as a relative low priority policy area contrasts with the explicit commitment to consumer policy as a 'horizontal measure' in European law. Under Article 153(2) EC, 'Consumer protection requirements shall be taken into account in defining and implementing other Community policies and activities'. Thus, in the European Union, consumer protection 'should be taken into account *inter alia* in the shaping of competition policy'.[131] In contrast, consumer protection seems to be considered an after-thought in Australia, despite Sylvan's recent suggestion for a 'reframing of the competition lens so it's seen from a consumer framework'.[132]

Thus, although competition is regularly described by the Australian Government as not being an end in itself, its actions suggest that competition, reduced market interference and reduced regulatory burdens, have now become the end game.

Conclusion

In this chapter, we have described the ways in which markets can fail consumers; with information asymmetry being the key problem. Consumer protection interventions to reduce market failures can lead to more competitive markets, often for the ultimate benefit of consumers.

However, we have also sought to describe the ways in which even competitive markets can fail consumers, using the consumer credit market in Australia as a case study. We have showed that, despite its competitiveness, the consumer credit market has particularly failed low income consumers through failing to provide appropriate products; imposing unfair contract terms; and offering unsafe products. These and other 'competition failures' should lead to calls for the imposition of regulatory requirements that are not necessarily 'competition-enhancing' rules, but are rules that reflect the more difficult to particularise concerns of social equity, fairness and the broader community welfare.

Our analysis shows that consumer protection rules are still essential, even in competitive markets. At a broad level, competition and competitive markets can

---

129 A. Fels and F. Brenchley, 'Consumers last in line', *Australian Financial Review*, 16 January (2007): 46.

130 For example, Productivity Commission, *Consumer Policy Framework*, p. 13.

131 S. Weatherill, 'The Links Between Competition Policy and Consumer Protection', in Howells et al (eds), *The Yearbook of Consumer Law 2007*, pp. 187–209 at p. 199, even if there may be some deficiencies in institutional backup.

132 Sylvan, 'A Global View of Consumer Issues: Then and Now', p. 8.

never be the complete answer to consumer problems because there is a difference in scale and perspective. Competition law and policy looks to the macro picture; it is not interested in the impact of competition on individual businesses and, similarly, it is not interested in micro-cases of unfairness.[133] It might influence the conduct of traders at a broad level, and over time, but does not directly impact on the time-specific relationship between an individual consumer and an individual trader.[134] However, consumers are very much interested in the micro-level, in the individual relationships that they have (or do not have) with traders. A perspective that competition will, over time, weed out rogue traders and unfair practices, does not offer much comfort to those affected by such practices today.

In contrast, consumer law can and should influence the daily individual transactions that occur across the market. This should particularly be the case in relation to consumer transactions in industries that exhibit information asymmetry problems at either supply or demand sides and provide essential services giving rise to considerations of social equity and access. The banking industry is one such industry and the consumer credit market has been used in this chapter as an example of a market exhibiting these features.

Competition law and policy is about economics and markets. But consumers are not just economic beings, doggedly seeking to get the best deal for themselves regardless of broader considerations. Among other things, the preference of at least some consumers for products and services that have minimal environmental impact; or that reflect fair trade and working conditions, illustrate the importance of other considerations. We acknowledge that traditional theories of markets encompass environmental considerations and other externalities, however, we suggest that economic policy in practice tends to ignore these issues.

Consumer law can and should sit alongside competition law and respond to both economic and social concerns and considerations. The alternative is that many consumers will be left to fend for themselves and inequities will prevail.

Competition law and consumer law are related, and are both equally important to the effective operation of markets in the interests of the community as a whole. The key here is the equal importance of the two aspects of law. Giving effective priority to competition, as appears to be the approach of the Australian Government in 2007, risks ignoring the needs and realities of many consumers, to the ultimate detriment of the community as a whole.

Consumer law and policy should not be a secondary consideration for Governments. It should be a high level priority in its own right. Responding effectively to consumer issues requires us to acknowledge the strengths and limitations of both competition law and consumer law; to articulate the problems and their genesis; and to identify one or more solutions without being blinkered by the mantra that competitive markets are always the answer.

---

133 K. Cseres, *Competition Law and Consumer Protection* (The Hague, 2005), p. 1.
134 E. Buttigieg, 'Consumer and competition policies: synergy needed', *Consumer Policy Review*, 15(5) (2005): 192–7, at 193.

5   The Consumer Protection Code: Regulatory Innovation from the Irish Financial Regulator

Mary Donnelly[1]

The Consumer Protection Code (the 'Code'[2]), drawn up by the Irish Financial Services Regulatory Authority (the 'Financial Regulator'), marks an important development in the regulation of financial services providers in Ireland. The Code, which came into force on 1 August 2006, is innovative in a number of respects. It effectively marries the enforceability of a statutory scheme with the flexibility more associated with 'soft law' regulatory frameworks. Further, it provides an integrated approach across all financial services providers, reflecting reality more accurately than the compartmentalisation which remains prevalent in regulation in this area. The Code also extends the definition of consumer and expands the obligations owed by financial services providers beyond the usual limits in voluntary codes. For lenders, this expansion has led to the imposition of responsible lending obligations. The Code may be seen as part of the ongoing development of a more vigorous approach to consumer protection in Ireland where, until recently, consumers had been underrepresented and the consumer voice had been largely absent from policy debates.[3]

This chapter presents the Code, concentrating on those aspects of the Code which may be of particular interest for other jurisdictions in considering appropriate models for the protection of consumers of financial services. In order to facilitate an understanding of the Code in this respect, the chapter begins with a general discussion of the context for consumer protection in relation to financial services

---

1   Senior Lecturer, Law Faculty, University College Cork. I am grateful to the referee for helpful comments.

2   The Code may be accessed at the Financial Regulator's website (www.ifsra.ie) under the heading 'Industry'.

3   On the underdeveloped nature of Irish consumer society, see generally M. Donnelly and F. White, 'The Effect of Information-Based Consumer Protection: Lessons from a Study of the Irish Online Market', in C. Twigg-Flesner *et al.* (eds), *Yearbook of Consumer Law 2008* (Aldershot, 2007), pp. 273–7. However, this underdevelopment is beginning to change through industry-specific initiatives like the Code and through the enactment of the Consumer Protection Act 2007, which commenced on 1 May 2007, and which established the National Consumer Agency.

and the regulatory mechanisms employed to provide this protection. The chapter then moves on to consider the legislative background to the Code, focussing in particular on the elevated role accorded to consumer protection within the relatively recently established office of the Financial Regulator. As will be seen, the legislative model employed has helped to create a climate which facilitates a dynamic approach to consumer protection. The chapter then outlines the more striking provisions of the Code.[4] The chapter concludes by asking whether the model adopted in the Code might usefully be drawn to the attention of regulators in other jurisdictions.

Consumer Protection in the Financial Services Context: An Overview

Although the financial services industry is, undoubtedly, heavily regulated, regulatory focus has traditionally been on the prudential aspects of the industry. While consumers have as much interest as the rest of society in ensuring the stability of financial services providers,[5] it is widely accepted that, from a consumer perspective, appropriate regulation must go beyond the prudential.[6] A number of rationales for consumer protection in respect of financial services may be identified. First, from an economic perspective, Cartwright identifies the primary rationale for regulation as being to address the unavoidable information asymmetry between the financial services provider and the consumer.[7] Asymmetry is unavoidable for a number of reasons. Certain financial products are 'credence' goods; that is their essential characteristics will only become known with the passage of time. Further, service providers will have an incentive not to provide potentially negative information which would place their product at a competitive disadvantage. This is compounded by the fact that, unlike in other markets,

---

4   This chapter does not attempt to provide a detailed breakdown of the Code: for this, see M. Donnelly, 'The Consumer Protection Code: A New Departure in the Regulation of Irish Financial Services Providers', *Commercial Law Practitioner*, 13 (2006): 271.

5   Indeed, P. Cartwright, *Banks, Consumers and Regulation* (Oxford, 2004), p. 6 argues that consumers may have an especially high degree of interest in the prudential stability of banks because the effect of bank failure may be particularly harmful to less affluent consumers who are likely to have proportionately more of their assets in banks.

6   However, there is not universal agreement on the utility of regulation in the financial services area: see for example, G. Bentson, *Regulating Financial Markets* (London, 1998), who argues that there is nothing intrinsically different about financial services when compared with many other products to justify a high degree of consumer protection. For an overview of the role of regulation in the financial services context, see D. Llewellyn, *The Economic Rationale for Financial Regulation*, (London, 1999); for a rebuttal of Bentson's argument regarding the non-specific nature of financial services, see Llewellyn, pp. 37–8.

7   See Cartwright, pp. 16–17.

competitors for the same market in financial services may not provide negative information about their competitors' products for fear of dissuading potential consumers from purchasing products of this kind at all.

The case for consumer protection may also be made from a social perspective. Cartwright argues that financial services regulation can be justified on the grounds of paternalism, distributive justice and community values.[8] At its simplest, paternalism protects people from the consequences of their own mistakes; it requires people to surrender some or all of the power to make their own decisions in return for this protection. Distributive justice is concerned with the distribution of resources on the basis of fairness or justice as opposed to simply on the basis of economics.[9] Consumer protection has the effect of redistributing power from the financial services provider to the consumer who is the weaker party in the relationship. Cartwright identifies community values as those values which 'we hold as a society which we want to see protected by regulation'.[10] Society has an interest in promoting characteristics such as trust, fair dealings and honesty in financial services providers and, to a degree at least, this may advanced through appropriate consumer protection.

A further justification for protecting consumers of financial services encompasses both economic and social rationales. Llewellyn notes that consumers demand protection in this area.[11] Thus, consumer protection is necessary because, in the words of the European Commission, 'the Internal Markets [in financial services] cannot function properly without consumer confidence'[12] and because as Llewellyn notes, consumers 'demand a degree of comfort that can only be provided by regulation'.[13]

While the case for consumer protection in the financial services context is widely accepted, there is more debate regarding the appropriate mechanisms to provide such protection. This is reflected in the range of approaches to consumer protection adopted. Leaving aside the important role played by entry and prior approval requirements,[14] there are several regulatory mechanisms to control how financial services providers conduct their business. First, in some contexts, there has been legislative intervention, in most cases emanating from the European Community. Thus, the Consumer Credit Directive;[15] the Unfair Terms in Consumer Contracts

---

8   *Ibid.*, p. 19.
9   *Ibid.*, p. 22.
10 *Ibid.*, p. 29.
11 Llewellyn, pp. 30–32.
12 Commission Communication, 'Healthier, Safer, More Confident Citizens – a Health and Consumer Protection Strategy', COM (2005) 115 final.
13 Llewellyn, p. 31.
14 For a discussion of the role played by the prior approval requirement as a consumer protection mechanism, see Cartwright, Chapter 4.
15 Directive 87/102/EEC as amended by Directive 90/88/EEC and Directive 2008/48/EC.

Directive[16] and the Distance Marketing of Financial Services Directive[17] all provide a protective framework directed specifically at consumers. In other contexts, legislation such as the Markets in Financial Instruments Directive ('MiFID')[18] extends beyond consumer protection but the general regulatory framework employed has the effect of extending the protections afforded to consumers. Most recently, the Payment Services Directive[19] introduces a split approach to protection, setting out a protective framework for all payment services users but allowing the parties to contractually agree derogation from the requirements where the user is not a consumer.[20] Of particular interest in the context of the discussion below is the provision in the Directive that Members States may extend full-scale consumer protection to 'micro-enterprises'.[21] While of increasing importance, legislation still covers only a small portion of the operations of financial services providers and clearly does not provide a comprehensive framework for the protection of consumers of financial services.

Secondly, a degree of consumer protection is provided through the body of case law enumerating the duties owed by bankers, insurers or other financial services providers to their customers.[22] In this regard, the fact that the customer is inexperienced in business matters may be a factor in delimiting the extent of the duty owed.[23] However, a difficulty with this form of protection is that it is inevitably haphazard, deriving, as it does, from the vagaries of the common law. Furthermore, even when a consumer protection type issue arises, the question before the court is whether the service provider has been in breach of its duty of care and not whether, in a broader policy sense, an appropriate degree of consumer protection has been provided. Thus, for example, in the absence of exceptional circumstances, there is no general duty for bankers to provide advice to their consumer customers about the wisdom of transactions entered into.[24]

A third consumer protection mechanism is the 'soft' law option of codes of practice. While widely utilised, the format for codes of practice has varied depending on the area of the financial services industry involved. In the context of banking and lending services, voluntary codes of practice have been the norm. A

---

16   Directive 93/13/EEC.
17   Directive 2002/65/EC.
18   Directive 2004/39/EC as amended by Directive 2006/31/EC and Directive 2006/73/EC. See also the Investment Services Directive (Directive 93/22/EEC).
19   Directive 2007/64/EC.
20   See Articles 30 and 51.
21   A 'micro-enterprise' is defined in Article 2 of Recommendation 2003/361/EC as an enterprise which employs fewer than 10 people and where the annual turnover and/or annual balance sheet total does not exceed €2 million.
22   In the context of banks, see E.P. Ellinger, E. Lomnicka and R. Hooley, *Ellinger's Modern Banking Law*, 4th edn (Oxford, 2006), pp. 152–63.
23   See, for example, *Verity & Spindler* v. *Lloyd's Bank plc* [1995] CLC 1557.
24   Although see *Verity & Spindler* v. *Lloyd's Bank plc*, *ibid.*, where, in the special circumstances of the case, a duty of care was held to exist.

voluntary code of practice for banks (*The Banking Code*) has been operational in the United Kingdom since 1992 and is currently in its eighth edition.[25] Voluntary banking codes also operate in many other jurisdictions, including Australia,[26] New Zealand,[27] South Africa[28] and Hong Kong.[29] Other jurisdictions, for example Canada, have chosen to focus on a range of codes to cover specific aspects of banking services.[30] Until the introduction of the Code, this was also the approach taken in Ireland. Voluntary codes of practice issued by the Irish Bankers' Federation (IBF) cover various aspects of banking business.[31]

In contrast to the largely voluntary approach in the banking and credit sectors, within the European Union, at any rate, investment services have been made subject to mandatory codes. The Investment Services Directive[32] required Member States to draw up rules of conduct which investment firms were obliged to observe at all times. Although, as a minimum harmonising measure, the Directive gave Member States a degree of flexibility in the rules drawn up, it did require that the rules must

---

25   *The Banking Code* (March 2008) is a joint publication of the British Bankers Association, the Building Societies Association and the Association for Payment Clearing Services. For discussion of earlier editions of the Code, see Cartwright, Chapter 5 and Ellinger, Lomnicka and Hooley, pp. 62–6.

26   See the *Code of Banking Practice* (Australian Bankers' Association, 1993). This Code was modified in 2003 and 2004. The Code may be accessed at: www.bankers.asn.au.

27   See *Code of Banking Practice*, 4th edn, New Zealand Bankers' Association, July 2007. The Code may be accessed at: www.nzba.org.nz.

28   See *The Code of Banking Practice*, Banking Council, 2004. The Code may be accessed at: www.banking.org.za.

29   See *The Code of Banking Practice*, Hong Kong Association of Banks and Deposit-taking Companies Association, 1997, as amended in 2004. The Code may be accessed at: www.hkab.org.hk.

30   There are separate Codes of Conduct in operation to cover cheque holds, online payments, consumer debit card services, transfers of registered plans, authorised insurance activities, electronic commerce, bank relations with small and medium sized businesses, plain language mortgage documents and unsolicited services. For full details, see the Canadian Bankers' Association (www.cba.ca).

31   See the Irish Bankers' Federation Code of Practice on Mortgage Arrears; the Code of Practice on Transparency in Credit Charges for Personal Customers; the Code of Practice for Small Business Customers; the Code of Practice for Personal Customers; the Code of Practice on Bank Restructuring; the Code of Ethics; the Code of Practice on Personal Account Switching; the Code of Practice on Business Account Switching. All of these Codes may be viewed at the IBF website: www.ibf.ie. In addition, in 2001, the Central Bank issued a brief, non-binding Code of Practice setting out general guiding principles but offering little in the way of concrete directions for either providers or consumers of banking services.

32   Directive 93/22/EEC.

implement certain principles.[33] Since the MiFID,[34] these rules of conduct have been put on a legislative footing and the flexibility afforded to Member States in drawing up rules has largely been removed.

Having set out in general terms the range of methods used to protect consumers of financial services, it now falls to consider the innovations in the Code. In order to do this, it is necessary to consider, in brief, the legislative background against which the Code operates.

The Irish Financial Regulator and the Role of Consumer Protection

The Financial Regulator is a relatively new body, established in 2003 as part of a legislative response to a series of banking scandals which came to light in Ireland towards the end of the 1990s. These included instances of deliberate over-charging of customers[35] and widespread complicity by banks in tax evasion by their customers.[36] In the light of these scandals, it became increasingly apparent that the existing regulatory structure failed to provide adequate protection for consumers. The difficulties arose in part at least from the fact that financial services regulation was split between two regulatory bodies which had little in common and had no interaction with each other. Prudential regulation was the function of the Central Bank[37] while consumer protection came within the ambit of the Office of the

---

33 These principles were that investment firms act honestly and fairly in the best interests of their clients and the integrity of the market; that they seek information from their clients regarding their financial situations, investment experience and objectives; that they make adequate disclosure of relevant material information and that they try to avoid conflicts of interest and if they cannot, that they ensure clients are fairly treated.

34 Directive 2004/39/EC as amended by Directive 2006/31/EC and Directive 2006/73/EC.

35 The charging policy at National Irish Bank (NIB) was the most high-profile of these scandals. Following a journalistic investigation, Inspectors were appointed (under section 8(1) of the Companies Act 1990) to investigate the way in which the NIB had conducted its business. The investigation concluded that the NIB had 'loaded' certain accounts of more troublesome customers in relation both to interest and bank charges (see *Report on the Investigations into the Affairs of National Irish Bank Ltd and National Irish Bank Financial Services Ltd by High Court Inspectors Mr Justice Blayney and Tom Grace FCA*, Office of Director of Corporate Enforcement (2004)).

36 This related to the collection of Deposit Income Retention Tax (DIRT) which is taxation on interest earned on bank deposits which had to be retained by banks on behalf of the Revenue Commissioners. See further M. Donnelly, *The Law of Banks and Credit Institutions* (Dublin, 2000), pp. 210–11.

37 Established by the Central Bank Act 1942.

Director of Consumer Affairs ('ODCA').[38] The regulatory gap was acknowledged by then Governor of the Central Bank who noted:

> I am acutely conscious of the viewpoint that we should extend our brief beyond prudential supervision; that we should actively ... take on a consumer protection role. There is, somewhere, a cross-over point where prudential supervision ends and what I might describe as consumer protection begins. I have to admit this is a grey area.[39]

While the need for enhanced regulation from a consumer perspective was generally accepted, there was debate regarding the appropriate locus for regulation in this regard. In particular, the question arose of whether Irish legislators should follow the UK lead and separate the regulatory function then exercised by the Central Bank from the role played by the Central Bank as lender of last resort.[40] In 1999, an influential policy report recommended that the regulation of all financial services should be the function of a single regulatory authority and that this authority should be separate from the Central Bank.[41] Unsurprisingly, this recommendation was vigorously opposed by the Central Bank. Following extensive debate, something of a compromise was reached. The Financial Regulator was established on 1 May 2003 as a distinct part of a newly established entity, the Central Bank and Financial Services Authority of Ireland (although, tellingly, in the legislation, the new entity is abbreviated as the 'Bank').[42]

The Financial Regulator is required to promote 'the best interests of users of financial services in a way that is consistent with (a) the orderly and proper functioning of financial markets and, (b) the orderly and prudent supervision of providers of those services'.[43] Additionally, the Financial Regulator is obliged to 'take such action as it considers appropriate to increase awareness among members of the public of available financial services and the cost to consumers, risks and benefits associated with the provision of those services'.[44] To ensure the promotion of consumer interests, the office of Consumer Director was established within

---

38 Established by the Consumer Information Act 1978. The ODCA was ineffective in many respects (see Donnelly and White, pp. 275–6) and has now been replaced by the National Consumer Agency.

39 Speech by the Governor of Central Bank, Mr Maurice O Connell, to the Joint Oireachtas Committee on Finance and the Public Service. For full text of Governor's speech, see Central Bank of Ireland Annual Report 1998, pp. 87–8.

40 The regulatory role played by the Bank of England was transferred to, what is now, the Financial Services Authority (FSA) by the Bank of England Act 1998. The FSA was established by the Financial Services and Markets Act 2000.

41 Report of the Implementation Advisory Group on the Establishment of a Single Regulatory Authority for the Financial Services Sector (Stationary Office, 1999).

42 Under the Central Bank and Financial Services Authority of Ireland Act 2003.

43 Section 33C(3) of the Central Bank Act 1942 (inserted by section 26 of the Central Bank and Financial Services Authority of Ireland Act 2003).

44 Section 33C(4) of the Central Bank Act 1942.

the Financial Regulator.[45] Within the structure of the Financial Regulator, the Consumer Director reports directly to the Chief Executive (as does the Prudential Director) and both offices are accorded equivalent status.[46]

The Consumer Director has the responsibility for 'monitoring the provision of financial services to consumers of those services to the extent that the Consumer Director considers appropriate, having regard to the public interest and to the interests of those consumers'.[47] As part of this role, the Consumer Director has the power to issue codes or impose requirements in the name of the Financial Regulator (after these have been approved by the other members of the Financial Regulator).[48] The consumer protection dimension of the Financial Regulator is further enhanced by the Central Bank and Financial Services Authority Act 2004. This Act establishes a Financial Services Consultative Consumer Panel[49] to monitor the Financial Regulator's performance of its consumer protection functions and to provide comments and suggestions for initiatives.[50] The Act also establishes the office of the Financial Services Ombudsman.[51] The principal function of the Ombudsman is to 'deal with complaints ... by mediation and, where necessary, by investigation and adjudication'.[52] The role of the Ombudsman in the context of the Code is discussed further below.

When compared with the regulatory structure adopted in the UK, there are two distinctive features of the Irish legislative approach. First, the Financial Regulator is the sole authority in relation to prudential regulation and consumer protection across all financial services. This is unlike the UK, where consumer credit is regulated by the Office of Fair Trading ('OFT') and other aspects of financial services are regulated by the Financial Services Authority ('FSA').[53] The fact of a single authority allows for an integrated approach across all financial services. Secondly, the status accorded to consumer protection by the creation (and elevation) of the office of Consumer Director within the Financial Regulator contrasts with the structure of the FSA. While consumer protection is one of the

---

45   Section 33Q of the Central Bank Act 1942.
46   Currently, the Consumer Director is a member of the Board of Directors of the Bank (and the Prudential Director is not). However, the Consumer Director does not have a statutory right of membership of the Board (see Board membership requirements listed in section 18B of the Central Bank Act 1942 (inserted by section 13 of the Central Bank and Financial Services Authority of Ireland Act 2003)).
47   Section 33S(1)(b) of the Central Bank Act 1942.
48   Section 33S(6) of the Central Bank Act 1942.
49   Section 57CW of the Central Bank Act 1942 (inserted by section 17 of the Central Bank and Financial Services Authority of Ireland Act 2004).
50   Section 57CY of the Central Bank Act 1942.
51   Part VIIB of the Central Bank Act 1942 (inserted by section 16 of the Central Bank and Financial Services Authority of Ireland Act 2004).
52   Section 57BK of the Central Bank 1942.
53   For a critique of this separation, see E. Lomnicka, 'Consumer Credit Bill' in G. Howells *et al* (eds), *Yearbook of Consumer Law 2007* (Aldershot, 2007), p. 401.

four objectives of the FSA under the Financial Services and Markets Act 2000 ('FSMA'),[54] there is no designated consumer office within the statutory structure.[55] Nor does the FSMA allow for the introduction of statute-backed codes of practice in the way in which the Irish legislation does. Bearing these features in mind, it now falls to consider how the Financial Regulator has used these statutory powers in the development of the Code.[56]

The Code: A New Approach to Regulation

Following an extensive consultation process[57] and the commission of market research into the practical issues of concern to consumers, the Financial Regulator published a public response, setting out in detail the bases for its decisions regarding the key provisions in the Code.[58] The Code itself came into force on 1 August 2006 (although full implementation of all aspects of the Code was not required until 1 July 2007). Since the Code's publication, the Financial Regulator has issued a number of clarifications regarding provisions in the Code.[59] The Code applies to all 'regulated entities' (these are financial services providers regulated by the Financial Regulator) with a very small number of exceptions, discussed further below. The Code is divided into seven chapters. Chapter 1 sets out general principles, such as the requirements to act honestly, fairly and professionally in the best interests of customers and the market and to act with due care and diligence. This chapter applies to all customers of financial services and not just consumers. This chapter reflects the Financial Regulator's view of itself as a principles-

---

54 The four regulatory objectives of the FSA are set out in section 2(2) of the FSMA 2000. In addition to consumer protection, these objectives are market confidence, public awareness and the reduction of public crime. The consumer protection objective is further elaborated in section 5 of the FSMA.

55 As with the Irish legislation, the FSMA provides for the establishment of a consumer panel to 'represent the interests of consumers' (see section 10).

56 In addition to the Code, the Financial Regulator has been responsible for the introduction of Minimum Competency requirements which apply to all individuals who provide advice or sell retail financial products to consumers and the commencement of more widespread financial education, including a user friendly website (see www. itsyourmoney.ie) and the publication of comparative tables regarding price and conditions for certain financial products.

57 In response to the invitation for consultation, sixty-one submissions were made by a diverse range of organisations representing, among others, service providers, consumer associations and the Law Society.

58 See *Consumer Protection Code: Public Response to CP 10*, December, 2005 (available at www.ifsra.ie).

59 See Consumer Protection Code Clarifications Document issued on 10 July 2007; Clarification on Provision 4.14 of the Consumer Protection Code issued on 26 November 2007 (available at: www.ifsra.ie).

based regulator which sets out the principles which represent broad expectations regarding how financial services providers should interact with their consumer customers.[60] Chapter 2 contains the common rules for all regulated entities and applies to consumers only. The remaining chapters set out rules covering the provision of specific financial services to consumers. Chapter 3 covers banking products and services; chapter 4 covers loans; chapter 5 covers insurance products and services and chapter 6 covers investment products. The final chapter covers advertising. In a number of respects, outlined below, the Code makes an important contribution to consumer protection.

A code with a statutory basis

Perhaps the most striking feature of the Code is that it is not voluntary but rather has a statutory basis.[61] The Code clearly states that regulated entities are required to comply with the Code as a matter of law and that the Financial Regulator has the power to administer sanctions for a contravention of the Code. In this regard, the Regulator has access to a tiered range of sanctions. These include the issue of a caution or reprimand, a direction to refund or withhold some or all charges imposed in respect of a financial service provided, the imposition of a penalty of up to €500,000 for service providers who are natural persons and €5 million for other service providers, and the issue of a disqualifying direction.[62]

The Code contains a number of provisions regarding compliance. First, regulated entities are required to have adequate systems and controls in place in order to ensure compliance with the Code.[63] Secondly, regulated entities are required to respond to the Financial Regulator's request for information regarding compliance by providing information that is full, fair and accurate in all respects within a reasonable time.[64] Thirdly, if the Financial Regulator considers that a meeting with personnel of the regulated entity is required, the regulated entity must use its best endeavours to ensure that appropriate personnel participate in

---

60   M. O'Dea, Consumer Director of the Financial Regulator, 'The Role of Consumer Protection Codes in Financial Services', *About Banking*, 1 (2005): 18.

61   The current voluntary codes of practice (see n. 31 above) continue to operate alongside the Code. The Code expressly states that, if there is a conflict between the Code and the voluntary codes, compliance with the Code must take priority. There is also the possibility that provisions currently covered by voluntary codes may become part of the Code. For example, the Regulator has warned (*Public Response to CP 10*, p. 15) that the IBF codes on account switching may become part of the statutory Code if future monitoring of the voluntary codes reveals insufficient progress in implementation.

62   These sanctions are set out in section 33AQ of the Central Bank Act 1942 (inserted by section 10 of the Central Bank and Financial Services Authority Act 2004).

63   Chapter 2, para. 57.

64   Chapter 2, para. 58.

the meeting.[65] Fourthly, the regulated entity must be able, if required to do so, to provide records showing compliance with the Code for any prior period specified by the Financial Regulator (up to a maximum of six years).[66]

All of these compliance provisions suggest that the primary enforcement mechanism for the Code is intended to be inspection of written information, supplemented if necessary by oral inquiry. However, this is effective only in relation to those aspects of the Code where evidence of compliance may be recorded in writing. For other aspects of the Code, the Financial Regulator will have to rely, to a degree at least, on private monitoring by individual consumers. This is most likely to occur through individual consumer complaints made to the Financial Regulator itself, or more likely, to the Financial Services Ombudsman. Where the Financial Regulator 'suspects on reasonable grounds' that the regulated entity is committing or has committed a 'prescribed contravention', it may hold an inquiry to investigate this.[67] A 'prescribed contravention' includes a contravention of a code.[68]

Obviously, the effectiveness of this kind of private enforcement mechanism is largely reliant on consumers being aware of the existence of the Code and of the regulatory obligations it imposes on financial services providers. Because the Code is directed at providers rather than consumers, its tone is legalistic, formal and not at all user friendly. This presented a real impediment to the possibilities offered by private monitoring by consumers and constituted a serious limitation regarding the potential of the Code.[69] However, the Code is now supplemented by a consumer-friendly summary,[70] which is much more accessible. This document specifically informs consumers about their right to complain if they consider that a financial services provider is not following the principles or rules of the Code and it directs consumers to bring such complaints to the Financial Services Ombudsman. Provided that this version of the Code is effectively publicised, this move increases the possibilities of private monitoring and suggests a genuine commitment on the part of the Financial Regulator to delivering an effective protective system.

An integrated approach to consumer protection

With a relatively small number of exceptions, the Code applies to all entities regulated by the Financial Regulator. Thus, financial services providers subject

---

65   Chapter 2, para. 59.
66   Chapter 2, para. 60.
67   Section 33AO of the Central Bank Act 1942 (inserted by section 10 of the Central Bank and Financial Services Authority Act 2004).
68   Section 33AN of the Central Bank Act 1942.
69   See the arguments made in Donnelly, 'The Consumer Protection Code: A New Departure in the Regulation of Irish Financial Services Providers': 283.
70   See *Consumer Protection Code: Your Little Red Book*, IFSRA, 2007 (available at: www.itsyourmoney.ie).

to the Code include all credit institutions, insurance undertakings, investment businesses (other than in providing MiFID services[71]), insurance and mortgage intermediaries and non-deposit lenders.[72] In all respects, the Code extends to entities authorised in another EU or EEA Member State if they are providing a financial service in Ireland on a branch or cross-border basis. By bringing together consumer protection in this way, the Code represents a more accurate reflection of the cross-sector nature of many aspects of financial services provision. However, the Regulator's decision means that some providers, particular providers of banking and credit services, experienced more of a regulatory 'culture shock' than providers who were more used to mandatory conduct of business rules.

Two exceptions to the Code merit mention. These are the exemptions for moneylenders and for most activities carried out by credit unions.[73] At the time the Code was introduced, there was concern about imposing a heavy compliance burden on these small-scale operations which, in the case of credit unions are non-profit, local organisations.[74] However, the omission meant that certain, typically lower income and more vulnerable consumers, were not afforded the protection of the Code. This is especially significant in the context of credit unions because of the extent of the role which credit unions play in the Irish financial services market.[75] In response to concerns regarding these exemptions, in March 2008, the Financial Regulator issued a Consultation Paper seeking views on a Draft Consumer Protection Code for Licensed Moneylenders.[76] It is expected that the Code will be in place by the end of 2008. In relation to credit unions, the Financial Regulator has adopted a different approach. Reflecting the separate regulatory

---

71   These are services or activities set out in Annex 1 of the MiFID. The listed services include portfolio management; investment advice; dealing on own account; and underwriting of financial instruments. Because the MiFID had not been transposed into Irish law at the time the Code was introduced, providers of services covered by the MiFID were not brought within the ambit of the Code.

72   The latter category of lender, typically operational in the sub-prime market, became subject to the regulatory authority of the Financial Regulator (and correspondingly to the Code) under the Markets in Financial Instruments and Miscellaneous Provisions Act 2007 with effect from 1 February 2008.

73   The Code applies to credit unions only in relation to activities which are not required to be authorised or registered with the Financial Regulator (these are the credit union's 'core services' as set out in the Credit Union Act 1997). The main activity which credit unions are likely to engage in, in this regard, is the provision of insurance services and therefore this is typically the only aspect of credit unions' conduct covered by the Code.

74   Credit unions are also excluded from the provisions of the Consumer Credit Act 1995 (which transposes the Consumer Credit Directive into Irish law).

75   There are over 525 credit unions in Ireland and Northern Ireland, which in total hold assets of approximately €15 billion and have an estimated membership of three million. See further: www.creditunion.ie.

76   Consultation Paper 33 (IFSRA, 2008).

regime for credit unions,[77] in March 2008, the Financial Regulator proposed a Draft Voluntary Code of Practice for Credit Unions.[78] The voluntary nature of the draft code reflects the current legislative position which does not provide a legal basis for the Financial Regulator to subject credit unions to a mandatory code. The Financial Regulator is not currently advocating an amendment of credit union legislation in this respect although, in the event of a general review of the Credit Union Act 1997, it has stated an intention to seek to have the Code placed on a statutory footing.

A new definition of consumer

The Code adopts a remarkably broad definition of 'consumer'. Unlike the commonly used legislative definition of a consumer as a natural person acting outside of his or her business, trade or profession, a 'consumer' under the Code is defined as any of the following:

a. a natural person acting outside their business, trade or profession;
b. a person or group of persons, but not an incorporated body with an annual turnover in excess of €3 million (for the avoidance of doubt a group of persons includes partnerships and other unincorporated bodies such as clubs, charities and trusts, not consisting entirely of bodies corporate);
c. incorporated bodies having an annual turnover of €3 million or less in the previous financial year (provided that such body shall not be a member of a group of companies having a combined turnover greater than the said €3 million); or
d. a member of a credit union.[79]

Thus, the category of consumer is no longer restricted to natural persons but extends to companies (provided they fall within the specified financial limits), partnerships, clubs, charities and trusts. Moreover, in order to be a 'consumer' under the Code, it is not necessary that the individual be acting 'outside their trade, business or profession'.[80]

---

77 Credit unions are regulated by the Credit Union Act 1997 and are subject to a separate regime within the structure of the Financial Regulator. The relevant regulatory body is the Registrar of Credit Unions which is a separate entity within the Financial Regulator.

78 Consultation Paper 32 (IFSRA, 2008).

79 Although a member of a credit union is included in the definition of 'consumer,' as noted above, the Code does not apply to credit unions' core activities.

80 In this regard, the definition may seem misleading – the first part of the definition, which is the standard definition of a consumer, is in fact unnecessary because the category is entirely subsumed within the second part of the definition.

Hardly surprisingly, this aspect of the Code caused some consternation during the consultation process. Industry submissions on the draft Code were opposed to the extension of the definition beyond natural persons, citing as difficulties the costs arising from the increased bureaucracy in cases where, it was argued, this is largely unnecessary.[81] In resisting industry pressures, the Regulator reiterated its commitment to the principle that small businesses should be able to avail of the protections of the Code.[82] The approach of the Code in this regard reflects recent developments at a European level. As discussed above, the Payment Services Directive recognises the category of 'micro-enterprises', which Member States may include within the scope of the protections afforded to consumers under the Directive.[83] Although the Code is somewhat more generous in the monetary limits used, the approach adopted recognises that the rationale for consumer protection outlined above – information asymmetry, distributive justice and community values – do not disappear simply because a customer is acting for business rather than personal purposes. Further, the Code's approach avoids the awkward question of whether an investor is to be categorised as a consumer or not. As Cartwright notes, investment is different to consumption, yet smaller investors share many of the features (and vulnerabilities) of 'consumers'.[84] Because of the breath of the Code's definition, this issue does not arise.

Access to services

Under the Code, regulated entities are prohibited, without prejudice to their legitimate commercial aims, from preventing access to basic financial services though their policies, procedures or working practices.[85] The intended ambit of this requirement is unclear. Certainly, it is broader in scope than the obligations arising under the Equal Status Act 2000, which prohibits discrimination in the provision of facilities for 'banking, insurance, grants, loans, credit or financing'[86] on nine stated grounds (which do not include socio-economic status).[87] However, there is uncertainty regarding exactly what kinds of policies, procedures or practices would fall foul of the Code under this provision and, to date, the Financial Regulator has done little to clarify the issue.[88]

---

81   See *Public Response to CP 10*, p. 7.
82   *Ibid.*
83   See text to n. 20 above.
84   Cartwright, p. 4.
85   Chapter 1, para. 11.
86   Section 2 of the Equal Status Act 2000.
87   The nine grounds are gender, marital status, family status, sexual orientation, religion, age, disability, race and membership of the travelling community (see section 3(2) of the Equal Status Act 2000).
88   The only further detail is found in Chapter 2, para. 7 which states that the statutory anti-money laundering requirements arising under the Criminal Justice Act 1994 to obtain photographic identification when opening an account or when providing

A recent study on financial exclusion in Ireland indicates that access to financial services constitutes a significant problem for many Irish people.[89] Based on a HBS survey, in 1999/2000,[90] almost 33 per cent of Irish households were without a current account.[91] This survey also found that, consistent with international trends in this regard, low-income households were significantly less likely to have a current account. A Eurobarometer survey in 2003 found that, across the EU15 countries surveyed, Ireland had the second highest number of respondents without a current account which comes with a payment card or cheque book.[92] In terms of other financial services, an EU-SILC survey found that over half the Irish adult population had difficulty saving income regularly and that 28 per cent of the population were without home-contents insurance.[93] Again, there was a clear link between socio-economic status and these forms of exclusion.

As is clear from the extensive literature, there are complex reasons for financial exclusion, especially among people in vulnerable socio-economic positions.[94] It is unlikely that the general provision in the Code will do much to address the issue of financial exclusion in Ireland and, without determined engagement by the Financial Regulator, this aspect of the Code could well be ignored by financial services providers. The Financial Regulator has indicated its intention to work with poverty organisations to analyse the difficulties encountered by some members of society in accessing financial services.[95] In this respect, there is a need for more

---

certain financial services are unaffected by the provision. The Consumer Protection Code Clarifications Document, above n. 59, does not refer to this aspect of the Code.

89   C. Corr, *Financial Exclusion in Ireland: An Exploratory Study and Policy Review*, Combat Poverty Agency, 2006.

90   *Household Budget Survey, 1999/2000* (Central Statistics Office, 2001).

91   Although there is no formal definition of what constitutes financial exclusion, the absence of a bank account is widely accepted as a relevant factor. See E. Kempson, C. Whyley, J. Caskey and S. Collard, *In or Out? Financial Exclusion: A Literature and Research Review*, Financial Services Authority (2000).

92   European Commission, *Public Opinion in Europe: Financial Services Report B* (2004). 46 per cent of Irish respondents did not have a current account with only Greece (with 80 per cent of respondents) having a higher number of respondents. The EU15 average was 19 per cent.

93   EU Survey on Income and Living Conditions 2004, Central Statistics Office (2005).

94   Kempson, Whyley, Caskey, Collard, Chapter 4 list as possible impediments to access: geographical location, disability, risk assessment methods, racism, marketing, lack of appropriate products, affordability, lack of financial literacy, psychological barriers and mistrust of suppliers, language and cultural factors and government regulations – for example money laundering legislation. See also I. Ramsay and T. Williams, 'Racial and Gender Equality in Markets for Financial Services', in P. Cartwright (ed.), *Consumer Protection in Financial Services* (London, 1999) regarding the role of freedom of contract ideology in perpetuating inequalities in access to financial services.

95   *Public Response to CP 10*, p. 14.

detailed empirical work to inform the development of policy in this area[96] and it may well be necessary for a detailed code aimed specifically at the issue of financial exclusion to be introduced.[97]

Information provision and warnings

The Code contains detailed information provision requirements.[98] This, of itself, is hardly unusual. Information provision has become established as the consumer protection mechanism of choice in relation to financial services.[99] What is notable about the Code, however, is that it addresses some of the more obvious difficulties that arise in the communication of information to consumers.[100] Chapter 2 of the Code contains detailed instructions regarding the ways in which required information must be communicated. All printed information must be of a print size to be clearly legible;[101] the information provided must be clear and comprehensible and the method of presentation must not disguise, diminish or obscure important

---

96   Corr's report for the Combat Poverty Agency, above n. 88, constitutes an important first step in this regard but this needs to be supplemented with focused surveys of the Irish financial services markets.

97   This is the suggestion made by Kempson, Whyley, Caskey, Collard and by Corr.

98   For example, Chapter 2 requires all regulated entities to draw up their terms of business and provide a copy of these to the consumer before doing business with the consumer. These terms must include details of complaints procedures and of any relevant compensation scheme. Information must also be provided regarding charges imposed and any conflicts of interest. Additional information requirements are imposed in relation to specified services.

99   See *Fair, Clear and Competitive: The Consumer Credit Market in the 21ˢᵗ Century*, Cm 6040 (DTI, 2003). Information provision is a fundamental component of EC consumer policy: see Commission Communication, 'Empowering Consumers, Enhancing their Welfare, Effectively Protecting Them', COM (2007) 99 final. See generally G. Howells, A. Janssen and R. Schultze (eds), *Information Rights and Obligations: A Challenge for Party Autonomy and Transactional Fairness* (Aldershot, 2005); G. Howells, 'The Potential and Limits of Consumer Empowerment by Information', *Journal of Law and Society*, 32 (2005): 349.

100 For discussion (from diverse perspectives) of the difficulties with information provision as a consumer protection mechanism, see W. Whitford, 'The Functions of Disclosure Regulation in Consumer Transactions', *Wisconsin Law Review*, 2 (1973): 400; T. Paredes, 'Blinded by the Light: Information Overload and Its Consequences for Securities Regulation', *Washington University Law Quarterly*, 81 (2003): 417; I. Ramsay, 'From Truth in Lending to Responsible Lending', in Howells *et al* (eds), *Information Rights and Obligations: A Challenge for Party Autonomy and Transactional Fairness*; pp. 47–66; Howells, 'The Potential and Limits of Consumer Empowerment by Information'; Donnelly and White, pp. 282–4.

101 Chapter 2, para. 22.

information.[102] Information must also be provided on a timely basis, which takes account of the time necessary for the consumer to absorb the information.[103]

The use of specific warnings for certain products is well established as a mechanism for information provision and this is widely adopted by the Code. The relevant documentation provided to consumers must contain special warnings regarding the risks in giving a guarantee;[104] the effects of missing a scheduled repayment;[105] the consequences of taking out a 'lifetime' (equity release) mortgage;[106] the use of illustrations in relation to investment products;[107] and the risks in tracker bond products.[108] There are also warning requirements in relation to advertisements for fixed rate and debt consolidation loans; variable rate mortgages; hire purchase and interest only mortgages and in relation to investment products.[109] All warnings required under the Code must be 'prominent', which is defined as meaning in a box, in bold type and of a larger font size than the norm.[110]

Responsible lending

The concept of 'responsible' lending has become more central to the consumer credit policy agenda in recent years.[111] In *Fair, Clear and Competitive*, the DTI noted that, while it is up to individuals to make responsible borrowing decisions, there is also a role for lenders in preventing over-indebtedness through responsible lending.[112] At a European level, the principle of responsible lending formed part of the basis for revising the Consumer Credit Directive in 2002.[113] The principle (albeit in a much diluted form) remains part of the current Directive.[114] Recital 26 of the Directive, as amended by the Parliament, states that Member States should take appropriate measures to ensure responsible practices during all phases of the credit relationship, taking into account the specific features of their credit market. The Recital also requires Member States to enact the necessary supervision to avoid creditors engaging in irresponsible lending and giving out

---

102 Chapter 2, para. 12.
103 Chapter 2, para. 13.
104 Chapter 4, para. 3.
105 Chapter 4, para. 9.
106 Chapter 4, para. 18.
107 Chapter 6, para. 4.
108 Chapter 6, para. 8.
109 Chapter 7.
110 Chapter 2, para. 6.
111 See Ramsay, 'From Truth in Lending to Responsible Lending'.
112 Above, n. 99, para. 5.61.
113 Proposal for a Directive of the European Parliament and of the Council on the Harmonization of the Laws, Regulations and Administrative Provisions of the Member States concerning Credit for Consumers (Brussels, COM (2002) 443 final 2002/0222 (COD)).
114 Directive 2008/48/EC.

credit without prior assessment of creditworthiness. Article 5(6) of the Directive requires Member States to ensure that creditors (and credit intermediaries) provide 'adequate explanations' to consumers in order to enable the consumer 'to assess whether the proposed credit agreement is adapted to his needs and to his financial situation'.

The Code goes further than the proposed Directive in giving effect to responsible lending principles. First, the Code bans some commonly used practices among credit providers. It prohibits regulated entities from offering unsolicited pre-approved credit facilities and from increasing a consumer's credit card limit unless there has been a specific request from the consumer to do so.[115] Predictably, these practice restrictions were resisted by lenders during the consultation prior to the introduction of the Code.[116] However, the Regulator retained the restrictions based on evidence that the prohibited practices could tempt consumers into overspending.

Secondly, the Code imposes an obligation on all regulated entities, including credit providers, to ensure the suitability of the product offered for the specific consumer. This is achieved through the imposition of a 'know your customer' requirement to the effect that, before a regulated entity provides a product or service to a consumer, it must 'gather and record sufficient information from the consumer to enable it to provide a recommendation or a product or service appropriate to that consumer'.[117] The regulated entity must then use this information and any 'other relevant facts about the consumer of which the regulated entity is aware' in order to ensure that any product or service offered to the consumer is suitable to that consumer and that any product recommended to the consumer is the most suitable product for that consumer.[118] These requirements do not apply where the consumer has specified the product and the product provider and has not received any advice; nor do they apply to the sale or purchase of foreign currency. They are also not applicable to the provision of a 'basic banking service'[119] provided that the regulated entity has alerted the consumer to any restrictions on the account and/or to the availability of a lower cost alternative. The effect of these requirements is that lenders must choose the most appropriate form of credit for each consumer

---

115 Chapter 4, paras 1–2. Compare the voluntary initiative taken by the ANZ Bank in Australia not to offer credit card limit increases to customers who have had a recent poor credit performance: see N. Howell, 'Preventing Consumer Credit Over-Commitment and Irresponsible Lending in Australia', in Howells *et al.* (eds), *The Yearbook of Consumer Law 2007*, p. 391.

116 See *Public Response to CP 10*, pp. 29–30.

117 Chapter 2, para. 24. Consumers may refuse to provide the information and, in this case, the refusal must be noted on the consumer's record. Regulated entities are also required to endeavour to have the consumer certify the information provided and, if the consumer refuses to do so, to note this in his or her records.

118 Chapter 2, para. 30.

119 This is defined as a 'current account, overdraft, ordinary deposit account or a term deposit account with a term of less than one year'.

based on the consumer's financial circumstances. This suggests that lenders must not make a loan if they do not consider that the consumer will be able to make the necessary repayments.

Conclusion: The Contribution of the Code to Consumer Protection

Having described the more notable aspects of the Code, it falls finally to ask what other jurisdictions can learn from the approach of the Irish Financial Regulator. In this discussion, it is important to recognise that the Code is still relatively new and that it would be premature to undertake a thoroughgoing assessment of the effectiveness of the Code from a practical perspective. Such an assessment will be necessary; the model can only be evaluated fully in light of what it actually delivers in terms of modification in suppliers' behaviour and practical developments in consumers' rights and confidence. For present purposes, the section to follow will concentrate on the Code as a regulatory model rather than attempt to evaluate the way in which the Financial Regulator has actually delivered on the Code.

An obvious first question is whether the Code's model of an enforceable code of practice constitutes a suitable regulatory device in the financial services context. There are two aspects to this question; first, is a statutory code preferable to legislation, and secondly, is a statutory code preferable to a voluntary code? Cartwright notes that, as regulatory devices, codes of practice have an advantage over legislation because of their flexibility and adaptability.[120] New developments can easily be incorporated into a code without having to wait for legislators' time and energy to be devoted to the enterprise. Furthermore, codes can set out requirements in language that would be difficult to incorporate into the formal legislative framework.[121] It is possible to leave more room for development and to adopt a more principles-based approach. Regulators are not left reliant on judicial interpretation, but can issue their own interpretations of key provisions as the need arises. This allows a more efficient and organic approach to be adopted. As against this argument, it must be recognised that legislation is more high-profile and likely to be more convincing for consumers who may be unfamiliar with the idea of a statutorily enforceable code. On balance, the approach of the Code may well be superior to legislation setting out conduct of business rules but it is important for regulators to recognise that this model requires extra efforts on the regulator's part to inform consumers of their rights.

The second issue is whether an enforceable code along the lines of the Irish model is superior to voluntary codes. In order to explore this further, it is necessary to consider the issue of enforceability of 'voluntary' codes of practice and ask what the addition of formal enforcement provisions adds to the regulatory framework. For the main part, voluntary codes will have some degree of in-built compliance

---

120 Cartwright, p. 123.
121 *Ibid.*, p. 124.

regimes. Cartwright outlines the compliance procedures set out in *The Banking Code* which allow the relevant monitoring body (The Banking Code Standards Board) to investigate breaches of *The Banking Code* by subscribers and to administer sanctions for these breaches.[122] These sanctions include the publication of details of the breach, the issue of warnings, the suspension of the subscriber and the public censure of the subscriber; in effect, one form or another of 'naming and shaming'. Cartwright argues that, while these kinds of sanction may be both significant and effective,[123] they should be approached with caution because they hand enforcement over to the 'capricious jury of public opinion'.[124] This creates a risk that the reality of the sanction may not reflect the extent of the breach of the code and that regulators will have no real control over the impact of the sanction.

Beyond the voluntary code's self-contained compliance regimes, there may also be some degree of legal backing for the provisions of voluntary codes through the imposition of civil liability. Arguments have been made that a bank's advertisement of adherence to a voluntary code may constitute an implied term in the banker/customer contract[125] and that consumers may raise a reasonable expectation argument regarding compliance with a voluntary code.[126] However, the law in this regard is by no means clearly established[127] and it would be a mistake to expect too much from the law in terms of enforcing voluntary codes of practice. Furthermore, the fundamental problem remains that only those providers who voluntarily subscribe to the code may be bound by it.

In addition to these issues, Cartwright expresses other doubts about the extent to which voluntary codes of practice can effectively protect the consumer.[128] First, there are issues of credibility and public belief in the regulatory process;[129] secondly, there are issues of visibility and public awareness of the existence of the code.[130] Finally, there are competition issues; voluntary codes may come to represent a lowest common standard which service providers will not exceed for fear of losing a competitive advantage.[131]

Ultimately, as Cartwright notes, a judgement on the effectiveness of voluntary codes of practice 'may only be made if we decide against what we are comparing them'.[132] While a persuasive argument may be made to the effect that codes of

---

122 *Ibid.*, pp. 141–2.

123 *Ibid.*, p 144.

124 Cartwright *ibid.*, citing B. Fisse and J. Braithwaite, *The Impact of Publicity on Corporate Offender* (Albany, 1983), p. 310.

125 See Ellinger, Lomnicka and Hooley, p. 63.

126 See A. Barron, 'Reasonable Expectations, Good Faith and Self-Regulatory Codes', in Howells *et al* (eds), *The Yearbook of Consumer Law 2007*, p. 3 onwards.

127 See Ellinger, Lomnicka and Hooley and Barron, *ibid.*

128 Cartwright, p. 146.

129 *Ibid.*, pp. 146–7.

130 *Ibid.*, p. 147.

131 *Ibid.*, pp. 147–8.

132 *Ibid.*, p. 148.

practices are superior to legislation, it is more difficult to justify voluntary codes when compared with an enforceable model along the lines of the Code. In this respect, the approach taken by the Irish Financial Regulator certainly merits serious consideration by other jurisdictions.

Having argued that a statutory code represents an appropriate regulatory device, the second question to consider is whether, at a level of detail, the approach taken by the Code has been the most effective utilisation of this device. As is evident from the discussion above, the Financial Regulator cannot be accused of having shirked its responsibility to engage with consumer protection issues. From the extended definition of 'consumer' to the imposition of responsible lending obligations, the Code takes a vigorous approach to consumer protection. It is difficult to imagine any circumstances in which a voluntary code of practice would have provided the scope of consumer protection afforded by the Code.

This does not, of itself, mean that the approach taken by the Code is inevitably the most appropriate response to consumers' protection needs. Broader social consequences of consumer protection must be recognised. For example, Ramsay shows that the imposition of responsible lending obligations on lenders may leave some (especially vulnerable) consumers with no choice but to move out of the regulated credit market and use unregulated credit providers.[133] It is essential that the Financial Regulator reviews the effectiveness of the Code, not just in terms of the enforcement of its requirements, but also as regards its impact on all aspects of the relationship between society, financial services providers and consumers. In this context, the Financial Regulator must engage more actively with the issue of financial exclusion. It is also important that the Financial Regulator maintains its policy of using market research and other empirical research in order to ensure the relevance of its approach for real consumers. On the whole, however, the Consumer Protection Code may fairly be regarded as providing a worthwhile model for regulators in other jurisdictions to consider in developing and revising their approaches to protecting consumers of financial services.

---

133 Ramsay, 'From Truth in Lending to Responsible Lending', p. 59.

6 Re-regulating Unsecured Consumer Credit in Japan: Over-indebted Borrowers, the Supreme Court and New Legislation[1]

Souichirou Kozuka[2] and Luke Nottage[3]

Consumer Over-indebtedness World-wide

Beginning in the US, but spreading also to Australia, Europe and Japan, consumer over-indebtedness has become a pressing socio-economic problem in most post-industrial capitalist democracies. Particularly since the 1980s, the liberalisation

---

1   This chapter first appeared on 1 September 2007 as *Sydney Law School Research Paper* 07/62, available at: http://ssrn.com/abstract=1019392; and was updated in January 2008 for the *Yearbook of Consumer Law 2009*. It is based on Parts I–III of our paper, 'Re-regulating Consumer Credit in Japan: Culture, Economics and Politics in Contemporary Law Reform', presented in July 2007 at conferences of the Law and Society Association (Berlin) and the Japan Studies Association of Australia (Canberra). Parts IV–V of that paper form the core of a manuscript completed in December 2007 for a collection edited by J. Niemi-Kiesilainen, I. Ramsay and W. Whitford, the main organisers of multiple panels on comparative consumer over-indebtedness at the Berlin conference: S Kozuka and L. Nottage, 'The Myth of the Cautious Consumer: Law, Culture, Economics and Politics in the Rise and Partial Fall of Unsecured Lending in Japan', in J. Niemi-Kiesilainen, I. Ramsay and W. Whitford, (eds), *Comparative Consumer Credit, Over-indebtedness and Bankruptcy: National and International Dimensions* (forthcoming). We are grateful for the opportunity to be involved in that project; for helpful comments by them and other conference participants; for the research assistance of Wan Sang Lung and Joel Rheuben (through a grant from the Legal Scholarship Support Fund); and to Tom Ginsburg, Colin Jones and Andy Pardieck. We warmly welcome further feedback, to L.Nottage@ usyd.edu.au or kozuka@sophia.ac.jp, as we complete a third companion paper drawing out more normative implications from this chapter and our book chapter: S. Kozuka and L. Nottage, 'Reforming Unsecured Consumer Credit Markets in Japan: Empirically-Informed Normativism', *Sydney Law School Research Papers* (2008) (Forthcoming).

2   Professor, Sophia Law School, Tokyo.

3   Associate Professor, Sydney Law School; Co-director, Australian Network for Japanese Law (ANJeL).

and globalisation of financial markets combined with advances in information technology (IT) have underpinned rapid expansion in the types and extent of loans to consumers. Governments generally have welcomed such lending to revive and expand economic growth through consumer spending. However, a growing portion of consumer debt has been used to finance present consumption rather than building up assets and wealth, resulting in individual over-indebtedness as well as concerns for long-term macro-economic stability. Major causes of consumer bankruptcy are typically the sudden loss of income due to job loss, family break-ups and (especially in the US) medical problems; but over-commitment or excessive credit is another important factor behind over-indebtedness. More deep-rooted causes include many behavioural biases infecting consumer decisions about credit, exploited directly or indirectly by lenders.[4]

Growing concern about consumer over-indebtedness has led to waves of regulatory responses world-wide,[5] going well beyond relief provided by traditional contract law through doctrines like 'unconscionability'.[6] Many responses are quite similar, but lags and emphases vary depending on the country. In the US fringe banking market, for example, a first wave of socio-economic concern over high-interest rate lending to consumers, particularly small unsecured 'payday loans', was partially addressed by enacting usury laws. The Model Uniform Small Loan Act of 1916 resulted in legislation in all states over the first half of the twentieth century. These laws generally restricted rates and required licensing. Developments in federal law short-circuited them in the 1970s, by allowing banks to lend inter-state from the minority of states retaining no interest rate restrictions,[7] but restrictions gradually have been re-imposed in recent years.[8]

Over the mid-twentieth century, most states added legislation extending usury restrictions to instalment sales of consumer goods, which ballooned as owning washing machines and other consumer durables became part of the American suburban dream. In the era ushered in by President Kennedy's 1962 declaration of basic rights for consumers, including the right to be informed,[9] the federal Truth in

---

4   R. Harris and E. Albin, 'Bankruptcy Policy in the Light of Manipulation in Credit Advertising', *Theoretical Inquiries in Law*, 7(2) (2006): 6; I. Ramsay, *Consumer Law and Policy: Text and Materials on Regulating Consumer Markets* (Oxford, 2007), pp. 243–9.

5   N. Howell and J. Hughes, 'Consumer Credit Regulation: An International Overview', *Centre for Credit and Consumer Law (Griffith University) Background Paper*, April 2005, available at: http://www.griffith.edu.au/centre/cccl/pubs/ccrio0405.pdf.

6   L. Nottage, 'Form and Substance in US, English, New Zealand and Japanese Law: A Framework for Better Comparisons of Developments in the Law of Unfair Contracts', *Victoria University of Wellington Law Review*, 26 (1996): 247.

7   J. White, 'The Usury Trompe L'oeil', *South Carolina Law Review*, 51 (2000): 445.

8   R.J. Mann and J. Hawkins, 'Just until Payday', *UCLA Law Review*, 54(4) (2007): 855, at 871–3.

9   See http://www.fairtrading.nsw.gov.au/shopping/shoppingtips/internationalconsumerrights.html.

Lending Act of 1968 standardised disclosure requirements for consumer credit.[10] Most state legislatures also constrained other deceptive practices in consumer contract negotiations more generally.

Over the 1970s, prompted by deregulation and mortgage-backed securitisation, the consumer credit boom increasingly involved larger loans, for automobiles as well as home equity involving lending against the home rather than to acquire it. Many consumer finance companies therefore 'moved onwards and upwards', beyond the pale of the Small Loan Acts, and credit card companies rapidly filled and expanded the market for small dollar credit.[11] The Oil Shocks exacerbated consumer indebtedness, leading to pro-debtor bankruptcy reform in 1978, partially rolled back only in 2005.[12]

By 2006, broadly similar patterns in consumer lending, over-indebtedness and regulatory responses had become evident in jurisdictions such as Australia, the European Union (EU), and Japan.[13] Although Japanese consumers, like their continental European counterparts, still do not use credit cards much for debt, consumer credit markets have grown strongly in recent decades.[14] As explained below, by 2006 about three million out of 14 million Japanese consumers with unsecured loans were probably over-indebted. The Japanese legal system has had trouble keeping up with the attendant socio-economic problems, but the main pieces have been put in place.

The Japanese Civil Code (Law No. 9 of 1898), although partly influenced by French law at the time, mostly followed German law and did not enact a general usury prohibition. However, caps were added by the Interest Rate Restriction Law ('IRRL', No. 100 of 1954); but with a precursor dating back to the Meiji Era (Ordinance No. 66 of 1877). Consumer protection was first enhanced through a Basic Law of 1965 (recently amended by Law No. 70 of 2004) and the Instalment Sales Law (No. 159 of 1961).[15] A second wave of concern for consumer issues,

---

10   C. Bruch, 'Taking the Pay out of Payday Loans: Putting an End to the Usurious and Unconscionable Interest Rates Charged by Payday Lenders', *University of Cincinnati Law Review*, 60 (2001): 1257, at 1262.

11   L. Drysdale and K. Keest, 'The Two-Tiered Consumer Financial Services Marketplace', *South Carolina Law Review*, 51 (2000): 590, at 618–25.

12   R.J. Mann, 'Bankruptcy Reform and the "Sweat Box" Of Credit Card Debt', *University of Illinois Law Review* (2007): 375.

13   N. Howell, 'Preventing Consumer Credit Over-Commitment and Irresponsible Lending in Australia', in G. Howells *et al* (eds), *Yearbook of Consumer Law 2007* (Aldershot, 2007) pp. 387–94; Productivity Commission, 'Review of Australia's Consumer Policy Framework: Draft Report', Vol. 2 (2007), available at: http://www. pc.gov.au/inquiry/consumer; Ramsay *Consumer Law and Policy: Text and Materials on Regulating Consumer Markets*.

14   R.J. Mann, 'Credit Cards and Debit Cards in the United States and Japan', *Vanderbilt Law Review*, 55 (2002): 1055.

15   P.L. Maclachlan, *Consumer Politics in Postwar Japan: The Institutional Boundaries of Citizen Activism* (New York, 2002).

beginning with enactment of the Product Liability Law (No. 85 of 1994),[16] included greater control over negotiations of consumer contracts as well as certain unfair terms (Consumer Contract Law, No. 61 of 2000). As economic stagnation and consumer bankruptcies nonetheless accelerated over the 1990s, even innovative case management techniques initiated by courts in Tokyo proved insufficient.[17] The Civil Rehabilitation Law (No. 225 of 1999) added a debtor-in-possession regime that has proved a popular alternative for over-indebted consumers since amendments in 2001, although regular insolvency cases under the Bankruptcy Law (No. 75 of 2004) have also grown strongly since the early 1990s.[18]

The most remarkable reforms in Japan were enacted on 20 December 2006, following a series of important judgments from its highest court since the late 1990s. In particular, on 13 January 2006 the Supreme Court held that 'grey zone' interest had to be returned because it could not be deemed to have been paid 'voluntarily' if the loan agreement (as is usual) contained an acceleration clause requiring repayment in full in the event of borrower default.[19] Taking the next step, as detailed below, by mid-2010 the legislative amendments will completely eliminate any 'grey zone' interest formed by the gap between the 29.2 per cent maximum under legislation distinct from the IRRL, which had capped interest at 20 per cent. The new legislation also brings in (by December 2007) a revamped 'suitability rule' requiring lenders to avoid 'unsuitable solicitation' in light of the borrower's knowledge, experience, finances and purposes. Although this does not provide direct public law sanctions for violations, teeth will be added from 2010 when lenders must check borrowers' annual income to ensure loans generally do not exceed one-third. Only a few jurisdictions in Australia and the US have extended such suitability rules to certain types of consumer loans, although there is growing pressure to strengthen such regimes following the subprime mortgage lending market collapse in the US since mid-2007.[20]

---

16   L. Nottage, *Product Safety and Liability Law in Japan: From Minamata to Mad Cows* (London, 2004).

17   Compare D.H. Foote, *Saiban to Shakai [Courts and Society]* (Tokyo, 2006).

18   K. Anderson, 'Japanese Insolvency Law after a Decade of Reform', *Canadian Business Law Journal*, 43 (2006): 2.

19   Supreme Court, 13 January 2006 (Minshu 60-1-1).

20   See K. Engel and P. McCoy, 'A Tale of Three Markets: The Law and Economics of Predatory Lending', *Texas Law Review*, 80(6) (2002): 1259; K. Engel and P. McCoy, 'Turning a Blind Eye: Wall Street Finance of Predatory Lending', *Fordham Law Review*, 75 (2007): 2039; OECD, 'The Report on OECD Member Countries' Approaches to Consumer Contracts', DSTI/CP(2006)8/FINAL, available at: http://www.oecd.org/dataoecd/11/28/38991787.pdf; A. Pardieck, 'Japan and the Moneylenders: Activist Courts and Substantive Justice', *Pacific Rim Law & Policy Journal* (2008), forthcoming. North Carolina, Ohio and Pennsylvania have all introduced suitability test requirements in some form, and most other states appear to be seriously considering, or in the process of adopting, similar measures. There is also traction for a Federal law governing predatory lending. For an overview of

The impact on Japan's unsecured consumer loan industry has already been massive. In the wake of the Supreme Court decision, the largest five lenders had to pay 176.9 billion yen to their borrowers and ex-borrowers for illegally accepting interest in excess of the grey zone during the year 2006.[21] By the time the new legislation is fully in force, in stages by June 2010, only 2000 out of around 14,000 registered lenders are expected to survive. Even the 'big seven', dominating 70 per cent of the market, are drastically cutting costs and operations.[22] A number of Japan's major banks, too, have already taken significant profit hits from their shareholdings in consumer lenders as well as the effects on their credit card divisions.[23] Over 2008 the 24 trillion yen market was expected to decline by three trillion yen, leading to a 1 percent drop in GDP just as Japan seemed finally to be pulling itself out of the economic doldrums.[24]

Oddly, however, the emergence and re-regulation of consumer credit in Japan has hardly been covered in the otherwise now voluminous academic literature on Japanese law in Western languages, especially in English.[25] A pre-eminent US scholar of consumer debt problems has produced a fine study contrasting a

---

developments nationwide, see the National State Attorneys General Program at Columbia University, available at: http://www.law.columbia.edu/center_program/ag/predatorylend.

21 See *Gekkan Shohisha Shinyo [White Paper on the Credit Industry]* (September 2007) p. 38.

22 Already, a mid-tier lender has gone bankrupt (M. Yasu and F. Flynn, 'Credia Files for Bankruptcy with Debts of 75.8 billion yen', *Bloomberg*, 14 September 2007), and top-tier Sanyo Shinpan has been forced to merge with the larger Promise ('Promise acquires Sanyo Shinpan', *The Japan Times*, 15 September 2007). However, generally lenders appeared to be back in the black by year's end: K. Takahara, 'Consumer lenders back to black after grey-zone ills', *The Japan Times*, 9 November 2007; M. Yasu, 'Aiful Turns to Profit as Loan, Refund Provisions Fall', *Bloomberg*, 13 November 2007.

23 'Mitsubishi UFJ Nicos to post ¥100 billion net loss', *The Japan Times*, 21 September 2007; 'Shinsei Bank lowers projected profit again', *The Japan Times*, 14 November 2007; K. Takahara, 'Sumitomo Mitsui logs 30% profit drop', *The Japan Times*, 20 November 2007.

24 'Shark-infested Waters: Consumer Lending in Japan', *The Economist*, 12 August 2006, p. 63; 'Cap on Loan Interest Raises Fear of Setback for Japan's Recovery', *Financial Times*, 14 December 2006, p. 2; 'Citigroup Expects Big Losses in Japan', *Financial Times*, 10 January 2007, p. 25. The number of registered lenders had already declined to less than 12000 by the end of March 2007. See statistics cited in *Gekkan Shohisha Shinyo*, p. 43. See also generally *Toyo Keizai* (2 December 2006), featuring the impact of the new Moneylenders Law on the consumer finance industry.

25 See generally H. Baum and L. Nottage, *Japanese Business Law in Western Languages: An Annotated Selective Bibliography* (Colorado, 1998), updated in H. Baum and L. Nottage, '*Auswahlbibliographie* [Selected Bibliography]', in H. Baum (ed.), *Handbuch des Japanischen Handels- und Wirtschaftsrechts [Japanese Business Law Handbook]* (Cologne, 2009), forthcoming.

narrower point: how credit cards in Japan have been used overwhelmingly as a payment mechanism and, hence, the slow uptake of debit cards.[26] One scholar described as a leader of the 'the new generation'[27] of Japanese law scholars outside Japan introduced broader developments in consumer credit and indebted consumers, but focused on the disturbing, but relatively small, proportion who end up committing suicide.[28]

Until 2007, the most comprehensive work published in English about the legal and practical issues of consumer debt was actually provided by a review essay included recently in the Journal of Japanese Law, which we help edit. The book reviewed was a bestseller published in 2003, where two non-lawyer authors explained legal and practical ways to 'not repay the money you owed' (*karita kane wa kaesuna*).[29] The essay offered a bittersweet taste of a voluminous literature in Japanese that has spread from the popular press squarely into mainstream legal writing.[30] Just as this essay was going to press, a US lawyer visiting from the University of Washington presented the results of his comprehensive study of the field in the United States.[31] Like our present work, he highlighted the role of the judiciary – first in the 1960s, and especially again in recent years – in developing the law, particularly through substantive controls over high interest rates, to assist consumer borrowers.

This virtual void in the English language world of 'Japanese Law', until now, may relate to its tendency to focus on commercial law topics.[32] Just as consumer law tends to be a junior partner to business law in countries like Australia and the US, comparative consumer law may struggle to find as much traction – or as many well-funded research grants – as comparative studies of more 'hard-core' business law areas such as corporate law. Even in the world of German-language studies of Japanese law ('*Japanisches Recht*'), which traditionally has been less dominated by commercial imperatives, very little work has been published about

---

26   Mann, 'Credit Cards and Debit Cards in the United States and Japan', incorporated into his broader comparative study of credit cards: R.J. Mann, *Charging Ahead: The Growth and Regulations of Payment Card Markets* (Cambridge, 2006).

27   K. Anderson, 'The New Generation: Milhaupt and West on Japanese Economic Law', *Michigan Journal of International Law*, 27(3) (2006): 985.

28   M.D. West, *Dying to Get out of Debt: Consumer Insolvency Law and Suicide in Japan*, (2003) SSRN, incorporated into selected essays: M.D. West, *Law in Everyday Japan: Sex, Sumo, Suicide, and Statutes* (Chicago, 2005).

29   C. Jones, 'Escaping Your Debts in Japan: Hiroyuki Yagi and Masakazu Kaji, Karita Kane wa Kaesuna [Book Review]', *Journal of Japanese Law*, 12 (23) (2007): 259.

30   See, for example, the special issue Vol. 77 No. 9 of *Horitsu Jiho* (August 2005).

31   Pardieck, see generally (e.g. fn 20).

32   T. Ginsburg, L. Nottage, *et al.*, 'The Worlds, Vicissitudes and Futures of Japan's Law', in T. Ginsburg, L. Nottage and H. Sono (eds), *The Multiple Worlds of Japanese Law* (University of Victoria, BC Canada, 2001), pp. 1–14.

consumer credit.[33] The present chapter therefore begins to fill a major gap in these two worlds, setting broad parameters for future study connecting more directly to the much bigger world of Japanese law studies in Japanese (*'nihon-ho'*).[34]

The gap so far is particularly surprising firstly because consumer credit issues raise many practical implications – a major driving force for comparative projects generally,[35] not just for many Japanese Law analyses in English. As mentioned further below, for example, two of the major providers of unsecured consumer loans are owned by American interests. GE Consumer Finance (also trading as 'GE Money') has developed the 'Lake' network since 1994, while Citigroup took over 'DIC' from 2000.[36] (Unsurprisingly, perhaps, the American press was sharply critical of the stricter interest rate caps enacted recently.) Foreign investors and Japan's mega-banks have also purchased significant shareholdings in other major consumer finance companies in recent years.[37] The mega-banks are finally clearing their massive bad loans problems partly thanks to their ever-growing supply of finance since the 1990s to such companies for on-lending to consumers. Such developments should be particularly important for the vast majority of

---

33 Exceptionally, see a section in a recent PhD thesis: M. Dernauer, *Verbraucherschutz und Vertragsfreiheit im Japanischen Recht [Consumer Protection and Freedom of Contract in Japanese Law]* (Tuebingen, 2006).

34 Our present chapter also helps fill a remarkable void even in the English-language literature by economists, apart from short news articles (especially recently) by financial journalists. For rare overviews of Japan's consumer credit market, see various publications by the Japan Research Institute (available at: http://www.jri. co.jp), owned by the Sumitomo-Mitsui Financial Group, since the late 1990s.

35 A. Riles (ed.), *Rethinking the Masters of Comparative Law* (Oxford, 2001).

36 Both Citigroup and GE Money have also been hard hit, with GE Money in particular considering an exit from the market: R. Layne, and M. Yasu, 'GE Considers Selling Japanese Consumer Credit Unit', *Bloomberg*, 21 August 2007. However, at the beginning of December a new US player (TPG, formerly Texas Pacific Group) has entered the market, planning on using Japan also as a base to move into consumer lending in China: M. Yasu, 'TPG to Pay $282 million for Stake in Japan Lender NIS', *Bloomberg*, 10 December 2007.

37 For example, Mitsubishi UFJ Bank (Japan's largest) holds 12.99 per cent of Acom: 'Consumer Finance Groups Facing Leaner Times under Japan's New Law', *Financial Times*, 12 January 2007, p. 24. Sumitomo Mitsui Banking Corporation owns 20 per cent of Promise, Japan's third largest consumer lender which is planning a tender offer for another now-struggling lender to create the market's largest lender: 'Promise, Sanyo Shinpan Close to Integration Deal', *The Japan Times*, 25 July 2007. GE Money may soon leave the Japanese market: 'GE Considers Selling Lake Credit Unit', *The Japan Times*, 22 August 2007. For an editorial critical of the Supreme Court's role in promoting reform in this field, see 'Consumer Finance Woes', *The Wall Street Journal Asia*, 19 July 2007, p. 11.

commentators who emphasise the importance of 'main banks' in promoting corporate governance in other Japanese firms.[38]

Recent re-regulation is also important for those highlighting the role of consumers as increasingly important direct stakeholders in Japanese corporate governance, particularly as the corporate sector embraces 'corporate social responsibility' to regain or promote legitimacy and long-term profitability. In addition, Japan's consumer credit saga offers many insights into governance not only of financial markets, but other spheres of Japanese business activity.[39]

The gap is remarkable, secondly, because this field offers insights into more theoretical issues that persistently emerge in the English language literature on the relationship between Japanese law and its socio-economic context.[40] As outlined in our Interim Conclusions, the growth of consumer lending may well be underpinned by 'culturalist' factors, including a strong sense of obligation and community still in some parts of Japan; but it is also explicable by the biases or heuristics uncovered by 'behavioural law and economics' in many other countries. To understand the recent re-regulation, however, a political theory of increasingly less 'patterned pluralism' is more plausible.

Another tentative conclusion from the following analysis, also sketched is that *ex post* legal responses, providing better private law remedies (particularly damages claims) and consumer bankruptcy procedures, are useful but insufficient to address such deep-rooted socio-economic problems. Like consumer product safety,[41] this

---

38   For example C.J. Milhaupt, 'On the (Fleeting) Existence of the Main Bank System and Other Japanese Economic Institutions', *Law and Social Inquiry*, 27 (2002): 425; D. Puchniak, 'Perverse Main Bank Rescue in the Lost Decade: Proof That Unique Institutional Incentives Drive Japanese Corporate Governance', *Pacific Rim Law & Policy Journal*, 16 (2007): 13; compare notably Y. Miwa and J.M. Ramseyer, *The Fable of the Keiretsu: Urban Legends of the Japanese Economy* (Chicago, 2006). More plausible is the compromise view that main banks did play a role in corporate governance, but have lost sway since the late 1990s. See for example L. Nottage and L. Wolff, 'Corporate Governance and Law Reform in Japan: From the Lost Decade to the End of History?', in R. Haak and M. Pudelko (eds), *Japanese Management: In Search of a New Balance between Continuity and Change* (New York, 2005); M. Aoki, G. Jackson, *et al.* (eds), *Corporate Governance in Japan: Institutional Change and Organizational Diversity* (Oxford, 2007).

39   Broadly M. Abe and L. Nottage, 'Japanese Law', in J. Smits (ed.), *Encyclopaedia of Comparative Law* (Cheltenham, 2006), pp. 357–371. On product safety, see for example L. Nottage, 'Product Safety Regulation Reform in Australia and Japan: Harmonising Towards European Models?', in C. Twigg-Flesner *et al.* (eds), *Yearbook of Consumer Law 2008* (Aldershot, 2007) pp. 429–45.

40   Compare generally L. Nottage, 'Translating Tanase: Challenging Paradigms of Japanese law and Society', *Sydney Law School Research Papers* (2006), available at: http://papers.ssrn.com/sol3/papers.cfm?abstract_id=921932, updated for *Victoria University of Wellington Law Review* (forthcoming 2009).

41   See L. Nottage, 'Redirecting Japan's Multi-Level Governance', in K. Hopt *et al.* (eds), *Corporate Governance in Context: Corporations, State, and Markets in Europe,*

area seems to generate and demand multiple levels of *ex ante* regulation, involving public authorities despite ongoing economic deregulation, in Japan as well as other advanced industrialised democracies. Both aspects are historically evident and normatively desirable for even minimalist welfare states committed also to market forces.[42] The real challenge then is to unwrap an integrated and innovative package.[43] Despite path-dependencies afflicting technology, markets, society and law particularly in this field, Japan's experience may offer some useful lessons for other countries struggling with similar dilemmas, just as the latter promise further insights for Japan.

Comparing Consumer Credit Markets in Japan

Despite Japan's 'lost decade' of economic stagnation from the 1990s, it remains the world's second-largest economy. By 2000, consumer debt in Japan had grown to reach 14.4 per cent of GDP, situating it among the group of top-ranking countries which includes the US, Canada, the UK and Singapore. Japan had pulled ahead of mid-ranking countries like Australia (11.6 per cent), as well as significantly less profligate developed countries like Germany (7 per cent) and developing countries like Taiwan (8 per cent) and Brazil (4.7 per cent).[44] Compared to household final consumption expenditure, consumer debt grew from 15 to around 27 per cent in 1991 and that ratio has remained almost constant.[45]

Of this roughly 68–76 trillion yen market in consumer debt (excluding home loans) since the 1990s, the proportion of 'sales credit' (*hanbai shinyo*, supplied so consumers can purchase specific goods or services) has grown from 40 per cent in 1991 to 55 per cent in 2004 (40 out of 74 trillion yen), with a corresponding decline in 'consumer credit' (*shohisha kinyu*, 34 trillion yen). In the latter category, the most dramatic change has been a decline in secured finance (10 trillion yen in 2004), and corresponding growth in unsecured 'consumer loans' (*shohisha roon*, 24 trillion yen), especially those provided by 'consumer credit companies' (*shohisha kinyu gaisha*, 10 trillion yen) as opposed to banks and non-banks. These credit companies' share of the consumer loan market grew from 18 per cent in 1991 to 43 per cent in 2004[46] and was a major target for the recent reforms.

Japan and the US (Oxford, 2005), pp. 571–598.

42 E. Posner, 'Contract Law in the Welfare State: A Defense of the Unconscionability Doctrine, Usury Laws and Related Limitations on the Freedom of Contract', *Journal of Legal Studies*, 24 (1995): 283.

43 Kozuka and Nottage, 'The Myth of the Cautious Consumer: Law, Culture, Economics and Politics in the Rise and Partial Fall of Unsecured Lending in Japan'.

44 Mann, *Charging Ahead: The Growth and Regulation of Payment Card Markets*, at p. 109.

45 TAPALS (ed.) *Tapals Hakusho [Tapals White Paper]* (Tokyo, 2006), at p. 2.

46 *Ibid.*, at p. 3.

Compared to other developed countries, such as Australia and especially the US, Japan's expansion in unsecured consumer loans has hardly involved loans associated with purchases made using credit cards. Although Japanese consumers now use credit cards quite extensively, they still use them overwhelmingly as a payment mechanism, paying off their balances in full every month rather than borrowing under 'revolving credit'.[47] Burgeoning consumer loans instead come primarily in the form of cash advances.

Mann convincingly identifies several main reasons for this contrast.[48] Credit cards were initially developed in the US primarily to facilitate payments while travelling inter-state for business, but Japan was a smaller country with a more unified banking system nation-wide. On the other hand, Japan also developed highly segmented financial markets. Banks focused on lending to businesses and were not allowed (directly or via affiliates) to issue cards with the full panoply of borrowing options typical of the industry in other countries.[49] In addition, high telecommunication charges, especially over the 1990s,[50] meant fewer real-time checks at point of sale, and correspondingly higher fraud and default rates than with credit cards in the US. Finally, the US (compared also, for example, to the EU, except in practice in the UK), allows more sharing of 'positive information' about consumers' good history of repaying loans and applying for credit limit extensions, allowing issuers then to target likely customers with offers of further credit.[51] By contrast, such information is only shared within each sub-sector of Japan's consumer finance market (consumer finance companies, credit card issuers, or, *shinpan gaisha* and banks); instead only 'negative information' about defaults is shared industry-wide.[52]

---

47   Mann *Charging Ahead: The Growth and Regulation of Payment Card Markets*, at pp. 78–9.

48   Mann 'Credit Cards and Debit Cards in the United States and Japan'; Mann *Charging Ahead: The Growth and Regulation of Payment Card Markets*.

49   Banks, but not their affiliates, were dissuaded by 'administrative guidance' (*gyosei shido*) under the Banking Law (No. 21 of 1927) from issuing credit cards until 1982, when the new Banking Law (No. 59 of 1981) came into effect. Drawing on a parliamentary resolution (*futai ketsugi*) related to instalment sales law reform in 1984, regulators then refused to permit banks or their affiliates from issuing cards allowing revolving credit loans. That began from 1992, as recommended by a law reform council in 1990. However, the latter's further recommendations for bank-affiliated card issuers to allow non-revolving credit options were not acted upon until 2001: Mann 'Credit Cards and Debit Cards in the United States and Japan': 1065.

50   Compare generally L. Nottage, 'Cyberspace and the Future of Law, Legal Education, and Practice in Japan', *Web Journal of Current Legal Issues*, 5 (1998), http://webjcli. ncl.ac.uk/1998/issue5/nottage.5.html.

51   Mann, *Charging Ahead: The Growth and Regulation of Payment Card Markets*, at pp. 113–17.

52   Mann, 'Credit Cards and Debit Cards in the United States and Japan': 33 n. 90.

Nonetheless, several other factors also seem to have played a role in constraining credit card lending in Japan, although these are arguably less important and sometimes less amenable to precise confirmation. First, the 'default rule' in contracts between card issuers and customers has been *ikkai barai*, that is, repayment in full at the end of the (interest-free) monthly cycle, unless the customer requests a different repayment schedule at the point of sale. However, rather than a cause, this appears to be a consequence of cards being used for payments (particularly since personal cheques are almost never used) instead of for borrowing. It may reflect the idea in Japan, at least among more reputable companies, that the 'customer is king'. Thus, suppliers seek to meet their expectations and needs, rather than shaping them.

However, at least one bank-issued card has recently offered cardholders the alternative of choosing as the default revolving credit with repayment divided up and outstanding portions accruing interest. Revolving credit is apparently being promoted by reducing the annual fee and increasing points acquired through shopping,[53] and the bank in question has developed a close relationship with the major consumer finance company 'Promise'. Further, even in 1999, one consumer finance company had inaugurated a popular credit card that permits consumers (as in the US or Australia) simply and freely to select their repayment schedule at the end of each billing cycle, rather than pre-committing at the point of sale.[54] Thus, norms involved may be evolving, with issuers more aggressively seeking to shape customer behaviour rather than to respond to it.

Secondly, even until recently banks may have been concerned 'about the adverse reputational effects that they would suffer if they became involved in the vigorous collection efforts and high interest rates that are typical of successful consumer lending', even by means of credit cards.[55] This point also deserves elaboration. Even though 'revolving credit' cards only became permissible from 1992, the unsecured consumer loan industry had already been developing since the 1970s, populated by much smaller lenders with much more dubious reputations. Bank affiliated issuers may be less concerned about moving into more card-based lending only now that Japanese consumers have gotten used to using cards at least for payments,[56] and now that consumer finance companies have grown in scale and

---

53 See the website of the card issuer at: https://www.smbc-card.com/mem/revo/mypace. jsp.

54 Mann, 'Credit Cards and Debit Cards in the United States and Japan': 32.

55 *Ibid.*, at 29, n. 75.

56 By contrast, other countries including several in Asia have largely leapfrogged credit cards as a payment mechanism, creating infrastructure and norms for the use of debit cards as payment mechanisms: A. Rosenberg, 'Better Than Cash? Consumer Protection and the Global Debit Card Deluge', *Thomas Jefferson Research Paper Series* (2005), available at: http://ssrn.com/abstract_id=740528. On the shifting perceptions of Japan's consumer finance companies, see JRI News Release, 'Consumer Survey on the Image of Consumer Finance Companies', 27 June 2005, available at: http://www. jri.co.jp/english/press/2005/jri_050627-1_e.pdf.

improved their image. That image has been tarnished in recent years, but it may be retrievable over the next few years as the smaller operators are driven out of the market, particularly after the 2006 reforms, while banks continue to collaborate with – or at least mimic – the remaining larger operators to a greater degree.[57]

Thirdly, other norms and institutions may help explain the slow uptake of credit cards as a borrowing device. Japan's overall consistently high savings rate bears no necessary relation to the numbers of borrowers or the amounts they borrow, and consumer debt per capita (or compared with GDP) is high in Japan. Mann also points out the high savings rate may be due to institutional factors such as stages of industrial development and that any cultural 'adversity to borrowing' may have been deliberately promoted especially after World War II.[58] On the other hand, the initial hesitancy towards using consumer finance companies and then credit cards, especially for borrowing, may reflect comparatively higher risk aversion among Japanese decision-makers.[59]

Norms about carrying and paying with cash may also lessen the attraction of credit cards even as a payment mechanism, yet Mann demonstrates that the latter function has grown in Japan. It also seems likely that certain establishments – as in Japan's large sex or gambling industries – still do not allow or encourage payment by card not because of cultural expectations, but simply so that no paper trail remains for both suppliers and consumers. Cash advances from consumer finance companies then become the only option. On the other hand, carrying around such cash becomes more realistic given comparatively low levels of theft.[60] In turn,

---

57   Similarly, in a seminar presentation at the University of Tokyo on 9 June 2006, a
      visiting professor from Houston suggested briefly that 'a change in consumer
      attitude (which ... could be accomplished by a sophisticated advertising effort)' may
      combine with other factors to result in Japanese consumers finding themselves 'using
      credit cards in a manner similar to their American counterparts': R.M. Alderman,
      'Consumer Credit, Debt Collection and Identity Theft: A Look at the United States
      and a Prediction for Japan [Seminar Report]', *ICCLP Annual Report* (2006): 12, at
      14. Japan's major banks and consumer lenders are certainly now collaborating more
      closely, especially in credit card lending.
58   Mann, 'Credit Cards and Debit Cards in the United States and Japan': 37. See further
      S.M. Garon, *Molding Japanese Minds: The State in Everyday Life* (Princeton, 1997).
59   This may also be a factor, for example, behind the 'reformist conservatism' in
      adding postgraduate 'Law School' programs in Japan recently: L. Nottage, 'Build
      Postgraduate Law Schools in Kyoto, and Will They Come – Sooner *and* Later?',
      Australian Journal of Asian Law, 7 (2005): 241. But an intense literature search has
      uncovered little systematic research comparing risk aversion generally, and again any
      such tendency may be highly dependent on fluctuating socio-economic constraints.
60   Compare Mann, *Charging Ahead: The Growth and Regulation of Payment Card
      Markets*.

the possibility of norms encouraging law-abiding behaviour independent of cost-benefit appraisals, including the chance of legal sanctions, cannot be ruled out.[61]

On other hand, Mann is more convincing in downplaying differences in consumer protection law and practice.[62] It is true that 'Japan has no analogue to TILA Article 170, which generally preserves the right of American cardholders to present against the issuer any defence to payment that they would have against the merchant'. Articles 30–4 and 30–5 of the Instalment Sales Law provide such protection only for the extension of credit (*kappu*), yet such *kappu* borrowing still does not occur much via credit cards. On the other hand, credit card usage for payments has risen significantly without any improvement in the latter Law for consumers. TILA Article 133 also caps at US$50 the liability of customers for unauthorised transactions. However, although there is no counterpart in Japanese law,[63] credit card companies have generally included similar protections in their contracts with consumers.[64]

Overall, therefore, mostly path-dependent historical factors in the US and Japan – geography, technology, financial markets regulation and possibly some independent social or cultural norms – have resulted in different trajectories in credit card usage. This is especially true for lending through this mechanism, but Japan's tendency to substitute cash loans from consumer credit companies may be coming under increasing threat. The comparison also uncovers some strong underlying commonalities in consumer credit market growth in these countries, as well as other jurisdictions such as Australia and the EU.

First, the rapid expansion of consumer lending has been associated with macro-economic slowdowns. In the US, these included the more intense Oil Shocks followed by weak economic performance over the 1980s, in Japan, the 'lost decade' since the 1990s.

Secondly and more importantly, automation and IT progressed dramatically among lenders first in the US, then in Japan. Economies of scale underpinned the emergence of several large consumer lenders, especially in Japan. That has

---

61   See for example the comparative 'drop tests' of wallets in Japan and the US, described in West, *Law in Everyday Japan: Sex, Sumo, Suicide, and Statutes*, along with his introduction therein to the (more respectable) 'love hotel' sector of Japan's sex industry. See also M.D. West, 'The Resolution of Karaoke Disputes: The Calculus of Institutions and Social Capital', *Journal of Japanese Studies*, 28 (2002): 301 on how both 'social capital' (one possible measure of culture) as well as cost–benefit analyses influences decisions to complain about *karaoke* noise in neighbourhood disputes; and E.C. Sibbitt, 'Regulating Gambling in the Shadow of the Law: Form and Substance in the Regulation of Japan's Pachinko Industry', *Harvard International Law Journal*, 38 (1997): 568 on gambling in *pachinko* parlours.

62   Mann, 'Credit Cards and Debit Cards in the United States and Japan', 39.

63   *Ibid.*, at p. 42.

64   See for example P. Crookes, 'Credit Card Fraud: How They Do It and How to Protect Yourself', *The Japan Times*, 26 April 2005, available at: http://search.japantimes. co.jp/cgi-bin/nb20050426a5.html.

probably been underpinned by greater potential for applying 'credit-scoring' techniques to 'positive information' within such companies, and possibly the banks that some of the largest Japanese companies are now associated with, given restricted data-sharing especially of positive information. In particular, Japan's consumer loans market took off in mid-1993 with the advent of automatic loan-dispenser booths. Now littering Japan's urban and even some rural landscapes, these allow applicants to obtain small, high-interest cash loans after a simple operation of the touch panel (monitored by the company staff through a video camera) and quick checks of credit history and identity documents (scanned and faxed). After the operation, a cash card is emitted from the dispenser with which the borrower can obtain money from an ATM installed alongside it.

Thirdly, clever television and media advertising accompanied the deployment of these booths, such as the *mujin-kun* series.[65] As well as emphasising anonymity and convenience, advertising has tried to project a 'safe' image for consumer credit company cash loans. Borrowers targeted were primarily stressed-out middle-aged 'salary men' with stable but low salaries, a home loan, and a few children generating rising outlays on educational services. In recent years, the larger lenders have also aimed at younger men earning low incomes. Accordingly to a survey in 2002 of the five largest companies, 72 per cent of new customers were male – of these, 44 per cent were in their 20s and 23 per cent in their 30s. Most (81 per cent) earned less than 5 million yen per annum – indeed, 65 per cent earned less than 4 million and 42 per cent less than 3 million.[66] Overwhelmingly, the advertising features attractive young women clerks.[67]

Fourthly, such demographics indicate strong parallels to the 'sweat box' business model of consumer lending perfected by credit card companies in the US. Unlike normal bank lending, epitomised by the mortgage loan, their most profitable customers are not those least likely to default; instead, the lender profits from large-scale information analysis and advertising likely to generate borrowing by the financially distressed. Credit card companies aim to get customers 'on their books' by issuing cards, then hope they will not only use them for payments, but stop regularly repaying at the end of each monthly cycle. High interest rates

---

65   *Mujin-kun* (meaning 'Mr Alone') is a nickname for the loan-dispenser booths installed by Acom. It was the first in this kind of booths, immediately followed by other major credit finance companies in installing similar loan-dispensers with equally trendy names. In 1990s, *Mujin-kun* was advertised on television at night featuring comical extraterritorial creatures dropping by on Earth to borrow some money by using the loan-dispensers. Most of the viewers of television programmes at night are young (often male) people, who have emerged as the main target of the credit finance companies.

66   S. Suda, *Karyugui – Shohisha Kinyu No Jittai [Devouring the Lower Class: The Reality of Consumer Finance]* (Tokyo, 2006), at pp. 84–6.

67   In fact, these are often top 'gravure idols' (pin-up girls): Inoue Waka was dumped a couple of years ago by Promise in favour of Nakagawa Shoko, while Acom uses Ono Mayumi.

will kick in, and there will also be more chance of late and over-limit fees. The objective is to keep the customer sweating on the debt treadmill as long as possible, with almost all resources going towards paying off interest and charges without running down the principal owed. Once customers become insolvent, major credit issuers increasingly sell that defaulted debt to smaller companies that may be able to collect more aggressively.[68]

Similarly, Japan's credit finance companies are uninterested in higher-income customers more likely to repay without default. For low-income borrowers, calculations show how very high interest rates make it drastically more difficult to pay off the loans.[69] Larger lenders are generally delighted to extend additional loans to existing customers (rollovers), or to customers of other large lenders, at already high rates or (very soon) rates close to the statutory limits. If borrowings begin to spiral out of control, risking repayment of the lender's principal advanced, the lender can prolong the agony by seeking repayments more vigorously. Compared to credit card lenders in the US, it is not common among Japanese finance companies formally to sell off their loans, partly because the law has applied the same regulations as for the original lenders, including the complicated rules over 'grey zone' interest.[70] However, as a functional equivalent, the large lender in Japan can introduce such a borrower to a multitude of smaller lenders who may charge even higher interest and ultimately enforce their own debts more aggressively, but whose advances can be used by the borrower for some period to keep paying off the loans from the original lender. One survey in mid-2006 confirmed that 2.7 out of 14 million borrowers were in default for three months or more. Over 3.5 million

---

68   Mann, 'Bankruptcy Reform and the "Sweat Box" Of Credit Card Debt': 384–92.

69   Suda, at pp. 84–9.

70   See generally Y. Kataoka and S. Yamamoto, *Shohisha Shin'yo Bijinesu no Kenkyu [Research into the Consumer Credit Business]* (Tokyo, 2001), pp. 196–206. The enactment of the Law on Special Rules to the Civil Code regarding the Transfer of Receivables (Law No. 104 of 1998, now renamed the Law on Special Rules to the Civil Code regarding the Transfer of Movables and Receivables), made possible the securitisation of consumer loans by firms under MoF jurisdiction. From 1992, securitisation had only been possible through special legislation, namely the Law on Securitisation of Certain Kinds of Assets (Law No. 77 of 1992, abolished in 2004), promoted by METI: see S. Nathoo, A. Lee *et al.* 'Japanese Consumer Loan Securitisation: A New Asset Class', *Hong Kong Lawyer*, August (1999): 26. Compared to the overall rapid growth in Japan's securitisation market, the securitisation of loans extended by consumer finance companies has remained relatively small until 2000: Kataoka and Yamamoto at p. 195. However, in 2002, consumer loan securitisation was the fastest growing market segment: M. Johnson 'Japan Securitisation: CLOs Bloom', *Euroweek*, 778 (2003): 18. For a critical analysis of the perverse and irresponsible practices involved in securitising consumer loans in the US, but focused on the sub-prime mortgage loan market that collapsed in mid-2007, see Engel and McCoy, 'Turning a Blind Eye: Wall Street Finance of Predatory Lending'.

had four or more lenders, and 30 per cent of them were in default.[71] The limited numbers of practising attorneys (*bengoshi*) allowed to engage in the legal aspects of debt collection, deregulated only partially by the Law on Special Measures for Servicing Business (known as the 'Servicer Law', No. 126 of 1998), encourage actual or threatened enforcement by gangsters (*yakuza*) and limit the potential for robust legal defences.[72]

There are even stronger parallels with predatory 'payday lending' in the US nowadays. Typically, that involves a customer writing a cheque for a small sum, dated for the next payday. The lender advances a smaller cash amount immediately, and later recovers the full amount by depositing the post-dated cheque. The annualised interest rates in such loans over a few weeks work out to be extremely high. They also differ from contemporary credit card loans, where repayment of both principal and interest can generally be postponed – adding to the debt burden for future monthly cycles, subject to the agreed credit limit.

In practice, however, many payday loans are rollovers, especially welcomed by lenders because fixed costs such as basic credit checks are proportionately less for high-frequency borrowers. There is also a strong pattern of borrowing from one lender to pay off another. Industry structure is also quite similar to that of consumer finance companies in Japan. 'Mom-and-pop providers' still comprise the bulk of the market, but national publicly traded providers have grown rapidly by establishing small outlets in as many locations as possible.[73] In addition, payday lenders have targeted insular groups such as military personnel, who are cash-poor, often do not own their own homes (important for credit-reporting and mainstream lending), yet are unlikely to be laid off or be paid wages late.

In 2007, the federal Talent–Nelson Amendment capped interest rates at 36 per cent for loans to such personnel and their dependents. There are also compelling calls for further usury law restrictions, limits on indefinite rollover loans, stricter transparency requirements (including improved TILA disclosure and bans on associated products such as insurance) and measures to encourage large national providers to further edge out less reputable lenders.[74]

Japan's consumer finance companies may have independently developed similar business strategies to foreign credit card companies and payday lenders. But larger companies in Japan have long been careful to benchmark against foreign developments, to which they are increasingly exposed.[75] Japan's credit

---

71 Suda, at pp. 180–81.
72 C.J. Milhaupt and M.D. West, 'The Dark Side of Private Ordering: An Institutional and Empirical Analysis of Organised Crime', *University of Chicago Law Review*, 67(1) (2000): 41.
73 Mann and Hawkins, 'Just until Payday': 864–7.
74 *Ibid.*, especially at 858 n. 3 and 871.
75 T. Kitagawa and L. Nottage, 'Globalization of Japanese Corporations and the Development of Corporate Legal Departments: Problems and Prospects', in W. Alford (ed.), *Raising the Bar* (Cambridge, Mass., 2007).

card industry also got a kick-start from an early appreciation of how 'monoline' issuers were supplanting bank issuers as technology and deregulation proceeded. Most directly, as mentioned above, since the 1990s US financial institutions have moved into the consumer lending business in Japan, just as they have taken advantage of other transformations in financial markets over the last decade.[76] GE Money arrived in 1994. US-based Associates First Capital had developed three fully-fledged consumer finance companies, inherited by Citigroup when it controversially bought out the firm for US$31 billion in 2000, while the lender was under investigation for predatory practices. Among other major lenders, foreign investors own large proportions of Aiful, Promise, Acom and Takefuji.

Whatever the precise causes and despite somewhat different manifestations, the expansion of unsecured consumer lending in Japan has led also to similar effects. More than three million struggling borrowers are associated with ever-growing inquiries and complaints to the government's many Consumer Lifestyle Centres and newly expanded 'Japan Legal Support Centres', continued rises in bankruptcy filings and one of the world's highest levels of suicides – mostly debt-related.[77] Particularly since 2006, media attention has increasingly focused on other tragedies afflicting borrowers as well as their families and communities. All this has generated intense reform debate and ultimately a strong re-regulatory response, albeit again with some Japanese characteristics.

---

76   See generally E.C. Sibbitt, 'A Brave New World for M&A of Financial Institutions in Japan: Big Bang Financial Deregulation and the New Environment for Corporate Combinations of Financial Institutions', *University of Pennsylvania Journal of International Economic Law*, 19(4) (1998): 965; and G. Tett, *Saving the Sun: A Wall Street Gamble to Rescue Japan from Its Trillion-Dollar Meltdown* (London, 2004). Firms from Europe and other parts of the world have also re-engaged with the Japanese market, but they have had less experience or interest in unsecured consumer lending.

77   See West, *Law in Everyday Japan: Sex, Sumo, Suicide, and Statutes*, and more recent information available at: http://www.kokusen.go.jp and http://www.moj.go.jp/ENGLISH/issues/issues02.html. Over 30,000 people committed suicide in 2006, only slightly down from 2005, despite growing social concern epitomised by a Basic Law introduced in October 2006: 'State Guidelines Aim for 20 per cent Cut in Suicide Rate', *Japan Times*, 9 June 2007. It is unclear whether debt-related suicides are declining. However, consumer insolvency filings increased between November 2000 and June 2002 due to implementation of the Civil Rehabilitation Law, not just macro-economic factors: Y. Jiang, *Empirical Consumer Credit Risk Analysis: Economic and Legislative Evidence from the Japanese Consumer Credit Market*, PhD dissertation, Queen's University at Kingston (2004).

Japan's Re-regulatory Responses

A legal system can adopt various approaches to address problems arising from consumer loans.[78] On its face, Japan has deployed most of them. However, the focus of judicial remedies and law reform has almost always been regulation over the interest rate charged. This Part first presents a comprehensive picture of the relevant regulations, before looking into the judicial and then legislative responses that have taken place recently.

When analysing regulation of consumer credit in Japan, it must be emphasised that credit extended in connection with the sale of goods has been treated separately from straight loans. The former 'sales credit' is governed by the Instalment Sales Law, applicable to the sales of goods or services for which the purchaser makes a payment in instalments of three or more times over two or more months, or by revolving credit. The IRRL and the Capital Funding Law (Law on Investments, Deposit Taking and Other Financial Transactions, No. 195 of 1954: the *Shusshi Ho*), which regulate the maximum interest rates for straight loans, have been held not to be applicable to sales credit.[79] This fragmented regulation is related to the different governmental agencies overseeing the industry. Sales credit, understood as an aspect of commerce, is subject to the oversight of the Ministry of Economy, Trade and Industry (METI), while the non-banks providing straight loans are subject to the supervision of the Financial Services Agency (FSA: formerly the Ministry of Finance: MoF) as a branch of financial sector. However, in the wake of the 2006 amendments to the statutory regime for unsecured straight loans to consumers, in December 2007 METI published a report aimed at strengthening the Instalment Sales Act in 2008.[80]

---

78   Engel and McCoy, 'A Tale of Three Markets: The Law and Economics of Predatory Lending': 1297.

79   Nagoya District Court, 8 February 1985 (554 *Hanrei Times* 281).

80   METI proposes to: add registration requirements for sales credit suppliers (besides credit card companies that have [originally 'are'] already required registration); require them to scrutinise the goods and services suppliers (shops) when entering into business with them; allow for cooling-off by the consumer; require refunds of their credit payments if a shop has defrauded the consumer; prohibit the extension of excessive credit (through using credit information bureaus); otherwise strengthen protection of privacy and credit card information; enlarge the Law's scope of application to include repayment upon one 'bonus' to income (not otherwise considered an instalment) and to include credit related to all goods and services (rather than designating them, as at present); and encouraging better self-regulation by industry. See http://www.meti. go.jp/topic/data/e71210aj.html (in Japanese) and 'Predatory sales driven by collusive credit firms', Yomiuri Shimbun, 3 December 2007.

The statutory regime until 2005

Price regulation: Interest rate caps The primary source of regulation over the interest rate in Japan is the IRRL. It provides that no loan may charge interest exceeding:

- 20 per cent per annum if the principal is less than 100,000 yen;
- 18 per cent per annum if the principal exceeds 100,000 yen but is less than 1,000,000 yen;
- 15 per cent per annum if the principal exceeds 1,000,000 yen.

Any excess interest is null and void. However, payment of excess interest cannot be reclaimed by the borrower if the latter makes the payment 'voluntarily' (Article 1). This means that the claim for the interest exceeding the cap under the IRRL is a 'natural obligation' (*shizen saimu* or *obligatio naturalis*), a concept derived from Roman law: the claim is unenforceable by the lender but not entirely without legal effect. In addition, if the lender is a registered non-bank and seeks interests of more than 109.5 per cent to the principal, the loan contract itself becomes null and void so that the lender cannot enforce even the repayment of the principal (Article 42-2, Moneylenders Control Law, No. 32 of 1983: the *Kashikingyo Kiseiho*).

Further regulation comes from the Capital Funding Law, adding penal sanctions. A professional lender (that is bank or non-bank) may be imprisoned for up to five years and/or fined 10,000,000 yen or less if it seeks interest constituting more than 29.2 per cent per annum on the principal (if the lender is not a professional lender, interest constituting more than 109.5 per cent per annum to the principal is open to such penalties: Article 5). Reading the Capital Funding Law together with the IRRL, a non-bank shall not be penalised for seeking interest at rates between 15 to 20 per cent and 29.2 per cent, though the agreement on interests of such a rate cannot be enforced as valid. This had been known as the 'grey zone' interest rate.

With regard to the 'grey zone' interest, the Moneylenders Control Law before amendments in 2006 provided that payment of such interest was deemed valid if the lender was a registered non-bank and had delivered to the borrower documentation of contract details and receipts for payments, complying with requirements under the Moneylenders Control Law (Article 43).

The legislative intent of the Moneylenders Control Law was to overrule the Supreme Court decisions (discussed in Part III.B below) that rendered the *obligatio naturalis* under the IRRL to be almost completely devoid of legal effect. By distinguishing 'good' (or 'less bad') non-banks from 'bad' ones by reference to compliance with the disclosure requirements, the Moneylenders Control Law intended to give the former the privilege to continue receiving 'grey zone' interest notwithstanding those judgments.

Disclosure rules Disclosure requirements enabling the borrower to make an informed decision are usually the first step in regulating consumer credit. When extending loans to customers, Article 17 of the Moneylenders Control Law required lenders to:

> (i) post a notice in their office showing the interest rate, method of repayment, term and frequency of the repayment, as well as the name of the person in charge of the office (Article 14);
> (ii) include in any advertisement or e-mail message the name and the registered number of the lender, interest rate and other items as required in (i) (Article 15); and
> (iii) deliver a document that states the contract details (name and address of the lender, date and amount of the loan, interest rate, method of repayment, term and frequency of the repayment, any liquidated damages or the like, and other items stipulated by Ministerial Order).

In addition, immediately upon receiving repayment, Article 18 required the lender to:

> (iv) deliver a receipt stating the relevant contract details and the outcome of the repayment (name and address of the lender, date of lending, amount of the loan, amount received and how the received amount is apportioned among the principal, interest and damages, date of receipt, and other items stipulated by Ministerial Order).

Such receipts can be understood as complementing the initial disclosure rules, since they can be expected to inform the borrower of the amount and details of the remaining debt. The documents and receipts under (iii) and (iv) cannot be delivered by electronic means. Delivery of the documents or receipts under (iii) and (iv) were therefore further preconditions for the non-bank lender to retain 'grey zone' interest as validly agreed and 'voluntarily' repaid. Thus, disclosure rules under the Moneylenders Control Law were connected to, and supported by, regulation capping interest rates.

Similarly, for sales credit, the current Instalment Sales Law imposes certain duties of disclosure on sellers. When concluding an instalment sale contract, Article 4 requires the seller to:

> (i) disclose the conditions of instalment sales by posting a notice in the office or delivery of a document at the time of the sale (in the case of the sale of an individual item) or when handing over the credit card (in the case of the sales by a credit card) (Article 3);
> (ii) deliver a document that indicates details of the sales (the price, amount of instalments, timing and method of payments, timing of the delivery of the goods or provision of the service, conditions of cancellation, any conditions

on transfer of title, and other items stipulated by Ministerial Order).
(iii) Delivery of such documents may occur via electronic means (Article
4-2).

In addition to these regulations specific to each industry, there are more general
laws requiring the lender to make necessary disclosure. First, the Consumer
Contracts Law (No. 61 of 2000) gives a consumer the right to cancel a contract
entered into as a result of a misunderstanding caused by the other party (Article
4). Secondly, the Law on Sales of Financial Products (No. 101 of 2000), under the
jurisdiction of the FSA, obliges the seller of any financial product to explain to the
customer about the possibility of losing the whole or part of the principal (Article
3). Otherwise, the customer may claim compensation for any damages suffered
(Article 5).

Regulating debt collection Non-bank consumer loans in Japan are renowned for
'three evils' (*sarakin san-aku*): high interest rates, excessive lending, but also
strict and aggressive collection.[81] To address the last-mentioned problem, the
Moneylenders Control Law prohibited a lender (registered or not), or a person
engaged by the lender, from harassing or interfering with the privacy of anyone
when collecting a loan (Article 21). Examples of such harassment or interference
with privacy are listed: making a telephone call or sending a fax at inappropriate
times of the day; visiting or calling places other than the residence of the borrower,
such as his or her office; not leaving the residence of the borrower even after the
request of the latter to leave; disclosing to the public the fact of borrowing by
posting a notice or otherwise; and so on.

There are both administrative and penal sanctions for the infringement of
the prohibition of aggressive collection. Under the Law before the amendments
in 2006, the administrative sanction was an order to cease business against a
registered non-bank that committed any of the prohibited actions in collecting its
loan (Article 36) or the revocation of the registration when the infringement was
serious (Article 37). On the other hand, any lender (registered or not), employee
or any other person that committed prohibited acts could be imprisoned for two
years or less and/or be fined three million yen or less (Article 47-2. now Article
47-3) The regulation of collection methods, however, was also connected to the
regulation of interest rates. Because the privilege to keep the 'grey zone' interest
arose only when the borrower repaid the loan voluntarily, amounts collected by
means of any of the prohibited acts did not qualify for privileged treatment.[82]

Ex post remedies When the borrower has borrowed too much and has become
insolvent, it may be appropriate to excise part of the debt and enable the borrower

---

81   Suda, at p. 24.
82   M. Omori, '*Kashikingyo Kiseiho Dai-43-jo ni Tsuite* [Article 43 of the Consumer
     Loans System Law]', *Hanrei Jiho*, 1080 (1983): 8.

to repay the remainder. The procedure used most for this purpose is to file for bankruptcy and petition for discharge (Article 248 of the Bankruptcy Law, No. 75 of 2004). In 2006, bankruptcy proceedings filed by individuals amounted to 166,339 cases, about two-thirds of the record high of 242,849 in 2003, but still more than double the volume ten years ago (71,683 in 1997).[83] Over-committed consumers are unlikely to retain any assets constituting a bankruptcy estate. In such a case, immediate closure of the bankruptcy procedure is declared (Article 216 of the Bankruptcy Law).

Another procedure now available to the borrower is civil rehabilitation. Provisions favourable to individuals were added in 2001 to the Civil Rehabilitation Law (No. 225 of 1999), originally enacted to enable SMEs to reorganise while the debtor remained in possession of the business, in order to address the increased number of over-extended consumers. The procedure is available to an individual expecting regular income who owes unsecured debts of 50 million yen or less. An over-indebted consumer can reschedule loans even if he or she does not qualify for discharge under the Bankruptcy Law. The rehabilitation plan must cover at least one-tenth (if the total amount of unsecured loans is more than 30 million yen) or one-fifth (if 30 million yen or less) (Civil Rehabilitation Law, Article 231). Further, it must not harm the general interest of the creditors. This is taken to mean that the total amount to be paid according to the rehabilitation plan must exceed the amount to be distributed under the bankruptcy procedure (Article 241(2)(ii)). The procedure has recently been used extensively. In 2006, the number of filings amounted to 26,113.[84]

When filing under either of these procedures, the borrower's lawyer first determines the actual amount of existing debt. In many cases, the borrower does not know about the IRRL and has been deceived into consenting to interest rates higher than the maximums. A lender as a registered non-bank may not have complied fully with the requirements to deliver documentation of contract details or receipts for repayment, and therefore is not entitled to keep 'grey zone' interest. In such cases, the lawyer negotiates to get the lender to give up trying to enforce interest above the maximum allowed under the IRRL, so that the total of the outstanding debt is reduced. Thus, here again, the interest rate restrictions are very important.

Prevention of excessive lending The Moneylenders Control Law imposed a duty on a non-bank to investigate the borrower's assets, outstanding loans and plans for repayment; and not to extend a loan that apparently could not be repaid by the latter (Article 13). In addition, advertisements of a non-bank were not to be too aggressive, seeking to limit lending exceeding the borrower's capacity to make repayments (Article 16). Both provisions were aimed at preventing excessive

---

83   M. Sato and M. Iwama, '*Heisei-18-nen ni okeru Tosan Jiken Moushitate no Gaikyo* [An Account of Bankruptcy Appeals for 2006]', *NBL*, 857 (2007): 12, at p. 12.

84   *Ibid.*, at pp. 13–14.

lending, but were not accompanied by specific criteria of what amount would be 'excessive'.

As voluntary self-regulation, the three major non-bank consumer finance companies agreed in 1997 not to extend loans to a borrower that had already taken loans from any one of the other lenders.[85] However, smaller lenders and credit card companies have not been bound by this agreement, let alone financiers providing sales credit by instalment sales. In reality, therefore, excessive lending was not effectively prevented.

A somewhat related issue is the sharing of credit history and other information on borrowers. In Japan there exist various reporting agencies, primarily: (1) the Federation of Credit Bureaus of Japan (FCBJ), consisting of a network of 33 credit bureaus for finance companies and the Tera Net organised by credit and leasing companies; (2) CIC Inc., compiling credit information for sales credit; (3) the Personal Credit Information Center (PCIC) of the Japanese Bankers Association, whose membership is limited to banks; and (4) CCB Inc., originally established by foreign finance companies. While the 33 bureaus under FCBJ have been sharing 'negative information' about borrowers (defaults and so on) with CIC and PCIC, the two networks under the FCBJ (the 33 bureaus and Tera Net) have shared only 'positive information' (amounts of outstanding loan). In addition, a number of finance companies and moneylenders belong to none of these credit bureaus.

This multiplicity of credit bureaus has made it difficult to regulate information sharing among lenders through formal legislation. Further complication comes from a seemingly odd argument by consumer groups in favour of information-sharing among lenders, with the hope that such sharing can prevent excessive lending. In the US, extensive information-sharing has led to consumers being increasingly inundated by tempting credit offers.[86] Consumer groups in Japan may be hoping for more restricted information-sharing that makes it possible for the major lenders to perform their self-enforced agreement to restrict lending. However, the argument for broader information-sharing encounters the reluctance of lenders, especially finance companies (as opposed to banks and credit card companies); to give away information that constitutes an essential part of their know-how. As a result, attempts to introduce privacy protection over the transfer or sharing of information on borrowers' credit history have made little progress. Even when the Study Group of the then-MoF (later: FSA) and MITI (later: METI) discussed the issue of privacy protection of borrowers, its 1998 report noted the need to facilitate the sharing of credit information for the sake of 'appropriate lending', albeit with a proposal to introduce legislation on privacy protection.[87] However, despite lessons from South

---

85   FSA Study Group (2006) *Kondankai ni okeru Koremade no Giron (Zachou to shiteno Chukan Seiri)* [Discussions of the Study Group to Date (Chair's Progress Report)] available at: http://www.fsa.go.jp/singi/singi_kasikin/20060421.html at 2.

86   Mann, *Charging Ahead: The Growth and Regulations of Payment Card Markets.*

87   MoF/MITI Study Group (1998) 'Report of the Study Group on the Use and Protection of Personal Credit Information', *Jurisuto*, 1144 (1998).

Korea and other countries where consumer lending has expanded recently,[88] Japan has not enacted legislation to facilitate information-sharing.

Private law restrictions Although loan agreements are obviously subject to more general rules of the Civil Code and other private law statutes such as the Consumer Contract Law, these were seldom employed to deny the validity of clauses in the loan agreement detrimental to the borrower. For example, the acceleration clause that puts pressure on the debtor to perform its obligation to repay was not challenged under the regulation of unfair clauses in the Consumer Contract Law, until the Supreme Court invalidated it by resorting to the Moneylenders Control Law (see below III. B.2(b)). One of the reasons for preferring such public law rules to private law may be that the formalistic or detailed rules of the former are easier for the lawyers to rely on, on behalf of the borrower, not to mention for the courts.

Courts stepped in only when the loan agreement was absurdly harsh on the borrower, such as when the interest rate per annum reached 1200 per cent,[89] or exceeded 500–800 per cent.[90] The court in the latter case invalidated the loan agreement as being exploitative (what jurists in Germany term '*Wuchergeschäft*') and contrary to public policy (Article 90 of the Civil Code). In the former, the court found there was no longer any loan agreement in any real sense, but a mere illegal scheme or sham under the guise of a loan. Interestingly, here again, the interest rates involved were the principal criteria emphasised when finding the (extreme) harshness impugned by these judgments. By contrast, unconscionability or undue influence doctrine in American and (especially) Anglo–Commonwealth law focuses – ostensibly – much more on procedural flaws in the contract negotiation process, rather than substantive unfairness of the resultant terms.[91]

---

88   See Mann, *Charging Ahead: The Growth and Regulations of Payment Card Markets*, at pp. 116–17.
89   Sapporo High Court, 23 February 2005 (1916 *Hanrei Jiho* 39).
90   Tokyo District Court, 25 March 2005 (1914 *Hanrei Jiho* 102).
91   Nottage, 'Form and Substance in US, English and Japanese Law: A Framework for Better Comparisons of Developments in the Law of Unfair Contracts'. Further, on appeal from a Summary Court ruling that refunds of excessive interest based on unjust enrichment were barred by the 10-year prescription period, on 13 November 2007 the Kobe District Court awarded the borrower damages in tort for the same amount (http://www.courts.go.jp/hanrei/pdf/20071214111256.pdf). Promise now states that it did not appeal further due to time pressure, but that it would resist further judgments like this: '*Shohisha Kinyu Kabarikin ni Baisho Meirei – Higaisha Kyusai no Han'I of Kakudai* [Compensation Order Against Excessive Consumer Finance Payments: Expanding the Scope of Protection for Victims]' *Asahi Shimbun*, 11 December 2007.

Court rulings on excessive interest[92]

Purposive interpretation of the IRRL in 1960s As mentioned above, the IRRL provides that interest exceeding the maximum limit may still be retained by the lender if it is paid 'voluntarily' (Article 1(2)). The legislative intent suggested by the literal reading of this text appears to be that the excess interest cannot be enforced but can be retained, as *obligatio naturalis*, as long as the payment was made without pressure being applied. However, the Supreme Court interpreted the provision more in favour of borrowers in the 1960s, an era when other consumer and social issues became more important in Japanese law and society.[93] Judgments revealed considerable activism in employing a purposive, rather than the textual, interpretation of the IRRL, in order to protect the weaker party. It seemed almost as if the original intent expressed by the legislation was being rejected.

A first judgment held that the excess interest paid by the borrower was to be converted into repayment of the principal.[94] The Court interpreted the statute as denying claims for recovery of the excess interest through litigation, but not excluding other types of treatment of the payment made for the excess interest. Then followed a case in which the amount paid by the borrower as excess interest was so large that it was more than the amount of the whole principal. The Supreme Court allowed the borrower to claim for recovery of the difference between the amount paid for the excess interest and that of the principal. The rationale was that when the whole principal was paid off, there was no debt to be paid so that the borrower was entitled to claim for unjust enrichment, not 'recovery of the excess interest'.[95]

The Moneylenders Control Law In 1983, the Moneylenders Control Law was enacted after political debates that had dragged on for many years. It introduced a provision to overrule the case law and enable the lender to retain payment of the excess interest. The Law employed the phrase 'the payment is deemed to be valid' instead of 'the lender may retain ...', as phrased in the IRRL, and explicitly justified the lender to keep the 'grey zone' interest paid voluntarily to it if the above-mentioned documentation of contract details and receipts were delivered in compliance with the Law.

In 1990, the Supreme Court affirmed that the payment was made voluntarily and allowed the lender to retain the 'grey zone' interest even when the borrower was not aware that he was paying interest above the maximum limit under the

---

92 For a more detail particularly about the case law development, and further information about the 2006 legislative reforms, see Pardieck.
93 Maclachlan; F.K. Upham, *Law and Social Change in Postwar Japan* (Cambridge, Mass, 1987).
94 Supreme Court, 18 November 1964 (Minshu 18-9-1868).
95 Supreme Court, 13 November 1968 (Minshu 22-12-2526).

IRRL. It certainly did not hold the excess interest portion to be null and void.[96] At this point, the legislative intent appeared to have been supported by the judiciary.

However, from the end of 1990s the Supreme Court reverted to activism in favour of consumers. In a series of cases brought by lawyers specialising in this area, the hurdles for the lender to benefit from the privilege under the Moneylenders Control Law were raised one by one, until finally in 2006 the provision was made almost defunct.

(a) Cases on Documentation of Contract Details and Receipts

With regard to the delivery of the documentation, the Supreme Court was able to be activist by sticking instead to textualism. The first of these cases was the decision of the Supreme Court in 1999. It held that the requirement to deliver the receipt 'immediately after' the payment was made was to be applied strictly even in the case of payments through an ATM and not over the counter.[97] A second decision, in 2004, that held that the delivery of receipt 20 days after payment through an ATM was too late to qualify as 'delivered immediately'. Although it might appear inevitable in the case of ATM transactions to have some time lag before the receipt is delivered, the Supreme Court refused to accept that as an excuse for the lender.[98]

Such textualism was then extended to the case of revolving credit, which was a type of transaction not imagined by the legislator that enacted the Moneylenders Control Law. The items to be stated in the document of contract details as stipulated in the Law as well as its Ministerial Order are not appropriate for revolving credit. Admitting that in the case of revolving credit the 'term and frequency of repayment' or 'amount of each payment' (as required by the Ministerial Order) was not determined in advance, the Supreme Court held that the lender should have stated equivalent information, that is the minimum amount to be repaid and the term of repayment in case the borrower chose to pay the minimum amount. It prevented lenders that had delivered documentation lacking such information from enjoying the privilege of retaining excess interest payments.[99]

Finally, in a high-profile judgment in January 2006, the Supreme Court declared void a provision in the Ministerial Order that admitted a simplified statement in the receipt (reference to the contract number instead of the date of execution and amount of the loan), as not complying with the overarching provisions in the Law. As a result, the lender that had delivered a receipt produced according to the Ministerial Order was unable to retain the grey zone interest.[100]

---

96   Supreme Court, 22 January 1990 (Minshu 44-1-332).
97   Supreme Court, 21 January 1999 (Minshu 53-1-98).
98   Supreme Court, 20 February 2004 (Minshu 58-2-475).
99   Supreme Court, 15 December 2005 (Minshu 59-10-2899).
100 Supreme Court, 13 January 2006 (Minshu 60-1-1). On 13 July, the Court further ruled that borrowers could claim interest on the grey zone interest to be refunded:

(b) Cases on 'Voluntary Repayment'

In a sharp contrast to such textualism, courts have reverted to purposive interpretation when interpreting the requirement of 'voluntary repayment' as another condition for the privileged retention of grey zone interest. This preference seems to be because such a flexible interpretation on this point is more likely to work in favour of the borrower. In January 2006, the Supreme Court held that an acceleration clause included in the loan agreement makes the repayment not 'voluntary', as the borrower may be afraid of triggering the acceleration when paying the excess interest. This means that payment of the grey zone interest will never be given the privilege if an acceleration clause is contained in the loan agreement, which is commonplace in order to facilitate enforcement.

(c) Cases on Non-bank's Duty to Disclose Lending History

The above cases were mostly the fruits of efforts by lawyers attempting to reduce the mountains of debt apparently owing, before filing for bankruptcy or personal rehabilitation. In some other cases the amount paid as excessive interest was found to exceed the principal plus interest as calculated according to the maximum rate under the IRRL. The borrowers in these cases could claim for recovery of the amount paid in excess.

In order to proceed with this kind of litigation, borrowers (or lawyers) need precise records of the history of borrowing. However, often the borrower has taken on too many loans without precise records. The Supreme Court also favoured borrowers by ordering lenders to disclose the history of loans, including rollovers, according to the books that it is obligated to keep under the Moneylenders Control Law. The Court held that denial of a request for disclosure of the loan history constituted a tort entitling the borrower to claim damages.[101] Successful 'statutory tort' claims for damages for regulatory statutes have been very rare in the consumer context in Japan.[102]

The 2006 reforms

The interim report by the FSA advisory council In the wake of these court decisions, mass claims were filed around the country by other over-indebted borrowers. Reform of the regulation over unsecured lending by non-banks therefore came

---

'Consumer lenders ordered to pay interest on refunds', *The Japan Times*, 14 July 2007. This will be at the five per cent rate fixed in the Civil Code, even though it is much higher nowadays than the market interest rate and is therefore itself likely to be changed by legislation: 'Legal 5% Interest Rate May Be Cut', *The Japan Times*, 16 July 2007.

101 Supreme Court, 19 July 2005 (Minshu 59-6-1783).
102 Dernauer, see generally (e.g. fn 33).

to the forefront of the legislative agenda. By chance, the Moneylenders Control Law was to be reviewed in 2006, so a Study Group (comprising leading scholars and various stakeholder representatives) had been set up within the FSA since the previous year. The Study Group met several times before the 'Interim Report' on 21 April 2006 was published under the name of the Chair, Professor Naoyuki Yoshino of Keio University's Faculty of Economics.[103]

The Interim Report stated, among other things, that the 'deemed valid payment' rules for grey zone interest were detrimental to both parties and should be discarded. It further suggested abolishing the grey zone itself. However, it did not make it clear how best to achieve such a result, namely whether the penalised rate under the Capital Funding Law should be lowered to the cap under the IRRL (supported by consumers) or *vice versa* (supported by non-banks). In analysing the issue, the Interim Report pointed out (at page 9) that both the borrower's demand for and lender's supply of the loan funds need to be considered. On the one hand, the maximum interest rate should ensure that the borrower can repay the debt in full – principal and all interests – without facing hardship. On the other hand, setting the cap too low might drive borrowers with poorer financial records out of the market and force them to resort to illegal financing.

Other issues raised in the Interim Report included: the regulation over the total amount of lending to one borrower, sharing of information on credit history of borrowers, regulation over advertisements by non-banks, regulation of collection, enhancing the entry conditions for non-banks, education of consumers on financial affairs, as well as counselling for borrowers who had taken out too many loans.

The Government response With various alternatives left in the Interim Report, the matter was handed over to the political parties. The governing coalition, the LDP and the Komeito, published on 6 July 2006 their Basic Policy.[104] It suggested diminishing the grey zone by lowering the penalised interest rate down to the maximum under the IRRL, while creating an exception for small loans. In other respects, the Basic Policy of the coalition was largely in line with the Interim Report. Main suggestions were to: enhance the entry conditions of non-banks; reorganise the industry association into a self-regulatory body; strengthen regulation over advertisements and collection; make it mandatory for non-banks to participate in an information sharing institution; promote effective counselling; and introduce regulation over excessive lending.

Achieving reform However, the Basic Policy was greeted by criticism, especially with respect to the exception for small loans. The public feared that such an

103 FSA Study Group *Kondankai ni okeru Koremade no Giron (Zachou to shiteno Chukan Seiri)*.

104 LDP and Komeito, *Kashikingyoseido to no Kaikaku ni kansuru Kihontekina Kangaekata* [Basic Policy on the Reform of the Regulation of Non-banks] (2006), available at: http://www.jimin.jp/jimin/seisaku/2006/seisaku-020.html.

exception would become a loophole in the entire scheme and completely undermine the aims of the reform. After political turbulence, the governing coalition decided not to include such an exception and consented to reform that simply equates the punishable interest rate in the Capital Funding Law with the maximum rate under the IRRL.

Thus, the amendments to the Moneylenders Control Law and related laws passed the Diet in December 2006. Besides revising the title of the Law to the 'Moneylenders Law' (removing 'control', so it becomes the *Kashikingyoho*), the reform included the following points:

- bringing down the interest rate penalised under the Capital Funding Law to 20 per cent per annum (abolishing the grey zone);
- requiring assets of 50 million yen for a non-bank to be licensed and operate;
- reforming the Federation of Moneylenders Association (*Zenkoku Kashikingyo Kyokai Rengokai*) into a nationwide Moneylenders Association as the self-regulatory body authorised under the Law on Non-banks;
- adding restrictions over various activities by the non-banks, including strengthening regulation on collection, and a new prohibition on them becoming beneficiaries under life insurance contracts taken out by their borrowers;
- suitability rules prohibiting a non-bank from 'unsuitable solicitation', and eventually from extending a loan exceeding one-third of the borrower's annual income;[105]
- obliging a non-bank to refer to the information-sharing institution every time it extends a loan, as well as to check the borrower's tax filings, in order to confirm his or her annual income when lending more than 500,000 yen.

These diverse aspects will be phased in gradually, by mid-2010. The final phase involves the grey zone abolition (although meanwhile lenders are already constrained by the Supreme Court rulings[106]) and full implementation of the 'suitability rules' aimed at limiting loans to borrowers beyond their likely repayment capacity.

---

105 This prohibition does not extend to housing or other exempted loans specified in the Ministerial Order. In addition, the Ministerial Order will provide some exceptions where the loan is found beneficial to the borrower. The draft Ministerial Order submitted for public comment lists six kinds of exempted loans and nine types of exceptions. The annual income of the borrower shall be examined by tax authorities' assessment of taxable income or other certificates to be specified by the Ministerial Order, so the draft Order lists ten. Thus, consumer loans under the new Moneylenders Law have come to be very awkwardly regulated. The draft Ministerial Order (available only in Japanese) is posted on the website of the FSA, available at: http://www.fsa. go.jp/news/19/kinyu/20070706-2.html.

106 All four major consumer lenders have already brought down their maximum rates to 18 per cent, while still returning to profitability. Compare, for example 'Takefuji Set to Bring its Interest Rate Down to 18%', *Kyodo News*, 18 December 2007.

Interim Conclusions

Japan's own struggle with consumers overburdened by unsecured loans is still playing itself. The 2006 amendments are already having major but complex effects on the market, as well as prompting movements for similar reforms to the Instalment Sales Law regime to address existing and potential future excesses regarding sales credit.[107] Nonetheless, this chapter already offers a firm basis for consumer lawyers and policy-makers interested in comparing Japan's evolving experience.

This outline of the rise of unsecured consumer lending and its significant decline recently, due to the recent legislative reforms building on considerable judicial activism, also opens a new field to explore for comparative lawyers perennially intrigued by how law interacts with socio-economic context in contemporary Japan. Rich insights can be gained by turning to various quite distinctive schools of thought that have tended to dominate the English language world of Japanese law studies.[108] Generally, a focal point in this literature has been Japan's comparatively low civil litigation rate. One explanation for that phenomenon, common amongst commentators during the 1960s and 1970s but still found especially in the popular press, is culturalist. Due to Confucian norms of harmony and the like, the Japanese just *don't* like law. A second explanation, propounded from the late 1970s and underpinning Japan's wave of civil justice reforms since 2001, is the existence of institutional barriers to litigation. These mean that the Japanese *can't* like law. A third explanation, influential from the 1980s as US 'revisionist' commentators began to emphasise that a distinctive form of capitalism in Japan required novel responses to lessen trade friction, is elite management. Bureaucrats, in particular, manage social problems so the Japanese are *made not to* like law.

By contrast, as the US economy regained ground over the 1990s, neoclassical economics provided a fourth explanation: the Japanese *do* like law, settling cases out of court in its relatively predictable shadow. As well as emphasising that legal rules often do matter in Japan, and indeed are often efficient, this 'Chicago School' approach argues increasingly stridently that the only other significant variable needed to understand Japanese socio-legal behaviour is straightforward market forces.[109]

However, a 'new generation'[110] of 'hybrid theorists' remains prepared to acknowledge the impact of socio-economic and cultural institutions (such as 'main

---

107 Above notes 18–21 and 80.
108 Abe and Nottage; Nottage, 'Translating Tanase: Challenging Paradigms of Japanese law and Society'.
109 C. Freedman and L. Nottage, 'You say Tomato, I Say Tomahto, Let's Call the Whole Thing Off: The Chicago School of Law and Economics Comes to Japan', *Centre for Japanese Economic Studies Research Papers*, 2006-4, available at: http://www/econ. mq.edu.au/docs/research_papers/2006-4_Freedman_Nottage.pdf.
110 Anderson, see generally (e.g. fn 18).

banks', *keiretsu* corporate groups and relational contracting) that are distinctive to Japan, at least compared to conventional neoclassical perceptions of how free markets operate. These theorists are also more eclectic in their methodology, balancing the sort of quantitative analysis favoured by neoclassical economists as the only way to true enlightenment with a renewed respect for qualitative analyses. Such approaches argue that the Japanese *sometimes* like law, but sometimes don't. They also tend to conclude that socio-legal behaviour and governance structures are undergoing gradual but significant transformations. By contrast, minimal change is perceived both by traditional culturalist theorists – communitarianism remains strong; and ironically by Chicago School economists – straightforward market forces and efficient legal rules have always characterised modern Japan.

Such views, particularly hybrid theories of Japan's 'gradual transformation', are helpful starting points for fruitful analysis and debate especially about law and socio-economic context impacts on behaviour, such as the role of various potential stakeholders in corporate governance.[111] Commentators leading these schools of thought have offered less convincing explanations of the necessarily messier processes by which key actors in turn shape both legal and social norms. Both aspects are important, especially for those who favour more social constructionist approaches to socio-legal studies,[112] but also for other social scientists interested in feedback loops.[113]

In one companion paper,[114] we conduct an extensive thought experiment of how some of these various schools of thought might explain not only the growth of consumer credit markets in Japan, in the light of legal and socio-economic institutions, but also the recent re-regulation. We conclude that the growth of consumer over-indebtedness may well be explained by culturalist theory, albeit reinterpreted in a contemporary light – for example, emphasising a strong rather than weak sense of contractual obligation held by many Japanese.[115] Explanations from Chicago School neoclassical economics, emphasising straightforward wealth-maximising rationalism on the part of borrowers as well as lenders, are

---

111 L. Nottage 'Nothing New in the (North) East? The Rhetoric and Reality of Corporate Governance in Japan', *CLPE Research Paper*, 01-1 (2006), available at: http://ssrn.com/abstract=885367, updated as Chapter 2 in L. Nottage, L. Wolff and K. Anderson (eds) *Corporate Governance in the 21st Century: Japan's Gradual Transformation* (Elgar, Cheltenham, 2008).

112 Nottage, 'Translating Tanase: Challenging Paradigms of Japanese law and Society'.

113 S.K. Vogel, *Japan Remodelled: How Government and Industry Are Reforming Japanese Capitalism* (Ithica, N.Y., 2006).

114 Kozuka and Nottage, 'Reforming Unsecured Consumer Credit Markets in Japan: Empirically-Informed Normativism', and Kozuka and Nottage, 'The Myth of the Cautious Consumer: Law, Culture, Economics and Politics in the Rise and Partial Fall of Unsecured Lending in Japan'.

115 L. Nottage, 'Changing Contract Lenses: Unexpected Supervening Events in English, New Zealand, Japanese, US, and International Sales Law and Practice', *Indiana Journal of Global Legal Studies*, 14 (2008) 385.

much less plausible than accounts drawing on the new paradigm of 'behavioural economics'.[116]

Turning from the growth of consumer credit and over-indebtedness to its re-regulation, however, insights from behavioural economics played little role in crafting specific reforms.[117] Instead, political theory emphasising a growing consumer voice in contemporary policy-making – even, perhaps, some excessive populism – provides a persuasive and relatively novel explanation for the array of measures introduced.

Other explanations for these reforms are less convincing, since key evidence is lacking. One is elite management theory, emphasising especially the resilience of Japan's financial mandarins in diverting political problems away from the courts.[118] The other is Chicago School 'public choice' theory, which likes to explain regulation as inefficiently promoted by certain industry groups to disproportionately undermine commercial rivals.[119]

A conventional culturalist account also struggles to explain how and why significant reforms have been introduced recently. Pardieck does acknowledge the important role of the judiciary in developing the law, which challenges such an account; but he argues that this field involves private rather than citizen-state relationships. He also draws parallels with the ongoing judicial and legislative emphasis on substantive controls, particularly through interest rate caps, and the willingness of (pre-1868) Tokugawa-era lawmakers and magistrates periodically to impose substantive justice despite realising the likely long-term effects on credit markets.[120] Pardieck contrasts the courts' retreat from the ideology of freedom of contract, which prevailed in the early twentieth century, with its persistence in the US since the nineteenth century.[121] Quite like other contemporary neo-culturalists,[122] he suggests that the renewed interest in substantive justice reaffirms a moral sense of community. However, substantive interventions in consumer credit markets have long been a feature of countries with very different cultural traditions.[123]

116 See for example Harris and Albin.
117 F. Hiruma '*Kashikingyoho Kaisei Mondai ni Kansuru Shogiron no Saikento: Kaketa Shiten Wa Nanika?* [Revisiting the Debates on Amending the Moneylenders Law: What is the Missing Viewpoint?]', *Credit Kenkyu*, 38 (2007): 6.
118 Compare, for example, G.D. Ruback, 'Master of Puppets: How Japan's Ministry of Finance Orchestrates Its Own Reformation', *Fordham International Law Journal*, 22 (1998): 185.
119 Compare, for example, J.M. Ramseyer, 'Public Choice', *Chicago Law School Law and Economics Working Paper*, available at: http://www.uchicago.edu/Lawecon/WkngPprs_26-50/34.Ramseyer.pdf.
120 Pardieck, see generally (e.g. fn 20).
121 See also generally Dernauer.
122 J.O. Haley, *The Spirit of Japanese Law* (Athens, 1998); and Tanase (introduced in Nottage, 'Translating Tanase: Challenging Paradigms of Japanese law and Society').
123 See for example, Howell and Hughes, 'Consumer Credit Regulation: An International Overview'.

Along with measures aimed at procedural fairness, such as adequate disclosure, they also remain a feature of consumer law worldwide since the 1960s.[124] Pardieck himself also remains sensitive to the new political environment that underpinned Japan's recent re-regulation.

Yet, that belated combination of measures must give pause as well to those modernists who perceive a sharp shift in Japan towards a liberal, rights-based social and legal order,[125] and especially to those proclaiming the 'Americanisation' of Japanese law.[126] Nonetheless, only public choice purists would be fervently opposed to such re-regulation. Their relatively low numbers, certainly in Tokyo and even perhaps around Chicago these days, help explain why these far-reaching reforms did get enacted in 2006.

Such interpretations should also be useful for specialists in consumer law less interested in Japan *per se*, but rather in the relative impact of culture, economics and politics in other countries facing similar challenges from consumer over-indebtedness.[127] In addition, Japan is quite distinctive now in pursuing ex ante interest rate regulation, and in the role played by the judiciary (especially the Supreme Court) rather than the legislature in addressing consumer lending issues. A view explored in our second companion paper is that a range of other re-regulatory tools, combining soft and hard law, needs to be deployed by a range of socio-legal actors to address such a serious and complex problem.[128] Meanwhile, we hope that this first paper in our trilogy begins to fill a major void in the English-language literature on the problem in Japan, revealing many broad commonalities with that afflicting other post-industrial capitalist societies.

---

124 See generally, for example, Ramsay, *Consumer Law and Policy: Text and Materials on Regulating Consumer Markets*.

125 See for example, C.J. Milhaupt and M.D. West, *Economic Organizations and Corporate Governance in Japan* (Oxford, 2004).

126 See, for example, R.D. Kelemen and E.C. Sibbitt, 'The Americanization of Japanese Law', *University of Pennsylvania Journal of International Economic Law*, 23 (2002): 269.

127 For example the UK: I. Ramsay, 'Functionalism and Political Economy in the Comparative Study of Consumer Insolvency: An Unfinished Story from England and Wales', *Theoretical Inquiries in Law*, 7 (2006): 625.

128 Kozuka and Nottage, 'Reforming Unsecured Consumer Credit Markets in Japan: Empirically-Informed Normativism'.

7 Consumer Collective Redress in the European Union: The 'Italian Case'

*Cristina Poncibò**

Introduction

In the 1970s and 1980s, the consumer rights movement in Europe primarily focused on improving consumer rights by way of changing the substantive law. From the second half of the 1980s onwards, consumer law increasingly became of interest to the European Union. According to the European Commission, consumer law was and is instrumental in the establishment and completion of the internal market.[1] As a result of this instrumentalist view of consumer law, the emphasis in European consumer law was often put on correcting information asymmetries by imposing duties to inform on sellers and service providers, often combined with the introduction of cooling-off periods and rights of withdrawal.[2]

Since the beginning of the twenty-first century, however, a new trend seems to, emerge and the attention is gradually shifting from improving consumer rights through substantive law to improving access to consumer justice.[3]

Actually, consumers often find it difficult to obtain redress through conventional judicial proceedings. Not only are they usually unfamiliar with the law; their claims often involve small amounts of money so litigation costs can easily exceed the amount of the claim. Thus, consumers tend to abandon their claims rather than pursue an economically unprofitable course. Moreover, businesses are typically 'repeat players' in legal controversies. They have more expertise in legal matters and possess economies of scale that allow for more efficient litigation. They also have an incentive to litigate for the creation of precedent as well as for immediate

---

*   Researcher, Comparative Private Law, Faculty of Law, University of Turin (Italy).
1   A. Coughlin, 'The Movement of Consumer Protection in the European Community: A Vital Link in the Establishment of Free Trade and a Paradigm for North America', *Ind. Int'l & Comp. L. Rev.*, 5 (1994): 143, at 158.
2   G. Brueggemeier, M. Bussani, H. Collins, A. Colombi Ciacchi, G. Comande, M. Fabre-Magnan, S. Grundmann, M.W. Hesselink, C. Joerges, B. Lurger, U. Mattei, M. Meli, J.W. Rutgers, C. Schmidt, J. Smith, R. Sefton-Green, H. Muir Watt and T. Wilhelmsson, 'Social Justice in European Contract Law: A Manifesto?', *European Law Journal*, 10:6 (2004): 653–74.
3   W.H. Van Boom and M.B.M. Loos (eds), *Collective Enforcement of Consumer Law; Securing Compliance in Europe through Private Group Action and Public Authority Intervention* (The Netherlands, 2007), p. 1.

gain; as a recurrent litigant, they are willing to spend resources to influence the making of legal rules. For these reasons, consumer problems were often cited as the paradigm of the problem of access to justice.[4]

In this chapter I consider Part V of the Italian Consumer Code ('Consumers' Associations and Access to Justice') and particularly the new Article 140-*bis* (Collective redress action) with the aim to broadly discuss the ways in which consumers can seek collective redress in the European Union.

With Legislative Decree of September 6, 2005 No. 206 the Italian Parliament issued the Consumer Code, which harmonised and reorganised the rules governing consumer transactions to ensure a high level of protection of consumers and users.[5]

The creation of a codified version of the domestic measures, transposing the *acquis communautaire* concerning the protection of consumers' economic interests into Italian law, serves to remedy the lack of coordination in the implementation of the individual directives. Prior to the adoption of the code, the legislation on the protection of consumers, almost entirely of Community origin, was fragmented in a whole series of uncoordinated and sometimes legislative instruments, including articles of the Civil Code.

From this standpoint the systematisation that has been achieved with Legislative Decree No. 206/2005 is undoubtedly significant: the codification of consumer law, on the basis of the French model, makes the whole subject matter more accessible, permits its homogeneous interpretation and allows the various aspects to be linked together in a unitary structure.[6]

Especially commendable is the decision to combine the treatment of the exercise of the right to withdraw from distance contracts and contracts negotiated away from business premises, which resolves the interpretative doubts caused by the earlier legislation (Article 64 'Right to withdraw').

The Consumer Code also espouses the principle of making information available to the consumer to increase his awareness of rights and remedies: 'Education of consumers and users is designed to encourage awareness of their rights and interests, the development of associations, participation in administrative procedures and their presence in representative bodies' (Article 4 'Consumer education').

---

4   M. Cappelletti, *Access to Justice* (Milan, 1978); M. Cappelletti (ed.), with the assistance of J. Weisner and M. Seccombe, *Access to Justice and the Welfare State* (Netherlands, 1981); C.E.F. Rickett and T.G.W. Telfer (eds), *International Perspectives on Consumers' Access to Justice* (Cambridge, 2003).

5   Legislative Decree 6 September 2005 No. 206 – Consumer Code Consumer Code pursuant to Article 7 of Law of July 29, 2003 No. 229, as modified by the art. 19 of the Law February 6 2007, no.13, the Legislative Decree August 2, 2007, no.146, the Legislative Decree October 23, 2007, no. 221 and the art. 1, paragraphs 445, 446, 447, 448 and 449 of the Budget Law 2008.

6   B. Pasa and M. Weitenberg, 'Improved Consumer Protection through New Codification? – First Comments on the New Italian Consumer Code', in G. Howells *et al.* (eds), *Yearbook of Consumer Law 2007* (Aldershot, 2007), pp. 295–308.

Nevertheless, the provisions of the Consumer Code will have little practical meaning without mechanisms which allow consumers to seek a quick, inexpensive and fair resolution of disputes. I agree with some authors arguing, while commenting on the '*Parmalat Case*', that: '... gatekeepers are substantially undeterred in Italy because of poor enforcement rather than legislative black holes.'[7]

Traditional approaches to enforcement focus on three areas: (1) individual action through citizen claims pursued in the courts or other forums; (2) collective actions by consumer organisations; and (3) government intervention in civil consumer protection laws.[8]

Although the Consumer Code outlines an enforcement framework involving each of these mechanisms and includes various provisions designed to encourage compliance with the law, the enforcement scheme – recently modified – shows a heavy reliance on actions by consumer organisations.[9]

Private Litigation

The costs of litigation represent a serious obstacle for consumers. This aspect should be considered in a civil proceeding characterised by the long duration of the processes and their uncertain outcomes. Consumers can quite rationally decide that the cost of attempting to secure redress is not justified if the amount involved is less than the cost of complaining. Accordingly, excluding personal injury, most consumer claims are not worth pursuing and, thus, there is no credible threat to litigate on the part of an aggrieved consumer since any defendant would be fully cognisant of the consumer's inability to pursue the claim. It also means that, since no or limited recoveries will be sought in the absence of some collective enforcement action, there will be a predictable under-deterrence of wrongdoing.

There are different solutions to reduce the problem of costs, including small claims courts, legal aid and Alternative Dispute Resolution (ADR) mechanisms that are briefly discussed in the following sections.

---

7   G.A. Ferrarini and P. Giudici, 'Financial Scandals and the Role of Private Enforcement: The Parmalat Case', ECGI Working Paper Series in Law, No. 40/2005, May 2005. Accessed 21 August 2007 at http://ssrn.com/abstract=730403.

8   F. Cafaggi and H.W. Micklitz, 'Administrative and Judicial Collective Enforcement of Consumer Law in the US and the European Community', August 2007, EUI LAW Working Paper No. 2007/22. Available at: http://ssrn.com/abstract=1024103. W.H. Van Boom and M.B.M. Loos, 'Effective Enforcement of Consumer Law in Europe: Synchronizing Private, Public, and Collective Mechanisms', January 2008; available at http://ssrn.com/abstract=1082913.

9   S. Chiarloni and P. Fiorio (eds), '*Consumatori e Processo. La tutela degli interessi collettivi dei consumatori, Atti del convegno tenutosi a Torino il 28-29 Maggio 2004*' (Torino, 2005).

Small claims

According to the EC Regulation on European Small Claims Procedure, the establishment of an efficient and effective 'small claims' court mechanism might contribute greatly in furthering the goal of consumer protection.[10]

Within the Italian legal system small claims, including consumer claims, are presently dealt with by the Justices of the Peace (*'Giudici di pace'*).[11] The objective of this was to re-route some matters that would have normally been dealt with by the ordinary civil courts into a specialist court with a lower jurisdictional limit.

Typically, small claims consumer cases involve issues of commercial law, private contracts, property rights and minor personal injuries. Other types of small claims cases might include landlord-tenant disputes, family law (for example, divorce and adoption), and decedent's estates.[12]

Before the Justice of the Peace procedures are simplified and the consumer can file a case at little or no cost; the parties need not file written legal briefs or comply with formal rules of evidence and trial procedures; and the consumer generally does not have to hire a lawyer. The small claims judge simply hears the testimony of both parties and others who have knowledge relevant to the dispute, and either attempts to mediate a compromise or makes a decision in favour of one party.

An important component of an effective small claims court system is the procedure for appeals. In Italy disappointed small claims litigants typically have an automatic right of appeal to the first level of the ordinary courts. As a practical matter, most cases are not appealed because the appeal will cost more than the amount in dispute.

This system addresses the consumer access to justice problem, first because it reduces legal costs. However, Justices of the Peace have come under strong criticism for their low level of training and the very limited accuracy of their decisions. Because procedural rules are relaxed and the parties present their cases without professional assistance, there may be a slightly greater risk that the decision will be inconsistent with some legal doctrine. It is debatable if the benefits of a simplified procedure may, therefore, justify the increased possibility of error.

---

10   Regulation (EC) No 861/2007 of the European Parliament and of the Council of 11 July 2007 establishing a European Small Claims Procedure [2007] OJ L 199, pp. 1–22. G. Haibach, 'The Commission Proposal for a Regulation Establishing a European Small Claims Procedure: An Analysis', *ERPL* (2005): pp. 593–601.

11   V. Varano, 'Machinery of Justice', in J.S. Lena and U. Mattei (eds), *Introduction to Italian Law* (Great Britain, 2002), pp. 101–103; P. Nebbia, *'Judex Ex Machina*: The Justice of the Peace in the Tragedy of the Italian Civil Process', *CJQ*, 17 (1998): p. 164.

12   Interesting in a comparative perspective, P. Lewis, 'The Consumer's Court? Revisiting the Theory of the Small Claim Procedure', *CJQ*, 25 (2006): pp. 52–69.

Legal aid

In consideration of the situation already described, one may expect that consumers would be granted access to justice by way of legal aid from the State. Nevertheless, this is not the case because consumers with insufficient means are entitled to legal aid[13] only in a limited number of civil proceedings (for example separation, custody of children or rulings regarding parental responsibility).

Anyone with a taxable income not exceeding €9,723.84, as shown on his or her latest tax return, is entitled to legal aid.[14] It corresponds to the Italian institution of 'advocacy in court paid for by the State' to protect defendants with insufficient means and involves exempting such persons from having to meet certain costs and the State paying other costs. Where there is an entitlement to legal aid, the person is not required to pay the standard charge, standard payments for official notification and certain fees (registry fees, judicial mortgage and land registry fees).[15]

The State has the right of reimbursement and, where it does not recover the money from the loser, it may claim repayment from the party eligible for legal aid, if the recipient wins the case or settlement of the dispute and receives at least six times the cost of the expenses incurred or if cases are discontinued or barred.

Applicants granted legal aid may nominate a lawyer from the lists of legal aid lawyers drawn up by the bar associations of the court of appeal circuit of the judge who knows the merits of the case or the judge before whom it is pending. They may also nominate expert witnesses, where allowed by law. If the case is at the appeal stage, the lawyer will be chosen from the lists drawn up by the bar associations of the court of appeal circuit where the judge who made the contested ruling has his or her chambers. The list of legal aid lawyers comprises professionals who have applied to be put on it and have the qualifications necessary to represent clients.

It should be noted that legal aid is too limited in its scope given that it covers only certain civil proceedings. At the same time, the criteria to receive legal aid are so stringent that very few consumers have been able to benefit from it. Both reasons undermine the potentiality of the system that does not receive adequate financial public support.

---

13 Presidential Decree, May 30, 2002 No. 115, *Testo unico delle disposizioni legislative e regolamentari in materia di spese di giustizia*, in OJ 139, 15.6.2002 – Supplement No. 126.

14 The income threshold is adjusted every two years by order of the Ministry of Justice to take account of variations in ISTAT's consumer price index.

15 The State pays the following: (a) counsel's fees and expenses; (b) travel costs and expenses incurred by judges, officials and judicial officers for performing their duties outside the court; (c) travel costs and expenses incurred by witnesses, court officials and expert witnesses who incurred expenses when performing their duties are also reimbursed; (d) the cost of publishing any notice regarding the judge's ruling; (e) the cost of official notification.

Out-of-court settlement of disputes

The Consumer Code promotes the development of mechanisms for the out-of-court settlement of disputes. This emphasis on alternative dispute resolution reflects the obstacles that judicial procedures can pose for consumers, particularly lower income ones, and the desire to increase the likelihood of consumer redress.[16]

At present, a system of mediation for consumers' claims is provided by the local chambers of commerce. Such mechanism is an informal and confidential procedure that makes it possible to find good solutions, acceptable to both parties, and to preserve commercial relations, thus managing both the legal and psychological aspects related to a dispute.[17]

The mediation is intended for consumers who wish to resolve disputes which may occur with a trader, regardless of their economic value, in a fast, friendly and confidential way. After receiving the request, the secretariat informs the other party (or parties) involved in the dispute and invites them to file the answer. If the other parties agree to join the proceeding, the secretariat appoints the mediator, who shall sign a statement of independence. The mediator is appointed by the chamber of commerce, having trained on mediation techniques, and helps them in finding the best solution. The proceeding should be as fast as possible in the physical presence of the parties.[18] If the mediation is successful, the parties sign an agreement that is binding as a contract. It should be remembered that the mediation procedure is voluntary,[19] thus the parties may withdraw at any moment, without any consequence, if they are not satisfied by the outcome. Further, all the parties involved in the procedure, including the mediator and any participant in the meeting, have a duty of confidentiality: they shall not disclose any information obtained during the proceeding.[20] There is evidence that mediation by the chamber of commerce is rarely used due to lack of information by the consumers, who are often not aware of such an opportunity. Consumers suffer from a lack of specific information about remedies and, more generally, the ways to enforce substantial

---

16 M. Cappelletti, 'Alternative Dispute Resolution Processes within the Framework of the Worldwide Access to Justice Movement', *Mod. L. Rev.*, 56 (1993): p. 282.

17 A specific mediation service is established for disputes arising in the tourism field, that has been established in close cooperation with consumers' and tour operators' organisations. Other examples of mediation concern telecommunication, postal and banking services. Moreover, the Ombudsman model, which allows complaints of individuals to be investigated by an independent person, is provided only for consumers' complaints concerning banking services.

18 Please note that the parties may choose the on-line procedure.

19 It should be noted that few trade associations have adopted voluntary codes of practice and the codes of practice have little relevance in consumer protection in Italy. See, on the contrary in the UK system, R. Lowe and G. Woodroffe, *Consumer Law and Practice* (London, 2004), pp. 178–212.

20 Each party shall pay a limited contribution to the expenses, which is determined according to the fee schedule.

rights provided by the Consumer Code. As a consequence of their limited awareness about remedies, consumers may not realise that their problem is subject to a remedy and thus they accept a solution by ignoring that it is below the legal standard (for example, the remedies provided for sale of goods by Article 130 of the Consumer Code). Or they may think that a problem is not sufficiently serious to make a claim or that they should be capable of tolerating the inconvenience. They may also be reluctant to admit that they have been 'ripped off'.[21]

Scarce measures have been taken to overcome this problem that still persists, coupled with a legal profession that does not want to share forensic knowledge with the general public. I underline the fact that access to justice is mainly available through lawyers and this seriously undermines the implementation of solutions involving the out-of-court settlement of disputes, as well as those providing for personal representation by consumers, as in 'small claims' cases before the Justice of the Peace.

Collective redress

In the absence of specific instruments for consumer collective redress, the Italian system has been developed through the adaptation of 'traditional' institutes such as the *litisconsorzio* (joinder of parties) and the *'costituzione di parte civile nel processo penale'* ('action instituted by a private person for damages').

The offices of the public authorities and, particularly, the *'Pubblico Ministero'* ('Attorney-General') play a major role in protection of consumer rights by 'acting' as substitutes for collective redress. When private parties join criminal proceedings, they can benefit from the evidence offered by the prosecutors and can thus minimise the burden of persuading the court (a burden that, in any event, stays with the prosecutor). However, civil claimants' compensation depends on conviction. In criminal actions the standard of proof is different because proof beyond a reasonable doubt is required. In contrast, standards of proof in civil cases are more relaxed – even though, at least in Italy, they are usually stricter than the standard of the preponderance of evidence. In other words, this type of action is not structured to recover consumers' damages in a mass-fault scenario and the outcome has often been insufficient.

The Attorney-General's success in assuming this new social role has considerably broadened its political power as an institution, and this phenomenon has evoked bitter criticism based on the idea that this power undermines the democratic doctrine of government.

More importantly, many cases that do not represent a criminal offence do not fall under the competence of the *Pubblico Ministero*.[22] Here, the institute of the *litisconsorzio* has been adapted as a device for mass litigation in cases concerning

---

21   C. Scott, J. Black, *Cranston's Consumers and the Law* (London, 2000), pp. 104–105.
22   The role of criminal law in consumer protection is not discussed in this chapter.

blood infection and asbestos, where a settlement has followed the courts' decisions in favour of consumer claims.[23]

In such context, individual actions still play a major role in protecting consumer rights, but certain characteristics of our judicial system reduce the effectiveness of private actions. As an author noted: 'In Italy there seems to be a sharp contrast between the law as it is written in the books and its operation in reality.'[24] Italian courts are slow and inefficient[25] and, actually, the consistent increases in the number of cases on each judge's cause list has, from time to time, created a large backlog.[26]

This endless increase, as well as the lack of resources (that is number of judges, court personnel, access to technology), have seriously affected the duration of the new proceedings.[27] In this context, a key role is played by the legal profession that is moving far away from traditional ethical ideals and that, doubtless, needs to be deeply reformed.[28]

Notwithstanding these negative experiences, the Consumer Code adopted in 2005 does not include any mechanism for consumer protection or for damages and the avenue of redress for mass defaults in the Italian legal system has been limited to collective actions brought by the public prosecutor. In the perspective of access to justice, the adoption of the Consumer Code represented, at that time, a missed opportunity.[29]

---

23 C. Poncibò, 'Le azioni di interesse collettivo per la tutela dei consumatori', *Riv. Crit. Dir. Priv.*, 4 (2002): pp. 659–69.

24 S. Chiarloni, 'Civil Justice and its Paradoxes: An Italian Perspective', in A. Zuckerman (ed.), *Civil Justice in Crisis, Comparative Perspectives of Civil Procedure* (Oxford, 1999), p. 263.

25 D. Marchesi, *Litiganti, avvocati e magistrati. Diritto ed economia del processo civile* (Bologna, 2003).

26 A.C. Reynolds, 'Dimensions of Justice in Italy: a Practical Review', *Global Jurist Advances*, 3/2 (2003), article 1; accessed 21 August 2007 at: http://www.bepress.com/gj/advances/vol3/iss2/art1.

27 *Ibid.*, p. 269.

28 For the analysis of the legal profession, Chiarloni, 'Civil Justice and its Paradoxes: An Italian Perspective', pp. 276–8.

29 Formally the Consumer Code has the scope to secure consumers' express rights, including the right to compensation and it contains provisions for consumer protection that do expressly grant the right to seek remuneration, such as Articles 94–5 about tourism and package travel, and Article 114 ('Liability for damage caused by defective products').

Public Enforcement

Traditional civil-law political ideology generally looks to the government for protection of the collective interests of the consumers. Unless there is a growing sense of its limited knowledge and resources, the Consumer Code assigns various functions to governmental organisations.

The National Council of Consumers and Users

The Consumer Code maintains the Directorate-General for Harmonisation and Protection of the Market ('*Direzione Generale per l'armonizzazione del mercato e la tutela dei consumatori*'), established in 1997 within the Ministry of Productive Activities. Its aim is to consolidate and coordinate consumer policies in cooperation with the European Union and with a view to reforming the Italian public administration in accordance with the principles of geographical decentralisation of powers and functions. Emphasis must be placed on the importance of the process of administrative decentralisation in the Italian public administration. Thus, the trend in defending consumer interests is to delegate as many activities as possible to local authorities, so that consumers and businesses can deal with the authority which is closest to them. At the same time, it is responsible for rectifying the current fragmentation of responsibilities among various bodies, at both local and national levels, in order to ensure the unity and coordination of administrative action. In this connection, the Directorate-General will be able to help promote practical collaboration between the ministries and other administrations (especially on the subject of product safety) and between the central and regional authorities.

Under the Consumer Code, private enforcement should be complemented by governmental oversight from the National Council of Consumers and Users ('*Consiglio Nazionale dei Consumatori e degli Utenti*').[30]

Article 136 of the Consumer Code gives administrative authority to the Council to represent the consumers' and users' associations nationwide. It is part of the Ministry of Productive Activities and its chair is held by the Minister or one of his delegates. At the moment the Council is composed of 17 recognised associations and a representative member of the Regions and Autonomous Provinces elected by the Regions–State Conference.[31]

The Council's main duties are those of expressing opinions, where requested, on preliminary draft legislation produced by the Government or draft legislation

---

30   The Council Website is available at: http://www.tuttoconsumatori.it.
31   The Council invites representatives from recognised Environmental Protection Associations and National Consumer Co-Operative Associations to its meetings. Representatives from bodies and organs with the functions of regulating or standardising the market, of the economic and social sectors concerned, competent public authorities and experts in the subjects under consideration may also be invited to attend.

produced by the members of parliament, as well as on draft regulations that affect the rights and interests of consumers and users.

In addition to its advisory function *vis-à-vis* the Parliament (at hearings), and *vis-à-vis* the Government (consultation sessions), the Council takes part in other regular consultation processes with other authorities and bodies by being a signatory to memorandums of understanding as well as by attending hearings on specific topics. It also promotes studies and research and expresses opinions, where required, on the features of regulations concerning the rights and interests of consumers and users, and formulates proposals in relation to the protection of consumers and users, also with reference to European programmes and policies. The Council has two other tasks consisting of drawing up programmes for the distribution of information to consumers and users and mainly in encouraging initiatives designed to improve consumers' and users' access to justice in order to settle disputes.[32]

Due to the inadequacies of private enforcement of consumer rights, a strong government authority would be extremely useful for consumer protection. Unfortunately, the National Council of Consumers and Users has very limited authority since it only represents a consultant for the Government and it carries on bureaucratic work that does not have direct impact on the welfare of Italian consumers.

The Italian Antitrust Authority

In cases of infringement of the provisions of the Consumer Code concerning misleading and comparative advertising (Articles 18–37), fines may be imposed by the Italian Antitrust Authority (*Autorità garante della concorrenza e del mercato*) established by Article 10 of Law October 10, 1990 No. 287.[33]

Competitors, consumers, their associations and organisations, the Minister of Productive Activities, and every other public authority having an interest in relation to its own institutional tasks, also following a complaint from the public, may request the Authority to ensure the restraint of acts of misleading or comparative advertising deemed to be unlawful, to ensure that the continuance of such acts

---

32   On the basis of its Article 2(3) Law No. 57 of 5 March 2001 concerning provisions in relation to the opening-up and regulation of the markets, the National Consumers' and Users' Council is authorised to co-fund information and guidance programmes targeting the users of insurance services backed by the consumers' and users' associations in order to distribute appropriate information to users about the premiums required for the compulsory insurance for third-party liability when driving a motor vehicle.

33   Since Article 148 of the Law of December 23, 2000 No. 388 ('*Legge finanziaria* 2001') the fines received in the form of administrative fines imposed for the infringement of the antitrust law 'by the authority operating as guarantor for competition and the market' are to be used to fund initiatives undertaken for the benefit of consumers.

be prevented and that their effects be eliminated. In any event, it shall notify the advertiser that the procedure has been opened and if the principal commissioning the advertisement is unknown, may demand all such information as may identify the principal from the owner of the medium that has spread the advertisement.

If the Authority finds the advertisement misleading or the comparative advertising not to be permitted, it shall allow the complaint, prohibiting advertising that has not yet been made public or ordering the cessation of advertising that has already commenced.[34] The decision upholding the complaint may include an order for that decision to be published in part or in full, and may include, in addition, an order for the publication of a special corrective statement to eliminate the continuing effects of the misleading or non-permitted comparative advertising.

Only recently, the Authority has been given, by the Government, a series of new competences to implement of the Unfair Commercial Practices Directive.[35] The Authority will also be responsible for the application of the Regulation on Consumer Protection Cooperation.[36]

Injunctive Relief by Consumer Organisations

Articles 139–140 of the Consumer Code prevent unlawful behaviour against the general consumer interest and implement the 'necessary measures in order to correct or eliminate the damaging effects of the violations'.[37]

Article 140 of the Consumer Code provides that:

---

34 Article 26, paras 10–11, Consumer Code:
   In case of failure to comply with interim measures and injunctions or measures for elimination of effects, the Authority shall impose an administrative fine of between 10,000 euro and 50,000 euro. In the event of repeated non-compliance the Authority may order that the firm's activities be suspended for no more than thirty days. For failure to comply with requests to furnish the information or documentation provided by paragraph 3, the Authority shall impose an administrative fine of between 2,000 euro and 20,000 euro. If the information or documentation supplied is untruthful, the Authority shall impose an administrative fine of between 4,000 euro and 40,000 euro.

35 Directive 2005/29/EC of the European Parliament and of the Council of 11 May 2005 concerning unfair business-to-consumer commercial practices in the internal market ('Unfair Commercial Practices Directive'), OJ L 149, 11.6.2005, pp. 22–39.

36 Regulation (EC) No 2006/2004 of the European Parliament and of the Council of 27 October 2004 on cooperation between national authorities responsible for the enforcement of consumer protection laws, OJ L 364, 9.12.2004, pp. 1–11.

37 Article 139 and followings of Consumer Code implementing Directive 98/27/EC of the European Parliament and of the Council of 19 May 1998 on injunctions for the protection of consumers' interests, OJ, L 166, 11.6.1998, pp. 51–5.

The parties referred to at Article 139 [the associations of consumers and users registered before the Ministry of Productive Activities; independent Italian public organisms and organisations recognised in another Member State of the European Union] are qualified to act to protect the collective interests of consumers and users by applying to a Court for[38] a) a prohibition order against actions damaging to the interests of consumers and users; b) suitable measures to remedy or eliminate the damaging effects of any breaches; c) orders to publish measures in one or more national or local daily newspapers where publicising measures may help to correct or eliminate the effects of any breaches.

The process of 'accreditation' is regulated by objective requirements established by the Ministry of Productive Activities, such as the number of association members, the length of incorporation, the non-profit organisation status, the democratic character of its deliberations and elections, the source of income, and the record of political, social and legal activism. These requirements should be sufficiently strict to exclude inadequate representatives, but strict accreditation requirements may reduce the number of authorized associations, strengthen the power of the few accredited ones and ultimately make them detached from individual members of the community.[39]

The Court shall set a deadline for compliance with the obligations set out in the order, and in the event of non-compliance, shall order (at the request of the party who instigated the proceedings or another party) the payment of a sum of money of between €516 and €1,032 for each instance of non-compliance or each day of delay, commensurate with the gravity of the breach. Such sums of money shall be paid into State funds to be re-allocated by an order of the Ministry of the Economy and Finance to a fund to be set up as part of a special basic budgetary section of the Ministry of Productive Activities to finance initiatives for the benefit of consumers.

The Italian experience confirms that effective private enforcement in turn requires mechanisms to aggregate the small and diffuse claims of consumers. In order for consumers to advocate on their own behalf, there must be a mechanism

---

38   A specific provision concern injunctions to prevent the use of unfair terms: 'Consumers' associations pursuant to Article 137, associations representing professionals, and Chambers of Commerce, Industry, Crafts and Agriculture, may bring proceedings against any professional or professional association that uses or recommends the use of contractual terms drawn up for general use, and may request the competent court to grant orders preventing the use of terms that have been found unfair pursuant to this Title' (Article 37 of the Consumer Code).

39   Decree 6-11-2003 (OJ No. 26 of 15.11.2003) ratified by Decree 16-12-2003 (OJ No. 299 of 27.12.2003) concerning the updating of the list of consumers' and users' associations entered on the list and on which 14 associations are registered. The Ministry for Production Activities updates the list annually by adding new associations.

to coordinate diverse consumers, to compel their cooperation so as to be able to pool resources against financially superior opponents.[40]

The Consumer Code indicates that consumers should rely on these associations as the primary means to resolve their concerns. Despite powers being granted to consumer organizations in the Act, they may find it difficult to guard the collective interests of consumers and the case-law reported before the courts is very limited (less than 15 cases).[41]

An Impact Assessment of Directive 98/27/EC

All of the redress mechanisms discussed above – private action in the courts and various forms of informal dispute resolution – suffer from one fundamental weakness: their outcomes depend significantly on the relative competence and power of the parties to the dispute.

These mechanisms isolate the individual's complaint, which often will seem small and hardly worth pursuing, and ignore the larger collective injury to consumers in the aggregate. By fragmenting consumer interests, these dispute resolution mechanisms thus attack only the 'tip of the iceberg' and the bulk of consumer injury remains undisturbed below the surface.

One solution to the problems encountered by the individual consumer in enforcing his/her rights may be to give collective standing to consumers' associations. The notion of collective injunction actions has clearly taken root in Europe, driven by European Law. Starting with the misleading advertisements directive, successive consumer protection directives included provision for injunction procedures.[42]

Drawing upon the diverse traditions within the Community these provided standing to either public bodies, whose task it was to protect consumers, or consumer organisations having the same function. Sometimes these were clearly alternatives, at other times it was arguable that the wording of the directives required Member States to give standing to consumer groups as well as public authorities.

---

40   G. Howells, R. James, 'Litigation in the consumer interest', *ILSA J. Int'l & Comp. L.*, 9 (2002): p. 1.

41   Ferrarini and Giudici, p. 41.

42   Council Directive 84/450/EEC of 10 September 1984 relating to the approximation of the laws, regulations and administrative provisions of the Member States concerning misleading advertising, OJ L 250, 19.9.1984, pp. 17–20. Directive 97/55/EC of European Parliament and of the Council of 6 October 1997 amending Directive 84/450/EEC concerning misleading advertising so as to include comparative advertising, OJ L 290, 23.10.1997, 18–23. Council Directive 93/13/EEC of 5 April 1993 on unfair terms in consumer contracts, OJ L 95 of 21.04.1993, p. 29.

This development culminated in the Directive 98/27/EC governing injunctions for the protection of consumers' interests (also indicated as the 'Injunctions Directive').[43] The legislative justification behind Directive 98/27/EC was the belief, by the European Parliament and Council, that infringements against the collective interests of consumers are an unacceptable distortion of free competition within the EU internal market.[44]

It provides a mechanism whereby aggrieved consumers may seek civil relief from wrongdoings which fall within the ambit of the law, but may only do so in an action commenced by an 'authorised national entity', as defined in Article 3 of the Directive. It provides for the granting of injunctions but not for money judgments, except for damages payable in the event that a losing defendant does not comply with the injunction.

The Directive covers only the protection of economic interests by excluding, for instance, product liability and product safety. However, it provides for minimum standards and some Member States, Italy for instance, extend the injunctive relief to health and safety issues. This interpretation is based on the necessity to ensure that the rights assigned to consumers by European and national laws are effective before the Courts. In particular, the collective interests are defined in Article 2 of the Consumer Code to include economic and non-economic interests, such as: health protection; the safety and quality of products and services; adequate information and correct advertising; and fairness, transparency and equity in contractual relations.

In one form or another, Directive 98/27/EC finds a counterpart in the national law of EU member countries (such as the above mentioned Articles 139–140 of the Consumer Code). The implementation of this provision demonstrates that there is no uniformity in the European Community: there are Member States that have laid enforcement in the hands of a competent ministry or an independent or dependent agency and there are others that have combined administrative and judicial enforcement or simply relied on judicial enforcement alone. The key actors then are public agencies, consumer organisations and sometimes also business organisations which may file an action for injunctions in the courts.

The 'Stuyck Report' underlines some of the shortcomings of this mechanism:

> First, the scope of an injunction is limited to the territory of one Member State; the order is not pan-European. Second, businesses can defy the enforcement of injunctions by changing only certain aspects of their violation. Only if a new infringement is, in its core, identical to the first one, can the judgment be enforced. Further criticism concerns the way in which the Directive has been implemented in the Member States.[45]

---

43   Directive 98/27/EC of the European Parliament and of the Council of 19 May 1998 on injunctions for the protection of consumers' interests, OJ L 166, 11.6.1998, pp. 51–5.

44   Preamble p. 4.

45   J. Stuyck, E. Terryn, T. Van Dyck, V. Colaert, N. Peretz and P. Tereszkiewicz, 'Study on alternative means of consumer redress other than redress through ordinary judicial

More important, the EU Consumer Law *Acquis* Database confirms that injunction procedures have been scarcely used in the Member States, probably due to the costs incurred by associations in bringing such actions.[46]

The collective action actually granted to consumer organisations by the Injunctions Directive suffers from a major critique coming from the lack of any action for damages capable of protecting consumers' rights in mass default scenarios.[47] On such a basis, an action for damages arising from liability represents an effective complement to injunctions and, actually, the landscape seems to have shifted in favour of expanding the availability of group proceedings devices.

In particular, some authors criticise it as being largely ineffectual and they define the threshold as to when an action becomes a 'class action' as where proceedings enable private suits to be brought which might otherwise be economically unfeasible and, because the Directive does not operate in such a way, it does not grant class actions.[48] As one author notes: 'The first factual observation is that it is only recently that some European jurisdictions have introduced a rule of court procedure on the recognition and management of multi-party actions.'[49]

The most significant developments in recent years were the adoption by Germany of 'model case proceedings'[50] and the introduction of the Group Litigation Order in England.[51]

Actually, the Member States have chosen a variety of ways to permit multi-claimant litigation to go forward and be managed. Notably, none of these bears much resemblance to the American 'Rule 23'. This is not surprising. With few exceptions,[52] European commentators and drafters of proposed legislation frequently cite examples of abuses of class actions in the United States and

---

proceedings (for the EU-25, Australia, Canada and the US)', 17 January 2007. Also 'Stuyck Report', p. 14.

46 H. Schulte-Nölke (ed.), in co-operation with C. Twigg-Flesner and M. Ebers, '*EC Consumer Law Compendium, Comparative Analysis*', April 2007. The Consumer Compendium was accessed on 21 August 2007 at http://ec.europa.eu/consumers/cons_int/safe_shop/acquis/comp_analysis_en.pdf.

47 D.J. Schwartz, 'Loose teeth in European Union consumer protection policy: the injunction directive and the mass default scenario', *Ga. J. Int'l & Comp. L.*, 28 (2000): pp. 527–54.

48 R.B. Cappalli and C. Consolo, 'Class Actions for a Continental Europe? A Preliminary Inquiry', *Temp. Int'l & Comp. L. J.*, 6 (1992): pp. 239–40.

49 C. Hodges, 'Multi-Party Actions: A European Approach', *Duke J. Comp. & Int'l L.*, 11 (2001): 321, at 327. Scott and Black, pp. 124–7.

50 H.W. Micklitz, 'Collective private enforcement of consumer law: the key questions', in Van Boom and Loos (eds), *Collective Enforcement of Consumer Law; Securing Compliance in Europe through Private Group Action and Public Authority Intervention*, pp. 13–33.

51 C. Hodges, *Multi-Party Actions* (Oxford, 2001).

52 R. Mulheron, 'Some difficulties with Group Litigation Orders – and Why a Class Action is Superior', *CJQ*, 24 (2005): pp. 40–68.

express concerns that American class actions are lawyer-driven, that they subject defendants to judicial blackmail and that the accompanying media coverage adversely impacts on share prices even if claims are not meritorious. Some features of the procedures they have adopted regarding multi-claimant litigation are directed at these concerns.[53]

Enlarging Associational Standing?

An effective system of consumer protection cannot operate when there are transnational mass damages and there is no effective aggregating device, because it leads to under-deterrence unless a very efficient public alternative is at work. In the internal market, a mechanism of aggregation should be considered necessary to allow consumers to have a better chance of access to resources with which to take on defendants, who are often corporations, financial institutions and insurance companies. Collective consumer redress is also necessary to obtain compensation for damages that concern a large number of consumers that, if handled individually, would never be brought before the courts by the damaged consumers due, for example, to the small amount of individual claims. Such action is needed to bridge the gap between the recognition of individual rights by EC Law and the effective possibility of enforcing those rights.[54]

The need to establish a common mechanism to increase consumer protection in the Single Market is acknowledged in the New Consumer Strategy 2007–2013 that envisages an in-depth assessment of how best to strengthen consumer collective redress:

> If consumers are to have sufficient confidence in shopping outside their own Member State and take advantage of the internal market, they need assurance that if things go wrong they have effective mechanisms to seek redress. Consumer disputes require tailored mechanisms that do not impose costs and delays disproportionate to the value at stake ... [55]

In itself, the idea of European collective action legislation is not a new concept.

In 1999, the EU Commission considered whether organisations should be permitted to bring injunctive or class actions under the Product Liability Directive.

---

53 Bundesministerium der Justiz, 'The German Capital Markets Model Case Act'. Bundesgesetzblatt Jahrgang 2005 Teil I Nr. 50, ausgegeben zu Bonn am 19 August 2005. English translation available at: http://www.bmj.bund.de/kapmug.

54 H.L.A. Hart, *The Concept of Law* (Oxford, 1961), p. 92.

55 'Communication from the Commission to the Council, the European Parliament and the European Economic and Social Committee, EU Consumer Policy Strategy 2007–2012, Empowering consumers, enhancing their welfare, effectively protecting them, Brussels', 13 March 2007, COM(2007) 99 final, p. 11.

At that time, the Commission concluded that there was 'no indication that action concerning access to justice specifically with regard to product liability cases would be appropriate'.[56]

It has been considered for some time at the European Commission level; having been suggested in the Commission's 2005 Green Paper '*Damages actions for breach of the EC antitrust rules*' as a possible mechanism to improve the ability of consumers to enforce their rights in relation to breaches of competition law.[57] Pursuant to the EU's 'Lisbon Policy', the Green Paper, suggests that 'collective actions' may be an improved and desirable way of protecting consumers harmed by breaches of antitrust law and of coupling public and private enforcement of those laws. It specifically suggests a twofold damages model, in which damages awarded to the plaintiff consumers' associations could be calculated, based upon the illegal gains of the defendant, and the damages awarded to the individual consumers (as members of the plaintiff association) could be calculated on the basis of the individual damages that each member suffered.

Recently, the White Paper "Damages actions for breach of the EC antitrust rules" issued on April 2, 2008 (the "White Paper")[58] suggests a combination of two complementary mechanisms of collective redress to address effectively those issues in the field of antitrust. A representative action for damages brought by entities with certain characteristics – such as consumer organizations, trade associations and State bodies – on behalf of identified or, in rather restricted cases, identifiable victims (not necessarily their members). And an opt-in collective action where the claims from individuals or businesses are combined in one single action. In such model of action, as opposed to representative actions as defined above, the claimant himself has suffered harm. These suggestions are part of the European Commission's wider initiative to strengthen collective redress mechanisms and may develop further within this context.

For example, the Green Paper may herald a model through which the EU standardises many of the procedural and access-to-justice rules, but the Member States retain a degree of local autonomy regarding such substantive issues as the quantum of damages. It may also herald applications of the model into consumer relief areas well beyond the field of antitrust, as has been the experience with Directive 98/27/EC.

---

56 Report from the Commission on the Application of Directive 85/374 on Liability for Defective Products, COM(2001)893 (31.01.2001), p. 27.

57 EC Commission, Green Paper 'Damages actions for breach of the EC antitrust rules', COM (2005) 672, 19 December 2005.

58 Commission (EC), 'White Paper on Damages actions for breach of the EC antitrust rules', COM (165) 2 April 2000 and 'Staff Working Paper accompanying the White Paper on Damages actions for breach of the EC antitrust rules', Brussels, April 2, 2008, SEC (404), 2 April 2008.

That said, one main option to reform the current mechanism concerns the possibility of granting consumer associations standing to recover damages on behalf of a group of consumers by amending the Directive 98/27/EC.

The main goal of this chapter is to discuss this option (also indicated as 'representative action') that provides a mechanism for organisations to represent, by mandate, the sum of individual interests, rather than the collective interest.[59] A question mark hangs over the issue of whether the European institutions even have legal competence to intervene in national civil procedure rules in the light of the principle of national procedural autonomy; moreover, as has been said: 'Article 6 of the European Convention on Human Rights and the relevant constitutional principles guaranteeing access for each citizen to a judicial decision maker form an obstacle to the introduction of US type class actions based on an opt-out system.'[60] However, intriguing though it certainly is, it goes beyond the ambitions of this chapter.

Article 140-bis of the Consumer Code

Article 140-*bis* of the Consumer Code – that it is expected to take effect on January 1, 2009 – goes precisely in this direction by granting associations standing to recover damages or to bring an action for restitution on behalf of consumers.[61]

In particular, the associations referred to in Article 139, paragraph 1 (see Injunctive relief, above) and, in general, the associations and the committees which duly represent collective interests, now have legal capacity to protect the collective interests of consumers and users by resorting to the court of the place where the company has its offices.

They may act in order to request the ascertainment of the right to be compensated for damage as well as in order to request that the defendant be ordered to return any due amounts to the individual consumers or users within legal relationships relating to agreements entered into pursuant to Article 1342 of the Italian Civil

---

59   Lord Chancellor's Department, Representative Claims: Proposed New Procedures (February 2001). In the United Kingdom, the notion of representative action was taken to heart by the Labour Government who set up a committee to look into how such a procedure should work not only in the consumer context, but also in any setting where a collective interest was at stake. Whilst the notion of representative actions for injunctions and declaratory relief were accepted in principle, there is more hesitation over including damages claims, although interestingly this possibility was not excluded in the final report.

60   Stuyck, Terryn, Van Dyck, Colaert, Peretz and Tereszkiewicz, p. 267.

61   Article 140-*bis* Legislative Decree September 6, 2005, No. 206 ('Consumer Code'). The article has been introduced by Article 1, sections 445–9 of the Law on December 24, 2007 No. 244 (*'Disposizioni per la formazione del bilancio annuale e pluriennale dello Stato. Legge finanziaria* 2008') in OJ 28 December 2007, No. 300, Supplement No. 285. In June 2008, the Italian Government has decided to postpone the entering into force of this provision to January 1, 2009.

Code, or as a consequence of tort liability, unfair trade practice or anti-competition behaviour, providing that such unlawful acts damage the rights of a plurality of consumers and users. Those consumers and users who intend to benefit from the protection afforded by this Article must notify the association in writing of their intention to join the collective action. It may be informed of this even during the appeal and up until the hearing scheduled in order for the parties to specify their conclusions.[62]

At the first hearing the court, after having heard parties and gathered brief information (to any necessary extent), shall declare the admissibility or inadmissibility of the claim by way of an order that may be challenged before the Court of Appeal, which shall rule in Chambers. The claim is declared inadmissible when it is clearly groundless, when there is a conflict of interest, or whenever the judge does not ascertain the existence of any collective interest deserving protection pursuant to this Article.[63]

Should the judge declare the admissibility of the claim, then the party who has initiated the collective action is ordered to duly advertise the content of the claim and actions are also taken for the continuation of the proceedings. Should the judge accept the claim, he or she shall also sets the criteria to be used in order to calculate the amount to be paid or given back to the individual consumers and users who have joined the collective action or who have intervened in the proceedings (the judge shall also establish the minimum amount to be paid to each consumer or user should this be possible on the basis of the documents at his or her disposal). Within 60 days of the service of judgment, the company shall make its offer for payment by way of a written deed to be served upon any entitled party and to be filed with the clerk's office.[64]

The decision that brings the proceedings to an end also has legal effects on those consumers and users who have joined the collective action. Those individual consumers or users who have not joined the collective action shall continue to have their right to bring individual actions. The provisions do not clarify what happens in the case of '*lis pendens*': two identical cases brought by two different associations or between the collective litigation and a corresponding individual action. It is also unclear whether the individual consumer may act to change the representative association because of its inappropriateness or whether she/he may appeal against the first judgment. Also, in the event that an association reached

---

62 The commencement of the collective action or the fact of joining it afterwards shall interrupt the statute of limitations pursuant to Article 2945 of the Italian Civil Code. Moreover, any individual consumer or user who wishes to file claims having the same subject matter may, in any case, intervene in the action.

63 The judge is entitled to postpone the assessment of the admissibility of the claim when preliminary investigations concerning the same subject matter are underway before an independent authority (primarily the Italian Antitrust Authority).

64 Any form of proposal accepted by the consumer or user shall be enforceable.

a settlement immediately before any litigation happened, it is unclear what the consumer might do to act against the collective settlement.

Should the company fail to make its offer within the period indicated, or should its offer remain unaccepted after 60 days of its service, the chief judge of the court shall appoint a sole *Camera di Conciliazione* (that is, conciliation committee) in order to set the amounts to be paid or given back to consumers and users who have joined the collective action and who so request it.

The conciliation committee is composed of a lawyer indicated by those who have brought the collective action and by a lawyer indicated by the summoned company, and it is chaired by a lawyer appointed by the chief judge of the court, chosen from among those entered in the special register for higher jurisdictions.

It shall set, by way of minutes to be signed by its chairman, the terms, methods and amounts to be paid in order to compensate the individual consumers and users for damage done. Alternatively, should the party who has promoted the collective action and the defendant jointly request, the chief judge of the court shall order an out-of-court settlement before one of the conciliation bodies referred to in Article 38 of Legislative Decree No. 5 on January 17, 2003, as subsequently amended, operating in the same municipality as that of the court.

Adequate representation?

The conflict between the principal and the agent Together with lawyers, consumer associations may be qualified as intermediaries in the provision of access to justice for individuals. They may influence the type of remedy, they mediate between business and consumers, consumers and private-attorneys; they heighten or dampen conflicts. But, do associations adequately represent individual consumers? In cases of legal actions taken by associations, the agency chain is lengthened and consequently there is room not only for the pursuit of self-interests of the private-attorneys, but also of the association and its personnel.[65] Additionally, the association cannot only partially distance itself from the interests of the injured, but can also be influenced by other interests including those of the attorneys. The associations have their own interests, which may be different from those of the injured consumers they seek to represent. For example, a consumer group which is interested in the safety of food may seek to represent individual consumers who were injured by it. The individual consumer will want to focus on proving that the producer is liable to him or her and the amount of damage he or she has suffered. In such context, a strategy which advances the interest of the association may not necessarily advance the individual's claims and may be, in fact, detrimental to those claims. In addition, consumers whom the association seeks to represent may

---

65   H.B. Schaefer, 'The Bundling of Similar Interests in Litigation. The Incentives for
       Class Action and Legal Actions taken by Associations', *European Journal of Law
       and Economics*, 9:3 (2000): pp. 183–213; M. Olson, *The Logic of Collective Action,
       Public Goods and the Theory of Groups* (New York, 1970), pp. 191–9.

have internal conflicts which makes it impossible to represent the group: some individuals who took a product already have suffered an injury; others may be concerned that their ingestion of the product will cause them to develop an injury in the future. Some may have serious or life threatening injuries or may have only minor complaints. Some may have been warned by their doctors of potential side effects; others may have received no warnings. These considerations draw attention to the importance of the discretionary decisions of the organisations and the dynamics between consumer and intermediary. As an author notes:

> A consumer association will be considered legitimate when its constituents democratically participate in the decision-making within the association, even if the outcome is not always the one desired by these constituents. This type of legitimacy is known as input legitimacy or political legitimacy.

Moreover, the consumer associations that are not based on democratic participation can still be considered legitimate if consumers are satisfied with the policy-outcomes (this form of legitimacy is known as output legitimacy).[66] In practice, input and output legitimacies are interlinked: as a result of the fact that only a very small percentage of consumers are actually members of a consumer association, its effectiveness is inherently impaired since it cannot compel consumers to participate in a boycott or in any other form of collective action. The low level of membership may well affect the ability of consumer associations to identify what constitutes the consumer interest and hence to represent the consumer interest effectively.

The possibility to act on behalf the consumers to recover damages seems to be less problematic because it provides for consumers' express consent on the basis of agency-theory; however, I note that in some cases consent is impractical for many of the groups of consumers that had large numbers of geographically dispersed members.

In the light of the above, adopting representative actions by granting consumer associations standing to recover damages on behalf consumers may present analogous problems as trying American-style class actions: substituting an association as the named claimant will not make these problems go away.

The legal standing In this paragraph I argue that the system of government accreditation for consumer associations currently provided under the Articles 140 and 140-*bis* of the Consumer Code is not fully convincing; while 'court certification' concerns the conduct of the representative in a specific lawsuit, the government accreditation is generic: the association is accredited as a 'fit representative'

---

66   O. Dayagi-Epstein, 'Representation of Consumer Interest By Consumer Associations – Salvation for the Masses?', *Competition Law Review*, 3:2 (2006): pp. 209–49, at 224–5 quoting S. Smismans, '*Law, Legitimacy and European Governance Functional Participation in Social Regulation*' (Oxford, 2004), at p. 72.

independent of the existence of an actual lawsuit.[67] I believe that the court should retain the power to control the adequacy of representation in a specific case,[68] although the previous government accreditation makes the judicial control of adequacy considerably easier. At this regard, I follow the considerations held by the Italian Supreme Administrative Court in a recent leading case on environmental protection.[69] It is understood that – for the functionality of the judiciary – the *locus standi* has to be limited especially in cases where the interests are, by their very nature, common and shared and the rights relating to those interests are liable to be held by a potentially large number of individuals. Nevertheless, the fact that particular interests are shared by the many, rather than the few, does not make them less deserving of legal protection through the judicial process. The problem is thus, how to limit the legal standing without infringing the right to a judicial remedy. According to the Italian Supreme Administrative Court this goal is to be pursued by an assessment of the concrete legal interest of the applicant in the case at issue and not on the basis of any abstract formal recognition by the Government; the latter approach would entail a denial of justice in all such cases where such interests are statutorily protected by non-recognised associations.

Incentives and liability

Consumer associations are not usually the most efficient enforcers because they cannot have access to the breadth of information that private parties naturally possess. More importantly, they have limited incentives to assume management of collective claims. Such organisations can be viewed as if they were 'maximisers' of (good) publicity. Publicity can be important for them in several ways: first, it may directly aid in promoting a cause by exposing the alleged governmental failures to the public; second, it may enhance the association's reputation and thereby facilitate effective negotiations and provide for new sources of funding.

Apart from publicity, incentives to act before the Court are not very strong and I bring the case of the '*action en representation conjointe*' to support my argument. In France, since 1992, a non-profit, government-authorised consumer organisation may seek compensation for damages that must have been caused by the same person and have a common origin, suffered on behalf of consumers (under Article L. 422-1 of the French Consumer Code). The organisations may file their actions before the civil or criminal courts and any damages are paid to the

---

67   Cafaggi and Micklitz.
68   Stuyck, Terryn, Van Dyck, Colaert, Peretz and Tereszkiewicz, p. 26.
69   Italian Supreme Administrative Court, judgment No. 5760 of 2 October 2006, *Comuna Bellis e Santuario* v. *Comune di Ostiglia*; comment by S. Gobbato, in *Journal of Environmental Law*, 19:2 (2007): pp. 259–65.

affected consumers.[70] However, very few actions of this kind have been brought (that is, three cases in about 20 years).

The reason is that this mechanism suffers serious shortcomings:

- the difficulty in collecting the mandates without adequate instruments of advertising (associations may seek potential claimants through the press but they are not allowed to advertise, send mailings or make public announcements on television or radio);
- the costs of running the collective actions;
- the complexity in managing a large group of consumers, and
- the risk of liability.

In 2005 the French President asked the government to propose legislation on 'collective actions' and a working group of ministers, consumer organisations, companies and lawyers was formed to prepare draft legislation for collective consumer actions ('*actions de groupe*').[71]

The aim of the new Bill was to introduce a 'French-style' collective action for consumers by reforming the *action en representation conjointe* or by enlarging the standing of the consumer associations '*à des demandes en réparation de préjudices individuels*' (that is, 'to recover individual damages').[72]

Accordingly, consumer organisations would have been able to bring an action on the question of liability on behalf a group of consumers they represent. Once the decision was handed down, publicity would be given to it, and consumers could decide whether to benefit from the decision or take their own action.

I question why a consumer organisation would wish to involve itself in such a procedure – and in the action now provided by the Article 140-*bis* of the Italian Consumer Code. It can, in any event, assist consumers to bring actions and this new procedure does not entitle it to claim damages in its own right. However, if consumer organisations are to participate in market surveillance, they need some encouragement, possibly in the form of allowing the recover of part of the damages or allowing the recovery of legal fees.

---

70   L. Bore, 'L'action en représentation conjointe: class action française ou action mortneé?', *Dalloz*, III, chr. (1995): p. 267.

71   A lively debate took place on such a reform. In April 2006 two bills were submitted to the Parliament – Sénat and Assemblée Nationale – one by socialist Members of Parliament, and the other by a Member of Parliament from the current majority rightwing party ('UMP'), to incorporate a system of collective action into the French legal system. However, the new bill on consumer rights, which comprised some provisions on collective consumer actions, was withdrawn from Parliament's agenda at the end of January 2007, probably owing to the upcoming presidential election. Nevertheless, the debate on the introduction of class actions in France is still open and the issue will be raised again after the election.

72   The parallel with the Article 140-*bis* of the Italian Consumer Code is evident.

The idea of the '*dommage collectif*' (that is 'not the simple accumulation of numerous individual claims, but rather a nominal, or a non-material, lump-sum that cannot be exactly calculated and proved'[73]) would therefore completely divorce the case from the individuals who suffered the actual loss. If the individuals with the actual losses are made irrelevant to the judicial process, the damages awarded are in fact a penalty imposed upon defendants.

Under the current situation, consumer associations have the threat of costs liability against them. In this sort of 'representative action' organisations may expose themselves to liabilities in terms of claims by consumers if they do not exercise their mandate properly and by producers if they damage their reputations unfairly. Under certain circumstances, they may also be held liable for the defendant's legal costs if the action.

Lack of funding and risk of capture

The lack of resources tends to be more pronounced for consumer organisations than for governmental agencies. The EC Consumer Compendium confirms that: 'the evidence to date shows that the cross-border procedure is not being utilised. One reason may be the question of costs for qualified entities from one member state to take action in another ...'[74]

Consumers' associations have, for a number of years, been funded from the activities they carry out, whether at national, regional or local level. The aim of the funding granted by national and regional authorities[75] (that in most cases is a percentage co-funding of the activity in question) is normally a project in connection with information and training programmes or activities connected with the associations' publications. Some specific public funding is granted to consumers' associations for their publishing activities.[76] Supporting publication is important for the information campaign, a fundamental element of consumer protection. This means to stress the importance of information dissemination activities undertaken by the associations with the aim of developing an understanding of the market on

---

73   H. Koch, 'Non-class group litigation under EU and German Law', *Duke J. of Comp. & Int'l L.*, 11 (2001): 355 at 361.

74   Schulte-Nölke at p. 610.

75   In Italy, for example, the associations receive funding for activities they carry out with the aim of providing information and advice to consumers by opening consumer information centres for which there is provision under related regional legislation. See, also, the Decree on 2 March 2006 of the Directorate-general for Harmonization and Protection of the Market providing funding for the initiatives for the benefit of consumers ('*Disposizioni per il finanziamento delle iniziative a vantaggio dei consumatori*'), OJ No. 70, 24 March 2006.

76   Article 137, para. 3, of the Consumer Code clarifies that consumers' and users' associations shall be forbidden from undertaking any promotional or commercial advertising activities relating to goods or services produced by third parties and any shared interests with production or distribution companies.

the part of consumers and of the channels open to them for the protection of their interests. Nevertheless, most of the funding of the associations is utilised for these primary goals and 'not for litigation'.

Moreover, while many consumer-directed associations are ideologically immunized from direct capture, a form of cooptation is nonetheless a risk.[77]

These organisations often measure their effectiveness by their ability to obtain audiences with powerful officialdom and by their ability to obtain resources from government sources, wealthy backers, or foundations. Each source of financial support is also a potential source of institutional compromise.

Conclusions

As a general consideration, I note that the proposals to enlarge associational standing under the Directive 98/27/EC should be understood within the process of 'the judicialisation of politics', that is, the ever-accelerating reliance on courts worldwide for addressing public policy questions, such as consumer and environmental protection. For a long time litigation has not been viewed in the Member States as the principal avenue to achieve policy goals: the welfare systems and the regulatory state, also through its agencies, have been considered the key-mechanisms to pursue policy goals. Nowadays there are, therefore, some examples of regulation by litigation in the European single market and the most evident is the increased use of litigation in protecting the consumer interest.[78]

In particular, I underline that the Injunctions Directive remains undeveloped before the courts in the Member States and, thus, any improvement based on such model of action, should be carefully considered.

I agree that such a system has the potential to reduce the costs of litigation to both the judicial system and the litigants. First and most obvious are the savings that aggregation makes possible when the alternative is individual trials and associations are doubtless 'repeat players' according to Olson's theory.[79]

Nevertheless, I am not fully convinced by 'the general assumption' that associations have the financial resources and the expertise to support the litigation: the considerations presented in the previous paragraphs show how crucial are 'in concrete' for associations the issues of incentives, funding of actions, as well as actions' management and liability. Any reform to enlarge the standing of European consumer associations to recover damages on behalf of consumers should consider

---

77 S. Issacharoff, 'Group litigation of consumer claims: lessons from the U.S. experience', *Texas International L.J.*, 34 (1999): p. 135.

78 R. Hirschl, 'The New Constitutionalism and the Judicialization of Pure Politics Worldwide', *Fordham Law Review*, 75:2 (2006): pp. 721–54; C. Poncibò, 'Regulation and Private Litigation: A Debate Over the European Perspective', 2nd Von Mises International Seminar, October 2005; available at: http://ssrn.com/abstract=1028527.

79 M. Olson, *The Logic of Collective Action* (Harvard, 1971).

the difficulties above addressed and ensure that consumer associations have not only the opportunities, but also the ability to adequately represent the consumer interest.

8 The Future of Consumer Law in the United States – Hello Arbitration, Bye-bye Courts, So-long Consumer Protection

*Richard M. Alderman**

Introduction

Ask any American middle-school student to explain his or her system of government and you will quickly be told of 'separation of powers' – the division between the legislative, judicial and executive branches of government – a system of 'checks and balances'.[1] Americans have long appreciated the way in which our founding fathers established an independent judiciary, and the important role courts play in the American system of law.[2]

---

* Associate Dean, Dwight Olds Chair in Law and Director of the Center for Consumer Law. Alderman@uh.edu.
1 A popular children's book states:
 There are three branches of federal government, charged with different responsibilities. The legislative branch (the House of Representatives and the Senate) creates laws for the nation. The executive branch (headed by the president of the United States) executes, or carries out, the laws. The judicial branch (The Supreme Court and other lower courts) interprets the law and can overrule them.
 In addition to separating powers, the Constitution also provides for numerous ways in which these bodies of government overlap. This is so they can check up on one another in case one body does something that isn't good for the country.
 M. Friedman, *Government* (2005), p. 12.
2 For example, two recent books on very different topics discussed our separation of powers and the importance of an independent judiciary. See C.T. Bogus, *Why Lawsuits are Good for America* (New York, 2001), p. 45 ('The division of powers among three branches of government is perhaps the most fundamental feature of American government. It is also the feature most distinctly American.'); and D. McCullough, *John Adams* (New York, 2001), p. 222; ('But it was through the establishment of an independent judiciary, with judges of the Supreme Court appointed, not elected, and for life, that Adams made one of his greatest contributions not only to Massachusetts but to the country, as time would tell').

At the highest level, American federal courts oversee the legislative and executive branch, ensuring compliance with constitutional principles. At the same time, state courts serve the even more significant additional role of providing remedies for those injured or wronged by others, often supplementing our justice system through the creation of common law rules and principles. It is the judicial system in the United States that protects the individual from the unreasonable exercise of legislative power, provides a forum for those who lack the ability to exercise significant influence over the legislative process, and provide a mechanism for individual to seek redress form abuses in the marketplace. As Justice Marshall long ago recognised in *Marbury* v. *Madison*, 'The very essence of civil liberty certainly consists in the rights of every individual to claim the protection of the law, whenever he receives an injury'.[3]

American consumers have benefited greatly from this Anglo-American legal culture. The American civil justice system has spawned judicial reform dealing with everything from a wide range of product safety issues,[4] to the establishment of premises liability, and the creation of performance standards in landlord–tenant[5] and service contracts.[6] Courts have become increasingly receptive to claims of

---

3   5. U.S. 137, at 163 (1803). See also, T. Phillips, 'The Constitutional Right to a Remedy', *N.Y.U.L. Rev.*, 78 (2003): 1309, wherein he quotes Sir Edward Coke:
   Every subject of this realm, for injury done to him in goods, lands, or person, by any other subject, be he ecclesiastical, or temporall, ... or any other without exception, may take his remedy by the course of the law, and have justice, and right for the injury done to him, freely without sale, fully without any deniall, and speedily without delay...
   Justice must have three qualities; it must be ... free; for nothing is more odious than Justice let to sale; full, for justice ought not to limp, or be granted piece-meal; and speedily, for delay is a kind of denial; and then it is both justice and right.
   Ibid., at 1321. (portions of quotation translated from Latin by Phillips).
4   'The single greatest development of the common law during the twentieth century has been the creation of a new area of law known as products liability.' Bogus, p. 137. See also, J.M. Feinman, 'Un-Making Law: The Classical Revival in the Common Law', *Seattle Univ. L. R.*, 28 (2004): 35; (While negligence cases are most numerous in tort law, the most significant area of development in neoclassical law was the law of products liability.).
5   For example, some courts have created an implied warranty of habitability in residential leases. See, for example, *Javins* v. *First National Realty Corp.*, 428 F.2d 1071 (D.C. Cir. 1970); *Pines* v. *Perssion*, 14 Wis. 2d 590, 111 N.W.2d 409 (1961). Similar protections have also been provided to commercial tenants. See *Davidow* v. *Inwood N. Prof'l Group*, 747 S.W.2d 373 (Texas 1988).
6   See, for example *Melody Home Manufacturing Co.* v. *Barnes*, 741 S.W.2d 349 (Texas 1987); (implied warranty of good and workmanlike performance in contract to repair or modify existing tangible goods or property). See also, *Humber* v. *Morton*, 426 S.W.2d 554 (Texas 1968); (implied warranty of good and workmanlike performance and habitability in contract for construction of new home).

overreaching,[7] and have liberally construed our many consumer protection laws to provide increased protection from false, misleading and deceptive acts.[8]

The recent movement to impose binding pre-dispute mandatory arbitration[9] in an increasingly large number of consumer contracts, however, threatens to eliminate this 'fundamental' branch of government from the consumer law arena, substituting a system of private, often secret, justice,[10] neither bound by precedent nor unable to create it.[11] This chapter considers how American consumers' rights

---

7   Perhaps the most notable decision to consider overreaching in a consumer context is *Williams* v. *Walker-Thomas Furniture Co.*, 350 F.2d 445 (D.C. Cir. 1965) (applying unconscionability to a consumer contract).

8   A recent book review comments upon the development of plaintiffs common law rights in tort:
In 1969 Robert Keeton wrote that 'the most striking impression that results from reading the weekly outpouring of torts opinions handed down by appellate courts across the nation for the decade commencing in 1958 is one of candid, openly acknowledged, abrupt change.' Keeton observed that the state courts had, between 1958 and 1968, 'candidly and explicitly' overruled precedents in a 'wide range of problems in the law of torts', and he listed ninety overruling decisions on at least thirty-five topics, ranging from eliminating or limiting common law immunity doctrines, to expanding the right to recover for pure emotional distress, to expanding the doctrine of strict liability. As Gary Schwartz famously commented, until the early 1980s these changes were 'almost all triumphs for plaintiffs; the collection of these cases could be referred to as "plaintiffs' greatest hit."'.
A.J. Sebok, 'Dispatches From the Tort Wars', *Tex. L. Rev.*, 85 (2007): 1465, at 1110–11; (reviewing W. Haltom and M. McCann, *Distorting the Law: Politics, Media and the Litigation Crisis*; H.M. Kritzer, *Risks, Reputations and Rewards: Contingency Fee Legal Practice in the United State*; and T. Baker, *The Medical Malpractice Myth*).

9   I have chosen to use the term 'pre-dispute mandatory arbitration' to emphasise that the practice under consideration is the use of arbitration agreements contained in a contract entered into prior to the existence of a dispute. As others have recognised, pre-dispute arbitration itself is often referred to as 'mandatory arbitration.' See, for example, R.E. Speidel, 'Consumer Arbitration of Statutory Claims: Has Pre-Dispute (Mandatory) Arbitration Outlived Its Welcome?', *Ariz. L. Rev*, 40 (1998): 1069. This chapter uses the phrases 'pre-dispute mandatory arbitration' and 'mandatory arbitration' synonymously.

10   In most cases, the decisions of arbitrators are private. In fact, it is not unusual for arbitrators to rule without any written opinion.

11   The 'threat' posed by the privatisation of law may already be real. In a recent article discussing the effect of arbitration on the development of contract law, Professor C.L. Knapp notes the diminishing number of decisions discussing contract issues. He notes, 'Far and away the most pervasive contract-related issue litigated during this period [2002] has been this: Will the court enforce an arbitration contract in the parties' written agreement?'; C.L. Knapp, 'Taking Contracts Private: The Quiet Revolution in Contract Law', *Fordham L. Rev.*, 71 (2002):761, at 763. See also, C.A. Carr and M.R. Jenks, 'The Privatization of Business and Commercial Dispute Resolution: A Misguided Policy Decision', *Ky. L. J.*, 88 (1999): 183.

might ultimately be impacted by this privatisation of the judicial system, which is gradually resulting from widespread use of pre-dispute mandatory arbitration.[12] It is suggested that as consumer access to the American civil justice system and juries is reduced or eliminated, consumer protection similarly decreases.[13] The chapter concludes with a bit of optimism that recently proposed legislation prohibiting pre-dispute binding arbitration may be enacted by Congress.

American Consumer Protection

As a 'movement,'American consumer protection is relatively young. Consumerism began in earnest in the 1960s.[14] Federal legislation, such as the Truth in Lending

---

12   I recognise that others have discussed the effects of the privatisation of law through arbitration agreements. See, for example, Charles L. Knapp, 'Taking Contracts Private: The Quiet Revolution in Contract Law', *Fordham Law Review*, 71 (2002) 761, 798, wherein the author concludes with a question and answer:
Can powerful private interests with the ability to control most of the terms of most of the contracts they make, deprive large segments of American society of their access to the courts for which all of us pay, and to which all of us have historically had access? The answer, until now, sadly, to some of us – they apparently can. And do. And will. See also, G. Szott Moohr, 'Arbitration and the Goals of Employment Discrimination Law', *Wash. & Lee L. Rev.*, 56 (1999): 395, (arbitration does not produce a uniform or consistent law). As will be discussed in this chapter, however, I believe that the impact of arbitration on consumer law is of particular concern because of the increasingly widespread use of mandatory arbitration in consumer cases, and consumers' inability to meaningfully bargain for an alternative.

13   Other authors have noted the broader impact arbitration may have upon our civil justice system. See, for example, J.R. Sternlight, 'The Rise and Spread of Mandatory Arbitration as a Substitute for the Jury Trial', *U. San Francisco L. Rev.*, 38 (2003): 17, at 38; ('If our society is to eliminate the civil trial right we should do so in the open, following a full public discussion. It is wrong to allow companies to use mandatory arbitration clauses to surreptitiously eliminate this precious right.').

14   'Webster's dictionary defines consumerism as "a movement for the protection of the consumer against defective products, misleading advertising, etc." Limited consumer protection was present until the 1950s and early 1960s. In the 1950s, a significant breakthrough occurred with the establishment of the product-liability concept, whereby a plaintiff did not have to prove negligence but only had to prove that a defective product caused an injury. In his 1962 speech to Congress, President John F. Kennedy outlined four basic consumer rights, which later became known as the Consumer Bill of Rights. Later, in 1985, the United Nations endorsed Kennedy's Consumer Bill of Rights and expanded it to cover eight consumer rights. Consumer protection can only survive in highly industrialised countries because of the resources needed to finance consumer interests. Kennedy's Consumer Bill of Rights included the right to be informed, the right to safety, the right to choose, and the right to be

Act,[15] attempted to level the playing field through meaningful disclosures and standardisation. Numerous other state and federal laws were enacted to deal specifically with false, misleading and deceptive practices and warranties. For example, at the federal level the Magnuson-Moss Warranty Act[16] attempted to establish minimum warranty standards, while the states enacted lemon laws and deceptive trade practice acts of varying scope and applicability.[17] Even the Uniform 'Commercial' Code provided some special protections for consumers, creating implied warranties, making it more difficult to limit damages, and easier to sue remote parties.[18]

Along with the enactment of new laws came a change in the manner in which consumer protection laws were enforced. Early in the twentieth century, the enforcement of consumer protection measures generally was left to federal and state governments. It was soon recognised, however, that private litigation and private remedies were necessary to achieve effective reform. Writing 37 years ago, Professor William Lovett[19] correctly noted the importance of private enforcement:

Consumer protection has achieved dramatic new popularity within the last few years, and as a result, significant progress has been made in regulating product safety, enforcing disclosures to the public, and in making deceptive trade practices unlawful at the state and local – as well as federal – levels of government. But much less has been done to provide adequate private remedies in the law against frauds or other deceptive trade practices which victimize consumers. There is still too little appreciation of the very healthy and complementary relationship that should exist between private and administrative remedies for deceptive trade practices, even though the potential for such complementary remedies is amply demonstrated in federal securities and antitrust law. What we need now in the deceptive trade practices area is comparable development of private remedies to match the recent growth of government investigation and prosecution efforts. *Without effective private remedies the widespread economic losses that result from these trade practices remain uncompensated and furthermore, private*

---

heard.' Answers.com, available at: http://www.answers.com/topic/consumer-bill-of-rights?cat=biz-fin.

15 15 U.S.C.A. §§1601–1667. Although there was some pre-1960s consumer protection legislation, it usually was directed primarily at attempts to increase competition or eliminate a very specific health or safety problem.

16 Manguson–Moss Warranty – Federal Trade Commission Improvement Act of 1975, Title 1, §§101-112, 15 U.S.C.A. §§2301-11. See generally, C. Reitz, *Consumer Protection Under the Magnuson–Moss Warranty Act* (2nd edn) (Philadelphia, 1987).

17 For a list of all state deceptive trade practice legislation, and an excellent discussion of the subject, see National Consumer Law Center, *Unfair and Deceptive Acts and Practices* (6th edn (and supp.)), (2004 and 2007). See generally R.M. Alderman and D. Pridgen, *Consumer Protection and the Law*, 2008 Edn (2008).

18 See, for example, sections 2-312, 2-316, 2-318 and 2-719 of the UCC.

19 See W.A. Lovett, 'Private Actions for Deceptive Trade Practices', *Admin. L. Rev.*, 23 (1970): 271.

remedies are highly desirable for additional consumer bargaining power and more complete discipline against fraud in the marketplace.[20]

Professor Lovett's desire for private remedies quickly came to fruition. Most American consumer statutes provided for liberal remedies and possible treble damages in a sufficient amount to justify litigation, and perhaps more importantly, for the award of attorneys' fees for a successful consumer.[21] Private litigation of consumer disputes did not just supplement public enforcement; it effectively replaced it.

The Role of the Courts – Interpretation and Creation of Law

Interpreting the law

As consumer litigation increased, American courts found themselves dealing more and more with consumer issues. For example, all of the newly enacted laws had to be applied and interpreted – consumer legislation was not always the best example of judicial clarity and precision. Perhaps more importantly, the gaps left by the failure of the legislature to act, or the enactment of ambiguous legislation, provided an opportunity for courts to create common law doctrine. During the past four decades, American consumer law has been created, modified, reformed, and refined by the courts. Perhaps no other area of law better demonstrates the role of the courts in the American civil justice system, and the relationship between its three branches of government.

A recent decision of the United States Supreme Court indicates how essential the courts are to implementing our consumer laws and maintaining their consistent application. In 1995, Congress amended section 1640(a)(2)(A) of the Truth-in-Lending Act, changing the remedy provisions for a violation of the Act.[22] Unfortunately, the language used by Congress was not the most precise, and courts gave differing interpretations to a significant issue – whether damages under this

---

20   *Ibid.*
21   For example, the Truth in Lending Act, a federal consumer credit law, provides that a successful consumer claimant shall be entitled to recover from the creditor 'the costs of the action, together with a reasonable attorney's fee as determined by the court,' as well as punitive damages between $100 and $1,000. TILA §130(a)(3); 15 U.S.C. §1640(a). The Texas Deceptive Trade Practices Act, a state consumer protection statute, allows for attorney's fees and punitive damages up to three times economic and mental anguish damages; Texas Bus. & Com. Code §17.50(a),(b). Most state consumer laws allow the recovery of reasonable attorneys' fees, see generally, Alderman and Pridgen; *Consumer Protection and the Law*, 2008 Edn; National Consumer Law Center, *Unfair and Deceptive Acts and Practices*.
22   Truth in Lending Act Amendments of 1995, Pub L 104-29, § 6, 109 Stat 274.

section were capped at $1,000.[23] In *Koons Buick GMC, Inc.* v. *Nigh*,[24] the United States Supreme Court was called on to resolve the controversy that had arisen, and provide an interpretation that would allow for consistent application of the law. The Supreme Court, with five separate opinions, held that the cap applied.[25] Without the ability of a court to review this statute, and render a decision that was binding on all other courts to consider the issue, lower courts would have continued a non-uniform application of the statute and consumers and businesses would remain uncertain as to how to apply the law. As demonstrated by *Koons Buick,* the American system of binding precedent and *stare decisis* ensures that damages under the Truth-in-Lending Act will now be computed is a consistent manner. All courts must now abide by the meaning given section 1640(a)(2)(A) by the Supreme Court.

Creating common law

In the American system of government, it also is not unusual for state courts to create legal rights. While the legislature enacts laws, courts 'legislate' through their interpretation of legislation, as well as enactment of the 'common law'. Every first year student at an American Law School is taught that precedent and *stare decisis* are the foundations of the common law. Courts are bound by precedent, and must follow decisions of higher courts, and all courts should give serious consideration to the rationale of others.[26] As Justice Stone noted almost seventy years ago, the common law's:

---

23   As the Supreme Court noted, 'We granted certiorari, to resolve the division between the Fourth Circuit and the Seventh Circuit on the question whether the $100 floor and $1,000 ceiling apply to recoveries under §1640(a)(2)(A)(i).' *Koons* v. *Buick GMC Inc.*, 543 U.S. 50 (2004), at 59.

24   543 U.S. 50 (2004).

25   *Ibid.*, at p. 64. The opinion was written by Justice Ginsburg, joined by Justices Rehnquist, Stevens, O'Connor, Kennedy, Souter, and Breyer. Concurring opinions were issued by Justice Stevens, joined by Justice Breyer; Justice Kennedy, joined by Chief Justice Rehnquist; and Justice Thomas. Justice Scalia dissented.

26   The importance of *stare decisis* was recently recognised by the Supreme Court:
Basic principles of *stare decisis,* however, require us to reject this argument. Any anomaly the old cases and *Irwin* together create is not critical; at most, it reflects a different judicial assumption about the comparative weight Congress would likely have attached to competing legitimate interests. Moreover, the earlier cases lead, at worst, to different interpretations of different, but similarly worded, statutes; they do not produce 'unworkable' law. Further, *stare decisis* in respect to statutory interpretation has 'special force,' for 'Congress remains free to alter what we have done'. Additionally, Congress has long acquiesced in the interpretation we have given.
John R. Sand & Gravel Co. v. *United States*, ___ U.S. ___ , ___ , 169 L. Ed. 2d 591, 599 2008 U.S. LEXIS 744 (2008) (citations deleted).

[D]istinguishing characteristics are its development of law by a system of judicial precedent, its use of the jury to decide issues of fact, and its all-pervading doctrine of supremacy of the law – that the agencies of government are no more free than the private individual to act according to their own arbitrary will or whim, but must conform to legal rules developed and applied by courts.[27]

Through this process of judicial precedent, courts create and mould legal rights, co-existent with and supplemental to, those created by statute.[28]

Although the current consumer protection movement is relatively young, American courts have attempted to deal with the problems presented by marketplace deception and product defects since the turn of the twentieth century. Both tort and contract theories have been used as methods of providing consumer redress. The development of traditional contract and tort theories to deal with consumer issues demonstrates the application of our common law tradition. For example, contract law, primarily warranty, offered consumers a cause of action that was often easier to establish than tort, however, it required privity and was easily limited or disclaimed. Tort liability, on the other hand, was available without privity, however, it was often more difficult to establish because of culpability requirements inherent in the concept of negligence or *scienter* requirements of fraud or misrepresentation. Gradually, both contract and tort requirements were judicially relaxed to permit liability for personal injury without regard to fault or

---

27 H.F. Stone, 'The Common Law in the United States', *Harv. L. Rev.*, 50 (1936): 4, at 5.

28 The need for a common law supplement to legislation has been described as follows: Our society has an enormous demand for legal rules that actors can live, plan, and settle by. The legislature cannot adequately satisfy this demand. The capacity of a legislature to generate legal rules is limited, and much of that capacity must be allocated to the production of rules concerning governmental matters, such as spending, taxes, and administration; rules that are regarded as beyond the courts' competence, such as the definition of crimes; and rules that are best administered by a bureaucratic machinery, such as the principles for setting the rates charged by regulated industries. Furthermore, our legislatures are normally not staffed in a manner that would enable them to perform comprehensively the function of establishing law to govern action in the private sector. Finally, in many areas the flexible form of a judicial rule is preferable to the canonical form of a legislative rule. Accordingly, it is socially desirable that the courts should act to enrich that supply of legal rules that govern ... [business] conduct – not by taking on lawmaking as a free standing function, but by attaching much greater emphasis to the establishment of legal rules than would be necessary if the courts' sole function was the resolution of disputes.
Carr and Jencks, note 11 at 193. See generally, Jay M. Feinman, 'Un-Making Law: The Classical Revival in the Common Law', *Seattle University Law Review*, 28 (2004) 1 (discussing changes and trends in the development of the common law).

privity, and provide a claim for false representations without regard to knowledge or intent.[29]

More recently, American courts have found less need for major doctrinal pronouncements, and a much greater demand for review of more specific scenarios. Decisions such as *Williams* v. *Walker-Thomas Furniture Co.,*[30] *Unico* v. *Owen*[31] and *Henningsen* v. *Bloomfield Motors, Inc.,*[32] refused to put form over substance and provided relief to consumers. Today, courts are often called on to deal with individual claims of overreaching and must regularly deal with the application of traditional principles to newly developed technology, such as the internet.[33]

The courts also provide a significant 'gap-filling' role, dealing with transactions that either slip through the cracks of legislation or simply were not dealt with. One of the most significant roles of the common law is maintaining consistency between similar rights in the absence of legislative action. For example, the Uniform Commercial Code comprehensively governs contracts for the sale of goods. Until the enactment of Article 2A, lease agreements were treated in a similar manner by common law analogy to Article 2.[34] Today, Articles 2 and 2A comprehensively regulate the creation of warranties, as well as disclaimers and damage limitations, in the sale or lease of goods. There is no similar statute, however, governing service contracts. Analogous law in the area of service contracts, therefore, is left to common law development by the courts.[35] The state of Texas provides a

---

29   See, for example, *McPherson* v. *Buick Motor Co.*, 217 N.Y. 382, 111 N.E. 1050 (1916) (eliminating the requirement of privity); *Greenman* v. *Yuba Power Products, Inc.*, 377 P.2d 897 (Cal. 1963) (imposing strict products liability). See generally W.L. Prosser, 'The Fall of the Citadel (Strict Liability to the Consumer)', *Minn. L. Rev.*, 50 (1966): 791. See also W. Seavey, 'Caveat Emptor as of 1960', *Tex. L. Rev.*, 38 (1960): 439; S.L. Hester, 'Deceptive Sales Practices and Form Contracts – Does the Consumer Have a Private Remedy?', *Duke L. J.*, (1968): 831.

30   350 F.2d 445 (D.C. Cir. 1965).

31   50 N.J. 101, 232 A.2d 405 (1967).

32   32 N.J. 358, 161 A.2d 69 (1960).

33   This is not to imply that recent decisions uniformly recognise the lack of bargaining in the typical consumer contract of adhesion. In fact, most courts use a traditional contract analysis to find assent and a valid contract. See generally, J. Braucher, 'The Afterlife of Contract', *N.W. U. L. Rev.*, 90 (1995): 49.

34   See, for example, *KLPR TV Inc.* v. *Visual Electronics Corp.*, 327 F. Supp. 315 (W.D. Arkansas 1971) (express warranty in leased equipment); *Sarafanti* v. *M.A. Hittner & Sons*, 35 App. Div.2d 1004, 318 N.Y.S.2d 352 (1970) (implied warranty in lease of automobile). See generally, W.D. Hawkland, 'Impact of the Uniform Commercial Code on Equipment Leasing', *Ill. L. F.*, (1974): 446. See also, A.H. Boss, 'The History of Article 2A: A Lesson for Practitioner and Scholar Alike', *Ala. L. Rev.*, 39 (1988): 575; E.E. Huddlesin, III, 'Old Wine in New Bottles: UCC Article 2A—Leases', *Ala. L. Rev.*, 39 (1988): 615.

35   For a general discussion of the development of the law with respect to the sale of goods and service transactions, see E. Taylor, 'Applicability of Strict Liability Warranty Theories to Service Transactions', *S.C. L. Rev.*, 47 (1996): 231.

good example of how this area of law has been developed and demonstrates the importance of the courts to the creation of consumer rights.

Until 1987, the Texas Supreme Court had not recognised an implied warranty in a service contract. In *Melody Home Manufacturing Co.* v. *Barnes*,[36] the court noted that the United States had shifted from goods to a service oriented economy. Based on a 'public policy mandate', the court imposed a warranty of good and workmanlike performance in any contract to repair or modify existing tangible goods or chattels. The court also defined the warranty as 'the quality of work performed by one who has the knowledge, training, or experience necessary for the successful practice of a trade or occupation and performed in a manner generally considered proficient by those capable of judging such work'.[37]

As with the development of any judicially created rule, *Melody Home* has been refined, modified, expanded and limited in the 21 years since it was decided. The Texas Supreme Court has cited the opinion no less than a dozen times, initially broadening its scope and recently sharply limiting it. For example, after some question,[38] the Texas Supreme Court held the warranty does not apply to professionals[39] and recently the court excluded certain 'incidental services'.[40] Meanwhile, more than 130 other Texas cases have cited *Melody Home* in their opinions. This is the life of the common law – a deliberate process of moulding doctrine to the times. It is also a process that probably would not have occurred if the problem that gave rise to the decision in *Melody Home* arose today. *Melody Home* involved a manufactured home. The likelihood is that today, the contract in *Melody Home* would have contained a clause mandating arbitration – precluding a court from considering any of the legal issues involved.

Consumer Arbitration – Bye-bye Courts

For some time now, arbitration has been heralded as a panacea for the ills of the American judicial system. It has been widely touted as a voluntary system of alternative dispute resolution that is more efficient, less expensive, and more flexible than our clogged and congested courts. The use of an alternative forum to hear consumer disputes would seem to be the best of both worlds; prompt resolution for consumers, and less expense for business.

---

36   741 S.W.2d 349 (Texas, 1987).
37   *Ibid.*, at p. 354.
38   In *Archibald* v. *Act III Arabians,* 755 S.W.2d 84 (Texas, 1988), the court suggested that the warranty could be applied to professional services.
39   *Murphy* v. *Campbell*, 964 S.W.2d 265 (Texas, 1998) (no implied warranty for professional services).
40   *Rocky Mountain Helicopter Inc.* v. *Lubbock County Hospital Dist.*, 987 S.W.2d 50 (Texas, 1999) (no implied warranty for services incidental to helicopter maintenance).

Arbitration is generally viewed by the courts reviewing it as nothing more than a voluntary forum selection clause, simply moving a dispute to a more convenient, efficient, and less expensive forum.[41] Recently, arbitration clauses have been embraced by American courts, particularly the Supreme Court, with open arms, uniformly adopting a pro-arbitration stance.[42] The support shown by the United States Supreme Court has been well documented,[43] and is demonstrated by the Courts recent decision in *Buckeye Check Cashing, Inc. v. Cardegna.*[44]

Cardegna involved the question of whether an arbitration clause in an illegal and void payday loan agreement was enforceable against a consumer. The supreme court of Florida held that the arbitration clause was not enforceable and the illegality of the contract was an issue for the courts. The United States

---

41   See, for example, *Scherk* v. *Alberto-Culver Co.*, 417 U.S. 506, 519 (1974) ('An agreement to arbitrate before a specified tribunal is, in effect, a specialized kind of forum-selection clause that posits not only the situs of suit but also the procedure to be used in resolving the dispute').

42   The provisions of the FAA [Federal Arbitration Act] manifest a 'liberal federal policy favoring arbitrations agreements'. *Gilmer* v. *Interstate/Johnson Lane Corp.*, 500 U.S. 20, at 25 (1991). This pro-arbitration stance of the Supreme Court began in earnest with the decision in *Moses H. Cone Memorial Hospital* v. *Mercury Construction Corp.*, 460 U.S. 1 (1983). Subsequent Supreme Court cases all evidence a strong pro-arbitration position. See, for example, *Circuit City Stores Inc.* v. *Adams*, 532 U.S. 105 (2001) (FAA's employee exception should be narrowly construed); *Green Tree Finance Corp.* v. *Randolph*, 531 U.S. 79 (2000) (Possibility of excessive costs is insufficient to defeat arbitration clause); *Doctor's Association, Inc.* v. *Casarotto*, 517 U.S. 681 (1996) (FAA pre-empts state statute restricting arbitration); *Shearson/ American Express, Inc.* v. *McMahon*, 482 U.S. 220, 226 (1987) (courts should 'rigorously enforce agreements to arbitrate').

43   'The Arbitration Act establishes that, as a matter of federal law, any doubts concerning the scope of arbitrable issues should be resolved in favor of arbitration, whether the problem at hand is the construction of the contract language itself or an allegation of waiver, delay, or a like to arbitrability.' *Moses H. Cone Memorial Hospital* v. *Mercury Construction Corp.*, 460 U.S. 1, at 24–5 (1983). See also *Shearson/American Express, Inc.* v. *McMahon*, 482 U.S. 220, 226 (1987) (stressing that courts should 'rigorously enforce agreements to arbitrate'); *Dickinson* v. *Heinold Sec., Inc.*, 661 F.2d 638, 643 (7th Cir. 1981) (describing the 'established federal policy that, when constructing arbitration agreements, every doubt is to be resolved in favor of arbitration'); *Wick* v. *Atl. Marine, Inc.*, 605 F.2d 166, 168 (5th Cir. 1979) (asserting that courts should stay proceedings pending arbitration 'unless it can be said with positive assurance that an arbitration clause is not susceptible of an interpretation which would cover the dispute at issue'); *Becker Autoradio U.S.A., Inc.* v. *Becker Autoradiowerk GmbH*, 585 F.2d 39, 44 (3d Cir. 1978) (recognizing that even in international agreements, the federal courts continue to favour arbitration of disputes); *Germany* v. *River Terminal Ry. Co.*, 477 F.2d 546, 547 (6th Cir. 1973) (acknowledging that using arbitration to resolve disputes, with consent of the parties, reduces 'court congestion').

44   546 U.S. 440 (2006).

Supreme Court disagreed. It noted three propositions for determining the validity of an arbitration clause:

> First, as a matter of substantive federal arbitration law, an arbitration provision is severable from the remainder of the contract. Second, unless the challenge is to the arbitration clause itself, the issue of the contract's validity is considered by the arbitrator in the first instance. Third, this arbitration law applies in state as well as federal courts.[45]

Applying these rules, the Court held that the issue of whether the contract was illegal was to be decided by the arbitrator, pursuant to the contract's arbitration provision. An arbitration clause, even if contained in an otherwise unenforceable contract, is none the less enforceable.

Consumer Arbitration – Substance over Form

As noted above, the courts 'strongly favour' arbitration clauses, even in consumer contracts, based on the notion that such clauses are valid contract provisions, knowingly and intentionally entered into, and that such clauses do not deny any substantive rights. In fact, however, consumer arbitration is not about an alternative forum for dispute resolution; it is about a modification of substantive rights. Consumer arbitration in the United States is often simply a way for a business to reduce the number of disputes, avoid the courts and juries, and achieve more favourable results. Arbitration is not about relocating or simplifying consumer dispute resolution; it is about eliminating consumer disputes and controlling their resolution.

For example, a recent article discussing damages for mental anguish in Alabama suggests that the current Alabama rule is an improper extension of the law, resulting in overly generous damage awards in cases involving the sale of automobiles and homes.[46] The authors provide strong support for the argument that the Alabama courts should review and modify this rule. The authors, however, may never see their article considered by the courts. The Alabama courts may never have the opportunity to modify the law in a way consistent with the premise of the article. Why? Because auto dealers and homebuilders have taken matters into their own hands and 'opted out' of our civil justice system. They have found a way to avoid the laws of Alabama, and achieve the results they want. As the authors of the article note:

---

45   *Ibid.*, at p. 446.
46   W. Scott Simpson, S.J. Ware and V.M. Willard, 'The Source of Alabama's Abundance of Arbitration Cases: Alabama's Bizarre Law of Damages for Mental Anguish', *Am. J. Trial Advoc.*, 28 (2004): 135.

The auto and home industries, fearing catastrophic verdicts before Alabama juries, now require customers, nearly across-the-board, to enter into pre-dispute binding arbitration agreements as a condition of doing business. These industries have effectively divorced themselves from the Alabama civil justice system in hopes of obtaining fairer and more just awards before arbitrators.[47]

As this excerpt indicates, American businesses dissatisfied with the civil justice system may privatise the dispute resolution process through arbitration, thereby controlling outcome as well as forum. The Alabama auto and homebuilding industries did not choose arbitration to promptly resolve disputes or provide consumers with an alternative forum. They imposed arbitration to avoid the legal rules of Alabama that would be applied by a court and jury.[48]

The use of arbitration to achieve substantive results different from what would be available in the courts not only circumvents our legal system, it also denies the courts the opportunity to review legal doctrine and make changes when appropriate.[49] The validity of arbitration clauses is based on the premise that they are a voluntarily chosen alternative forum of dispute resolution. In the consumer context, arbitration is anything but voluntary and it is becoming the norm, not

---

47   *Ibid.*, at 177. The authors also note that, 'It is virtually impossible now for Alabama consumers to purchase a new automobile or home without first signing a pre-dispute arbitration agreement.' *Ibid.*, at 138.

48   Although the auto and home industries have 'divorced' themselves from the Alabama civil justice system, I assume that if the courts adopted a more pro-business stance these same industries would again 'opt-in' to the civil justice system by removing their arbitration provisions. Because the decision of whether to include an arbitration provision rests exclusively with the business, businesses alone can determine when to arbitrate and when to allow a matter to proceed to court.

49   'As a general rule, a court may not review the decision of an arbitrator. A federal court may set aside an arbitration award under the FAA only upon a finding that certain statutory or judicial grounds are present.' *The Andersons, Inc.* v. *Horton Farms, Inc.*, 166 F.3d 308, 328 (6th Cir. 1998). Those statutory grounds are:
(a) In any of the following cases the United States court in and for the district wherein the award was made may make an order vacating the award upon the application of any party to the arbitration—
(1) where the award was procured by corruption, fraud, or undue means;
(2) where there was evident partiality or corruption in the arbitrators, or either of them;
(3) where the arbitrators were guilty of misconduct in refusing to postpone the hearing, upon sufficient cause shown, or in refusing to hear evidence pertinent and material to the controversy; or of any other misbehavior by which the rights of any party have been prejudiced; or
(4) where the arbitrators exceeded their powers, or so imperfectly executed them that a mutual, final, and definite award upon the subject matter submitted was not made.
9 U.S.C. § 10. It is extremely unusual for a court to find a basis upon which to set aside an arbitrator's decision.

an alternative. A recent study of commercial arbitration clauses supports the proposition that the widespread use of arbitration in consumer cases may be in fact based on something other than the efficiency benefits of an alternative forum:

> We present evidence that large corporate actors do not systematically embrace arbitration. International contracts include arbitration clauses more than domestic contracts, but also at a surprisingly low rate. Our results have implications for the justifications for the widespread use of arbitration clauses in consumer contracts. If the reasons that some have advanced to support the use of arbitration in the consumer context – that it is simpler and cheaper than litigation – are correct, it is surprising that public companies do not seek these advantages in disputes among themselves. In the simple economic view, our results suggest that corporate representatives believe that litigation can add value over arbitration.[50]

Consumer Arbitration Under Attack

In response to this privatisation of justice, arbitration in America, particularly pre-dispute consumer arbitration, has come under attack by consumer advocates and others who have found fault with both the manner in which arbitration is agreed to, the process itself, and the results of arbitration proceedings.[51] For example, the

---

50   T. Eisenberg and G.P. Miller, 'The Flight From Arbitration: An Empirical Study of Ex Ante Arbitration Clauses in the Contracts of Publicly Held Companies', *DePaul L. Rev.*, 56 (2007): 335, at 373–4.
      A recent article discusses arbitration, and compares it with an alternative, a contract to modify the rules of litigation: H.S. Noyes, 'If You (Re)Build It, They Will Come: Contracts to Remake The Rules Of Litigation in Arbitration's Image', *Harv. J.L. & Pub. Pol.*, 30 (2007): 579. As the article points out, contractual modification of the rules of litigation can offer the parties substantial procedural and cost benefits over the current alternative, arbitration. Parties do not, however, use such contractual agreements in consumer arbitration, and it is unlikely they will. As discussed above, this is because arbitration in consumer cases is not used to provide a simpler, quicker, more efficient and less costly alternative to litigation. It is used to change the substantive results of the civil litigation system. As Professor Noyes points out, if business truly wanted a better alternative to our current litigation system, it could contractually modify the rules to effectuate cost and time reductions, while maintaining the traditional roles of the courts.
51   See, for example R.M. Alderman, 'Pre-Dispute Mandatory Arbitration in Consumer Contracts: A Call for Reform', *Houston L. Rev.*, 38 (2001): 1237; A. Brafford, 'Arbitration Clauses in Consumer Contracts of Adhesion: Fair Play or Trap for the Weak and Unwary?', *J. Corp. L.*, 21 (1996): 331; F.L. Miller, 'Arbitration Clauses in Consumer Contracts; Building Barriers to Consumer Protection', *Mich. B.J.*, 78 (1999): 302; D.S. Schwartz, 'Correcting Federalism Mistakes in Statutory Interpretation: The Supreme Court and the Federal Arbitration Act', *Law & Contemp. Problems*, 67 (2004): 5; D.S. Schwartz, 'Enforcing Small Print to Protect Big Business: Employee

adhesive nature of the contracts upon which arbitration is based is often cited as a reason to not impose arbitration on the consumer.[52] Courts and commentators alike have also noted the often-excessive costs of arbitration, which may deny access to those unable to pay.[53] A recent dissenting opinion in a Florida arbitration decision summarises the situation most consumers face:

---

and Consumer Rights Claims in an Age of Compelled Arbitration', *Wis. L. Rev.*, (1997): 33; R.E. Speidel, 'Consumer Arbitration of Statutory Claims: Has Pre-Dispute [Mandatory] Arbitration Outlived its Welcome?', *Ariz. L. Rev.*, 40 (1998): 1069; J.R. Sternlight, 'Rethinking the Constitutionality of the Supreme Court's Preference for Binding Arbitration: A Fresh Assessment of Jury Trial, Separation of Powers, and Due Process Concerns', *Tul. L. Rev.*, 72 (1997): 1.

52 One of the few challenges to arbitration provisions that has met with limited success is unconscionability. See, for example, *Circuit City Stores, Inc.* v. *Adams*, 279 F.3d 889 (9th Cir. 2002) (employer's 'Dispute Resolution Agreement' is unconscionable and unenforceable); *Gibson* v. *Neighborhood Health Clinics, Inc.*, 121 F.3d 1126, 1131 (7th Cir. 1997) (declining to enforce an employment arbitration agreement in the absence of consideration); *Hull* v. *Norcom, Inc.*, 750 F.2d 1547, 1550 (11th Cir. 1985) (holding that 'the consideration exchanged for one party's promise to arbitrate must be the other party's promise to arbitrate at least some specified class of claims' and, absent such an exchange, an arbitration provision in an employment agreement is invalid and unenforceable); *Ting* v. *A.T.& T.*, 182 F. Supp.2d 902 (N.D. Cal. 2002) (agreement unconscionable where consumer had no meaningful choice); *Kloss* v. *Edward D. Jones*, 2002 Mt. 123, 54 P.3d 1 (Montana 2002) (arbitration agreement in contract of adhesion not enforceable); *Armendariz* v. *Foundation Health Psychare Services Inc.*, 6 P.3d 669, 694 (California, 2000) (refusing to enforce an agreement to arbitrate employment disputes and finding the agreement unconscionable because it required arbitration for claims brought by employees but did not require arbitration of claims brought by the employer); *Stirlen* v. *Supercuts, Inc.*, 60 Cal. Rptr. 2d 138, 158–9 (California Ct. App. 1997) (declaring an arbitration clause in an employment agreement unenforceable, unconscionable, and against public policy because it was adhesive, the duty to arbitrate was unilateral, and the terms unfairly benefited the employer).

53 The United States Supreme Court recently had an opportunity to rule on this point in *Green Tree Fin. Corp.* v. *Randolph*, 531 U.S. 79 (2000). The court side-stepped the issues, however, noting that although '[i]t may well be that ... large arbitration costs could preclude a litigant ... from effectively vindicating her federal statutory rights, ... [t]he "risk" that Randolph will be saddled with prohibitive costs is too speculative to justify the invalidation of an arbitration agreement'. *Ibid.*, at 91. For examples of cases that have considered the effect of excessive costs, see *Paladino* v. *Avnet Computer Technologies, Inc.*, 134 F.3d 1054 (11th Cir. 1998); *Cole* v. *Burns International Security Services*, 105 F.3d 1465 (D.C. Cir. 1997); *Dunlap* v. *Berger*, 567 S.E.2d 265 (West Virginia 2002); *Armendariz* v. *Foundation Health Psychare Services, Inc.*, 6 P.3d 669, 694 (California 2000).
    Although most small claims courts provide a judge and jury for less than $100, the costs of arbitration far exceed this amount. A recent study by Public Citizen concludes that the costs of arbitration almost always exceed the costs of litigation; *The Costs of*

What we have begun to see is that virtually all consumer transactions, no matter the size or type, now contain an arbitration clause. And with every reinforcing decision, these clauses become ever more brazenly loaded to the detriment of the consumer – who gets to be the arbitrator; when, where, how much it costs; what claims are excluded; what damages are excluded; what statutory remedies are excluded; what discovery is allowed; what notice provisions are required; what shortened statutes of limitation apply; what prerequisites even to the right to arbitrate are thrown up – not to mention the fairness or accuracy of the decision itself. The drafters have every incentive to load these arbitration clauses with such onerous provisions in favour of the seller because the worst that ever happens, if the consumer has the resources to go to court, is that the offending provisions are severed. The state courts, demoralized by the United States Supreme Court's disapproval, have too often allowed these overreaching provisions to succeed. Most consumers can't read them, won't read them, don't understand them, don't understand their implication and can't afford counsel to help them out.[54]

An additional problem inherent in the widespread use of arbitration is the fact that an arbitration clause may preclude the use of the class actions device.[55] Although

---

Arbitration, April 2002. (The report's publication number is B9028. It is available from Public Citizen, www.citizen.org.) For example, AAA cites $700 per day as the average arbitrator's fee in 1996; K. May, 'Labor Lawyers at ABA Session Debate Role of American Arbitration Association', *Daily Lab. Rep. (BNA)*, 31 (15 February 1996): A-12. Judicial Arbitration and Mediation Services arbitrators charge an average of $400 per hour. R. Alleyne, 'Statutory Discrimination Claims: Rights "Waived" and Lost in the Arbitration Forum', *Hofstra Lab. & Emp. L J.*, 13 (1996): 381, 410 n. 189. Fees up to $600 per hour are not uncommon. See M.A. Jacobs, 'Renting Justice: Retired Judges Seize Rising Role in Settling Disputes in California', *Wall Street Journal*, July 26, 1996, at A1; D. Segal, 'Have Name Recognition, Will Mediate Disputes', *Washington Post*, Dec. 16, 1996, Washington Business, at 5. The CPR Institute for Dispute Resolution estimates arbitrators' fees of $250–$350 per hour and 15–40 hours of arbitrator time in a typical employment case, for total arbitrators' fees of $3,750 to $14,000 in an 'average' case; CPR Institute for Dispute Resolution, *Employment ADR: A Dispute Resolution Program for Corporate Employers* I-13 (1995).

54   *Mercedes Homes, Inc.* v. *Colon*, 966 So. 2d.10, 28–9 (Florida.Ct. App 2007) (Griffin, dissenting).

55   In *Greentree Financial Corp.* v. *Bazzle*, 399 U.S. 444, (2003), the Court recognized class arbitration, and held that the interpretation of an arbitration provision in an arbitration clause was to be decided by the arbitrator.

Courts sitting to consider whether such clauses preclude a class action have reached differing results. For example, in *Discover Bank* v. *Superior Court of Los Angeles*, 36 Cal. 4th 148, 167, 113 P.3d 1100, 1110, 30 Cal. Rptr. 3d 76, 87 (2005), the California Supreme Court found a class action prohibition unconscionable and unenforceable, stating:

We do not hold that all class action waivers are necessarily unconscionable. But when the waiver is found in a consumer contract of adhesion in a setting in which disputes between the contracting parties predictably involve small amounts of damages, and

widely criticised, the class action device often proves a valuable tool for achieving consumer redress, and controlling the market place. In *Greentree Financial Corp.* v. *Bazzle*,[56] the Supreme Court recognised that an arbitration clause was not invalid when applied to a request for class action status and relief, and that arbitration could be conducted as a 'class arbitration'. The Court also held that the interpretation of an arbitration provision in an arbitration clause was to be decided by the arbitrator. Thus, whether the proceeding may be maintained as a class action and the procedures employed to do so, are questions for the arbitrator.

---

when it is alleged that the party with the superior bargaining power has carried out a scheme to deliberately cheat large numbers of consumers out of individually small sums of money, then, at least to the extent the obligation at issue is governed by California law, the waiver becomes in practice the exemption of the party 'from responsibility for [its] own fraud, or wilful injury to the person or property of another.' Under these circumstances, such waivers are unconscionable under California law and should not be enforced.

The Ninth Circuit reached a similar conclusion with respect to a cell phone contract. See *Shroyer* v. *New Cingula Wireless Services*, 498 F.3d 976 (9th Cir. 2007) ('Applying that law to the class arbitration waiver at issue here, we conclude that under the test set forth in *Discover Bank* v. *Superior Court of Los Angeles*, 36 Cal. 4th 148 (Cal. 2005), the waiver is both procedurally and substantively unconscionable and, therefore, unenforceable.') See also *Scott* v. *Cingular Wireless*, 156 Wn.2d 1001; 135 P.3d 478 (2007) (arbitration class action ban unenforceable); *Champ* v. *Siegel Trading Co., Inc.*, 55 F. 3d 269 (class action waivable under FAA). However, the Supreme Court of North Dakota, in *Strand* v. *U.S. Bank National Assoc.*, 693 N.W.2d 918 (2005), recently upheld a class action prohibition, noting:

Nor has Strand established that he will be left without an effective remedy if the 'no class action' provision is enforced. The arbitration provision here requires that the arbitration take place in Strand's home jurisdiction and provides for advancement of fees and costs by the Bank. Furthermore, if Strand prevails in his claim against the Bank he will be entitled to an award of attorney fees ... under the facts of this case the arbitration provision between Strand and the Bank creates a chance that Strand can be made whole through individual arbitration.

[t]he facts certified to us have failed to show that enforcement of the disputed contractual provision would leave Strand without an effective remedy. We therefore conclude Strand has failed to demonstrate that the 'no class action' provision is substantively unconscionable.

Because a showing of both procedural and substantive unconscionability is required to declare a contractual provision unconscionable and unenforceable, we conclude that, under the facts of this case, the 'no class action' provision is not unconscionable.

Ibid., at 927. See also *Gay* v. *CreditInform*. 511 F.3d 369 , 2007 U.S. App. LEXIS 29302 (3d Cir. 2007). See generally, A.S. Kaplinsky and M.J. Levin, 'Consensus or Conflict? Most (but not all) Courts Enforce Express Class Action Waivers in Consumer Arbitration Agreements', *Business Law*, 60 (2005): 775; J.R. Sternlight, 'As Mandatory Binding Arbitration Meets the Class Action, Will the Class Action Survive?', *William & Mary L. Rev*, 42 (2000): 1.

56   539 U.S. 444; (2003).

More significantly than what the court proclaimed, however, is what it did not discuss. The *Bazzle* Court did not resolve the question of whether an arbitration clause could prohibit class relief. In light of the deference shown to an arbitration clause and the weight given to the notion of freedom of contract when interpreting them, it appears that in light of *Bazzle*, a contractual prohibition on class action status will be enforceable.[57] It may be just a matter of time before 'anti-class action clauses'[58] are included in all agreements, possibly eliminating the consumer class action.[59]

It may be argued, as it has been with arbitration in general, that all the Court did in *Bazzle* was shift the forum for class actions from the courts to arbitration. Even assuming the correctness of this statement, and that in fact arbitration provisions are not drafted to preclude class action, the arbitration class action and arbitrations in general do not provide the same relief in terms of either procedure or substance. Even in the event of a class action arbitration is held, there may be no requirement that the process comply with the due process requirements imposed upon the courts.[60]

---

57   See generally, Sternlight, 'As Mandatory Binding Arbitration Meets the Class Action, Will the Class Action Survive?'.

58   For example, many arbitration provisions contain clauses similar to this one:
      PLEASE READ THIS AGREEMENT CAREFULLY. IT PROVIDES THAT ANY DISPUTE MAY BE RESOLVED BY BINDING ARBITRATION. ARBITRATION REPLACES THE RIGHT TO GO TO COURT. YOU WILL NOT BE ABLE TO BRING A CLASS ACTION OR OTHER REPRESENTATIVE ACTION IN COURT SUCH AS THAT IN THE FORM OF A PRIVATE ATTORNEY GENERAL ACTION, NOR WILL YOU BE ABLE TO BRING ANY CLAIM IN ARBITRATION AS A CLASS ACTION OR OTHER REPRESENTATIVE ACTION. YOU WILL NOT BE ABLE TO BE PART OF ANY CLASS ACTION OR OTHER REPRESENTATIVE ACTION BROUGHT BY ANYONE ELSE, OR BE REPRESENTED IN A CLASS ACTION OR OTHER REPRESENTATIVE ACTION.
      American Express contract provision received by the Author.

59   'Bazzle's twin holdings – and just as importantly, the manner in which arbitration administrators and courts have responded to them – make it possible for corporations to draft arbitration clauses so as to virtually guarantee that claims will not be arbitrated on a classwide basis.' Note: 'Beyond Unconscionability: Preserving the Class Mechanism Under State Law in the Era of Consumer Arbitration', *Tex. L. Rev.*, 83 (2005): 1715, at 1721. Although many courts have continued to uphold such clauses and prohibit class action arbitrations, the recent trend appears to be to invalidate limits on class action arbitrations. Compare *Gay* v. *CreditInform*, 511 F.3d 369, 2007 U.S. App. LEXIS 29302 (3d Cir. 2007) (class action ban enforceable) with *Dale* v. *Comcast*, 498 F.3d 1216 (11th Cir. 1007) (ban on class arbitration is unenforceable); *Scott* v. *Cingular Wireless*, 156 Wn.2d 1001, 135 P.3d 478 (Washington, 2007) (ban on class action arbitration unenforceable); *Kinkel* v. *Cingular Wireless*, 223 Ill. 2d 1; 857 N.E.2d 250 (2006) (class action ban is unconscionable).

60   See, for example, C.J. Buckner, 'Due Process in Class Arbitration', *Fla. L. Rev.*, 58 (2006): 185, at 263; ('State action may require due process in some models of class

Finally, consumers forced to arbitrate are also subject to what is perceived as the unfair advantage for the repeat player.[61] It has been argued that the repeat player, such as the business that has thousands of arbitrations a year compared to the consumer who has just one, has an unfair advantage due to its greater familiarity with the process, as well as the process itself. In most arbitrations, either party as the right to 'strike' an arbitrator. The repeat player, therefore, may be favoured by the arbitrator because of the possible consequence of ruling against it. Arguably, the arbitrator, who could be precluded from hearing a large number of cases, will consciously or subconsciously favour the repeat player rather than risk offending him and be 'blackballed' in the future.[62]

Due to the secret nature of most arbitrations, and unavailability of public data, it is hard to verify or dispel the repeat player advantage. The *Christian Science Monitor*, however, recently evaluated available data from the National Arbitration Forum [NAF], one of the largest arbitration organisations:

> A *Monitor* analysis of the last year of available data from NAF found that arbitrators awarded in favour of creditors and debt buyers in more than 96 per cent of the cases. Such results may be similar to outcomes in court. It also found that the 10 most frequently used arbitrators – who decided almost 60 per cent of the cases heard – decided in favour

---

arbitration, and perhaps would not require such protections under other models').

61   This theory is based on the seminal work by M. Galanter, 'Why the "Haves" Come Out Ahead: Speculations on the Limits of Legal Change', *Law & Society Rev.*, 9 (1974): 95. Galanter's thesis was rather simple: repeat-players with substantial assets can use the legal system to their advantage. This conclusion was based on his observations concerning the ability of the 'Haves' as repeat-players to manipulate the legal system to optimize long-term results. Those with a greater stake in the outcome of future litigation will attempt to optimize long-term results. See also S.S. Silbey, 'Do The "Haves" Still Come Out Ahead?', *Law & Society Rev.*, 33 (1999): 799; ('Since its publication in 1974, Galanter's paper has been cited more often than any other piece of socio–legal scholarship, and it stands among the most well cited law review articles of all time.' (citing F.R. Shapiro, 'The Most-Cited Law Review Articles Revisited', *Chi. Kent L. Rev.*, 71 (1996): 751, at 766, which ranks Galanter's article as thirteenth on the list of most cited law review articles)).

Whether the 'haves' come out ahead in consumer arbitration is virtually impossible to prove or disprove. In the consumer context, there is almost no data available. Even in the employment area, where the most data is available, it is hard to come to any meaningful conclusions. This is due, in part, to the fact that the most meaningful statistic would be one that compared not only arbitration numbers, but also similar cases in the courts. See, for example, *Cole* v. *Burns International Security Services*, 105 F.3d 1465, at 1485 n. 17 (D.C. Cir. 1997); ('It is hard to know what to make of these studies without assessing the relative *merits* of the cases in the surveys.'). It must be assumed, however, that if businesses are increasingly imposing mandatory arbitration provisions on consumers, they see some benefit in precluding resort to the courts.

62   See generally, *ibid.*

of the consumer only 1.6 per cent of the time, while arbitrators who decided three or fewer cases decided for the consumer 38 per cent of the time.

The *Monitor* also found support for the notion that arbitrators who rule against business are 'blackballed' and not selected again. '[T]wo former NAF arbitrators say banks took them off of cases after they issued rulings unfavourable to the institution.'[63]

All of the above arguments against the use of arbitration clauses in consumer contracts are to some extent valid; some even compelling. Yet none of these arguments will be discussed here. Instead, the remainder of this article will focus on a different, and perhaps substantially more significant, problem inherent in the widespread use of consumer arbitration – the elimination of a core component of the American justice system.

The Real Problem

As binding pre-dispute arbitration is increasingly used and consumer access to the American civil justice system is proportionately denied, consumer protection in the United States will be diminished as business structures a system of private dispute resolution that it finds acceptable.[64] Arbitration clauses and arbitration procedures will be designed to choose the system of arbitration that most favours business, and clauses will be drafted in a manner that precludes attack and limits redress, within the limits imposed by the courts.[65] For example, language will

---

63   'Consumer Advocates Slam Credit-Card Arbitration', July 16, 2007 available at: http://www.csmonitor.com/2007/0716/p13s01-wmgn.htm. The Christian Science Monitor report is not alone in finding that consumers do not fare well in arbitration. In a recent study of nearly 34,000 arbitration cases conducted by the National Arbitration Forum in California, it was found that the business prevailed in over 94 per cent of the cases. The study also found that arbitrators charge up to $10,000 a day and some make $1 million a year. The report, entitled, '*The Arbitration Trap: How Credit Card Companies Ensnare Consumers*', shows that 'binding mandatory arbitration is a rigged game in which justice is dealt from a deck stacked against consumers'. The complete 74 page study is available through Public Citizen at: htpp://www.citizen. org.
64   Because pre-dispute arbitration clauses are drafted by the business and presented to the consumer on a take it or leave it basis, the business has the ability to draft an arbitration clause in whatever manner is most beneficial to the business. For example, the business may select the arbitration forum, specify the time and location of the arbitration, designate what claims will or will not be subject to arbitration, whether class–action arbitrations will be permitted, and whether there will be a written opinion.
65   One of the results of litigation against arbitration clauses is that even when consumers prevail, the result is often simply a stronger clause used in the future. Many pro-

be included to prevent the use of class actions, and costs will be structured to be sufficiently low enough to meet unconscionability and due process standards, yet sufficiently high enough to deter many valid consumer claims.

Under current American law, it appears inevitable that consumer arbitration will eventually replace litigation.[66] As consumer dispute resolution is privatised, the development and application of consumer law in America gradually will be

---

consumer opinions strike specific language and do so with such specificity that it enables the business to modify its arbitration clause in a manner that complies with the law.

66   In fact, this is already happening. Many have noticed that jury trials are vanishing in the United States, and that this has been caused at least in part by the increased use of arbitration clauses. Much has been written recently about the privatization of justice and the vanishing jury trial. See generally *The Privatization of Justice? Mandatory Arbitration and the State Courts – Report of the 2003 Forum for State Appellate Court Judges* (2006 Pound Civil Justice Institute). See also, *2004 ABA Annual Meeting – Program Materials: Bench and Bar: The Vanishing Jury Trial*, available at: http://www.abanet.org/abanet/litigation/mo/premium-lt/prog_materials/2004_abaannual/20.pdf (membership required); G.A. Ballard, Jr., 'The State of Trial Work – 2007', *Houston Lawyer*, 44 (2007): 6; I. Blanco and T.C. Edwards, 'Arbitration v. Litigation Pros and Cons: What Business Lawyers Need To Know (Arbitration and the Vanishing Jury Trial)', *Tex. Bar Journal* 69 (Oct. 2006): 858; S. Brister, 'Decline in Jury Trials: What Would Wal-Mart Do?', *S. Tex. L. Rev.*, 47 (2005): 191; D.J. Drasco, 'The American Jury Project and the Image of the Justice System', *Litigation No.* 2, 32 (2005): 1, available at: http://www.abanet.org/litigation/journal/opening_statements/05winter_openingstatement.pdf; J. Fleming, 'Using Best Practices to Draft Arbitration Agreements (Arbitration and the Vanishing Jury Trial)', *Tex. Bar Journal*, 69 (2006): 866, at 868; N.L. Hecht, 'The Vanishing Civil Jury Trial: Trends in Texas Courts and an Uncertain Future', *S. Tex. L. Rev.*, 47 (2005): 163; P.E. Higginbotham, 'Point-Counterpoint: Two Judges' Perspectives on Trial by Jury: Mahon Lecture', *Tex. Wesleyan L. Rev.*, 12 (2006): 501; E. Kinkeade, 'Point-Counterpoint: Two Judges' Perspectives on Trial by Jury: Introduction', *Tex. Wesleyan L. Rev.*, 12 (2006): 497; D.T. López, 'Arbitration and the Vanishing Jury Trial: Realizing the Promise of Employment Arbitration', *Tex. Bar Journal*, 69 (2006): 862; J. Mazzone, 'Symposium: Justice Blackmun and Judicial Biography: A Conversation with Linda Greenhouse: The Justice and the Jury', *Brook L. Rev.*, 72 (2006): 35; T. Walters McCormack, 'Privatizing the Justice System' (Symposium), *Rev. Litig* 25 (2006): 735; T.R. Means, 'Point-Counterpoint: Two Judges' Perspectives on Trial By Jury: What's so Great About a Trial Anyway? A Reply to Judge Higginbotham's Eldon B. Mahon Lecture of October 27, 2004', *Tex. Wesleyan L. Rev.*, 12 (2006): 513; K.W. Schuler, 'Note: ADR'S Biggest Compromise', *Drake L. Rev.*, 54 (2006): 751; Task Force on the Vanishing Jury Trial, Boston Bar Association, *Jury Trial Trends in Massachusetts: The Need to Ensure Jury Trial Competency Among Practicing Attorneys as a Result of the Vanishing Jury Trial Phenomenon* (2006); M.R. Trachtenberg and C.F. Cozier, 'Risky Business: Altering the Scope of Judicial Review of Arbitration Awards by Contract', *Tex. Bar Journal*, 69 (2006): 868; P. Tynes, 'Design Your Own Arbitration: Redesigning Arbitration to Fit Your Dispute? (Arbitration and the Vanishing Jury

skewed toward those who control the process. For example, in most arbitrations, arbitrators are selected through a process that enables either side to eliminate potential arbitrators. In commercial arbitrations, arbitrators must be concerned with fairness because either party may exercise its pre-emptive strike against that arbitrator in a future dispute. For example, an arbitrator who rules 'unreasonably' in favour of one party or the other will soon be without work.[67] The fact that both sides to the dispute will have the right in the future to again select an arbitrator helps ensure fairness. Common sense tells us that one of the reasons an arbitrator must be fair and impartial is that an arbitrator will not be inclined to rule in a manner one side finds offensive, and which may adversely affect his or her future selection.[68]

This concept works well in commercial arbitrations, but not in the consumer context. Unlike commercial arbitration, where each party has the same potential to be involved in future disputes and exercise equal influence over the selection process, in consumer arbitration one party is involved in multiple arbitrations, while the other is a one-shot player. For example, a bank or credit card company may be involved in hundreds or even thousands of arbitrations a year. The consumer is generally involved in one. Arbitrators, consciously or unconsciously, are probably aware of the fact that a few adverse decisions could preclude him or her from selection in the future. Consumers are not repeat players, and lack the ability to obtain information from others regarding arbitration decisions because such decisions generally are not published. A system of private justice will always favour those who control access and the purse strings.[69] As noted above, this is

---

Trial)', *Tex. Bar Journal*, 69 (2006): 872; W.G. Young, 'Vanishing Trials, Vanishing Juries, Vanishing Constitution', *Suffolk U. L. Rev.*, 40 (2006): 67.

67   In the typical arbitration, the parties are presented with a list of arbitrators and are allowed to delete some or all members of the list. The arbitrators for that specific dispute are then selected from the remaining names. In other words, a party may not select the arbitrator but he may prevent someone from serving. If an arbitrator were viewed as unreasonable, he or she could effectively be out of work because neither side would want to run the risk of an unfair decision. An unfair or unreasonable commercial arbitrator would have his or her name deleted from the list of acceptable arbitrators.

68   American arbitrators generally are well compensated, and many rely upon being selected as an arbitrator as their sole means of income. As discussed above, if an arbitrator were deemed to be 'unfair' or 'unfit' he or she would effectively lose all income because both sides to a dispute would 'strike' him or her. In the context of consumer arbitration, however, an arbitrator viewed as unfair by the consumer loses little. The consumer is involved with one arbitration and is not a repeat-player. On the other hand, many businesses are involved in thousands of arbitrations a year. Being deemed unfair by business would preclude most future employment.

69   A similar problem may exist with respect to financial contributions to the campaign of judges. Spending on judicial elections has been skyrocketing, and data suggests that the spending is often rewarded with favourable rulings. See, for example, A. Liptak

explicitly recognised in Alabama, where auto dealers and homebuilders have chosen to 'opt-out' of the civil justice system to obtain the substantive benefits of arbitration.[70]

Precedent and *Stare Decisis*

Even assuming an arbitrator is committed to impartially following the law; he or she still cannot create or shape it. Therein lies perhaps the most serious problem with increased use of arbitration. The interpretation of our statutes, the development of the common law, and the courts' ability continually to establish and refine legal rights depends upon litigants, cases, public written opinions, and appeals regarding questions of law.[71] Arbitration eliminates litigation, preventing our appellate courts from playing the role they were designed to play in the American justice system.[72]

Unlike court opinions, most of which are published, most decisions of arbitrators are secret, and are often not even accompanied by a written opinion. Even when published and made available to the public, the decision of one arbitrator or panel of arbitrators, is in no way binding on any other arbitrator or panel. In fact, arbitrators generally are not compelled to follow the law, and their decisions are not appealable.[73] Arbitration precedent and *stare decisis* do not exist. Arbitrators

and J. Roberts, 'Campaign Cash Mirrors a High Court's Rulings', *New York Times*, October 1, 2006, available at: http://www.nytimes.com/2006/10/01/us/01judges.html. Whether and to what extent contributions to judges affect their decisions is still an open question.

70　See notes 46 and 47 and accompanying text, above.

71　'As trials shrink as a presence within the legal world, they are displaced from the central role assigned them in the common law. [C]ommon law procedure has been defined by the presence of this discreet plenary event, to which all else was a prelude or epilog.'; M. Galanter, 'The Vanishing Trial: An Examination of Trials and Related Matters in Federal and State Courts', *J. Empirical Legal Studies*, 1 (2005): 459, at 524.

72　As one author discussing arbitration has stated: 'A private civil justice system is evolving, one that is relatively unconstrained by law and relatively uninformed by systematic empirical research.' Using what is described as 'Dispute Resolution Darwinism,' the author concludes that: 'We may already be witnessing the first mass extinction as large institutional organisms move in to occupy entire habitats in the civil justice ecosystem'; L.B. Bingham, 'Self-Determination in Dispute System Design and Employment Arbitration', *U. Miami L. Rev.*, 56 (2002): 873.

73　As a general rule, decisions of arbitrators are not appealable. Under the Federal Arbitration Act (FAA), a court has very limited authority to vacate an arbitrator's award. Federal Arbitration Act, 9 U.S.C. § 10 (1994) (indicating that an arbitral award can be vacated only on narrow grounds including corruption, fraud, partiality, and misconduct). In most cases, the award may not be appealed based on the incorrect application of law or an improper factual finding. The review process was nicely

can interpret the law, but the interpretation of one arbitrator is not binding upon another. Consequently, arbitration lacks the ability to formulate policy, impose consistency, or change existing law. Most would argue, and I concur, that this is the way it should be. Arbitrators are not elected judges; they do nothing more than decide the single dispute before them.[74] The problem, however, is that our beliefs regarding the value of arbitration are based on the underlying assumption that arbitration is an 'alternate' method of dispute resolution. In other words, many disputes will remain within our civil justice system and our courts will continue to actively mould the common law. Consider the possible effects, as this alternative system of justice becomes the norm.

Return to the development of the warranty of good and workmanlike performance in Texas, beginning with the Texas Supreme Court's decision in *Melody Home Manufacturing Co.* v. *Barnes*.[75] *Melody Home* involved a dispute over services performed on a manufactured home. The likelihood today is that the contract for the sale of that home would include an arbitration provision. The Barnes would be in arbitration, not court. The arbitrators would apply the law, not create it, and implied warranties in service contracts would not exist.

Arbitration precludes the courts from creating substantive rights through the common law. It also prevents the modification of existing rights. The common

---

explained in *Stark* v. *Sandberg, Phoenix & Von Gontard*, P.C., 381 F.3d 793 (8th Cir. 2004) as follows:

When reviewing an arbitral award, courts accord 'an extraordinary level of deference' to the underlying award itself, because federal courts are not authorized to reconsider the merits of an arbitral award 'even though the parties may allege that the award rests on errors of fact or on misinterpretation of the contract.' Indeed, an award must be confirmed even if a court is convinced the arbitrator committed a serious error, so 'long as the arbitrator is even arguably construing or applying the contract and acting within the scope of his authority.'

Ibid., at 798. See also *Major League Baseball Players Association* v. *Garvey*, 121 S. Ct. 1724, 1728 (2001) ('Courts are not authorized to review the arbitrator's decision on the merits despite allegations that the decision rests on factual errors or misinterprets the parties' agreement'); *Universidad Interamericana* v. *Dean Witter Reynolds, Inc.*, 208 F. Supp.2d 151 (D. Puerto Rico 2002); (courts do not sit to hear claims of factual or legal error by an arbitrator). For a general discussion of the grounds for vacating an arbitrator's award, see S.L. Hayford, 'Law in Disarray: Judicial Standards for Vacatur of Commercial Arbitration Awards', *Ga. L. Rev.*, 30 (1996): 731.

74   Not only are arbitrators without authority to develop the law, they also have little incentive to do so. Because their decisions are final and limited to the purpose of resolving the immediate dispute, arbitrators have little motivation to explain their awards in a way that makes them useful to future litigants or the general public. See generally Moohr, 'Arbitration and the Goals of Employment Discrimination Law': Note 12 at 436.

75   741 S.W.2d 349, discussed at note. 36 and accompanying text.

law allows the courts to create the law, and it also allows them to change it.[76] In theory, this consequence of precluding access to the courts favours neither side to a dispute. It is neither pro-consumer nor pro-business.

For example, in *Melody Home*,[77] the Texas Supreme Court created a very pro-consumer warranty, of apparently broad applicability. Recent decisions, however, have limited its scope and drawn into question its continued validity.[78] Because most consumer contracts now contain a mandatory arbitration clause, the case that gave rise to the opinion in *Melody Home* may never have arisen, or there might not have been subsequent decisions that limited it. In other words, arbitrators could find themselves applying law that a court, if given the opportunity, might modify, or even reverse. Arbitration has the potential to 'freeze' the common law as it exists at the time universal arbitration is imposed, creating a 'time warp' of consumer protection, unable to accommodate change.

But this analysis ignores an important fact: arbitration in consumer contracts is imposed almost as a matter of right by businesses. American consumers have no choice but to agree, businesses have the choice to leave out an arbitration provision whenever they wish to pursue litigation, or waive arbitration and proceed to court. Through the sophisticated use and enforcement of mandatory arbitration provisions, business may engage in a form of selective creation of the common law. That is, selecting which disputes, if any, our courts will be allowed to deal with. In other words, consumer arbitration may stall the development of the common law, or even worse, it may allow business to control common law development to accommodate the needs of business.

Consumer Arbitration is Different

It is recognised that most of the above discussion applies to all forms of arbitration, not just consumer arbitration. For example, employment, securities or commercial arbitration also have the potential to preclude resort to the courts.[79] It is suggested, however, that in America, consumer arbitration presents a unique situation that exacerbates the problems inherent in arbitration. What is special about consumer arbitration and why does it present problems different from those presented in other contexts, such as commercial agreements or employment contracts? First, in

---

76 'There is another characteristic of litigation in the Anglo–American system, however, much less frequently manifested but perhaps of equal importance: the ability to *depart* from precedent.'; Knapp, 'Taking Contracts Private: The Quiet Revolution in Contract Law': Note 12 at 785 (emphasis in original).

77 741 S.W.2d 349 (Texas 1987).

78 See, for example, *Rocky Mountain Helicopters, Inc.* v. *Lubbock County. Hospital District*, 987 S.W.2d 50 (Texas 1998) (no implied warranty found).

79 This fact has been noted and discussed elsewhere, *see generally* Knapp, *supra* note 12, Moohr, *supra* note 12 and Carr and Jencks, *supra* note 11.

the United States, arbitration is not used with the same frequency in non-consumer contexts. Commercial parties actually bargain for an arbitration provision, and many commercial contracts do not include such provisions. In the employment context, many employees do not work subject to a written arbitration provision.[80] Further, even a valid arbitration clause in an employment contract does not prevent litigation from being brought by a federal agency on behalf of the employee.[81] In the consumer context, however, there is in fact no bargain and arbitration provisions are becoming universal. For example, all of the major American credit card companies, most banks, most home builders, and many service providers, including professional service providers, currently include an arbitration provision in their agreements.[82] As businesses realise the advantages of arbitration, more and more begin to include such provisions. Based solely on my personal experiences and anecdotal stories from friends and colleagues, it appears that today, most written consumer agreements contain an arbitration provision.

Second, commercial parties have the resources to influence legislators and government agencies to deal with problems through legislative or administrative rulings. For example, automobile dealers who found it unfair that they be forced to arbitrate recently successfully encouraged Congress to amend the federal Arbitration Act to prevent automobile manufacturers from imposing arbitration on dealerships.[83] Similarly, employees have labour organisations, as well as federal

---

80   Section 2 of the FAA requires that the arbitration provision be contained in a written contract. It is also interesting to note that some have argued that employers are better off not including an arbitration provision. See, for example, M.Z. Green, 'Debunking the Myth of Employer Advantage from Using Mandatory Arbitration for Discrimination Claims', *Rutgers L. J.*, 31 (2000): 399, at p. 470; ('The increasing use of mandatory arbitration by some employers has constituted an ill-advised departure from the overwhelmingly successful experience of employers in the court system').

81   See, for example, *Equal Employment Opportunity Commission* v. *Waffle House, Inc.*, 534 U.S. 279, 122 S.Ct. 754 (2002); (An agreement between an employer and an employee to arbitrate employment-related disputes does not bar the EEOC from pursuing victim-specific judicial relief, such as back-pay, reinstatement, and damages, in an ADA enforcement action).

82   See, for example, J. Harrington, Comment, 'To Litigate or Arbitrate? No Matter – The Credit Card Industry is Deciding For You', *J. Dispute Resolution* (2001): 101.

83   The Motor Vehicle Franchise Fairness Act has been codified at 15 U.S.C. §1226 and reads as follows:
§ 1226. Motor vehicle franchise contract dispute resolution process
(a) Election of arbitration.
(1) Definitions. For purposes of this subsection –
(A) the term 'motor vehicle' has the meaning given such term in section 30102(6) of title 49 of the United States Code; and
(B) the term 'motor vehicle franchise contract' means a contract under which a motor vehicle manufacturer, importer, or distributor sells motor vehicles to any other person for resale to an ultimate purchaser and authorizes such other person to repair and service the manufacturer's motor vehicles.

regulatory agencies such as the Equal Employment Opportunity Commission (EEOC), to represent their interests within legislative and regulatory communities. Consumers, on the other hand, have almost no effective lobbying group and little in the way of support from agencies such as the Federal Trade Commission. Consumers have historically relied upon litigation and the courts to provide relief from false, misleading, deceptive and unconscionable practices.

Finally, consumer law is a newer body of law and consequently is undergoing more changes than might be seen in other areas. Until 40 years ago, there were few consumer statutes and *caveat emptor* reigned. Federal and state consumer law is still being actively interpreted by the courts and common law doctrines of fraud, deceit, misrepresentation and warranty continue to undergo substantial change.

In other words, although pre-dispute mandatory arbitration may present problems in the context of commercial or employment agreements, consumer arbitration poses the greatest challenge to the American common law tradition. Consumers in the United States must rely more upon the courts to establish and refine rights. Yet at the same time, they are being precluded from the courts with greater frequency.

Conclusion

As discussed above, binding pre-dispute mandatory arbitration clauses are quickly becoming the norm in American consumer contracts. Mandatory arbitration is imposed on consumers who lack the knowledge or bargaining power knowingly to agree to waive their right to use the courts, and in a manner that imposes significant increased costs and substantial deterioration of substantive rights. For these reasons alone, steps should be taken to slow down or stop the advance of pre-dispute mandatory arbitration clauses in consumer contracts. But as this article has pointed out, there is an additional and perhaps more compelling reason businesses should not be allowed to unilaterally preclude access to the courts.

The American civil justice system relies on courts and juries to regulate the marketplace. Unlike many other countries, private lawsuits are the means by which

---

(2) Consent required. Notwithstanding any other provision of law, whenever a motor vehicle franchise contract provides for the use of arbitration to resolve a controversy arising out of or relating to such contract, arbitration may be used to settle such controversy only if after such controversy arises all parties to such controversy consent in writing to use arbitration to settle such controversy.

(3) Explanation required. Notwithstanding any other provision of law, whenever arbitration is elected to settle a dispute under a motor vehicle franchise contract, the arbitrator shall provide the parties to such contract with a written explanation of the factual and legal basis for the award.

Interestingly, many of those same dealers who found it unfair that they should be forced by the manufacturer to arbitrate, often impose arbitration on their customers.

American consumers are compensated for damage caused by over-reaching, and most American consumer protection laws have been enacted based on the premise that they will be enforced by private lawsuits in our courts.

The common law is the system that America has adopted and developed over the centuries for ensuring the law stays current with rapidly changing social and economic conditions. As Justice Harlan F. Stone noted: 'If one were to attempt to write a history of the law in the United States, it would largely be an account of the means by which the common–law system has been able to make progress through a period of rapid social and economic change.'[84] The American judiciary is much more than just a check on the legislative and executive branches of government. It is an independent branch of government, often looking out for the rights of those who lack the power or influence to receive the attention of our elected representatives. The American common law tradition is an essential part of the development and continuation of consumer protection;[85] arbitration destroys it.

Pre-dispute mandatory arbitration must not be allowed to preclude consumer access to the courts and circumvent the American civil justice system. Courts must be able to decide issues of statutory interpretation, and precedent must be established to maintain consistency of results and provide certainty in the decision making process of parties who must predict the result of legal challenges. For example, it is extremely doubtful any of the legal issues surrounding the use of credit cards and credit card agreements will again see the light of a courtroom. Thus, questions such as the one recently addressed by the United States Supreme Court in *Koons Buick GMC, Inc.* v. *Nigh*,[86] will be left to individual arbitrators, who will be free to decide the case as they see fit, with no consistency of results and no applicable standard the next time the same issue arises.

As I have noted elsewhere,[87] the only way to prevent the continued growth of arbitration and the degeneration of consumers' rights in the United States, is through a change in federal law, namely amending the Federal Arbitration Act. Current law assumes the validity of arbitration provisions and makes it extremely difficult to avoid enforcement. Exceptions to the current law, designed to ensure arbitration agreements are voluntary and consumers are provided a meaningful choice, must be enacted. The simplest change is to preclude pre-dispute arbitration clauses in consumer contracts, while permitting parties to agree to arbitration after

---

84   H.F. Stone, 'The Common Law in the United States', *Harv. L. Rev*, 50 (1936): 4, at 11.
85   Our common law tradition, while not perfect, generally ensures that parties to a dispute can rely on the fact that similar cases will be dealt with in a similar manner. The consistency and predictability of the common law is lost in arbitration.
86   350 U.S. 50 (2004), discussed at n. 24, and accompanying text.
87   See R.M. Alderman, 'Pre-Dispute Mandatory Arbitration in Consumer Contracts: A Call for Reform', *Houston L. Rev.*, 38 (2001): 1237, at 1264–7 (proposing amendments to the Federal Arbitration Act).

a dispute has arisen and other alternatives have been considered.[88] The law must ensure that American consumers retain the right to resolve disputes through the civil justice system, and that the common law tradition continues to be a viable part of the American system of justice. What are the chances that will soon happen?

On 12 July 2007, Senator Russell Feingold and Representative Hank Johnson introduced the Arbitration Fairness Act[89] in Congress. The Act prohibits the use of pre-dispute binding arbitration clauses in consumer and employment contracts. If enacted, it will restore the consumers' right to sue and ensure that American courts continue to play a significant role in the development of consumer rights. Hopefully, Congress will see the wisdom in this bill and promptly enact it. My fear, however, is that the business lobby is too strong for consumers to expect any prompt and favourable action.[90]

---

88   For example, Congress has recognized the 'unfairness' of arbitration clauses and prohibited the inclusion of pre-dispute arbitration clauses in contracts between automobile dealers and manufacturers. Motor Vehicle Franchise Contract Arbitration Fairness Act of 2002, 15 U.S.C. §1226. See, for example, *Volkswagen of America, Inc.* v. *Sud's of Peoria, Inc.*, 474 F.3d 966 (7th Cir. 2007).

89   Arbitration Fairness Act, S. 1782, H.R. 3010, 110th Cong. (2007).

90   On December 12, 2007, I testified before the Senate Judiciary Committee in support of the Arbitration Fairness Act. A copy testimony was based in large part on this article. A copy of the text and a video of my testimony may be found at http://www.peopleslawyer.net/arbitration.html. A copy of my testimony may also be found at, http://papers.ssrn.com/sol3/papers.cfm?abstract_id=1155245.

Part 2: Current Developments

9   The Unfair Commercial Practices Directive – Alternatives in UK Law

*Alan Barron**

Introduction

This chapter follows an earlier paper in which the role of soft law codes was considered in a consumer context.[1] There it was suggested that the concept of reasonable expectations could be employed to impose direct liability on a code subscriber for failure to comply with the terms of a code.[2] However, that paper was prepared prior to the publication of much of the material relating to the Directive on Unfair Commercial Practices ('the Directive').[3] The purpose of this chapter, therefore, is to consider the provisions of the Directive relating to soft law codes and their impact on code subscribers where they have failed to comply. Within the context of UK law, alternative means of imposing liability on code subscribers will also be considered. Liability will be discussed in two senses: firstly, civil liability directly enforceable by the consumer in the civil courts and, secondly, criminal liability under existing consumer protection legislation, enforceable by the State.

---

*   Lecturer in Commercial Law, University of Abertay, Dundee.

1   A. Barron, 'Reasonable Expectations, Good Faith and Self-Regulatory Codes', in G. Howells, A. Nordhausen, D. Parry and C. Twigg-Flesner (eds), *The Yearbook of Consumer Law 2007* (Aldershot, 2007), pp. 3–30.

2   This chapter is not concerned with liabilities imposed by code owners or ombudsmen which, in this context, might be described as forms of indirect liability. The chapter is concerned with rights that are directly enforceable in courts. For a chapter providing a detailed consideration of these indirect liabilities and the availability of judicial review see, P. O'Shea and C. Rickett, 'In Defence of Consumer Law: The Resolution of Consumer Disputes', *Sydney Law Review*, 28 (2006): 139.

3   Directive 2005/29/EC concerning unfair business-to-consumer commercial practices in the internal market and amending Council Directive 84/450/EEC, Directives 97/7/EC and 2002/65/EC of the European Parliament and the Council and Regulation (EC) No 2006/2004 of the European Parliament and of the Council.

The Terms of the Directive[4]

What is a code?

First, it will be useful to define a code for these purposes. The Directive refers to 'Codes of Conduct' which are defined in Article 2(f) as:

> [A]n agreement or set of rules not imposed by law, regulation or administrative provision of a Member State which defines the behaviour of traders who undertake to be bound by the code in relation to one or more particular commercial practices or business sectors.

From this definition, Howells was able to make a number of observations. The use of the word 'agreement' is unlikely to require agreement in a strict contractual sense. Indeed, it would seem that there is nothing to require that a code be in writing, although in practice written codes are apt to be the norm.[5] Further, a trader does not need to have formally signed up to a code. It would be sufficient to have agreed to follow an agreement satisfying the other required characteristics of a code.[6]

Who has responsibility?

Under the Directive, responsibility for codes is placed in the hands of what is termed a 'Code Owner', defined as: '[A]ny entity, including a trader or group of traders, which is responsible for the formulation and revision of a code of conduct and/or for monitoring compliance with the code by those who have undertaken to be bound by it.'[7]

The breadth of this definition raises an interesting point. Howells noted that it would be open to code owners to impose conditions on traders before they could claim to abide by a code. Being able to make such a claim is obviously significant as it may be a factor that influences a consumer's decision to transact with that trader.

---

4   It is not the purpose of this paper to provide an overview of the scheme and aims of the Directive. Instead, readers are directed to the *Yearbook of Consumer Law 2007* in which a range of papers considered the role of the Directive more generally. See also, G. Howells, H. Micklitz and T. Wilhelmsson, *European Fair Trading Law* (Aldershot, 2006); H. Collins, *The Forthcoming EC Directive on Unfair Commercial Practices: Contract, Consumer and Competition Law Implications* (The Hague, 2004) and M. Radeideh, *Fair Trading in EC Law: Information and Consumer Choice in the Internal Market* (Groeningen, 2005).
5   Howells, Micklitz and Wilhelmsson, p. 203.
6   Howells gives the example of the trader whose membership of a trade association binds him to its rules and conditions of membership, one of which could be compliance with a code. *Ibid.*, p. 203.
7   Article 2(g).

A code owner can require that a trader uses a particular redress scheme or pays a fee before being able to claim to comply with a code. If drafted into the code, it would then be misleading for the trader to fail to accept those conditions and claim compliance.[8] However, it might be questioned whether there are situations where a trader might fall through a gap with the result that the Directive does not apply. For instance, if the trader is required to pay a fee in order to be able to claim compliance but fails to do so because of a bank error or insolvency, what is the outcome? The claim of compliance may well have influenced a consumer's decision to transact. On that basis, the Directive would appear to be relevant. However, can liability be imposed where the reason for non-compliance is beyond the control of the trader or where imposition of liability would be financially futile? In other words there may be instances where a claim to be code compliant is *prima facie* misleading, but in reality is not. Arguably, the Directive would in any case impose liability in light of the provisions contained in Article 6.

Article 6

This Article imposes liability where a trader misleads a consumer. It provides, in relation to codes of conduct that:

> A commercial practice shall ... be regarded as misleading if, in its factual context, taking account of all its features and circumstances, it causes or is likely to cause the average consumer to take a transactional decision that he would not have taken otherwise, and it involves ...
> (b) non-compliance by the trader with commitments contained in codes of conduct by which the trader has undertaken to be bound, where:
> (i) the commitment is not aspirational but is firm and is capable of being verified, and
> (ii) the trader indicates in a commercial practice that he is bound by the code.

This provision is relatively narrow in scope.

> It is not concerned with whether there are legal means for ensuring compliance with codes, nor with whether non-compliance ... can be treated as unfair or misleading conduct ... It is simply concerned with the situation where a trader claims to be abiding by a code and then does not do so.[9]

This provision appears to go beyond the situation where the trader intended not to comply, and would cover mere non-compliance.[10] On this view, liability is, in effect strict. This may be questioned. The reference in the opening text of the Article

---

8   Howells, Micklitz and Wilhelmsson, p. 203.
9   *Ibid.*, p. 207.
10   *Ibid.*

to the factual context and all the facts and circumstances of the practice would suggest that intention may well be relevant. Mere non-compliance with a code would therefore not give rise to liability if it is not misleading. An example might help to illustrate this. One could imagine the situation where a trader had initially subscribed to a code, but later decided to withdraw that subscription. Indeed, it may have been withdrawn by the code owner. Early marketing material that is still in circulation might have referred to that subscription. Would the publication of later marketing material with no reference to code subscription countermand the earlier material, particularly where there is a time lag between a consumer receiving the material and making a transactional decision? It may be that it would be unfair to impose civil liability in these circumstances. However, under existing UK law, criminal liability could attach following the case of *Wings* v. *Ellis*.[11] In that case a travel tour operator was found guilty of the offence of making a false statement, notwithstanding that the mistake had been identified and attempts had been made to correct it.[12] Further, what if the trader or code owner published a circular or public advertisement stating that the trader no longer subscribed to a code? Clearly, it could be argued that the trader had no intention to mislead and took active steps to prevent consumers from being misled. Although the situation described may seem remote, the point is an important one. The Directive, like any piece of legislation, is apt to prove imperfect once in operation. The result is likely to be that there may be unusual situations that will fall outwith its scope. Later in this chapter I intend to consider alternative bases of liability. It will be argued that, notwithstanding the absence of liability under the Directive, there may be other ways in which a trader could be held liable for non-compliance with a code. First, it will be useful to consider in a little more detail the remaining provisions of Article 6.

Before a trader will be bound by a failure to abide by a code, his commitment to it must be firm and not aspirational. Much will, therefore, turn on the language the trader has chosen to express his commitments. It has been noted that the 'firm' aspect seems to have two components. First, the claim must amount to a binding undertaking, and second, it must be clear what is being promised.[13] It has also been noted that many codes are expressed in soft language, with terms such as 'will do our best' and 'will aim to provide', featuring prominently.[14] The result is likely to be that many cases will involve a debate about the language employed by the trader and whether it is sufficient to amount to a firm commitment. This aspect may ultimately give traders the greatest opportunity to market their subscription to codes, but in such a way that it will not give rise to liability. Again, this raises

---

11   [1985] A.C. 272.
12   Under s. 14(1)(a) of the Trade Descriptions Act 1968. However, later it will be noted
        that this provision is likely to be repealed by the legislation that will implement the
        Directive in UK law.
13   Howells, Micklitz and Wilhelmsson, p. 209.
14   *Ibid.*

questions about how else consumers might seek to impose liability where the Directive falls short.[15]

The trader's commitment to a code must also be capable of verification. In most cases it seems likely that this will be straightforward. Howells does, however, note that problems may arise where the commitment is subjective. He gives the example of a commitment to deal politely with customers. Since perceptions of politeness are inherently subjective, it may be impossible to objectively verify such commitments.[16]

Finally, Article 6 also requires that a firm, non-aspirational, verifiable commitment be accompanied by an indication in a commercial practice that a trader is bound by a code. Again, this ought to be straightforward. Many traders will no doubt refer to code subscriptions in their marketing materials, thus providing evidence of an indication that they are bound. Less clear will be situations where the trader has only verbally indicated that he is bound by a code of conduct. Further, the indication must have arisen through a commercial practice aimed at a consumer.[17]

From this short review of Article 6(2) one can see that the consumer has considerable ground to cover in establishing that a trader's failure to comply with a code of conduct should give rise to liability. If any of the components are missing, the consumer's claim will fail. As has been identified, there are likely to be novel situations not considered by the drafters that will undermine the claims of consumers. Before considering the possible alternative means of holding traders to codes, there is one final feature of the Directive that is relevant.

Practices that are always unfair

The Annex to the Directive contains a long list of trading practices that will always be unfair. Those concerning codes of conduct are:

1. Claiming to be a signatory to a code of conduct when the trader is not.
2. Displaying a trust mark, quality mark or equivalent without having obtained the necessary authorization.
3. Claiming that a code of conduct has an endorsement from a public or other body which it does not have.

This seems uncontroversial since it imposes a species of strict liability. Intention is not relevant in the way in which it might be under Article 6.

---

15 Howells does, however, note that the provision must be sensibly interpreted so as not to deprive it of any force whatsoever. Otherwise, as he says, traders will jump on to any ambiguity or caveat to evade liability. *Ibid.*

16 *Ibid.*, pp. 209–210.

17 *Ibid*, p. 210. Thus, claims made elsewhere, for example in trade journals or annual reports, would not be sufficient.

Alternative Forms of Liability

In this section I will consider alternative means of imposing liability on traders where they have failed to follow a code, but for whatever reason, the Directive does not apply. Some limited examples of when such situations might arise were given above.

Civil liability – implication of the terms of a code

Howells has suggested that the terms of a code can be implied into the contractual arrangements between a trader and consumer. If this is so, the result would be that a breach of the code by the trader would be a breach of contract.[18] The case cited in support of that proposition was *Bowerman* v. *Association of British Travel Agents Ltd*.[19] This was a decision of the English Court of Appeal. Bowerman was a pupil at a secondary school. She had booked a place on a skiing holiday organised by her school, paying for the holiday herself. The price included a sum representing an insurance premium. The school booked the holiday through a tour operator that was a member of the Association of British Travel Agents ('ABTA'). A feature of ABTA membership was that if a tour operator became insolvent ABTA would refund any monies that had been paid for the aborted holiday. That is what happened in this case. The tour operator became insolvent and a claim was made to ABTA for a refund. ABTA gave a refund, but did so subject to a deduction of £10 to represent the insurance premium, which ABTA claimed was not covered by its scheme. Bowerman raised an action to recoup the £10 based on the argument that the ABTA scheme ought to cover that also. The sum involved seems small, but this case acted as a test case for a number of others where ABTA had made refunds, subject to the insurance premium deduction.[20]

Codes of conduct were a feature as tour operators, when selling the holiday packages, advertised that they were members of ABTA and were thus covered by the ABTA scheme. Indeed, it is still common practice for tour operators to publish details of the ABTA scheme in their offices. Ultimately, the decision came down to a consideration of the specific terms of the ABTA scheme contained in the notices displayed in tour operators' premises.

This was a majority decision of Waite L.J. and Hobhouse L.J.[21] Lord Justice Waite began by considering the perspective from which the ABTA notice should be considered. The perspective was said to be that of the 'member of the public'.[22]

---

18   *Ibid*, p. 197.
19   [1996] C.L.C. 451. Unfortunately, Howells does not analyse the decision, merely referring to it in a footnote.
20   See the editorial comment in *International Travel Law Journal* (1997): 87.
21   Hirst L.J. dissenting.
22   [1996] C.L.C. 451, at 456.

However, his Lordship went further, elucidating the characteristics that such a person might possess. He said:

> Such a reader would be aware of the vulnerability of agents and operators in a highly competitive market where failures are not uncommon, and of the disappointment and financial loss which members of the public have experienced in the past as a result of sudden cancellations following financial collapse. The reader would appreciate, too, that ABTA is not a charity or a friendly society, but (as its full name makes clear) an association, for the purposes of trade, of persons and firms carrying on the business of travel agent. He or she would, further, be aware that it is in the interests of such an association to win trade for its constituent members by inspiring public confidence. There should also be imputed to the reader common knowledge that those who wish to disclaim legal liability for public representations frequently say so – in large print or in small. Finally, it is to be assumed that such a person would read the whole notice – neither cursorily nor with pedantic analysis of every nuance of its wording, but with the ordinary care to be expected of the average customer who is applying money they could not easily afford to lose in buying a holiday which it would be a serious disappointment to forego.[23]

This seems very straightforward. The general point is that the perspective is that of the reasonable person, taking account of all the circumstances. In this case, it was the circumstances, rather than the perspective, that caused the difficulty. The problem arose because the ABTA notice contained language that varied in tone. In parts it was in general terms, in others it undertook to use best endeavours and in others still it used language that was apparently binding in nature. Thus the lack of consistency in tone and language made it unclear whether ABTA intended the notice to create legal relations or whether the notice merely expressed ABTA's ambitions for its scheme.

Regarding the potentially binding nature of notices displayed to the public, the starting point in UK law is the early case of *Carlill* v. *Carbolic Smoke Ball Co.*[24] The smoke ball was a device intended to ward off the influenza virus. In its advertising the company promised a reward to anyone who used the smoke ball according to the instructions for a period of time and yet still contracted influenza. Mrs Carlill contracted the virus having used the smoke ball as instructed. The company resisted her claim, arguing that the promise of a reward in its advertising was not intended to create legally binding obligations. The company was held liable to make the payment due to the unequivocal language employed in the advertising.

Lord Justice Waite felt that this case was unhelpful in resolving the issue of the ABTA notice as it did not use unequivocal language, but language that was capable of a range of meanings, only some of which were unequivocal.[25]

---

23   *Ibid.*
24   [1893] 1 Q.B. 256.
25   [1996] C.L.C. 451, at 457.

Ultimately, his Lordship was persuaded that the ordinary member of the public would understand the terms of the notice as 'importing an intention to create legal relations with customers of ABTA members'.[26]

The exact wording of the ABTA notice said that: 'Where holidays or other travel arrangements have not yet commenced at the time of failure, ABTA arranges for you to be reimbursed the money you have paid in respect of your holiday arrangements.' It was held that the ordinary person would regard this as a clear promise and wide enough to cover any amount included in the price to represent insurance premiums.

Lord Hobhouse reached the same result, although he was persuaded that the *Carlill* case was of greater relevance. This was because ABTA's arguments before the court mirrored those used by the company in the *Carlill* case.[27]

Looking at this more generally, a number of points can be made. It is clear that the court does not view this as a matter of implication of terms into a contract. The question of whether the terms of a code can be implied into a contract with a consumer was dealt with in my earlier article.[28] However, a fundamental point has to be made. It is not easy to imply terms into any contract under UK law as the legal threshold for doing so is very high.

The issue for the court in *Bowerman* was whether the notice was sufficiently precise to amount to a legally binding offer. Indeed this is the view taken in all of the academic commentary on this case.[29] What is significant about this case is that, unlike the advertisement in *Carlill*, the ABTA notice involved the use of mixed language, only some of which was unequivocal in its terms. In light of this, *Bowerman* seems to represent a relaxation of the law following *Carlill* where the language used was entirely unequivocal. As one commentator has said: 'Clearly issues of construction of the particular words will remain important. However, manufacturers' warranties and the like are very influential in people's market choices and should generally be a matter of obligation not discretion for those who issue them.'[30] Thus, if the document *as a whole* coveys an impression to be bound by its terms, then the party issuing the document will be bound.

It is also important to note that the terms of the code in *Bowerman* were enforced against the code owner, not the code subscriber. In the present context, where the focus is on the liability of traders to consumers, that case might be

---

26   *Ibid.*
27   Ibid., p. 459.
28   Barron, 'Reasonable Expectations, Good Faith and Self-Regulatory Codes'.
29   See M. McMeel, 'Contractual Intention: The Smoke Ball Strikes Back', *L.Q.R.*, 113 (1997): 47; S. Mason, 'Carlill v. Carbolic Smoke Ball Company Revisited', *Commercial Lawyer*, 4 (1996): 6; B. Thomas, 'The Carbolic Smoke Ball Case', *Legal Executive* (1996): 30; R. Lawson, 'Commercial Reporter', *Sol. J.* 48 (1995): 1260; 'Editorial, The Ruined Holiday', *Consumer Law Today* (1996): 1; M. Whincup, 'Case Commentary', *Consumer Law Journal*, 4 (1996): 6.
30   McMeel: 49.

thought to be of limited assistance. However, that is not to say that where a code states that the trader will do something in terms sufficiently precise as to amount to a binding offer that they cannot be bound. Ultimately, it will come down the wording in the particular document.

Returning to the terms of the Directive, the effect of the *Bowerman* decision is very similar to the effects of Article 6(2)(b). However, due to the precise requirements of the Directive where it must be shown that the trader's code commitments are not aspirational, but firm and verifiable, it may be easier to establish a commitment at common law following *Bowerman*. It will ultimately come down to how courts view the terms 'aspirational' and 'firm' when interpreting the Directive. If interpreted restrictively, the view might be taken that these terms mean that a document that uses a mixture of equivocal and unequivocal language might not be sufficiently 'firm' as to give rise to binding obligations. However, as Howells has pointed out, it seems likely that a more relaxed interpretation will prevail. Nonetheless, a consumer, when raising an action against a trader, might be well served to have a common law line of argument to fall back on should the court reject an argument based on the Directive.

An additional argument might, however, be open to a consumer. This concerns the potential existence of a collateral contract.[31] The advantage of this is that the collateral contract would exist between the consumer and the trader and would be enforceable directly against the trader. This often arises where there is a written contract, supplemented by further oral representations amounting to a separate contract.[32] This will not apply where the collateral contract varies or contradicts a term set out in the primary contract.[33] In the circumstances under discussion, one could see that, in addition to the primary contract created through the promises made in a code by a traders' organisation, representations by the trader could amount to an enforceable collateral contract. Arguably, a representation by a trader that they always adhere to the terms of a code could potentially import the terms of the code into a collateral contract.

A further point of similarity between the Directive and the common law position concerns the hypothetical consumer who has been induced to enter a contract by a trader's claims relating to codes. As already noted, in *Bowerman*, the perspective taken was that of the ordinary member of the public. The perspective in the Directive is that of the 'average consumer'. Article 2(a) defines a consumer as 'any natural person who, in commercial practices covered by [the] Directive is acting for purposes which are outside his trade, business or profession'. However, although the 'average consumer' is referred to throughout the Directive, in particular in Articles 5 and 6, that term is not defined. Instead, recourse must be had to the case-law of the European Court of Justice where that concept was

---

31   For an overview of this area in English law, see G.H. Treitel, '*The Law of Contract*', 11th Edn (London, 2003), pp. 199–200.

32   See, for example, *Mann* v. *Nunn* (1874) 30 L.T. 526.

33   *Angell* v. *Duke* (1874) 32 L.T. 320 and *Henderson* v. *Arthur* [1907] 1 K.B. 10.

developed.[34] It should be noted, however, that rather than adopting a unitary standard throughout, the Directive appears to contain a variable standard. Articles 5 and 6, for example, employ differing versions of the 'average consumer'. The Articles differ in that Article 5 goes somewhat further. In addition to the 'average consumer' test it also refers, as an alternative, to the average member of the group when a commercial practice is directed to a particular group of consumers.[35] In addition, there is reference to the protection of vulnerable consumers.[36] No reference to these additional considerations is made in Article 6. This obviously raises the question whether a variable standard applies throughout the Directive[37] and is to be contrasted with the UK conception of the average consumer discussed above.

The fundamental features of the average consumer are that he or she is reasonably well-informed and reasonably observant and circumspect. Although it was originally proposed to include a definition of average consumer within the Directive, that approach was ultimately rejected. It has been observed that this could mean one of two things. On the one hand, this could suggest that the Directive represents a new beginning and therefore departs from pre-existing notions of the average consumer. On the other hand, it could mean that the term average consumer is so well understood that it goes without saying that the definition of the European Court of Justice is to be adopted. It seems likely that the latter approach will be preferred.[38] This is particularly so when one considers the concern that to enshrine the definition in the Directive could prevent it developing over time in line with the jurisprudence of the Court of Justice.[39]

The view that the average consumer is reasonably well-informed, observant and circumspect is virtually identical to Waite L.J.'s conception of the ordinary member of the public. Both of these hypothetical individuals would no doubt read the terms of any notice adverting to codes of practice. They would also be reasonably well aware of the market conditions against which the commitments in those codes have to be understood. Nothing therefore turns on whether one is an average consumer under the Directive or an ordinary member of the public at common law. This might be cited as an example of how the average consumer

---

34　Case C-470/93 *Mars* [1995] ECR I-1923, Case C-210/96 *Gut Springenheide* [1998] ECR I-4657, Case C-303/97 *Seketkelleriei Kessler* [1999] ECR I-513, Case C-220/98 *Lifting-Crème* [2000] ECR I-117. See also the commentaries in Howells, Micklitz and Wilhelmsson, chapters 3 and 4.

35　Article 5(2)(b).

36　Article 5(3).

37　For an analysis of these provisions see Howells, Micklitz and Wilhelmsson, pp. 111–16 and 131–6. The authors suggest, however, that the 'average consumer' will be the norm, and the additional considerations in Article 5 will be regarded as the exceptions. Thus, the existing case-law of the European Court of Justice on this matter would remain in point.

38　Howells, Micklitz and Wilhelmsson, pp. 111–12.

39　Radeideh, p. 255.

standard, when so interpreted, assists consumer protection, contrary to the general view that it weakens it.

One difference, however, is that the Directive takes express account of circumstances where a trading practice is aimed at vulnerable consumers. The result is that where the practice is likely to materially distort the economic behaviour of a particularly vulnerable group of consumers, the perspective taken is that of the average member of that vulnerable group.[40] On the face of it, this seems wider than the 'ordinary member of the public' perspective at common law. In reality, this is unlikely to be the case. In *Bowerman*, the consumer was a school pupil, exactly the type of consumer who might be unduly influenced by certain trading practices. Indeed, in that case it was accepted in evidence that the consumer was aware of the existence and general import of the ABTA scheme and had made her transactional decision accordingly. Although the court did not differentiate between vulnerable and 'other' consumers, the ordinary member of the public perspective, given its objective and fact-based nature, is broad enough to take account of the vulnerabilities of certain groups of consumers. Again, therefore, nothing turns on whether the common law approach, or the approach of the Directive, is preferred.

Nonetheless, taking the pessimistic view that the Directive may be found wanting once implemented in national legislation, it is worth reiterating that a common law argument may be a useful bolster for consumers pursuing traders for failure to live up to commitments expressed in codes of conduct. Alternative forms of redress exercisable directly by the consumer become particularly important when one considers the approach of the Directive to the availability of compensation.

Article 13 requires Member States to lay down penalties for infringement of national unfair commercial practices legislation. There is also a requirement to ensure that all necessary steps concerning enforcement of these provisions are taken and that any penalties should be effective, proportionate and dissuasive. As to whether this would result in a direct claim for compensation by a consumer for breach of the provisions of the Directive will depend upon the attitude of individual Member States and the extent to which they are willing to grant individual consumers the right to sue traders directly.[41] However, it has been observed that the Directive generally aims for collective protection of the consumer interest rather than individual protection.[42] Indeed, this approach is reflected in the draft Consumer Protection from Unfair Trading Regulations 2008. Whilst not yet in force, the Regulations may be taken as indicative of the UK attitude on this issue. Nowhere do they provide a mechanism for a consumer to raise a civil action directly against a trader for breach of the duty to trade fairly. The Regulations are predominantly criminal in character, containing a range of offences and penalties

---

40   Article 5(3).
41   Howells, Micklitz and Wilhelmsson, pp. 221–2.
42   *Ibid.*

enforceable against a trader who engages in unfair commercial practices.[43] The right of enforcement is reserved to 'enforcement authorities'.[44] The issue of compensation only arises where a person is prosecuted and acquitted of an offence and any goods seized as a result of the prosecution are lost, damaged or deteriorate.[45]

So far we have been considering civil remedies exercisable by a consumer. In the following section, criminal liability exercisable by the State will be considered.

Criminal liability – trade descriptions offences

So far, the alternative arguments have concerned a means of creating direct liability against a trader. However, there are alternatives in UK law by which liability can be created indirectly by enforcement bodies, rather than by a consumer. For example, section 14(1) of the Trade Descriptions Act 1968 makes it a criminal offence in the course of a trade or business for any person to make a statement which he knows to be false.[46] It is also a criminal offence recklessly to make a statement which is false where that statement relates *inter alia* to the provision of services, the nature of the services provided, the timing of the provision of services, and the examination of services.[47] However, it should be noted that once the Directive is implemented in the UK this may well result in the repeal of the existing criminal sanctions.[48]

Clearly, section 14 appears wide enough to include statements made by a trader relating to subscription to a code where that statement is false or the trader ought to have known that it was false. This view is supported by case-law. For example

---

43   The offences are contained in Draft Regs 8–12, and the penalties are contained in Draft Reg. 13. There is, however, a due diligence defence is contained in Draft Reg. 17.
44   Draft Reg. 2.
45   Draft Reg. 26.
46   Section 14(1)(a).
47   Section 14(1)(b)(i)–(v). For an overview of the statutory provisions and the explanatory case-law, see G. Howells and S. Weatherill, *Consumer Protection Law*, 2nd Edn (Aldershot, 2005), chapter 8.
48   Part 3 of the Draft Consumer Protection from Unfair Trading Regulations 2008 would introduce criminal offences relating to general unfair commercial practices (Reg. 8) and misleading actions of omissions (Regs 9 and 10), together with offences concerning aggressive commercial practices (Reg. 11) and specific practices included in a Schedule to the Regulations (Reg. 12). Schedule 1 of the draft Regulations includes the offence of claiming to be a signatory to a code when that is not the case. The types of conduct giving rise to criminal liability in the Schedule mirror the unfair practices listed in the Annex to the Directive. In addition, Schedule 2, Part 1, of the draft Regulations explicitly states that s. 14 of the Trade Descriptions Act 1968 would cease to have effect.

in *Architects Registration Council* v. *Breeze*[49] a consumer engaged the services of, what he thought was, a qualified architect. The engagement was made on the basis of an entry in a telephone directory where, after the individual's name, there was stated a series of letters indicating membership of a professional body. It transpired that the individual was, in reality, only a student and was not therefore entitled to describe himself as an architect. As the Lord Chief Justice put it in explaining why an offence had been committed:

> [S]uppose that a motor mechanic sets up in business to repair motor cars, and suppose that he announces to his prospective customers that he did a five-year apprenticeship with Rolls Royce when that is not the fact. We think that in a case of that kind it could perfectly properly be said that the man in question, in the course of a trade or business, had made a statement which he knew to be false and that it was a statement as to the provision of services which he offered, because it goes without saying that a qualified man is likely, in general, to do a better job than an unqualified man, and the fact that a man has qualifications such as an architect or an apprentice with five years' experience with Rolls Royce, is the sort of factor which goes to the likely quality of the service which he will perform, and is, we think, without any straining of language, properly to be taken to be within the term that the statement is made as to the provision of services ...[50]

One can see the analogy between this situation and the situation where a trader claims to subscribe to a code but in fact does not. The statutory provision creates criminal liability for making false statements as to the quality of services. The existence of professional qualifications is, according to the court, a factor central to the quality of the services to be provided. By analogy therefore, if a trader were to falsely claim compliance with a code of conduct which contains commitments as to the nature and quality of the services or goods to be provided, that also would amount to a criminal offence.

Of interest also is that liability can be imposed even where the false statement did not induce the consumer to enter the contract but was, in fact, made after the contract was concluded.[51]

Useful as such a criminal provision may be; one might question the relevance of this in a field where private law rights are primarily at issue. However, there is an

---

49 (1973) 57 Cr. App. R. 654. See also *Re V.G. Vehicles (Telford) Limited* (1981) 89 ITSA Monthly Review 91 in which a motor dealer was found guilty of an offence under s. 14(1) of the 1968 Act by falsely claiming to have complied with the Motor Industry Code of Practice. See Weatherill, *Consumer Protection Law*, p. 591 for a short commentary. In any case, should the Draft Consumer Protection from Unfair Trading Regulations 2008 be implemented, these cases would be impliedly overruled.

50 *Ibid*, p. 658.

51 *Breed* v. *Cluett* [1970] 2 Q.B. 459. In this case the builder of a house falsely claimed, after building had commenced, that defects would be covered by the ten-year guarantee provided by the National House-builders Registration Council.

important evidential point that can be made here. In the UK, a criminal conviction can be used as conclusive evidence in a subsequent civil suit.[52] That being so, where a consumer's civil claim follows upon a criminal conviction of a trader under the Trade Descriptions Act, this could pave the way for the successful resolution of a civil dispute in the consumer's favour.

Conclusion

The suggested means of imposing direct liability are based on the pessimistic view that the Directive may not find a solution in every case. It may be that once implemented in national legislation, the Directive will prove to be more effective than this chapter suggests. If so, all is well and good. That said it must also be borne in mind that the Directive is only concerned with unfair commercial practices that affect consumers. It is not concerned with such practices as they affect business-to-business transactions, no matter how small the consumer business might be. This is not the place to explore arguments about extending consumer legislation to small businesses.[53] However, the arguments set out above would be of potentially greater use to the consumer business where the supplier has failed to meet their stated commitments in a code of practice.

A further point of relevance in relation to the potential impact of the Directive in the UK concerns the maximal harmonisation nature of the Directive.[54] The first point to make is that the UK is very familiar with, and extensively uses, codes of conduct as a means of market regulation. This is to be contrasted with the position in other Member States where the use of codes is much less extensive and the legal position much less sophisticated.[55] That is not to say that some Member States do not have an equally sophisticated position to the UK concerning codes. Rather, the point is a simple one: those States that rely extensively upon codes will find the provisions of the Directive discussed above of much greater relevance than those that do not. One potential consequence of this is that the UK (and some other States) may well figure prominently in the development of the jurisprudence on codes of conduct in the future.

---

52   Civil Evidence Act 1968, s. 11. See H.M. Malik, J.Auburn and R. Bagshaw, *Phipson on Evidence*, 16th Edn (London, 2005), chapter 44 for a commentary on the operation of the statutory provisions and the accompanying case law.
53   For a paper supporting that argument, see E. Hondius, 'The Notion of Consumer: European Union versus Member States', *Sydney Law Review*, 28 (2006): 89.
54   Created by Article 4, the internal market clause. For a discussion of the maximal harmonisation nature of the Directive, see Howells, Micklitz and Wilhelmsson, chapter 2 and G. Howells, 'The Rise of European Consumer Law – Whither National Consumer Law?', *Sydney Law Review*, 28 (2006): 63.
55   Howells, Micklitz and Wilhelmsson, pp. 197–8. The author uses German law as the comparator, citing the paper by G. Teubner, 'Legal Irritants: Good Faith in British Law or How Unifying Law Ends Up in New Divergencies', *Modern Law Review*, 61 (1998): 11. See also, I. Ramsay, 'Consumer Law, Regulatory Capitalism and the "New Learning" in Regulation', *Sydney Law Review*, 28 (2006): 9.

However, if the point of maximal harmonisation is to provide a level playing field across Member States, it might be argued that consumers in the UK will be better protected than those in States where codes are less significant. Consumers in those States will be forced to rely primarily upon the protections contained in Articles 5 and 6(1). The Article 6(2) protections discussed above will be broadly irrelevant, or at least much less useful than in the UK. The corollary of this is that UK traders, who operate in markets where code subscription is the norm rather than the exception, will find that they are thus more heavily regulated that some of their European counterparts. Arguably, this rather subverts the purpose of maximal harmonisation.

There is no doubt that, from a consumer perspective, the Directive is to be welcomed. However, the purpose of this chapter has been to sound a cautionary note. As already noted, it is only once it has been implemented in national legislation and national courts have had an opportunity to test its effectiveness in fact-specific situations, that any real deficiencies will become apparent. For that reason, it has been worth considering at this stage whether there are any alternative forms of direct liability that can be utilised against traders for failure to comply with a code of conduct. In addition, it must also be considered that the UK approach to implementation, discussed above, does not seem to allow direct claims for compensation by consumers. Should the Directive prove a resounding success in practice, then these arguments may prove to be redundant. Taking a more pessimistic view, however, one might argue that to be forewarned is to be forearmed. Only time will tell.

10 Recent Amendments to Maltese Consumer Law – Transposition of the Unfair Commercial Practices Directive and Changes to the Regulatory Regime

*Paul Edgar Micallef**

Background

On 29 January 2008 Act Number II of 2008 amending the Consumer Affairs Act, the Commercial Code and the Doorstep Contracts Act[1] was enacted.[2] The main objects of these amendments are to transpose the Unfair Commercial Practices Directive[3] ('UCP Directive'), to ensure the proper transposition of a number of European Union ('EU') consumer protection directives and to improve upon the existing regulatory tools.[4] Malta, as a member of the EU, was required to apply the measures contained in the UCP Directive by not later 12 December 2007.[5] The process to comply with the requirements of this Directive was initiated in May 2007 when Government issued a public consultative document with proposals to transpose the UCP Directive and to introduce other measures relating primarily to compliance and regulatory matters.[6] As part of this document Government also submitted for public consultation various draft laws. These included a law transposing the UCP Directive which also catered for the introduction of

---

*   Dr. Micallef is a member of *l-Ghaqda tal-Konsumaturi* and is the Chief Legal Adviser to the Malta Communications Authority.
1   This chapter reflects only his views.
     Respectively Chapters 378, 13 and 317 of the Laws of Malta.
2   The Act provides that unless otherwise provided, its provisions shall be deemed to have come into force on 12 December 2007.
3   Directive 2005/29/EC of the European Parliament and of the Council of 11 May 2005 concerning unfair business-to-consumer commercial practices in the internal market.
4   See the objects and reasons of Bill No. 112 presented before Parliament on 16 November 2007.
5   See UCP Directive, Article 19.
6   The consultation was issued on 10 May 2007 and the general public was given up to 30 May 2007 to respond.

administrative fines and for the creation of a new appeals board[7] to deal with contestations of decisions taken by the Director of Consumer Affairs relating to unfair commercial practices, a law on product liability and other laws amending the Consumer Affairs Act, the Commercial Code and the Doorstep Contracts Act.[8] Subsequently on 16 November 2007 a Bill entitled the Consumer Affairs (Amendment) Act was published in the Government Gazette[9] thereby initiating the legislative process before Parliament, culminating in the enactment of Act II of 2008.

Act II of 2008, whilst including many of the proposals made in the consultation undertaken by Government, introduces some important changes to those proposals. It consists of amendments to three laws namely the Consumer Affairs Act, the Commercial Code and the Doorstep Contracts Act. Unlike what was originally proposed, the bulk of the changes are included as amendments to the Consumer Affairs Act, with the transposition of the UCP Directive being incorporated as a new Part to the Consumer Affairs Act, whereas the proposal to have separate laws on unfair commercial practices and on product liability is done away with.[10] The changes originally proposed to the Commercial Code and to the Doorstep Contracts Act have been retained.

Changes to Enforcement and a New Appellate Forum

Act II of 2008 focuses strongly on the strengthening of the enforcement regime. The UCP Directive requires Member States to provide for penalties that are 'effective, proportionate and dissuasive' and to take 'all necessary measures to ensure that national provisions adopted in the application of the Directive are enforced'.[11] The amendments to the Consumer Affairs Act, in adherence to these requirements, improve significantly on the previous enforcement tools and sanctions, primarily as a result of the introduction of administrative fines. The

---

7   The nomenclature of this tribunal was the Unfair Commercial Practices Appeals Tribunal. As proposed, this tribunal would have had a remit to hear appeals from decisions of the Director relating to any breach of the law transposing the UCP Directive including a decision imposing administrative fines.

8   There was no official communication about the responses received to this consultation.

9   Bill No. 112 of 2007. Most of the legislative proposals in the Bill have been retained in Act II of 2008 with the only notable additions being those concerning the Consumer Claims Tribunal.

10   The proposal in the consultation of May 2007 was to delete Part VII of the Consumer Affairs Act on liability for defective products and rewrite that Part as a new separate law on product liability. The reason given for this proposal was to clarify that the remedies available under Part VII: 'are available to all members of the general public, irrespective of whether or not they are "consumers"'.

11   UCP Directive, Article 13.

Director of Consumer Affairs is now empowered to impose an administrative fine on any person who is found to have committed an infringement of the Consumer Affairs Act or of any regulations issued under that Act. The quantum of such fine may vary from between a minimum of 465.87 Euros to a maximum of 46587.47 Euros.[12] Furthermore, in case of non-compliance with a compliance order, the Director may also impose a daily fine of not more than 232.94 Euros for each day of non-compliance.[13] What is especially noteworthy is that the law also establishes parameters to guide the Director in determining the quantum of the fine to apply for any given infringement. Hence gravity and duration of the infringement or the amount of gain improperly made as a result of the infringement are considered as aggravating factors and consequently the Director may impose a higher administrative fine than the basic amount established at law; whereas evidence that the non-compliant person took adequate measures to reduce the negative effects of the infringement he committed is considered to be a mitigating circumstance.[14] The main shortcoming is that, whilst the introduction of administrative fines is a welcome measure, the maximum fine of 46,587 Euros[15] is too low to be adequately dissuasive in all instances of non-compliance.

The amendments to the Consumer Affairs Act detail the process that the Director of Consumer Affairs has to follow when investigating an alleged infringement whereby the Director is required to inform the person investigated of the alleged infringement giving that person a minimum of 15 days in which to make his submissions.[16] In case of urgency, where there is risk of immediate and serious harm to the collective interests of consumers, the Director may order interim measures to remedy the situation prior to the taking of a final decision.[17] The Director, apart from undertaking investigations of his initiative, may also do so upon a 'reasonable allegation in writing' of an infringement of the Consumer Affairs Act or of any regulations made under that Act.[18] The law in this regard does not place any restrictions as to who may make such allegations and whether the complaining person needs to show that he has somehow been negatively impacted by the alleged infringement.

---

12   Consumer Affairs Act, Article 106A(1).

13   *Ibid.*, Article 106A(1).

14   *Ibid.*, Second Schedule.

15   The previous maximum fine was half that amount. The new figure of 46,587 Euros reflects the fine of 20,000 Maltese Liri, as the enactment of Act II of 2008 was caught in between the changeover from the former Maltese lira currency to the Euro currency, which became legal tender as of 1 January 2008.

16   Consumer Affairs Act, Article 14A. The Director has the option of seeking an undertaking in lieu of taking a decision finding that the person concerned has committed an infringement of the law.

17   *Ibid.*, Article 14B.

18   *Ibid.*, Article 12A.

Under Part X of the Consumer Affairs Act, entitled 'Compliance Orders',[19] the Director can now also issue a compliance order against any person engaging or proposing to engage in any unfair commercial practice. In doing so, the Director may require that person to discontinue or refrain from the practice or to take any measures as may be specified in the order. The Director, in his order, may further require that person to make a corrective statement.[20] Significantly the list of entities that may now request the Director to issue a compliance order have been extended to include independent public bodies which have an interest in ensuring the protection of the collective interest of consumers in Malta or in any other EU Member State, voluntary organisations in other EU Member States whose purpose is to protect the collective interest of consumers and any qualified entity in any other EU Member State recognised as such.[21]

One notable innovation, introduced by these amendments, is the establishment of a new adjudicative tribunal entitled the Consumer Affairs Appeals Board. This Appeals Board, which is appointed by the Prime Minister, is composed of three persons namely a chairman who must be an advocate of at least seven years practice and two other members able 'to properly assess the fairness or otherwise of commercial practices'.[22] The Appeals Board is independent in the performance of its functions and appeals may be presented to it from a decision, order or measure that the Director may take under the Consumer Affairs Act,[23] including any decision taken by the Director relating to the issue of a compliance order or the imposition of an administrative fine.[24] Any decision of the Appeals Board

---

19 This Part of the Consumer Affairs Act transposes Directive 98/27/EC of the European Parliament and of the Council of 19 May 1998 on injunctions for the protection of consumers' interests. The legislative measures transposing that Directive were first enacted in 2000 by amending the Consumer Affairs Act. The present amendments complete that transposition process in line also with most recent legislative developments in the EU including the application of the Injunctions Directive to the UCP Directive.

20 Consumer Affairs Act, Article 94(1)(b). There is a similar power requiring corrective statements in relation to any order issued to ensure compliance with any provision of the Consumer Affairs Act, any regulations made under that Act or any other consumer law as the Minister responsible for consumer affairs may designate, see Consumer Affairs Act, Article 94(1)(c).

21 The nomenclature previously used was that of 'qualifying bodies'. This has now been replaced by the term 'qualified entities'. See Consumer Affairs Act, Article 2, definition of the term 'qualified entity'. Previously only consumer associations, duly recognised under the Consumer Affairs Act, and any other bodies, whether constituted in Malta or elsewhere as may be designated by the Minister, were recognised as 'qualifying bodies'.

22 Consumer Affairs Act, Article 110A.

23 *Ibid.*, Article 110B.

24 The Appeals Board may, on appeal, confirm, revoke or change a compliance order on any terms or conditions it considers appropriate. See Consumer Affairs Act, Article

may, in turn, be appealed from on a point of law before the Court of Appeal in its inferior jurisdiction.[25]

The Transposition of the UCP Directive

The transposition of the UCP Directive has been undertaken by inclusion of a new Part to the Consumer Affairs Act[26] using similar, if not identical wording, to that used in the Directive. Articles 51A to 51E of the Consumer Affairs Act effectively replicate Articles 2 (definitions), 5 (prohibition of unfair commercial practices), 6 (misleading actions), 7 (misleading omissions), 8 (aggressive commercial practices) and 9 (use of harassment, coercion and undue influence) of the UCP Directive, whereas the First Schedule of the Consumer Affairs Act faithfully transposes the list of commercial practices which in all circumstances are considered as unfair as carried in the Annex to the UCP Directive. It is pertinent to note that prior to these amendments, the Consumer Affairs Act did have a provision stating that consumers are entitled 'to protection from unlawful or unfair trading practices'. This provision, which has been retained, is not directly enforceable at law, and is considered to be a declaration of principle laying down a basic consumer right which is to be adhered to in the interpretation and implementation of the Consumer Affairs Act and of any regulations made under that Act.[27]

Also related to the transposition of the UCP Directive, is the deletion of the provisions under the Consumer Affairs Act regulating misleading and comparative advertising and the amendment of the Commercial Code to include provisions regulating comparative and misleading advertising. As distinct from what was previously provided for under the Consumer Affairs Act, where the Director of Consumer Affairs was empowered to intervene to ensure compliance with the then existing provisions regulating advertising, under the Commercial Code it is the 'injured trader' only who may seek civil redress before the ordinary courts if there is a breach of the provisions under that Code regulating comparative or misleading advertising.[28] It is not clear why the legislator opted for such a procedure effectively eliminating any regulatory intervention by the Director in such instances. The

---

97(2).

25   Consumer Affairs Act, Article 110F. Such right of appeal is available to all the parties to the appeal before the Appeals Tribunal including the Director of Consumer Affairs.

26   *Ibid.*, Part VII entitled 'Unfair commercial practices and illicit schemes'. Part VII is divided into two titles, Title I deals with unfair commercial practices whereas Title II deals with illicit schemes including the so-called chain letter schemes and other misleading representations about certain schemes and activities.

27   *Ibid.*, Article 43. This provision has been retained.

28   See Commercial Code, Articles 32A and 32B which deal with comparative and misleading advertising and Article 37 which provides for the remedies a trader impacted negatively by such advertising has under the Code.

May 2007 Consultation, which had initially proposed such amendments, gave no reasons for these amendments other than to state that the removal of the reference to 'consumer' in the revised Misleading and Comparative Advertising Directive[29] justified the removal of such provisions from the Consumer Affairs Act since that Directive as amended by the UCP Directive referred only to business-to-business advertising.

Changes Relating to the Consumer Claims Tribunal

During the discussion of the Bill in Parliament, some important changes were introduced relating to the enforcement of, and appeal from, decisions taken by the Consumer Claims Tribunal. An issue that has consistently undermined the effectiveness of this tribunal as an alternative forum where consumers can seek redress against traders was the failure by a small minority of traders to abide with final tribunal decisions ordering them to compensate aggrieved consumers. At law, a decision of the Tribunal can be enforced as if it is a decision given by a court of law. The issue here is that, especially in instances involving small monetary values, many consumers simply consider that it is not worth their time and money to pursue the enforcement of favourable tribunal decisions, given that if a trader fails to abide with the Tribunal's decision then the aggrieved consumer must apply to the Courts to issue an executive warrant.[30] In order to dissuade traders who fail to comply with tribunal decisions, a provision has now been inserted whereby any person failing to comply with a tribunal decision within three months from the date when that decision becomes final shall be guilty of an offence and is liable to a fine of not more than 500 Euros.[31]

Other new measures relating to the Tribunal include changes to the right of appeal whereby appeals from tribunal decisions where the monetary value in dispute exceeds 1,200 Euros can now be appealed without any limitation, whereas if the amount in dispute is below that value, the right of appeal is limited to issues of jurisdiction, prescription or non-observance by the Tribunal of the rules of natural justice during the course of the proceedings.[32] The amendments further provide that the Court of Appeal may impose a penalty not exceeding 200 Euros if it considers that the appeal lodged is frivolous or vexatious. Another amendment, which positively impacts on the rights that consumers have, is the increase in the

---

29   Council Directive 84/450/EEC of 10 September 1984 relating to the approximation of the laws, regulations and administrative provisions of the Member States concerning misleading and comparative advertising as amended by Directives 97/55EC and 2005/29/EC.

30   This would be either a garnishee order or an executive warrant of seizure.

31   Consumer Affairs Act, Article 25A.

32   *Ibid.*, Article 22.

amount of moral damages that the Tribunal can award a consumer in determining a claim lodged before it.[33]

Whilst these amendments are an important step forward, the opportunity to undertake a more comprehensive review of consumer law was not taken up. From a regulatory standpoint various positive measures have been introduced including notably the introduction of administrative fines and the changes to ensure better compliance with decisions of the Consumer Claims Tribunal, however no significant measures have been taken to revisit the existing regulatory executive and advisory structures. The Director of Consumer Affairs and the Consumer Affairs Council have now been in place since 1994.[34] The only substantive change that has been effected since that date was the merging of the Department of Consumer Affairs and of the Office of Fair Competition within one comprehensive administrative set-up entitled the Consumer and Competition Division. Otherwise, the regulatory executive set-up remains that of a government department which set-up is not necessarily endowed with the required degree of autonomy and flexibility from the government of the day. The next, and it is submitted overdue, step is for Government to review the current regulatory structures, to see whether as presently structured these are effectively fulfilling their role or whether there are other more feasible options.

---

33   *Ibid.*, Article 21. The Tribunal can award a consumer moral damages for any pain, distress, anxiety and inconvenience that the consumer may have suffered.

34   The Consumer Affairs Act of 1994 creating these bodies came into force on 23 January 1996 and the Director and Council assumed their powers under that law on that date.

11   Secret Commissions and Overseas Purchases: The Good News for Consumers in 2007

James Ross[1]

In a year which was overcast by the sub-prime lending crisis and the ensuing debacle surrounding Northern Rock, two appellate decisions in the field of consumer credit may nevertheless bring a degree of relief to debtors. The case of *Office of Fair Trading* v. *Lloyds TSB plc*[2] provided much needed clarification in respect of creditors' liabilities to debtors under section 75(1) of the Consumer Credit Act 1974 ('the 1974 Act') for suppliers' breaches of contract or misrepresentations. The House of Lords held that the protection given to consumers by section 75 extends to overseas supply transactions. In *Hurstanger Ltd* v. *Wilson and Burton*,[3] the Court of Appeal held that a debtor could recover a commission paid by a creditor to the debtor's broker without the debtor's fully informed consent. The court also indicated that it had the discretion to order the rescission of loans entered into as a result of such a payment, a point which has already caused considerable disquiet amongst lenders.

Office of Fair Trading v. Lloyds TSB plc

Credit cards have become a part of everyday life for many consumers, both as a means of obtaining credit and as a convenient alternative to payment by cheque or cash. The use of credit cards for overseas holiday purchases is particularly attractive since it eliminates the need to carry local currency. It may be that most consumers are not aware of a further advantage that arises when paying by credit card: under section 75(1) of the 1974 Act, the consumer acquires a right of recourse against the UK card issuer in respect of breach of contract or misrepresentation on the part of the supplier. A long standing dispute arose between the OFT and UK card issuers over whether this protection extends to the use of credit cards in relation to foreign

---

1   The writer is a barrister at Gough Square Chambers, whose new series of law reports *Consumer and Trading Law Cases* (CTLC) is now available to subscribers: see www. goughsq.co.uk for details.
2   [2008] 1 AC 316.
3   [2007] 1 WLR 2351; [2007] CTLC 59.

supply transactions. In the House of Lords, the OFT, as respondents, maintained that section 75(1) does so extend, whereas the appellant representatives of the UK credit card industry took the opposite view.

Section 75(1) provides as follows:

> 75 liability of creditor for breaches by supplier
>
> (1) If the debtor under a debtor-creditor-supplier agreement falling within section 12(b) or (c) has, in relation to a transaction financed by the agreement, any claim against the supplier in respect of a misrepresentation or breach of contract, he shall have a like claim against the creditor, who, with the supplier, shall accordingly be jointly and severally liable to the debtor.

The reference to sections 12(b) and (c) simply indicates that section 75 applies only to situations in which there are pre-existing or anticipated future 'arrangements' between the creditor and the supplier. When the 1974 Act was drafted, relationships between card issuers and suppliers were rather more intimate than they are today: a card issuer authorised certain suppliers to accept its cards and made arrangements to reimburse each supplier in relation to transactions entered into by card holders. This system is still operated by American Express and Diners Club.

The majority of card issuers, however, have become members of one of the two main international credit card networks, VISA and Mastercard. The card networks make arrangements whereby a supplier agrees to honour any of the network cards and is reimbursed through the network clearing system, but not necessarily by the relevant card issuer itself. At first instance and in the Court of Appeal, the card issuers sought to argue that in such situations, it could not be said that there were 'arrangements' between the card issuer and the supplier such that sections 12(b) and (c), and hence section 75, applied. This argument was rejected on both occasions on the basis that the term 'arrangements' was well capable of embracing the modern relationships between card issuers and suppliers under the VISA and Mastercard networks. The House of Lords refused permission to appeal on this point.

Given the rather one-sided debate that was to ensue before their Lordships, it is perhaps surprising that the card issuers were given permission to appeal in respect of the Court of Appeal's ruling that section 75(1) applied to foreign supply transactions. The first argument put forward by the appellants, referring to the presumption that statutes do not have extra-territorial effect, was roundly rejected by their Lordships. The proposition that a UK card issuer may incur a liability to a UK consumer raises no issue of extra-territoriality merely because the extent of that (domestic) liability must be quantified by reference to a foreign transaction.[4]

---

4   The question of what amounts to a UK credit agreement remains outstanding, not having been raised by either party. The answer is not entirely clear but is presumably framed by reference to a number of factors, primarily the location of the debtor: see R. Goode, *Consumer Credit Law and Practice* (London, 1999), paras 49.82–49.90; A.G.

The second main argument made by the card issuers was that liability under section 75(1) was intended to be limited to situations where the card issuer could obtain an enforceable indemnity against the supplier, as provided for by section 75(2). Lord Hoffmann dealt with this point briefly as follows:[5]

> The appellants submit that section 75(1) should be limited to cases where the supplier would have a right of indemnity under section 75(2). The two subsections should be treated as indissolubly linked. It seems to me, however, that if Parliament had wanted to limit the application of section 75(1) by reference to the enforceability of section 75(2) it would have said so. It is not obvious why there should be such a link. Section 75(1) is consumer protection legislation for the benefit of the customers of United Kingdom creditors. It cannot be excluded by agreement between debtor and creditor. Section 75(2) is a default provision to regulate relations between creditor and supplier. It applies only in the absence of contrary agreement and can be supplemented by the terms of the contract or (if foreign) the governing law. If card issuers choose to authorise the use of their cards by foreign suppliers or join [network] schemes under which their cards may be so used, they can be expected either to make their own arrangements about indemnity against liability under section 75(1) or accept that the commercial advantages of allowing foreign use outweighs the absence of a right of indemnity.

Their Lordships were unanimous in rejecting the card issuers' appeal. Despite the difficulties that might be faced by a card issuer in enforcing an indemnity against a foreign supplier, it was thought that such recourse would be still more difficult at the instance of the individual consumer. Nevertheless, the potential exposure of card issuers after this ruling should not be underestimated. As Mr Hapgood QC argued for the appellants, a card issuer must stand as guarantor for each of the 29 million suppliers worldwide who have been enlisted by its card network. A degree of protection is available through the card networks by way of the 'charge back' system and provision is made for the expulsion of delinquent suppliers. However, the card issuers' perennial concerns in relation to 'super complaints' will not be assuaged by such measures. The liability to which a creditor is exposed by virtue of section 75(1) is not limited to the value of the transaction (whose cash price will be between £100 and £30,000). This leaves the possibility of card issuers being faced with cases where the value of the claim far exceeds the value of the transaction: consider the case of relatively low cost plastic surgery which goes badly wrong, for example.

Difficulties also arise in respect of relatively low value claims where the cost to the card issuer of investigating and defending the claim will be disproportionate to the sum in issue. The example cited in argument was the pending case of *Boyack* v. *The Royal Bank of Scotland*, where it is alleged that oral misrepresentations were made by a clock vendor in Dubai. The practical difficulties faced by UK card

---

Guest and M.G. Lloyd, *Encyclopaedia of Consumer Credit Law* (London, 2006), para. 2-194/2 onwards.

5   [2008] 1 AC 316; 320.

issuers in meeting such a claim are obvious. There would appear to be plenty of scope for unscrupulous holidaymakers to take advantage of the situation and little that the card issuers can do to protect themselves: the point made in argument was that UK card issuers have little bargaining power to renegotiate the network rules due to the dominance of American issuers. It is submitted, however, that the practical effect of this decision will not weigh too heavily upon the card issuers. The risk of 'super complaints' may be insured against and the card issuers have considerable experience in taking a pragmatic view of cases such as *Boyack*. The outcome for consumers is likely to be a degree of reassurance in respect of overseas purchases at the expense of marginally higher interest rates.

Hurstanger Limited v. Wilson and Burton

Of less general interest to consumers but of greater concern to the credit industry is the decision of the Court of Appeal in *Hurstanger Limited* v. *Wilson and Burton*. At first instance, the argument centred upon whether the credit agreement was compliant with the Consumer Credit (Agreements) Regulations 1983 ('the Regulations'), which require that agreements contain certain prescribed information and terms.[6] Sections 61 and 65(1) of the 1974 Act provide that an agreement which does not comply with the Regulations is improperly executed and may not be enforced without an order of the court. Section 127(3) precluded the making of such an order in circumstances where the agreement does not contain the terms prescribed by Schedule 6 of the Regulations.

In a judgment which has received widespread acclaim for its clarity and insight, Mr Recorder Douglas QC held that Schedule 6 imposes a basic requirement that the agreement contain the prescribed terms, as a matter of construction, and not as imposing any standard of clarity for the statement of those terms, clarity being a matter addressed by Schedule 1.[7] On appeal, the Recorder's decision in relation to the individual terms, as well as his analysis of the Regulations, was upheld. It is unnecessary to enter into a detailed discussion of the consumer credit arguments in this work: Schedule 6 prescribed terms will be of decreasing importance in the future given that section 127(3) was repealed on 6 April 2007 in relation to agreements entered into after that date, thus bringing to an end the possibility that an agreement is irredeemably unenforceable through failure to include a prescribed term.

The point of wider application in the case arose in relation to a commission of £240 paid by the lender to the borrower's broker. A document signed by the borrower acknowledged that, in certain circumstances, the lender would pay commissions to brokers. No further mention was then made of a commission. It was accepted by both parties that where a person (in this case the lender) makes

---

6   See Schedules 1 and 6 of the Regulations.
7   See [2007] CTLC 9 for the Recorder's judgment.

a payment to the agent of another person with whom he is dealing (in this case the borrower) knowing of the agency and fails to disclose that he is making the payment, the other is entitled to rescind the contract. The factual issue therefore arose of whether the commission paid by the lender was secret. The Recorder held that the document signed by the borrower was sufficient to negate secrecy and consequently refused to grant relief to the borrower.

On appeal, Mr Say, on behalf of the borrower, argued that it was incumbent upon the lender to obtain the borrower's fully informed consent in relation to payments made to his agents: a statement that payments might be made was not sufficient. In delivering the judgment of the court, Lord Justice Tuckey held as follows:[8]

> Obviously if there has been no disclosure the agent will have received a secret commission. This is a blatant breach of his fiduciary duty but additionally the payment or receipt of a secret commission is considered to be a form of bribe and is treated in the authorities as a special category of fraud in which it is unnecessary to prove motive, inducement or loss up to the amount of the bribe ... Furthermore the transaction is voidable at the election of the principal who can rescind it provided counter-restitution can be made ... But 'the real evil is not the payment of money, but the secrecy attending it' (Chitty L.J. in the leading case of *Shipway* v. *Broadwood* [1899] 1 QB 369, 373). Is there a half way house between the situation where there has been sufficient disclosure to negate secrecy, but nevertheless the principal's informed consent has not been obtained? Logically I can see no objection to this. Where there has only been partial or inadequate disclosure but it is sufficient to negate secrecy, it would be unfair to visit the agent and any third party involved with a finding of fraud and the other consequences to which I have referred, or, conversely, to acquit them altogether for their involvement in what would still be breach of fiduciary duty unless informed consent had been obtained. There is no authority which sheds any light on this question.

Their Lordships took the view that since the commission was not fully secret, the borrower did not have the right to rescind the credit agreement. However, since the fully informed consent of the borrower had not been obtained, the court had a discretion in equity to grant rescission. In the circumstances of the case, their Lordships held that rescission would be disproportionate and instead ordered that the lender pay the borrower the amount of the commission plus interest by way of equitable compensation.

This decision has caused considerable disquiet amongst lenders because the payment of commissions to credit brokers is standard industry practice. In many cases, the borrower will be required to sign a declaration acknowledging that such commissions may be paid. It will be relatively rare, however, for a borrower to be told the actual amount of commission: the provision of such information creates a number of practical difficulties and is generally unattractive in a situation where the borrower has already paid the broker a substantial sum. It may be that in the

8   [2007] 1 WLR 2351, 2363; [2007] CTLC 59, 70.

future it will become increasingly common for debtors to seek disclosure of the commission paid by lenders to brokers in order either to recoup that commission or argue that the court should exercise its discretion to allow rescission. Nevertheless, it is submitted that the possibility of rescission should not trouble creditors as much as the historic spectre of irredeemable unenforceability under the 1974 Act: a lender will at least be entitled to recover the principal sum loaned. On a practical note, it should also be remembered that many debtors will have difficulty in making counter-restitution in any event.

12   A Critical (Re)view of the Spanish Act on Improvement of Consumers Protection Concerning Long Term Contracts (Act 44/2006, of 29 December)

*Susana Navas Navarro**

Introduction

Article 51 of the Spanish Constitution (1978)[1] affirms that consumer protection has to be seen as one of the fundamental principles of social and economic policy, whose application the public authorities shall guarantee. The above-mentioned provision distinguishes between *consumers' basic rights* (for example, safety, health, economic interests) and *consumers' instrumental rights* (information, education and representation through associations).[2] Article 51 of the Spanish

---

*   Professor of Civil Law, Autonomous University of Barcelona, Spain. Whilst the present article is being printed the Consumers Protection Act referred to in the article has been modified most recently by the Royal Legislative Decree 1/2007, of 16th November, by which the revised text of General Law for the Protection of Consumers and Users and other additional laws (Official Journal of Spain, BOE, Nr. 287, of 30 November 2007). However, this new legislation has not materially changes Act 44/2006 of 29 December and that the statements and assumptions made by the author therefore remain fully valid.

1   For an English version of the Spanish Constitution see: www.constitucion.es/constitucion/lenguas/ingles.html.

2   Article 51:
1. The public authorities shall guarantee the protection of consumers and users and shall, by means of effective measures, safeguard their safety, health and legitimate economic interests.
2. The public authorities shall promote the information and education of consumers and users, foster their organizations, and hear them on those matters affecting their members, under the terms established by law.
3. Within the framework of the provisions of the foregoing paragraphs, the law shall regulate domestic trade and the system of licensing commercial products.

Constitution should be seen in connection with Article 53 para. 3.[3] The latter Constitutional rule considers consumer protection as a principle, which is not only guided by social and economic policy, but influences the Spanish legal system in general, in order to pursue a worthy quality of life.[4] This principle of consumer protection extends even to judicial practice and the actions of the public authorities.

The Spanish Consumers Protection Act of 19 July 1984[5] has been enacted and several times modified[6] in accordance with this principle. The last modification was made by Act 44/2006, of 29 December, on Improvement of Consumers Protection.[7] With this last modification, the Spanish legislator aimed to protect consumers from unfair practices and unfair contract terms that take place in some specific fields affecting the consumer.[8]

The Spanish legislator used Act 44/2006 in order to comply with the judgment of the European Court of Justice of 9 September 2004[9] condemning Spain for having improperly implemented Article 5 and Article 6 para. 2 of the Unfair Contract Terms Directive 93/13/CE of the Council of 5 April 1993.[10] This judgment obliged the Spanish legislator to modify Articles 10 para. 2 and 10-*bis* para. 3 of the Consumers Protection Act of 1984 and Articles 3 para. 2 and 6 para. 2 of the Standard Contract Terms Act of 13 April 1998.[11]

---

3   Article 53:

3. Recognition, respect and protection of the principles recognized in Chapter 3 shall guide legislation, judicial practice and actions by the public authorities. They may only be invoked before the ordinary courts in accordance with the legal provisions implementing them.

4   A. Bercovitz and R. Bercovitz, *Estudios jurídicos sobre protección de los consumidores* (Madrid, 1987), p. 136.

5   See, BOE, Nr. 176, of 24 July 1984. In Spain the self-governing Communities have legislation on consumer protection. However, for the purpose of this chapter we take only into consideration the consumer provisions of the Spanish legislator.

6   The three most important modifications are: first, the modification made by the Standard Contract Terms Act of 13 April 1998 (BOE, Nr. 89, of 14 April 1998), which aimed to implement the Unfair Contract Terms Directive 93/113/EC; secondly, the modification made by the Act 39/2002, of 28 October, on the implementation of different Directives in order to protect consumers (BOE, Nr. 259, of 29 October 2002) and finally, the modification made by the Sale of Consumer Goods and Associated Guarantees Act of 10 July 2003 (BOE, Nr. 165, of 11 July 2003), which implements the Directive 1999/94/EC.

7   See, Official Journal of Spain (BOE), Nr. 312, of 30 December 2006 (www.boe.es).

8   For some examples, see next section of this chapter.

9   C-70/2003 (*Commission* v. *Spain*).

10   OJ L 95, 21.4.1993, pp. 29–34.

11   Article 5 of Directive 93/13/EC makes an exception to the rule that the most favourable interpretation to the consumer shall prevail. Indeed, it affirms that 'this rule on interpretation shall not apply in the context of the procedures laid down in Article 7(2)'. Nevertheless, when Article 10 para. 2 of the Consumers Protection

This chapter will only discuss the legal modifications made by the Spanish legislator in order to improve consumer protection concerning long term contracts in the Spanish legal system.

The Pretended Improvement of the Consumers Protection in Spanish Law Concerning Long Term Contracts

It is the aim of Act 44/2006, of 29 December, on Improvement of Consumers Protection to reinforce consumer protection and fair competition. Therefore, this Act said that it has introduced some modifications in the field of consumer contract law. *Is this really the case?*

In the internal Spanish market it was (and still is) usual that large companies (for example, mobile phone companies) impose on consumers that intend to terminate a long term contract several burdensome and disproportionate

---

Act and Article 6 para. 2 of the Standard Contract Terms Act implemented this rule on interpretation, they did not make any restriction in order to exclude from the application of this rule proceedings which aim to have a decision to prevent the continued use of unfair terms ('*acciones colectivas de cesación*'). See: F.J. Infante Ruíz, 'La exclusión de la regla *contra proferentem* en el procedimiento de control abstracto (A propósito de la Sentencia del TJCE, Sala 1ª, de 9 de septiembre 2004 – Comisión Europea versus Reino de España- Asunto C-70/03)', *Revista de derecho patrimonial*, 15 (2005): 159–63. Moreover, Spain has implemented Article 6 para. 2 of Directive 93/13/EC introducing a restriction that is not present in the Directive. This provision states that 'Member States shall take the necessary measures to ensure that the consumer does not lose the protection granted by this Directive by virtue of the choice of the law of a non-Member country as the law applicable to the contract if the latter has a close connection with the territory of the Member States'. Article 10-*bis* para. 3 of the Spanish Consumers Protection Act has restricted the protection of consumers – it affirms that consumers protection is given independent of the choice of the law made by the parties – but in accordance with Article 5 of the Roma Convention on Contractual Obligations (Roma-I). The judgment of the European Court considers that Article 6 para. 2 of Directive 93/13/EC applies to all business–consumer contracts. On the contrary, Article 5 Roma-I only applies, as widely known, to certain contracts. Therefore, the Spanish legislator has introduced a restriction, which does not conform to the Directive. Consequently, Spain was forced to modify Article10 para. 2 and Art. 10-*bis* para. 3 of the Consumers Protection Act and Articles 3 para. 2 and 6 para. 2 of the Standard Contract Terms Act. (See, on the Spanish doctrine, A. Quiñones Escámez, 'Incorrecta transposición de la noción <<vínculo estrecho con el territorio comunitario>> de las Directivas de consumo (STJCE de 9-9-2004, as. 70/3, Comisión c/ España)', *Revista de derecho comunitario español*, 21 (2005): 537–50.)

obstacles.[12] These unfair commercial practices are usually accompanied by unfair contract terms.[13]

Unfair terms in long term contracts

An overview of the most common unfair terms within the Spanish internal market concerning long term contracts has to distinguish between (A) terms which exclude the right to terminate the contract and (B) terms which limit the exercise of the right to terminate the contract.

Contract terms excluding the consumer's rights to terminate the contract Such terms may consist in the following:

> a. terms expressly excluding the right to terminate the contract;
> b. terms enabling the professional and not the consumer to terminate the contract;
> c. renewal clauses. In Spanish case law some judgments are reported in this field. Typically, these judgments concern equipment service contracts (for example, servicing of computers, cars, electronic equipments, lifts[14]). The contract contains a duration clause stating that the contract shall be indefinitely prorogued. Judges have found such a term to be unfair because of a lack of transparency; furthermore, it has been found in some cases that the duration clause has not been indicated in the part of the contract reflecting its fundamental requirements; finally, such a term implies a disproportion between the reciprocal rights and duties of the parties;[15]
> d. contract terms which foresee a surprising period of time (for example, 2–3 days) to give notice of the consumer's intention to terminate the contract;

---

12   A '*long term contract*' comprises two situations: first, the contract, which is undefined and, secondly, the contract, which has a term, but this term is too long or disproportionate in relation to the content of the contract. In this kind of contract parties have the right to terminate the contract, although this right would not be stipulated or addressed in the contract itself. The only duty that they have to fulfil is to give due notice of the termination of the contract. In Spanish law there is not a general rule concerning this issue. However, case law and prevailing doctrine in Spain admit this right to terminate the contract (for example, E. Bosch Capdevila and A. Giménez Costa, 'Las cláusulas abusivas en los contratos celebrados con consumidores', *Revista crítica de derecho inmobiliario*, 692 (2005): 1757, at 1779).

13   On unfair contract terms, see the study of E. Bosch Capdevila and A. Giménez Costa, 'Las cláusulas abusivas en los contratos celebrados con consumidores'.

14   *Court of Appeal of Balearic of 23 June 1994* (AC 1994, p. 1036) and of *1 October 1996* (AC 1996, p. 1938).

15   With similar arguments, we could cite the judgments of the *Court of Appeal of Asturias of 12 February 2004* (JUR 2004, p. 82689) and of the *Court of Appeal of Girona of 30 April 2004* (JUR 2004, p. 181582).

e. contract terms which establish a disproportionate period in order to give notice of the termination of the contract (for example, 90 days), if compared with the duties and obligations of the parties stipulated in the same contract.

Contract terms which limit the consumer's right to terminate the contract

a. contract terms including additional costs for consumers if they exercise their rights to terminate the contract (such as punitive clauses,[16] compensation for damage that is not actually caused, the right of the professional to retain sums of money that consumers have advanced, excessive loan interest[17]);
b. contract terms introducing the payment for services that the professional has not provided;
c. calculation of the prices in favour of the professional service provider (for example, 'round up').

Analysing the recent Spanish case law, such round up is usually seen in banking contracts, in particular in mortgage loans with variable interest.[18] In these cases, judges consider such terms invalid because (i) they are unfair and (ii) they introduce a disproportion between rights and duties of the parties under the contract. Consumers pay more than they should.[19] A similar situation can be found, for instance, in car parking contracts.[20] Indeed, it was usual and common practice to round up the fee for using the car park to the next hour although the car might only have been, for instance, stationed a few minutes into the next hour, for example, only a fraction of the billed time. The court did not identify any legal justification which legitimates such commercial practices and therefore concluded that such terms are unfair.[21] Similar situations can be seen in cases in which the round up is

---

16   If the term concerning the duration of the contract services is invalid, the punitive clauses in relation to it, shall be declared invalid as well. This is the opinion of the majority of the Spanish case law: for example, *Court of Appeal of Vizcaya*, sect. 5, of 21 June 2000 (AC 2000, p. 1751); *Court of Appeal of Asturias*, sect. 5, of 14 November 2002 (AC 2002, 1928); *Court of Appeal of Cantabria*, sect. 2, of 20 January 2003 (JUR 2003, p. 121542) or *Court of Appeal of Girona*, sect. 2, of 3 May 2004 (JUR 2004, p. 181512).
17   *Court of Appeal of A Coruña*, sect. 1, of 2 May 1996 (AC 1996, p. 862).
18   F. Olivia Blázquez, 'Nulidad por su carácter abusivo de la cláusula de redondeo al alza (Comentario a la SJPI núm. 50 de Madrid de 11 de septiembre de 2001)', *Revista de derecho patrimonial*, 8 (2002): 235–47.
19   *Court of Appeal of Madrid*, sect. 11, of 10 October 2002 (AC 2002, p. 1417), *Court of Appeal of Balearics*, sect. 5, of 17 March 2003 (AC 2003, p. 1624), *Court of First Instance of Barcelona*, of 17 October 2003 (AC 2003, p. 1625), *Court of Appeal of Barcelona*, sect. 13, of 29 March 2005 (AC 2005, p. 855).
20   N. Álvarez Lata, F. Peña López and J.M. Busto Lago (eds), *Reclamaciones de Consumo* (Pamplona, 2005), pp. 605–607.
21   *Court of Appeal of Murcia*, sect. 2, of 1 February 2000 (AC 2000, p. 774), and of 31 March 2000 (AC 2000, p. 1282), *Court of Appeal of Madrid*, sect. 14, of 8 September

made by phone companies (in particular, regarding mobiles): instead of billing for the exact time a phone call lasted, phone companies used to round up the cost of the call in certain fractions to the detriment of consumers.[22]

Measures to improve consumers' protection?

In order to prohibit these unfair commercial practices in business-to-consumer contracts, Act 44/2006 introduces some modifications to the Consumers Protection Act prohibiting these unfair contract terms.

First of all, the Spanish legislator declared that contract terms limiting the exercise of consumers' rights are prohibited (revised Article 12 para. 2, Consumers Protection Act). In particular, contract terms which exclude or obstruct the consumer's right to terminate the contract are prohibited (revised Article 12 para. 3, Consumers Protection Act). Before Act 44/2006, such contract terms were not expressly prohibited, but considered unfair contract terms, similar to the Directive 93/13/EC,[23] by Article 10-*bis* para. 1 and the additional provision Nr. 1 of the Consumers Protection Act. The sanction was (and still is) the invalidity of such contract terms (Article 10-*bis* para. 2, Consumers Protection Act).[24] Now, with the new Act, the sanction is the same (invalidity), but not because these contract terms are unfair. They are invalid because the introduction of them within the contract is made against a prohibited provision (Article 6 para. 3, Spanish Civil Code). Under

2005 (AC 2005, p. 1554).

22 *Commercial Court of Madrid*, Nr. 4, of 21 November 2005 (AC 2005, p. 1791).

23 These unfair contract terms were expressly mentioned by the annex of Directive 93/13/CEE:
Terms referred to in article 3(3) 1. Terms which have the object or effect of:
(d) permitting the seller or supplier to retain sums paid by the consumer where the latter decides not to conclude or perform the contract, without providing for the consumer to receive compensation of an equivalent amount from the seller or supplier where the latter is the party cancelling the contract;
(e) requiring any consumer who fails to fulfil his obligation to pay a disproportionately high sum in compensation;
(f) authorizing the seller or supplier to dissolve the contract on a discretionary basis where the same facility is not granted to the consumer, or permitting the seller or supplier to retain the sums paid for services not yet supplied by him where it is the seller or supplier himself who dissolves the contract;
(g) enabling the seller or supplier to terminate a contract of indeterminate duration without reasonable notice except where there are serious grounds for doing so;
(h) automatically extending a contract of fixed duration where the consumer does not indicate otherwise, when the deadline fixed for the consumer to express this desire not to extend the contract is unreasonably early.

24 For a commentary on this Article 10-*bis* para 2, see M.C. Gete-Alonso and S. Navas Navarro, in I. Arroyo Martínez and J. Miquel Rodríguez, (eds), *Comentarios a la Ley sobre Condiciones Generales de la Contratación* (Madrid, 1999), pp. 289–96.

these circumstances, it cannot really be affirmed that the Spanish legislator has improved consumers' rights.

Secondly, it shall be clear and comprehensive within the contract that the consumer has the right to terminate it (revised Article 12 para. 1, Consumers Protection Act introduced by Act 44/2006). However, the existing Article 10 para. 1, Consumers Protection Act affirms that all contract terms shall be clear, intelligible, concrete and comprehensive. In so far as these contract terms are considered standard contract terms,[25] they are not part of the contract if they are incomprehensive, unclear, ambiguous and obscure (Article 7 Standard Contract Terms Act). Therefore, no real legal change exists.

Moreover, the revised Article 12 para. 4, Consumers Protection Act, introduced by Act 44/2006, states that the contract shall reflect the procedure that the consumer should follow in order to terminate the contract. In this case, if contract terms concerning this procedure are considered standard contract terms, they are subjected to the Standard Contract Terms Act of 1998 (Article 10 para. 3, Consumers Protection Act). The reference to this Act means that these contract terms shall pass the incorporation and the contents control that it imposes (Articles 5 and 7, Standard Contract Terms Act). If they do not pass these two controls, they have to be considered as invalid (Article 8 Standard Contract Terms Act) and the contract shall be integrated (Article 6 para. 3, Standard Contract Terms Act). The integration of the contract is the solution as well, when the professional has not introduced contract terms concerning the above-mentioned procedure (Article 10-*bis* Consumers Protection Act in relation to Article 1258 of the Spanish Civil Code). In the Spanish system, the integration of the contract is a general hermeneutical tool, which is applied to the contract like Articles 1258 and 1287 of the Spanish Civil Code show. However, when these terms exclude or limit the consumer's right to terminate the contract, as discussed earlier, Act 44/2006 states the invalidity of these terms as a legal consequence because they violate a prohibited rule. In this case, it can be questioned whether this new Act has really improved the consumer's rights system.

Thirdly, the revised Article 13 para. 1(g) of the Consumers Protection Act sets up a specific precontractual duty in order to inform consumers about how they can terminate a long term contract. Such information must be given free of charge, without any additional costs. Nevertheless, provision of pre-contractual

---

25 A classical study, but still very important on this issue is J. Álfaro Águila-Real, *Las condiciones generales de la contratación* (Madrid, 1991), p. 1 onwards, J. Álfaro Águila-Real, 'El Derecho de las condiciones generales y las cláusulas predispuestas', *Revista jurídica de Cataluña*, 1 (2000): 10–32; R. Bercovitz Rodríguez-Cano (ed.), *Comentarios a la ley de condiciones generales de contratación* (Madrid, 1999), p. 21 onwards; F. Llodrá Grimalt, *El contrato celebrado bajo condiciones generales* (Valencia, 2002), p. 1 onwards; J. Pagador López, *Condiciones generales y cláusulas contractuales predispuestas. La Ley de condiciones generales de la contratación* (Madrid, 1999), p. 12 onwards.

information in general, and the duty of professionals to inform about all circumstances concerning goods or services, were already expressly mentioned in Articles 8 para. 1 and 13 of the Consumers Protection Act.[26] In cases where such pre-contractual information has not been given or has been withheld, such information – as long as relevant to the consumer – will be part of the contents of the contract according to the rule of the integration of the contract established in Article 1258 of the Spanish Civil Code, as the revised Article 12 para. 6 of the Consumers Protection Act reaffirms. Again, no real legal change exists.

Finally, the information concerning prices of goods or services (and the public display thereof)[27] shall be presented in a detailed matter and subdividing the different components of which the price comprises: taxes, additional sums or discounted sums, costs that consumers have to assume, additional costs for additional services or for financing and, in general, sums in excess of the standard price (revised Article 13 para. 1(d) Consumers Protection Act). Nevertheless, Article 8 para. 1 of the Consumers Protection Act had already introduced a duty of professionals to inform consumers about all circumstances or aspects concerning goods or services, an important one of these being the price. It can again be questioned whether this Act has actually improved consumers' rights.

Conclusions

The real reason to modify the Consumers Protection Act was the unfair commercial practices that were taking place in the internal market. *But does Act 44/2006 actually improve consumers' protection?* The answer is no. As demonstrated before, the theoretically new provisions were already contained in other articles of the Spanish Civil Code, the Consumers Protection Act or/and in the Standard Contract Terms Act. *So, where is the consumer protection improvement?* In fact, the underlying intention of the Spanish legislator is to eliminate unfair commercial practices specifically cherished by large companies. We might want to ask why the Spanish legislator has not taken the opportunity properly to implement Directive 2005/29/EC of the European Parliament and of the Council of 11 May 2005 concerning unfair business-to-consumer commercial practices in the internal market,[28] instead of modifying partially the Consumers Protection Act without any imminent necessity to do so. The answer probably lies in the lack of coordination on part

---

26 E. Gómez Calle, *Los deberes precontractuales de información* (Madrid, 1994), p. 12 onwards; P.A. Pérez García, *La información en la contratación privada: en torno al deber de informar en la Ley general para la defensa de los consumidores y usuarios* (Madrid, 1990), p. 25 onwards.
27 From the perspective of the control of terms which express the substance of the bargain (*core terms*), see: S. Cámara Lapuente, *El control de las cláusulas <<abusivas>> sobre elementos esenciales del contrato* (Pamplona, 2006), p. 13 onwards.
28 OJ, L 149/22, of 11 June 2005.

of the Spanish legislator in implementing the European provisions. It is necessary for a global reform (modernisation) of the Law of Obligations[29] that should take into consideration consumers' protection and, of course, the implementation of the European legislation.

This legal situation could be more complicated if the Spanish legislator implements Directive 2005/29/EC in the same manner it usually does, that means, copying almost literally the EU Directive and without a major (global) view of the whole legal system or almost the whole consumer protection system. We hope that this will not be the case.

---

29 A.M. Morales Moreno, *La modernización del derecho de obligaciones* (Madrid, 2006), p. 1 onwards.

13   France: A New Law for 'The Development of Competition for the Benefit of Consumers'

Alexandre Regniault[1]

French law No. 2008-3 of 3 January 2008 in favour of 'the development of competition for the benefit of consumers', also called the 'Chatel Act', after the Minister who promoted the Bill (hereafter the 'Act'), entered into force on 5 January 2008.

The first section of the Act ('modernisation of commercial relationships') is aimed at reforming the sophisticated legal framework of commercial trading and cooperation. This follows prior legislation (the 'Dutreil Act' of 2 August 2005), which itself was inspired by a report filed in 2004 by a group of experts, which identified a number of factors hindering retail price competition in France. These factors were said to include the means of calculating the minimum resale price (which cannot be below the 'resale at a loss' threshold), especially having regard to the development of the so-called 'back margins'. 'Back margins' are the amounts paid by suppliers to their own distributors for services aimed at promoting their products (such as in-store means of product promotion, advertising in catalogues or leaflets, information or statistics concerning specifically the supplier's products, and so on).

Under the new law, each year a supplier and a distributor must enter into a written agreement that specifies the conditions for the sale of the products or services, resulting from the negotiations between the parties. The annual agreement must also describe, in detail, the conditions under which the distributor shall render services to the supplier, whether or not such services are directly related to the resale of specific and identified products or services. The annual agreement between the supplier and the distributor (or the framework agreement that will be followed by application agreements) must be executed before 1 March of each year.

The calculation of the 'resale at a loss' threshold now includes all the amounts paid back by the supplier to its distributor, under the annual agreement described above. This way, distributors should now be in a position to lower retail prices. The Government's intention is, through this technical measure, to favour competition through prices on a more realistic basis, namely the price actually paid by the

---

1   Avocat à la Cour, Simmons & Simmons.

distributor to the supplier, taking into account all the financial compensations obtained by the former from the latter.

At the end of this section of the Act, Members of Parliament introduced an article authorising 'retail furniture stores' to open on Sundays.

The second section of the Act is dedicated to 'sectoral measures in favour of purchasing power'.

Amongst the provisions of the chapter on electronic communications, consumers terminating a contract for electronic communications services (for example, access to the internet) will now be entitled to have their deposit or any amount paid in advance refunded within a specific deadline (ten days from the date of payment of the last invoice or restitution of the material). The notice period for the termination of the contract will no longer exceed ten days, unless the consumer requires otherwise. When the operator offers a free trial period, this offer may no longer be extended into a paying-basis contract unless the consumer expressly agrees to that. Conditions are placed upon minimum contract terms demanded by service providers, and upon contract termination fees. Payments made for calls to hotlines are subject to new rules limiting the powers of service providers.

Measures relating to the banking sector include the extension of the possibility to resort to mediation for disputes between banks and their clients acting as individual consumers (this dispute resolution technique had a limited scope and should now generally cover disputes relating to loans and savings). In addition, banks will now be obliged to send their clients an annual comprehensive list of the fees and expenses paid in relation to the management of their deposit account. This must be sent each year in January in relation to payments made during the previous year. Loan contracts for the acquisition of real estate must now include specific information on the financial impact of variable interest rate on the amounts due by the debtor in the course of time. As for these loan contracts with a variable interest rate, the bank will now have to inform the debtor each year on the amount of the outstanding amount in capital.

New statutory provisions give consumers an unconditional right to withdraw from their agreement, within two weeks, when they have agreed to enter into an insurance contract further to an unsolicited offer made to them at home or at work. Other provisions place additional conditions on the timeframe for delivery of a good ordered by a consumer, and on consumers' right of retraction. For example, when a consumer withdraws his/her agreement to an offer for a good or service, any amounts paid by the consumer in advance must be refunded to him/her within 30 days.

The provisions introduced by Parliament in January 2005 on the automatic extension of long-term contracts (the professional service provider must inform the consumer of the possibility not to renew the contract, between 1 and 3 months before the initial term expires) shall now apply 'to consumers and non-professionals', which extends the scope of these provisions to professionals acting outside of their sphere of activity (for example, a person renting a photocopy machine for the purpose of his/her professional activity).

Lastly, the Act implements Directive 2005/29/EC of 11 May 2005 concerning unfair business-to-consumer commercial practices in the internal market (which was supposed to be adopted and published by 12 June 2007). Accordingly, French law now lays down a general prohibition of 'unfair commercial practices'. A commercial practice is unfair if it is 'contrary to the requirements of professional diligence' and if 'it materially distorts or is likely to materially distort the economic behaviour of a normally informed and reasonable careful consumer, with regard to a good or service'. The Act redefines misleading advertising, now encompassed into a wider definition of misleading commercial practices. The Act also places criminal sanctions upon 'aggressive commercial practices', which are defined as altering the consumer's freedom through 'repeated and insisting solicitations or the use of a physical or moral constraint'.

14   EC Passenger Law Running on Track – The Regulation on Rail Passengers' Rights and Obligations

Jens Karsten[1]

The adoption, on 23 October 2007, of Regulation (EC) No. 1371/2007 on rail passengers' rights and obligations[2] (hereinafter 'Regulation 1371') – beyond the amenities it brings for railway passengers – is a momentous event in the development of EC passenger law and European private law.

For EC passenger law that so far has focused on the protection of the interests of air passengers, Regulation 1371 is the first true non-air transport-related constituent. It implements the policy principally outlined by the European Commission (the Commission) in the White Paper 'European transport policy for 2010: Time to Decide'[3] and the Communication 'Strengthening passenger rights within the European Union'[4] pushing for user rights for all modes of transport. The attention paid to passenger interests in transport legislation has, therefore, given birth to EC passenger law as a novel, but independent, strand of Community consumer policy.[5] Constitutionally, it is linked to the integration requirement of Article 153(2) EC (to become Article 12 of the Treaty on the Functioning of the European Union[6]) and to Article 38 of the Charter of Fundamental Rights of the European Union,[7] but it is based on Articles 70–80 EC (to become Articles 90–100 of the Treaty on the Functioning of the European Union) which define a *sui generis* concept of 'consumer protection' for transport users. As part of the wider

---

1   L.L.B. (Frankfurt am Main 1994), LL.M. in European Law (University of Nottingham 1996), German Bar Exam (Wiesbaden 1999).
2   OJ L 315, 3.12.2007, p. 14.
3   COM(2001) 370 final of 12 September 2001, pp. 82–3.
4   COM(2005) 46 final of 16 February 2005. See also Commission press release IP/05/182 of 16 February 2005, 'Transport with a human face: new rights for passengers', and website: http://europa.eu/scadplus/leg/en/lvb/l24124.htm (visited 20.12.2007).
5   On the notion of EC passenger law see: J. Karsten, 'Passengers, Consumers and Travellers – The Rise of Passenger Rights in EC Transport Law and its Repercussions for Community Consumer Law and Policy', *Journal of Consumer Policy*, 30 (2007): 117–36.
6   Treaty of Lisbon amending the Treaty on European Union and the Treaty establishing the European Community, (OJ C 115, 9.5.2008).
7   OJ C 303, 14.12.2007, p. 1.

agenda of intermodal passenger lawmaking, Regulation 1371 is not to be the last of its kind. The Common Position on a Regulation on the liability of carriers of passengers by sea in the event of accidents[8] ('the Athens Regulation') is the portent of the extension of EC passenger law in 2008 to maritime transport (though not for inland waterway transport, as initially proposed).[9] Furthermore, according to a Commission 'Working Document'[10] preparing the review of the 1990 Directive on Package Travel[11] in the context of the Green Paper on the Review of the Consumer *Acquis*,[12] a proposal for a Regulation on the rights of international bus and coach passengers[13] will be published (a study has already been tendered[14]). A Regulation on the rights of passengers with reduced mobility in the maritime sector[15] was announced in the same Commission document.

Regulation 1371 also adds substantially to the body of European private law.[16] First, it incorporates a convention of international law on civil liability into the *acquis communautaire* (like the Athens Regulation will do; the air transport Montreal Convention has been ratified by the EC[17]). Secondly, it provides additional rules of a private law nature which are the original product of EC law. A discussion of these provisions, however worthwhile, is not possible in the space of this chapter. What the chapter shall attempt instead is to present the Regulation's origins and to name its key provisions. It shall ponder the common elements

---

8   Common Position (EC) No. 19/2008 of 6 June 2008 (OJ C 190E, 29.7.2008, p.17).

9   For a discussion of the original proposal see: J. Karsten, 'European Passenger Law for Sea and Inland Waterway Transport', in G. Howells, A. Nordhausen, D. Parry and C. Twigg-Flesner (eds), *Yearbook of Consumer Law 2008* (Aldershot, 2007), p. 201.

10   Working Document on the Council Directive 90/314/EEC of 26 July 2007.

11   Directive 90/314/EEC on package travel, package holidays and package tours (OJ L 158, 23.6.1990, p. 59). Article 4(6)(2nd subparagraph, 2nd indent) and Article 5(2)(3rd subparagraph) plus recital 19 thereof directly refer to passenger law.

12   Commission Communication COM(2006) 744 final of 8 February 2007 (OJ C 61, 15.3.2007, p. 1). Also see European Parliament Resolution of 6 September 2007 and EESC Opinion (OJ C 256, 27.10.2007, p. 27).

13   COM(2007) ... Also see the Proposal for a Regulation on common rules for the international carriage of passengers by coach and bus [recast] (COM(2007) 264 final of 23 May 2007).

14   Study on passenger transport by coach in Europe (OJ S 208, 27.10.2007).

15   Commission staff working paper, 'Strengthening the protection of the rights of passengers travelling by sea or inland waterway in the European Union' – Public consultation document of the Directorate-General for Energy and Transport of 13 January 2006. Invitation to tender concerning a public consultation with citizens on passengers' needs for maritime transport and international coach transport', (OJ S 128-136075 of 8.7.2006).

16   J. Karsten, '*Droit communautaire des passagers et droit privé européen*', Revue Européenne de Droit de la Consommation, vol.4, 2006, pp. 257–272.

17   Council Decision of 5 April 2001 on the conclusion by the European Community of the Convention for the Unification of Certain Rules for International Carriage by Air (OJ L 194, 18.7.2001, p. 38).

between passenger and consumer law thinking, of which the Regulation provides a significant hint. Private international law also alludes to passenger law's allocation within Community law and hides a problem for the jurisdiction of courts. The adoption of the Regulation will finally provide an occasion to show that rules for the reservation of railway tickets and for intermodality between rail and air transport ought to have a place in today's EC railway passenger legislation. By sketching these points, the paper intends to show on which tracks the European legislator has set to run EC railway passenger law.

Travaux Préparatoires

Moving towards an integrated European railway area, the Commission says, includes the development of high-quality international passenger services.[18] Providing quality services encouraging more travellers to choose train travel requires, as a corollary, legal guarantees for passengers. To implement this policy, and starting from a description of the situation with rail passenger services and how passenger rights should be affirmed,[19] the Commission, therefore, asked, in its Second Railway Package of January 2002,[20] for a mandate to negotiate the accession of the Community to the modernised *Convention relative aux transports internationaux ferroviaires* (COTIF or Convention concerning International Carriage by Rail of 9 May 1980, amended by the Vilnius Protocol of 3 June 1999)[21] and proposed formal accession in November 2003.[22] The COTIF, which established the Intergovernmental Organisation for International Carriage by Rail (OTIF),[23] includes in its Appendix A 'Uniform Rules concerning the Contract for International Carriage of Passengers and Luggage by Rail'. This 1999 CIV Appendix, which entered into force 1 July 2006, is binding for twenty-one EU

---

18   Commission Communication 'Towards an integrated European railway area' (COM(2002) 18 final of 23 January 2002, p. 30 onwards) accompanying the Second Railway Package.

19   *Ibid.*, Annex II (pp. 53–9).

20   Commission press release IP/02/118 of 23 January 2002 'Revitalising the railways: Commission makes proposals to speed up establishment of an integrated railway area'.

21   COM(2002) 24 final of 23 January 2002.

22   Proposal for a Council Decision on the conclusion by the European Community of the Agreement on the Accession of the European Community to the Convention concerning International Carriage by Rail (COTIF) of 9 May 1980, as amended by the Vilnius Protocol of 3 June 1999 (COM(2003) 696 final of 17 November 2003). The European Parliament approved the conclusion of the agreement in its Report of 19 February 2004.

23   Available at: http://www.otif.org. On the accession to OTIF from an EU perspective see: http://europa.eu/scadplus/leg/en/lvb/l24011.htm (visited 20.12.2007).

Member States[24] (and a number of countries outside the EU[25]). It represents the elaborate basis in international law governing the contractual relationship between railway carriers and railway users, that is, passengers.[26]

However, the Commission did not wait for the CIV 1999 to enter into force or EC accession to OTIF to conduct consultations on railway passenger rights and to proceed, in its Third Railway Package of March 2004,[27] with a proposal for a Regulation on *international* rail passengers' rights and obligations.[28] This rush however resulted in a proposal that was, in parts, incompatible with the liability regime and the rules on contracts of international law. After going through its first reading,[29] the Commission document was thoroughly redrafted in the Common Position adopted in July 2006[30] which, as its most important amendment, included the CIV 1999 in an annex. This change was carried in the subsequent negotiations which revolved around the extension of its scope to *domestic* transport. The minutiae of the proposal's path through the EU legislature including the reconciliation procedure are documented on-line.[31]

Key Provisions

The Regulation establishes rules as regards the following:

    a)   the information to be provided by railway undertakings, the conclusion of

---

24   It has been ratified by all EU Member States with the exemption of Cyprus, Estonia (not yet a member of OTIF), Ireland, Italy, Malta and Sweden.

25   COTIF/CIV 1999 has also been ratified by the countries of the Western Balkans as well as Iran, Syria, Tunisia, Turkey and Ukraine.

26   For more information about international rail transport also see the website of the *Comité international des transports ferroviaires* (http://www.cit-rail.org).

27   Commission press release IP/04/291 of 3 March 2004 'With a quality European railway system the aim, the Commission is proposing the opening up of the market for international passenger services in 2010', available at: (http://ec.europa.eu/transport/rail/package2003/new_en.htm (visited 20.12.2007)).

28   COM(2004) 143 final of 3 March 2004.

29   Opinion of the Committee of the Regions on the legislative proposals of the Third Railway Package (OJ C 71, 22.3.2005, p. 26); Opinion of the EESC on the Proposal for a Regulation on international rail passengers' rights and obligations (OJ C 221, 8.9.2005, p. 8); European Parliament Opinion (OJ C 227E, 21.9.2006, p. 490).

30   Common Position adopted by the Council with a view to the adoption of a Regulation on international rail passengers' rights and obligations of 24 July 2006 (OJ C 289E, 28.11.2006, p. 1) followed by the European Parliament legislative resolution of 18 January 2007.

31   DG TREN website: 'What happened since the Commission adopted the package?' http://ec.europa.eu/transport/rail/package2003/next_en.htm (visited 20.12.2007) or Pre-Lex (http://ec.europa.eu/prelex: key in 'COM(2004)143').

transport contracts (Articles 4–6), the issuing of tickets and the implementation of a Computerised Information and Reservation System for Rail Transport (Articles 7–10),

b) the liability of railway undertakings (Article 11 referring to Annex I, that is, the incorporated CIV 1999) and their insurance obligations (Article 12) for passengers and their luggage (plus advance payments; Article 13),

c) the obligations of railway undertakings to passengers in cases of delay (and missed connections and cancellations; Articles 15–18),[32]

d) the protection of, and assistance to, disabled persons and persons with reduced mobility (PRMs) travelling by rail (Articles 19–25),

e) the definition and monitoring of service quality standards, the management of risks to the personal security of passengers and the handling of complaints (Articles 26–8), and

f) general rules on information and enforcement (Articles 29–31).

As stated, Annex I contains a near-complete *verbatim* reproduction from the CIV 1999 which so incorporates private law rules agreed in the international system of OTIF into the *acquis communautaire*. The Regulation duly affirms that it will assiduously abide by the convention as it is 'built on the existing system on international law on that subject contained in [the CIV 1999]'.[33] But it also states that 'it is desirable to extend the scope of this Regulation and protect not only international passengers but domestic passengers too'[34] which hints where supranationality extends the scope of protection. Annex II contains a list of minimum information to be provided by railway undertakings and/or ticket vendors. Annex III lists minimum service quality standards referred to in Article 28.

The 'Weaker Party' Status of the Passenger

Although these provisions all merit an in-depth analysis, this is beyond the scope of this chapter. However, the prologue given to the operative part of the Regulation is worth examining as it sets a salient political note. Article 253 of the EC Treaty[35] requires that the recitals of the preambles to Regulations and Directives 'state the reasons on which they are based' and thereby enlighten the background to legal

---

32 Interestingly, Article 16 modifies the concept of 'delay' (defined in Article 3 No. 12 as late arrival only), as it requires standardised and immediate assistance to passengers also in case of late departure.

33 Recital 6 of the Regulation's preamble.

34 *Ibid.*

35 Article 253 EC was to become Article I-38(2) of the – abortive – Constitutional Treaty. It is now, reworded, to become Article 296 of the Treaty on the Functioning of the European Union (n. 6 above).

acts of the Community.[36] Considering this ancillary nature, the significance of the message of recital 3 of the Regulation may far exceed the usual. It perhaps even formulates a tenet for the nascent doctrine of EC passenger law by succinctly stating: 'Since the rail passenger is the weaker party to the transport contract, passengers' rights in this respect should be safeguarded.'

That is a remarkable statement that, as far as can be seen, has not been affirmed in EC passenger law so far. To state that the passenger, a natural person entering into a contract of carriage,[37] by definition is the weaker party in the contractual relationship to a carrier, is to base the Regulation on a fundamental assumption underpinning traditional EC consumer law. That is all the more interesting as today's consumer policy seems to drift towards a concept of the confident consumer. But still much of the contract law *acquis* giving the consumer contractual rights proceeds from the assumption of imbalance in the trader/consumer relationship. This is explicit in Article 3(1) of Directive 93/13/EEC on unfair terms in consumer contracts[38] but a pattern repeated in other Directives as well. The Unfair Terms Directive deals with the 'substantive fairness' of a business-to-consumer (B2C) contract.[39] The ECJ stated in the *Océano* case[40] that 'the system of protection introduced by the Directive is based on the idea that the consumer is in a weak position *vis-à-vis* the seller or supplier, as regards both his bargaining power and his level of knowledge.' Recital 3 makes the same pattern (of rebalancing rights and duties in the name of substantive fairness) explicit for passenger law in a way that prolifically contributes to European contract law, along with the Regulation's Article 4 (transport contracts) referring to Articles 6–25 of its Annex I (the CIV 1999).

---

36   Case C-380/03, *Germany* v. *European Parliament and Council*, ECR [2006] I-11573, paragraph 107: Although the statement of reasons required by Article 253 EC must show clearly and unequivocally the reasoning of the Community authority which adopted the contested measure, so as to enable the persons concerned to ascertain the reasons for the measure and to enable the Court to exercise its power of review, it is not required to go into every relevant point of fact and law [*with further references to case law*].

37   The notion of 'passenger' is not defined in the Regulation. For what 'passenger' nevertheless implicitly means in Community law see Karsten, 'Passengers, Consumers and Travellers – The Rise of Passenger Rights in EC Transport Law and its Repercussions for Community Consumer Law and Policy': 131.

38   OJ L 95, 21.4.1993, p. 29.

39   S. Weatherill, *EU Consumer Law and Policy*, 2nd edn (Cheltenham, 2005), p. 115.

40   Joined Cases C-240/98 to C-244/98, *Océano Grupo Editorial SA* and *Rocío Murciano Quintero* (C-240/98) and *Salvat Editores SA* v. *José M. Sánchez Alcón Prades* (C-241/98), *José Luis Copano Badillo* (C-242/98), *Mohammed Berroane* (C-243/98), *Emilio Viñas Feliu* (C-244/98), ECR (2000) I-4941.

One may wonder whether recent developments in private international law (PIL)[41] also impinge an imbalance paradigm in the passenger/carrier relationship. Regulation (EC) No. 593/2008 on the law applicable to contractual obligations ('Rome I') has recenty been adopted[42] replacing the Rome Convention[43] (compare Article 24 of 'Rome I'). In the new numbering introduced by this Regulation, Article 5(2) on 'contracts of carriage' provides that in the absence of an express choice of law,[44] 'the law applicable shall be the law of the country where the passenger has his habitual residence provided that either the place of departure or the place of destination is situated in that country'.

Even though Article 5(2) also says that 'if these requirements are not met, the law of the place where the carrier has his habitual residence shall apply' and paragraph 3 states that 'where it is clear from all the circumstances of the case that the contract, in the absence of a choice of law, is manifestly more closely connected with a country other than that indicated in ... paragraph 2, the law of that other country shall apply', the key point remains the passenger's residence. This differs from Article 5(4)(a) of the Rome Convention on consumer contracts which excluded (and Article 6(4)(c) of 'Rome I' which still excludes) contracts of carriage other than those part of a package travel deal and subjected passengers to the general rules of the Convention. Plainly, this new conflict-of-law rule, principally based on the passenger's country of residence, enunciates the resolution to protect passenger interests better.[45] The motivation driving this change is given in recital 32 of 'Rome I' that reads: 'Owing to the particular nature of contracts of carriage ... specific provisions should ensure an adequate level of protection of passengers ...'

Just how advantageous this change may be for the passenger in reality is still to be seen. Yet it is remarkable, in defining the role of the passenger in the regulations designed for the purpose of his protection, that a weaker party status is becoming prevalent in the *acquis*.

---

41 On PIL in future Union law read Article 81 of the Treaty on the Functioning of the European Union.

42 OJ L 177, 4.7.2008, p. 6.

43 Convention on the law applicable to contractual obligations of 19 June 1980, as amended by the first and second protocol (consolidated version published in OJ C 334, 30.12.2005, pp. 1–27).

44 Limited to either the law of the country where (a) the passenger has his habitual residence, or (b) the carrier has his habitual residence (compare Article 19), or (c) the carrier has his place of central administration, or (d) the place of departure or (e) of destination is situated.

45 The author of this chapter was, in good faith, clearly wrong stating in his paper: 'European Passenger Law for Sea and Inland Waterway Transport', p. 228, that PIL was 'unlikely to grant the passenger consumer-like status in any future amendment.' This statement was made under the impression of legislative immobility and before, in Council deliberations, the clause that is now Article 5 of 'Rome I' was introduced.

Jurisdiction

Continuing this brief excursion into PIL, it is noteworthy that Annex I of Regulation 1371 does not incorporate Article 57(1) ('Forum') of the CIV 1999. If included, this clause would stipulate that:

> actions based on these Uniform Rules may be brought before the courts or tribunals of Member States [*of CIV*] designated between the parties or before the courts or tribunal of the Member State on whose territory the defendant has his domicile or habitual residence, his principal place of business or the branch or agency which concluded the contract of carriage. Other courts or tribunals may not be seized.

Reneging international law this way is no editorial slip. It is a deliberate omission and attempt to circumnavigate the problem that this PIL-clause deviates from Regulation (EC) No. 44/2001 on jurisdiction and the recognition and enforcement of judgments in civil and commercial matters ['Brussels I'].[46] This presents a predicament for the 21 EU-Member States which have ratified COTIF/CIV and are bound by it. Article 42 COTIF 1999 only allows declarations and reservations to the Convention when they are 'expressly provided for by the provisions themselves', which is not the case with Article 57 CIV.[47] The relationship between the *lex specialis* CIV and 'Brussels I' will thus have to be worked out in the application of Article 71 of the 'Brussels I' Regulation. Interestingly, this flaw in Regulation 1371 might be the first to be discussed again in the legislature as the Commission's forthcoming application report (Article 73 of 'Brussels I') purveys a catalyst to stimulate a debate.

Complementing the Regulation

A review of actual developments in EC railway passenger law is incomplete without reference to passenger information policy and the impetus for air-rail intermodality.

Rail transport included in air transport computer reservation systems (CRS)

Since its latest amendment 1999, Article 21b of the (air transport) Regulation on Computer Reservation Systems of 1989 (CRS Regulation)[48] includes a clause on

---

46   OJ L 12, 16.1.2001, p. 1, as last amended by Regulation (EC) No 1791/2006 (OJ L 363, 20.12.2006, p. 1).

47   Compare Karsten, 'European Passenger Law for Sea and Inland Waterway Transport', p. 230.

48   Regulation (EEC) No 2299/89 on a code of conduct for computerised reservation systems (OJ L 220, 29.7.1989, p. 1), as amended by Regulation (EEC) No 3089/93

rail transport products in its code of conduct on air transport CRS. CRS connect travel agents to airlines in a 'one-stop shop' for travel reservations. Where rail services are included in the principal display of an air transport CRS, Article 21b commits CRS providers to non-discriminatory treatment of these. The new CRS Regulation proposed on 15 November 2007[49] 'shall also apply to rail-transport products which are incorporated alongside air-transport products into the principal display of a CRS' (Article 1(2)). Without change in policy, this will ensure that rail services are given continued non-discriminatory treatment in the CRS.[50]

Rail transport CRS

For rail-only transport products, Article 3 No. 14 of Regulation 1371[51] defines its own notion of 'Computerised Information and Reservation System for Rail Transport' (CIRSRT). Article 10(1) on travel information and reservation systems expressly encourages the use of CIRSRT by railway undertakings and ticket vendors. Article 10(2)–(4) refer to the technical specifications for interoperability of the rail transport *acquis*[52] and the role of the European Railway Agency (ERA),[53] the technical arm of EC railway transport policy, in the information set out in Annex II of the Regulation. These clauses (and Article 8 of the Regulation) underline the importance of information policy for passenger protection.

Air–rail intermodality

Intermodality is a policy advocated in the 2001 Transport White Paper[54] favouring intermodal transport solutions such as integrated ticketing and baggage handling

---

(OJ L 278, 11.11.1993, p. 1) and Regulation (EC) No 323/1999 (OJ L 40, 13.2.1999, p. 1).

49 Proposal for a Regulation on a Code of Conduct for computerised reservation systems (COM(2007) 709 final of 15 November 2007). See also Commission press release IP/07/1702 "More choice and lower costs when booking airline tickets: the Commission advocates more competition in airline ticket distribution" and Memo/07/463 "Q&A on the revised rules for computerised airline ticket reservation systems" of the same date. On the result of the first reading: European Parliament press release "More competition in airline reservation systems – with protection for consumers" of 4 September 2008.

50 Explanatory Memorandum, p. 8. Refer also to Recital 9 of the preamble to the proposal.

51 Also see Recitals 8 and 9 of the preamble.

52 Directive 2001/16/EC on the interoperability of the trans-European conventional rail system (*OJ L 110, 20.4.2001, p. 1) establishes guidelines for trans-European rail networks according to Articles 154-6 EC.*

53 See http://www.era.europa.eu.

54 COM(2001) 370 final of 12 September 2001, pp. 80–81.

and continuity of journeys.[55] As shown above, air-rail intermodality was already partially dealt with back in 1999 in the second amendment to the CRS Regulation.[56] Other than this, the promotion of intermodality between the air and rail transport modules was subject to the report of the Rail Air Intermodality Facilitation Forum (RAIFF),[57] which made detailed suggestions, including some which could eventually lead to legislative initiatives.[58] More studies are available on air and rail competition and complementarity[59] while, also for environmental reasons, rail transport is promoted as a viable alternative to air transport.[60]

Now, the opening-up of international rail passenger services by Directive 2007/58/EC[61] grants open access rights for international rail passenger services including by 2010 the right of cabotage (that is, the right to take passengers and let them disembark on a national section of an international journey). It has been suggested that this measure would encourage airlines to operate rail services.[62] That would be practically still not being without obstacles. An airline would have to set up a railway undertaking, get a railway licence in a Community country, get qualified staff and appropriate rolling stock, apply for a safety certificate in the country(ies) of planned operations and ask for train paths. But the prospect that airlines (or airports) may run rail services to serve air hubs is an interesting development for passenger law as it will further the erosion of the regulatory barriers between different modes of transport.

Conclusions

The practical use of the Regulation is still hampered by limitations of its scope. Proposed by the Commission as a measure for international transport, it was

---

55   Commission web-page on intermodality: http://ec.europa.eu/transport/intermodality/ passenger/index_en.htm (visited 20.12.2007).

56   Note 47 above.

57   Available at: http://ec.europa.eu/transport/intermodality/raiff/index_en.htm (visited 20.12.2007).

58   Final Report, Annex II (Legal Issues) on 'seamless liability for air-rail intermodal passengers' and Annex III (distribution and passenger information) including computer reservation systems.

59   Available at: http://ec.europa.eu/transport/rail/studies/doc/2006_08_study_air_rail_ competition_en.pdf (visited 20.12.2007).

60   Written Question P-2449/07 by MEP Jean Lambert, 'Viable alternatives to air travel'.

61   Directive 2007/58/EC amending Directive 91/440/EEC on the development of the Community's railways and Directive 2001/14/EC on the allocation of railway infrastructure capacity and the levying of charges for the use of railway infrastructure (OJ L 315, 3.12.2007, p. 44).

62   *The Economist* (http://www.economist.com) of 7 July 2007 (pp. 61–2): 'A high speed revolution'.

only under pressure from the European Parliament that its reach was eventually extended to cover domestic transport as well.[63] This compromise, however, came at the cost of agreeing to considerable transition-periods and national opt-outs that could delay the full application of the Regulation until as long as the 2020s.[64] While basic passenger rights on ticketing, on liability for passengers and luggage under the terms of international law, on insurance, on key PRMs rights and on rules on personal security will apply as of 3 December 2009 (Article 2(3)), Member States may exempt domestic transport (Article 2(4)), urban, suburban and regional transport (Article 2(5)), and particular services or journeys partly operated outside the Community (Article 2(6)) for generously calculated transitional periods.

Still, Regulation (EC) No. 1371/2007 is of immediate significance for consumer lawyers for the vast amount of legal material it provides and the numerous questions that it will therefore inevitably incite. The points raised above are just a few highlights of a complex piece of European law (which, as far as the CIV 1999 is concerned, also qualifies as private law for the European region[65]). Moreover, it will be made known to travellers instilling widespread awareness of its existence. Article 29 of the Regulation on 'information to passengers about their rights' is an important provision as it will make sure that passengers will not remain ignorant about this directly applicable (Article 249(2) EC[66]) law. Soon, simply by entering a ticket office or a railway station, everybody will realise that, with its rail transport component, EC passenger law has coming of age.

---

63   The arduousness of the negotiations is perhaps best illustrated by the trail of European Parliament press releases of 2007: 'Parliament at odds with Council on the Community's railways' (10.1.2007); 'Third rail package: no agreement between EP and Council' (18.1.2007); 'No conciliation agreement on third rail package' (6.6.2007); 'Parliament and Council reach agreement on third rail package' (21.6.2007); 'Third railway package approved – opening up of the rail market and European licences for train drivers' (25.9.2007); 'Council go-ahead for third railway package respects Parliament's signals' (23.10.2007).

64   Urban, suburban and regional services may even be granted an indefinite exemption.

65   Note 25 above.

66   To become Article 288 of the Treaty on the Functioning of the European Union (n. 6 above).

15　Future Prospects for 'Class Actions' in Europe

*Andrew Laidlaw**

The year 2008 could prove to be an important one for the development of litigation in Europe and the UK. The issue of collective redress (or class actions) is being debated, or legislated on, by lawyers, policymakers and legislators, both in Brussels and other EU capitals. Meanwhile, the number of examples of mass litigation being brought in Europe continues to grow.

The EU Policy Imperative

The EU has long tried to engage directly with the European citizen in order to ensure that the rights it provides are made effective. The European Court of Justice has contributed significantly to this. Since the early days of its existence, the Court has developed concepts, such as direct effect[1] and primacy,[2] so that rights enshrined in European treaties and legislation can be enforced directly by individuals in domestic courts. The Court has also set down principles as to when the State may be liable to individuals for damages which are due to its failure to implement Community law correctly.[3] More recently, the Court confirmed the right to compensation from other individuals for loss suffered as a result of action that breaches directly effective Community law, such as the Treaty's antitrust provisions.[4]

In attempting to ensure that European citizens appreciate the value of European integration, policy makers have become increasingly concerned with guaranteeing the effectiveness of Community law. The ability to bring mass or multi-party litigation in order to enforce Community law rights, in particular for consumers, has thus become one of the many avenues being explored.

---

* 　Deputy Head, Joint Brussels Office of the Law Societies.
1　Case 26/62 *Van Gend en Loos* [1963] ECR 1.
2　Case 6/64 *Costa* v. *ENEL* [1964] ECR 585.
3　Joined Cases C-6/90 and C-9/90 *Francovich* [1991] ECR I-5357.
4　Case C-453/99 *Courage* [2001] ECR I-6297.

The Need for a European Model

At the EU level, the European Commission is examining the issue on two fronts: competition (antitrust) law and consumer protection law. The term 'class action' has, however, become synonymous with the US class action and all the apparent excesses that go with it. Severe punitive damages catalysed by civil jury trials, contingency fees and an opt-out system have led to a culture of litigation that finds little favour in European circles. Traditionally, European policymakers tend to favour instituting methods of public enforcement before facilitating private litigation.

In the EU context, the term 'collective redress' has been chosen to distinguish the EU debate from the US. The Commission in particular is keen to emphasise that the aim of its work is to address a deficit that exists in respect of the consumers' ability to seek redress and not to generate income for lawyers.[5] The same drivers of the US system, however, do not exist in most EU legal systems. EU jurisdictions do not have rules on fees or damages that equate to those in the US nor do many opt-out mechanisms exist. As such, the fixation with the nomenclature is political rather than legal.

Competition Law Litigation

Since the modernisation of competition law in 2004 and the decentralisation of enforcement, the Commission's Directorate General for Competition has been looking to facilitate private litigation based on competition law (antitrust) as a means of supplementing enforcement by public authorities and offering restitution to those who have suffered harm as the result of a cartel. Further to its 2005 Green Paper, it is set to publish a White Paper early in 2008, in which the issue of collective redress could feature.[6]

As a study for the Commission by the law firm Ashurst concluded: there is 'total underdevelopment' in this field in the EU.[7] In the UK, for instance, damages

---

5   'To those who have come all the way to Lisbon to hear the words "class action", let me be clear from the start: there will not be any. Not in Europe, not under my watch', Commissioner Meglena Kuneva, European Commissioner for Consumer Protection, 'Healthy markets need effective redress', at the Conference on collective redress, Lisbon, 10 November 2007. Available at: http://ec.europa.eu/consumers/redress_cons/docs/mku_cr_lisbon_final.pdf.

6   Green Paper: *Damages actions for breach of the EC antitrust rules*, COM (2005) 672 final, 19 December 2005.

7   *Study on the conditions of claims for damages in case of infringement of EC competition rules*, Ashurst, 31 August 2004, available at: http://ec.europa.eu/comm/competition/antitrust/others/actions_for_damages/study.html.

have rarely been awarded in relation to such litigation, a fact that is attributable, at least in part, to the high rate of settlement in many antitrust cases.

There are: however, signs of development. Interim damages were awarded by the Competition Appeal Tribunal for the first time in this type of case only in November 2006.[8] Also, the consumers' organisation, 'Which?', has used new powers under the Enterprise Act 2002 to bring a representative action against JJB Sports PLC (JJB). This 'follow-on' action was preceded, in 2003, by a decision by the Office of Fair Trading that JJB and others had been involved in price fixing in relation to the retailing of replica football shirts.[9] Which? is the only organisation yet to be designated a 'specified body' by the Secretary to State, capable of bringing claims on behalf of consumers in relation to antitrust infringements under the Act. It sought damages on behalf of a number of the consumers who had bought the shirts in question. Because of the current 'opt-in' arrangements under the Enterprise Act 2002, however, only a fraction of those affected were actually party to the litigation. The case settled out of court early in 2008 with the company paying compensation to consumers and the legal costs of Which?.

The interest amongst law firms in developing this practice area is evident. In addition, a number of US class-action law firms are establishing offices in London, with a view to becoming involved in some of the most high profile cases in this field. The pressure is therefore mounting on governments and other policymakers to develop their thinking on the issue and propose solutions to the perceived hurdles faced in such proceedings, which are appropriate to UK and EU legal traditions.

Collective Consumer Redress

In tandem to the aforementioned work, the European Commission's Directorate General for Health and Consumer Protection is examining how to improve the ability of consumers to seek redress, particularly with respect to rights found in Community legislation. As well as carrying out an overhaul of the substantive consumer law in 2007 and 2008, EU officials believe that facilitating effective collective redress, especially in a cross-border context, is an important element to creating a truly integrated internal market for consumers.

Speaking at a conference in Lisbon on 10 November 2007, Commissioner Meglena Kuneva announced that she was working to publish a communication on collective redress by the end of 2008.[10] In doing so, she set out a number of 'benchmarks' against which the Commission would evaluate the effectiveness of Member States' legal systems. For instance, she noted that 'the mechanism should enable consumers to obtain satisfactory redress in cases which they could not otherwise adequately pursue on an individual basis'. She continued: 'information

---

8   *Healthcare at Home Limited* v. *Genzyme Limited*, [2006] CAT 29.
9   OFT Decision No. CA98/06/2003, 1 August 2003.
10   See n. 5.

networking preparing and managing possible collective redress actions should allow for effective "bundling" of individual actions.'

Evidence, much of it anecdotal, has been presented to the Commission in an attempt to demonstrate why existing legal systems do not offer useful collective redress to large groups of consumers who have suffered the same damage. Such examples often focus, however, on the failings of individual jurisdictions. Providing concrete empirical data on the need to introduce a collective redress system within one jurisdiction is difficult. Proving the need for measures at an EU level would seem even more challenging.

The Which? case, mentioned above, is one example where only a small proportion of affected consumers opted in to the litigation. The inconsistency in the treatment of a multitude of claims by UK bank customers in respect of unauthorised overdraft charges has recently led the Office of Fair Trading to bring a test case before the International Dispute Resolution Centre, thus suspending individual claims.[11] While this may suggest the need for a collective redress mechanism in the UK, and possibly an opt-out mechanism, few cases demonstrate the need for a Europe-wide mechanism.

A number of cases brought under the Dutch Collective Settlement of Mass Damages Act 2005 (creating a court-approved settlement mechanism) do suggest, however, that in relation to matters such as securities, there will often be claimants in a number of EU jurisdictions.[12] A first small step in addressing the need to facilitate Europe-wide actions has already been taken in the EU's recently adopted Rome II Regulation, Article 6 of which provides that the law of one country may be applied in relation to a claim for damages that have been suffered in more than one Member State as a result of anti-competitive behaviour.[13]

---

11   Available at: http://www.oft.gov.uk/news/press/2008/6-08.
12   For instance, non-US shareholders of Royal Dutch Shell from across Europe were involved in seeking damages against the company in respect of losses caused by the 2004 drop in share value linked to the company's downward revision of its oil and gas reserves.
13   Regulation (EC) No 864/2007 of the European Parliament and of the Council of 11 July 2007 on the law applicable to non-contractual obligations (Rome II), OJ L 199, 31.7.2007, pp. 40–49.
      Article 6(3)(a) The law applicable to a non-contractual obligation arising out of a restriction of competition shall be the law of the country where the market is, or is likely to be, affected.
      (b) When the market is, or is likely to be, affected in more than one country, the person seeking compensation for damage who sues in the court of the domicile of the defendant, may instead choose to base his or her claim on the law of the court seized, provided that the market in that Member State is amongst those directly and substantially affected by the restriction of competition out of which the non-contractual obligation on which the claim is based arises; where the claimant sues, in accordance with the applicable rules on jurisdiction, more than one defendant in that court, he or she can only choose to base his or her claim on the law of that court if the restriction

Measuring the economic detriment suffered by consumers and by the economy at large as a result of the absence of effective collective redress mechanisms is less straightforward. With particular regard to its 'better regulation' agenda, the Commission has to be rigorous in producing studies and impact assessments containing empirical data that back up its proposals. Consequently, studies intended to measure the effectiveness of existing national legal regimes and to produce evidence of a need for the introduction of collective redress mechanisms are to be carried out for the Commission in 2008.

Future Prospects

Beyond the preparatory initiatives outlined above, it is unlikely that the Commission will be able to achieve much else before the European elections and the expiry of its own mandate in 2009. Legislative initiatives would appear to be out of the question.

It seems probable that it will be left to the next Commission to decide whether to propose an EU-wide system for collective redress. Political expediency may dictate that measures would be limited to cross-border claims. This has been the case for previous EU civil justice initiatives.[14] It may also dictate that future initiatives are conservative in other ways, such as limiting the ability to bring such cases to consumer bodies or approved organisations – something that already finds a precedent in some of the EU's consumer legislation.

Domestic Policy Developments

The policy debate is not limited to Brussels and the EU institutions, as developments across the EU attest. A bill to introduce class actions in France was to be published by the end of 2007. In Denmark, an opt-out system, operated through an ombudsman, is coming into operation. In the UK, the Ministry of Justice, HM Treasury and the Department for Business, Enterprise and Regulatory Reform are all considering the issue of collective redress. In Scotland there is an ongoing review of civil procedure rules, which includes a review of multi-party actions. The Civil Justice Council has already published recommendations to Government

---

of competition on which the claim against each of these defendants relies directly and substantially affects also the market in the Member State of that court.

14　Regulation (EC) No 861/2007 of the European Parliament and of the Council of 11 July 2007 establishing a European Small Claims Procedure, OJ L 199, 31.7.2007, pp. 1–22.

on litigation funding and will soon do so on the need for reforms in relation to collective actions.[15]

In November 2007, the Office of Fair Trading published its own recommendations to Government on private actions in competition law.[16] Interestingly, it recommends that, in relation to antitrust matters, representative actions should be available to both consumers and businesses and that judges should be able to decide on a case-by-case basis whether such claims should be brought on an opt-in or opt-out basis.

The UK Government is expected to consult on possible reforms in 2008 but it seems improbable that the US model of class action will be followed. Indeed, the UK may choose to mirror the more moderate models of other common law jurisdictions such as Canada or Australia. Irrespective of nomenclature, it is becoming increasingly apparent that changes in the legal market and political imperatives are driving increasingly towards the introduction of some form of class action in the UK and Europe.

There is a need for legal practitioners and consumer law experts to engage in this debate. The list of issues under discussion is long: opt-in versus opt-out systems; the certification of classes; the avoidance of spurious litigation; rules on evidence; the types of damages available; the quantification and distribution of damages; rules on costs and lawyers' fees; and the funding of litigation. While there may be multiple options for addressing the perceived need for collective actions in Europe, it is unlikely that many of them will be able to be pursued by the EU institutions.

---

15   Civil Justice Council, 'Improved Access to Justice – Funding Options and Proportionate Costs, The Future Funding of Litigation – Alternative Funding Structures', June 2007. Recommendations on collective actions should be published by the end of 2007.

16   *Private actions in competition law: effective redress for consumers and business*, Recommendations from the Office of Fair Trading, November 2007. Available at: http://www.oft.gov.uk/shared_oft/reports/comp_policy/oft916resp.pdf.